FOREIGN DIRECT INVESTMENT AND CITIES

Presenting a rich collection of insights into investment by foreign corporations into different types of cities around the world, *Foreign Direct Investment and Cities* uses original and revelatory case studies to help readers to turn theory into practice.

The book offers a structured set of case study chapters, with a diversity of location, setting, and industry, focusing on macro-, meso-, and micro-level factors, and outcomes in economic and non-economic terms. The chapters are authored by a diverse collection of international experts. The text is also supported by digital learning resources, including PowerPoint slides and video clips.

Foreign Direct Investment and Cities will be relevant to courses in international business and economic geography and will be key reading for academic researchers in business schools and wider social sciences, as well as the global practitioner community in investment promotion.

Christopher Williams (PhD) is Professor in the Strategy, Entrepreneurship and International Business Department at ESSCA School of Management in Paris. His research interests include international strategy, innovation in international firms and contexts, R&D and organizational resilience.

Martin Kaspar (PhD) is Vice President of Strategy and Corporate Development at Fränkische Industrial Pipes, a German Mittelstand's company and hidden champion in the automotive industry, where he is primarily responsible for internationalization projects.

In the International Business (IB) field there is an increasing emphasis on the societal impacts of IB (including its interactions with government policies and geopolitical relationships), and on the role of IB at the level of cities. This book nicely brings these themes together through some rich case study comparisons.

John Cantwell, *Distinguished Professor, Rutgers University, US*

As the saying goes, "all politics is local". This book brings an extremely useful collection of stories of regional / city foreign direct investment experiences. Fascinating real-life stories told by experts from different regions of the world, inviting a reflection on challenges and successes. And they are fun to read too!

Victor do Prado, *SciencesPo Paris, former Director of Council and Trade Negotiations Committee at the WTO*

The authors have put together a remarkable collage of FDI case studies on a city/regional level that can serve as roadmap and offer invaluable lessons to many local and regional IPA's on how to focus resources, shape strategy and win in the highly competitive FDI attraction contest.

Viktor Mizo, *Vice President Government Affairs at Kostal Group and former CEO of Invest in Macedonia*

FDI has the potential to reinvent cities and regions, and this book captures that dynamic perfectly. Its practical and academic perspectives make it an indispensable guide for understanding the evolving world of investment.

Andrew Wrobel, *Chief Reinvention Officer, Emerging Europe*

FOREIGN DIRECT INVESTMENT AND CITIES

Global Case Studies for Theory and Practice

Edited by Christopher Williams and Martin Kaspar

Routledge
Taylor & Francis Group
LONDON AND NEW YORK

Designed cover image: Igor Kutyaev/Getty Images®

First published 2026
by Routledge
4 Park Square, Milton Park, Abingdon, Oxon OX14 4RN

and by Routledge
605 Third Avenue, New York, NY 10158

Routledge is an imprint of the Taylor & Francis Group, an informa business

British Library Cataloguing-in-Publication Data
A catalogue record for this book is available from the British Library

ISBN: 978-1-032-77491-6 (hbk)
ISBN: 978-1-032-77481-7 (pbk)
ISBN: 978-1-003-48341-0 (ebk)

DOI: 10.4324/9781003483410

Typeset in Optima
by KnowledgeWorks Global Ltd.

Access the Support Material: www.routledge.com/9781032774817

CONTENTS

CONTRIBUTORS

Akil Amiraly is an associate researcher at i3-CRG, Management Research Center (a research unit of Ecole Polytechnique, CNRS, IP-Paris), and at the Chair Energy and Prosperity (Institut Louis Bachelier). His research concerns the provision of basic services (water, electricity/energy, mobility) by public and private operators in developing cities (mostly in India and in East Africa). He looks at the diffusion and appropriation of novel technical elements (e.g. metering water, electrifying mobility) in existing urban infrastructure systems. With an interdisciplinary perspective, he studies the interaction between these service providers, their technologies, and human behaviour, based on empirical fieldwork. His interest lies in describing in a comprehensive approach the sociotechnical context and the impact of technological devices on consumption practices.

Joachim Arnold is OCO Global's Deputy CEO based in Frankfurt, Germany. Within the OCO Global Group, Joachim is responsible for the Service Line Solutions which is managing trade and investment promotion programs. Joachim has more than 15 years of experience in the field of Foreign Direct Investment (FDI) and Trade Promotion, Corporate Location Advisory and International Market Expansion. He provides strategic consulting, research and business development services to governments and companies expanding to new markets.

In this role, Joachim has advised many of the world's leading economic development agencies on their strategy to attract Foreign Investments and its implementation through organizational design and international FDI lead generation. He is a certified international consultant with UNCTAD and delivers training and capacity building for investment promotion agencies. Joachim is

Senior Advisor to C Studios, a digital place marketing agency founded as Joint Venture between OCO Global and US-based marketing agency DCI, offering digital solutions for investment, trade and talent attraction.

Prior to joining OCO, Joachim worked as a representative to Invest in Morocco for the German-speaking markets. He started his career at the State Investment Promotion Agency Hessen Trade & Invest, promoting inward investments from the US, Japan and Korea. Joachim holds a PhD in Economic Geography from the University of Bayreuth, Bavaria, Germany.

Tom Becker is an economist at the United Nations Economic and Social Commission for Asia and the Pacific and Senior Advisor at NxtZones. Before this, Tom worked at the Financial Times' London office, in the fDi Intelligence specialist division of the FT, focused on foreign investment. Tom is advising governments on investment policy, promotion and sustainable development. He has worked with, developed and implemented investment attraction action plans, investment and incentive policies and Special Economic Zone frameworks for numerous countries across Europe, Asia-Pacific, the Middle East, Africa and Latin America – from in-country missions to the implementation phase. Tom has contributed to and published a number of works, including for the UN ESCAP, UNCTAD and OECD, as well as magazines and journal articles (forthcoming).

Davide Castellani is a professor and Head of International Business and Strategy at Henley Business School, University of Reading. His research lies at the intersection of International Business, International Economics and Economic Geography. He has extensively studied the determinants and effects of firms' internationalization strategies, including exports, imports and foreign direct investment, with particular emphasis on location decisions, productivity, innovation and economic performance. Davide has published over 60 peer-reviewed articles in leading academic journals such as *Journal of International Business Studies*, *Journal of International Economics*, *Research Policy*, *Regional Studies*, *Journal of World Business* and *Global Strategy Journal*. He has provided expert advice to various organizations, including the Department for International Trade, the Productivity Commission, NIESR, the National Centre for Universities and Business and the European Union. He is a fellow of The Productivity Institute, a member of the High-Level Group on Trade Policy Innovation, Editor-in-Chief of the *Journal of Industrial and Business Economics*, and a former Chair of the Academy of International Business UK & Ireland Chapter.

Ana Colovic, PhD, HDR is Full Professor of Strategy and Entrepreneurship at NEOMA Business School. Her research interests include business models, industrial clusters, inter-firm networks, entrepreneurial innovation, internationalization and innovation policy. She has held several visiting research positions in the United Kingdom, the United States and Japan. She has been involved in projects focusing on cluster policies in several countries. She has conducted research at the National Institute for Science and Technology Policy (Tokyo, Japan), and the National Association for Technological Research (Paris, France). She is a fellow of the Japan Society for the Promotion of Science. Ana has published in academic journals such as *European Management Review*, *Entrepreneurship & Regional Development*, *Journal of Business Research*, *Journal of World Business*, *Long Range Planning*, *Public Administration Review* and *Management and Organization Review*.

Jacopo Dettoni is the editor of fDi Intelligence and spearheads the title's editorial vision and strategic growth. A seasoned journalist, Jacopo has reported on some of the world`s most dynamic economies and transformative industries in Europe, Asia and Latin America for international and local media. He is a regular speaker and moderator at forums on international trade and investment and holds a master's degree in Economics and Finance from the Catholic University of Milan.

Juana Du is Professor in the School of Communication and Culture at Royal Roads University. Du receives her PhD in communication from Hong Kong Baptist University, an MS in Human Resource Management from New York University and an MA in International Communication from Peking University. Her research interests include intercultural communication in a globalized world, cross-cultural adaptation of sojourners, expatriate training and relocation, organizational diversity and culture, organizational learning and knowledge management, and subsidiaries of multinational enterprises and innovation. She has presented at many international academic conferences and published more than 30 book chapters and journal articles. She has been on the organizing committee of leading international academic conferences, including her role as Caucus Chair for the Academy of Management (AOM, 2023) and Track Chair for the Academy of International Business – Northeast chapter (AIB-NE, 2019-2023). She won the 2023 Best Paper Award of the *Journal of Comparative International Management*.

Harriet Fear, since January 2024, has enjoyed a portfolio career, which includes a range of consultancy, pro bono and charitable work. She is Chair of Cambridge Ahead and Chair of Cambridge Science Centre. She is also the founder of Harriet Fear Associates Ltd, her advisory/consultancy company which sees her advising a range of highly innovative international organizations with regard to their interests in Cambridge and the wider UK.

Harriet was a Diplomat for over 20 years with the British Foreign Office. She served in 17 countries, in various roles, including Deputy Ambassador

3 times, Head of Press and Public Affairs and Head of Commercial Services. She regularly served in hostile environments, trouble-shooting specific crises, including in the Congo, Cambodia and Ethiopia.

Half of her diplomatic career was spent in the commercial field, helping SMEs trade internationally. For 5 years, she was the head of the Government's National Life Sciences and Healthcare Trade Team.

Harriet was Chief Executive of One Nucleus from 2009 to 2017, which became the largest life science and healthcare membership body in Europe under her leadership and won a major award as 'Best Global Life Sciences and Healthcare membership organisation' in 2016. She was involved in the thinking behind Cambridge& from its earliest days in 2018 and led it from incorporation in February 2020 until the end of 2023.

Harriet was the Prime Minister's Business Ambassador for Life Sciences for 5 years to 2018. She has worked at the heart of the Cambridge business ecosystem since 2003. She was awarded an MBE in the Queen's Birthday Honours List 2016 for her services to Healthcare and Life Sciences.

Courtney Fingar is a London-based journalist, commentator and consultant specializing in foreign direct investment (FDI). She has covered business stories in all major regions of the world and has been on assignment to more than 80 countries.

She is the founder of Fingar Direct Investment, a boutique consultancy advising governments on investment promotion, investor outreach and location marketing. She also serves as a senior advisor for the World Association of Investment Promotion Agencies. She is a member of the advisory board of Halkin Investments and is a Global Fellow for the Woodrow Wilson International Center for Scholars.

She previously served as the editor-in-chief of Investment Monitor, a digital publication focused on cross-border investment, and before that spent 15 years with the Financial Times where she ran the group's specialist FDI publication. Among her ongoing media work, she writes a column for Forbes.com on FDI and is a contributing editor for Real Asset Media.

Kristian Hoelscher is a Research Professor at the Peace Research Institute Oslo (PRIO). His research interests lie at the intersection of cities, markets, politics, conflict and development in the Global South. He has worked in Sub-Saharan Africa, South Asia and Latin America, using both quantitative and qualitative methods. He holds a PhD in Political Science from the University of Oslo, an MSc. in Population and Development Studies from the London School of Economics and Political Science, and a BA in Business Management and BSc (Hons.) in Psychology from the University of Queensland in Brisbane, Australia.

Alex Irwin-Hunt is a reporter at fDi Intelligence, a specialist publication at the *Financial Times* focused on foreign direct investment and economic development. Alongside extensive reporting on innovation, tech entrepreneurship and start-up ecosystems, he has reported on business stories in markets around the world. He specializes in sourcing, visualizing and analysing data trends through his weekly newsletter Graph Time and is a regular speaker at international conferences. He has moderated panels on topics, including tourism, sustainability, urban planning, real estate, technology and investment climates.

Martin G Kaspar, as Vice President Strategy and Corporate Development of a German Mittelstand's company and hidden champion in the automotive industry, is primarily responsible for strategy development and internationalization projects (M&A as well as Greenfields).

Having completed his Ph.D. at Durham University on the role of Investment Promotion Agencies (IPA) in the location-decision making processes, he is a regular speaker/panellist at national and sub-national IPAs, International Organizations (UNCTAD, OECD, ILO) and professional bodies (WAIPA).

He has also been invited to become a member of the Commentary Group on Investment Facilitation and is a regular attendee at the BoKoWiTa, bilateral multi-party coordination meetings and Ditchley.

Martin has a bi-monthly column in fDi intelligence (the FDI-focused magazine of the FT group) and is regularly publishing articles in Investment Monitor and UNIDO-IAP.

Charles Krusekopf is Professor in the School of Business at Royal Roads University. Krusekopf has a Ph.D. in Economics from the University of Washington, an M.A. in International Relations and China Studies from Johns Hopkins School of International Studies and a B.A. in Economics and Management from Rice University. Krusekopf has worked with organizations including the World Bank, the Soros Foundation, the Albright Stonebridge Group, GLG, Fortune Magazine, the Office of the US Trade Representative and the US Department of State. He is the founder of the American Center for Mongolian Studies and has managed over $7 million in grants to support academic exchange and research in Asia. He served as a visiting professor at universities in Austria, Germany and China, and was a Fulbright Lecturer in Mongolia. He teaches across a range of fields including international trade and the global political economy, international business strategy, and environmental economics and policy.

Katiuscia Lavoratori is an Assistant Professor of International Business at Henley Business School, University of Reading (UK). Prior to joining Henley, she was a research fellow at Warwick Business School, University of Warwick (UK). Her research lies at the intersection of International Business and Economic Geography, with special reference to the economic analysis of location choices, the relation between agglomeration and productivity, Industry 4.0 and the new geography of global value chains. Katiuscia's work on these topics has won several awards, including the Copenhagen Business School Prize, the Global Strategy Journal Best Paper Award and the European International Business Academy Best Paper Award. Her work has appeared in leading journals such as the *Journal of International Business Studies, Regional Studies, Global Strategy Journal, Management International Review* and the *Journal of Regional Science*.

Michel Lemagnen is the co-founder of MCJ Lemagnen Associates Ltd. Michel is a dual national British-French and studied European Business Management in London and Reims. He has worked in FDI consultancy since 1997 and in international trade and investment since 1989. Michel first visited Finland in December 1993, a time when the Finnish Markka was the currency. In late 2007, Michel began his close relationship with the Greater Helsinki region of Finland in an FDI context, working with and for the fledgling Greater Helsinki Promotion agency through its various reorganizations to its present-day incarnation as Helsinki Partners. Michel and Julia co-founded MCJ Lemagnen Associates Ltd in December 2009, the intention being to move to Finland, and it was at the beginning of 2010 that Michel developed his enduring passion for Finland, the Baltics and the Nordics. He has witnessed the effects of the 2009 global economic crisis, Nokia's fall from its mobile phone leadership, the beginnings of the Finnish start-up boom, smart cities innovation and the realignment of the relationships with Russia since 2014 and especially since 2022.

Duncan McCunn has spent the majority of his career in Banking and Finance.

Working for NatWest, IBM and Barclays, he has specialized in Corporate Banking, directly and leading teams providing Capital Markets, Corporate Finance, Working Capital and Payment Solutions to SMEs and Global Corporates.

As a founder Director of Cambridge Ahead, he started to work more deeply within the Cambridge Ecosystem 10 years ago and is now CEO of Cambridge&, an organization focussed on growing Foreign Direct Investment into Cambridge and the Economic Impact of Cambridge more broadly across the United Kingdom and globally.

He is also a board member of the Oxford to Cambridge Supercluster where he looks to help grow Economic Impact more broadly across the region.

Iiris Saittakari is an Assistant Professor of International Business at Aalto University School of Business, Finland. Her research centres around multinational corporations' location processes and associated tensions, as well as city attraction games for multinationals' activities, including green investments and headquarters.

Petra Smith is a seasoned professional with over 20 years of experience across multiple industries, specializing in supporting startups and especially startup leaders through their early stages and first few years of growth. A self-proclaimed startup junkie and culture enthusiast, Petra thrives on building relationships and fostering People First Cultures by developing People First Leaders. Over the past two decades, she has taken on various roles within both small and large global organizations, leading diverse teams in Germany and the US. Her expertise spans industries such as publishing, technology, grocery retail, SaaS, and quick commerce. Some of the startups no longer exist, others have moved on to be very successful. Among the organizations Petra worked for are Lidl US, Gorillas and BRP US Inc.

Petra is passionate about working with international teams, and her hands-on experience in multiple sectors allows her to provide valuable insights and leadership to emerging businesses.

Ruxandra Victoria Steriu is a recent alumnus of Imperial College London, where she completed her Master of Business Administration and works as a Procurement Manager at GSK. With extensive commercial experience across multiple industries, she has worked in various business strategy roles, including business analysis, managing contracts as well as developing and implementing commercial strategies. Her academic research interests are international strategy and business for peace topics.

Dylan Sutherland undertakes research explaining the emergence of Chinese MNEs considering current international business theory, with an interest in knowledge and capability-building FDI. He works at Durham University Business School in the Management and Marketing Department.

Douglas van den Berghe (Ph.D.) is a global speaker and expert on FDI, SEZs, corporate international strategy and innovation. He is the CEO of NxtZones: a global advisory firm for SEZs and FDI. He has been an advisor to many governments in successfully developing FDI and SEZ policies for economic development increasing the competitiveness of cities. He has been a visiting professor at the Rotterdam School of Management, Erasmus University and the University of Maastricht both in the Netherlands.

Frans Van der Colff is an Executive Fellow at Henley Business School Africa, an Associate Professor of Practice at the University of Johannesburg, and a Sessional Lecturer at the University of Witwatersrand Business School.

Prior to his academic career he was a director of two of the largest retailers in South Africa and opened retail stores in twelve countries on the African continent.

He has worked on research for both Henley Africa and the University of Johannesburg and is currently researching authentic African Leadership as well as critical success factors for African entrepreneurs.

Christopher Williams is Professor in the Strategy, Entrepreneurship and International Business Department at ESSCA School of Management in Paris. His research interests include international strategy, innovation in international firms and contexts, R&D and organizational resilience. Before entering academia in 2007, Dr Williams spent two decades in industry, mostly in innovative and international environments, including 10 years with IMS Health. His research appears in journals such as *Research Policy, Journal of World Business, Journal of Management, Journal of Management Studies, Technovation, Asia Pacific Journal of Management, International Business Review, Journal of Business Research* and *Journal of International Management*. He has also published a range of teaching cases on strategy and innovative issues in international contexts with Ivey Publishing and is author of Venturing in International Firms: Contexts and Cases in a High-Tech World (Routledge, 2018), Management Consultancy for Innovation (Routledge, 2019), Organizing for Resilience (with J. You) (Routledge, 2021), and Strategic Business Case Analysis (Routledge, 2023).

Maurice Wokke, MSc is a Ph.D. researcher in International Business and Sustainability, specializing in sustainability, energy transition and innovation in hard-to-abate sectors. With more than 20 years of international experience in the steel industry, Maurice has held senior management positions, including Deputy Company Secretary of Tata Steel Nederland, Company Secretary of Tata Steel Nederland Holdings, Member of the Comité Exécutive of Tata Steel France Holdings and Managing Director of Tata Steel Germany.

He began his career as a maintenance engineer at the rolling mills, energy department and blast furnaces in IJmuiden. Maurice later played a crucial role in the asset strategy for Tata Steel Europe's captive power generation, covering the integrated steel sites in IJmuiden, Scunthorpe and Port Talbot. In IJmuiden and Port Talbot, he was crucial in developing the site's strategic asset roadmap, a programme that improved the firm's product range and profitability.

Additionally, Maurice served as the Programme Management Office (PMO) lead for the decarbonization and energy transition programmes at the IJmuiden site, a multibillion-euro project and the intended joint venture between Thyssenkrupp and Tata Steel Europe. Maurice's extensive experience in strategic asset development, international projects and energy transitions makes him a recognized expert in the global steel industry.

Ludan Wu is a Lecturer in International Business at Manchester Metropolitan University. Prior to joining the business school, she has completed her Ph.D. at Durham University Business School. She has presented her research at several international conferences and published in peer-reviewed journals. She actively engages in the academic community, contributing as a member of various international business organizations.

Haiyan Zhang is professor of international business at NEOMA Business School and founding director of the NEOMA Confucius Institute for Business. He holds an M.A. and a Ph.D. in public administration and Management from the University of Antwerp. His research interests include international business activities of Chinese and overseas Chinese-owned enterprises, management issues of international joint ventures in transition economies, high-tech industrial agglomeration in China, Chinese outward FDI in Europe, EU-China FDI relations, etc.

Zhiping Zhu is currently head of international teaching and programme development at China Executive leadership Academy-Pudong in Shanghai. After his master degree from Nanjing University, he has been programme manager and director of tailored leadership training programmes for government officials and business executives for more than 20 years. His research interests include business leadership, international investment of Chinese enterprises, M&A of Chinese SOEs, Chinese outward FDI and settlement of investment disputes. He has also offered consultation to government institutions and multinational companies on various topics such as China-EU relations and foreign enterprises in China.

PREFACE

Foreign Direct Investment (FDI) into cities is a key driver of social and economic development, shaping the fortunes of the places in which more than half of the world resides.[1] It is no coincidence that the vast majority of FDI is targeted towards cities given the markets for human, technological and financial capital that increasingly agglomerate in cities and the opportunities for returns that cities offer investors. Cities have emerged as critical nodes in the global economy, regularly competing for investment under their own banners. In some parts of the world, up to 80% of the population of a country lives in its cities. Cities are important places for humans to live, work and thrive, and the benefits they offer inhabitants in financial and social terms can depend heavily on the inward investment that flows into cities from foreign investors.

The phenomenon of FDI into cities is a complex one that can be examined in many ways, with many questions, and many ways of answering these questions. What are the drivers of FDI in cities? Why should a company choose city A over city B for investing shareholder capital? What are the outcomes of investment in social and economic terms? Is FDI into cities always a positive story, or are there outcomes from attempts at FDI into cities that disappoint stakeholders? Some researchers and analysts use quantitative methods to answer these questions, while others adopt a more qualitative approach. Some use a combination of both quantitative and qualitative data to report on FDI at the city level and help us understand the phenomenon. Some academics approach the topic by using theoretical lenses. But an overarching question eludes all these approaches: do we *really* understand the phenomenon of FDI and cities?

We (the Editors, Chris and Martin) have been reflecting on this over the past 3 years. We have been exploring and learning about the phenomenon somewhat differently to many others, having both worked in MNEs and then conducted academic research on them. Firstly, by working in MNEs and having firsthand experience of investment decisions and international operations conducted by MNEs in cities, we developed a connection to the phenomenon that many academic scholars might lack. We reflected on this and concluded that there are many different perspectives on FDI and cities such that a fruitful way of gaining understanding is by listening to the stories as told by a diverse range of experts who have been close to the phenomenon. Secondly, we ran a series of workshops in 2022 and 2023 at the University of York in the United Kingdom, in collaboration with NEOMA Business School in France, in which we invited experts from different domains to share their research, experiences and thinking on the topic. We listened to their stories, and they confirmed our hunch. The workshops allowed insights to be shared between academic scholars, and consultants, practitioners and policymakers in the real world of investment promotion at city level. We arrived at the same conclusion: there are stories to be told about FDI and cities from a multiplicity of vantage points, stories, which deserve to be compiled and shared for a wider audience.

This book seeks to explore FDI in the context of cities and offers new insights for academic audiences – including students at all levels, and more established professors – as well as practitioners in the business world. The pairing up of cities and MNEs may sound simple as if there was a formula for how to calculate a location choice, an investment amount, and a way of managing in a city by an MNE, as well as a way of wooing investors, and retaining their commitment to a city over time by a city's 'sales force'. The insights kindly offered by the contributors to this book suggest that such an online dating app for the global economy does not exist. There are some fabulous success stories, and there are some clear failures. And in many cases, there is a messy middle ground of exploration, action, learning, tenacity and re-working, all of which happen over time.

The temporal dynamics of FDI and cities are often not told. While many teaching cases in international business do exist, they can often lack an explicit focus on a given city and its peculiarities. Yet the outcomes of FDI are felt by the cities and the nations in which those cities belong over many years. And in the same country cities often compete against each other for the same investment in processes that can take months to years. Seismic events for cities, such as hosting an Olympic Games, occur in time, not just in space, and what happens before, during and after these events can be highly informative from an investment promotion angle. The stories we heard told us that investment opportunities in cities develop temporally and that time is a critical – if not *the* critical – contextual factor. We also learned that how foreign investment contributes to vitality and growth in cities can be told in the form of a diverse array of well-researched stories, or cases.

By presenting a diverse array of cases on FDI and cities, the primary objectives of the book are to:

1 Provide a comprehensive compendium of case data on FDI at city level in order to share knowledge of the phenomenon as told by those with detailed insight – often firsthand – into specific cases at city level.
2 Give students in business schools (international business, economic development) and social sciences (economic geography, development studies, urban development) deeper insight into the phenomenon of FDI at city level than they might otherwise have access to, to complement their study-based theoretical learning and to help them develop leadership skills and empirical knowledge through engagement with the phenomenon.
3 Offer a source of thought-provoking and substantive knowledge to assist decision-making by practitioners in (1) companies (MNEs) considering international investment into cities, (2) non-governmental organizations (NGOs) and inter-governmental organisations (IGOs), (3) investment promotion agencies (IPAs – there are 131 IPA members of WAIPA – the world association of investment promotion agencies) and (4) others such as independent consultants acting as investment facilitators in the field.

We hope that readers of the book will benefit from the storytelling style of the case data, its global diversity and city-level detail, and its structuring into topical themes and subjects. The goal is to allow readers to stay current and up-to-date in the field while also developing their heuristics concerning the relationship between FDI and cities as the global economy changes. We gave ourselves an interesting challenge in terms of how to structure and present the case data to meet this goal. One option would have been to present the cases by city name or size. Another option was to divide them into those written by academics and those by practitioners. In the end, we chose to group the cases into four thematic blocks, each with its own narrative and discourse. That said, there are overlaps between the blocks, and it will be possible to make links between themes across the various cases in the book. Indeed, we invite the reader to do so. The four thematic blocks are:

1 Cities in advanced economies as locations for FDI: issues relating to the organization of investment promotion, whether business models that work in one city in one developed country will work in another city in another developed country, the influence that a powerful home country

enterprise has in attracting FDI into a city, how advanced economy cities both attract and resist investors such that they end up being deterred, and how advanced economy cities can entice investors in a world of uncertain investment.

2 Cities in transitioning and developing countries: the institutional changes that occur over long periods of time that influence economic growth in cities through FDI, how FDI into developing country cities can expand into peri-urban areas over time, how political instability and change can alter the hopes and aspirations of inward investors, how cities once noted for their industrial prowess can transition and attract new and emerging industries to invest in order to diversify the city economy.
3 Technology, FDI and cities: how concerted and orchestrated initiatives can attract FDI from companies engaged in developing cutting-edge technology including Greentech, how there can be mixed outcomes – growth and inequality - for cities that develop a strong tech-base facilitated through FDI, how tech ecosystems can evolve over decades long initiative and investment in China, how 'cousin' cities help promote tech capacity development in cities in other countries.
4 Sustainable development and resilience in cities through FDI: how the transfer of know-how and practices between rich and poor countries through FDI at the city level can be difficult to implement, how FDI into cities plays a vital role in warzones and contexts beset by violence, how the re-purposing of land and labour in cities for new FDI allows industrial decline to give way to new economic development, and how FDI at city level matters for innovation in sustainable solutions.

This book would not have been possible without the hard work, research and commitment of all the case authors involved. While many are professional writers in their academic, consulting or journalistic capacity, not all had written case material on this topic at a level of detail that we pushed for. We thank all the authors contributing to this book enormously for their involvement and work over the last year. Many of the authors participated at our earlier workshops in York and Paris in 2022 and 2023, as speakers or audience delegates. We thank them for their time and involvement and for sharing their experiences in the field or as researchers of the topic. On that note, we thank the University of York, School for Business and Society, and NEOMA Business School for supporting these workshops.

We hope you enjoy reading and reflecting on the cases in this book as much as we have had in working with the various authors in compiling the cases. The universe of case data on FDI and cities is potentially unlimited and unbounded and evolves with every minute of every day somewhere in the world. While the stories contained here are not exhaustive, they exemplify the diversity and complexity of FDI and cities and can act to develop heuristics of the phenomenon for all interested parties. We welcome feedback and comments on the cases and look forward to future events at which we can share new case stories on FDI and cities as the world moves towards higher levels of city agglomeration with FDI playing a role in their social and economic performance.

Christopher Williams and Martin Kaspar
Rouen and Munich, Fall, 2024

Note

1 https://ourworldindata.org/urbanization

INTRODUCTION

FDI and cities in the context of globalization

In an era in which globalization is slowly turning towards deglobalization while urbanization and climate-related pressures endure, cities have become pivotal hubs of economic growth, innovation, and human enterprise. According to the World Bank, 56% of the world's population lives in cities.[1] This is expected to continually increase, and it is projected that 7/10ths of the world's population will live in cities by the year 2050. At the same time, 80% of global GDP is generated in cities. Foreign Direct Investment (FDI) – the investments made by actors in one country into another country – topped $1.3 trillion in 2022. Most of this is attributed to the investments made by Multinational Enterprises (MNEs), with the vast majority directed towards cities (Bono et al., 2024) in countries foreign to the home country of the MNE. While global flows of FDI fluctuate year-to-year, the general trend over the past five decades for FDI into cities has been upwards.

While the positive economic benefits of FDI on cities have been documented, such as knowledge spillovers that can boost development in both target and nearby cities (Ning et al., 2016), questions have been raised about its effects on social outcomes, including inequality (Basu & Guariglia, 2007; Chintrakarn et al., 2012). Some have shown that FDI can contribute to increases in property prices, as has been the case in Ireland (Agnew & Lyons, 2018). This in turn can create social tensions and drive the local population to the city periphery and beyond. One argument has been that FDI will benefit skilled and educated workers, with lower skilled workers benefiting less, if at all. In this line of thinking, some workers will become 'left out' because of FDI in their city. MNEs will bring in their own capabilities, intellectual property (IP)

DOI: 10.4324/9781003483410-1

and ways of doing things. The cumulative effect of many investment projects on cities can raise issues in terms of land use policy and the physical environment. It can result in population growth as workers are attracted to the city in search of jobs. Population growth and increases in population concentration can be problematic unless FDI projects are undertaken with urban growth management (UGM) in mind (Vongpraseuth & Choi, 2015).

The counter argument to this is that FDI can provide employment opportunities and is a source of innovation (Wang et al., 2013), as well as finance and tax for cities and their national governments (ALshubiri, 2024). For the MNEs investing in cities, new markets are opened. The same can be said of the cities too. Their firms will have access to new knowledge networks and trade links with the outside world through the MNEs that set up shop in the city. MNEs will also enable upskilling for the city's workforce, transferring knowledge, and IP that can have benefits throughout the labour market. This extends to practices for environmental management and sustainability. Demena and Afesorgbor (2020) found that the effect of FDI on emissions is negligible after accounting for heterogeneity. In Williams and Steriu's (2022) study of Heineken's investment in breweries in Addis Ababa, Ethiopia: '280 new local jobs were created, barley was sourced locally from smallholder farmers, local materials were used in the design of the brewery, and new health and safety practices implemented' (p. 6). In this line of argument, FDI into cities is a positive force for both MNE and city.

Competition amongst cities for FDI

Given that potential downsides to FDI in cities can be managed through adequate planning, and that benefits are seen to outweigh them, the competition between cities for FDI has become intense. Scholars note how younger cities with skills demographics that are advantageous to MNEs are particularly attractive to MNEs (Iammarino et al., 2018). Such cities act as disruptors, challenging the hegemony of long-standing cities that have failed to keep pace. Others have described how cities can shrink, particularly when instituted social behaviour (i.e., the prolonging of old industrialized mentalities) and spatial mismatches occur (Reckien & Martinez-Fernandez, 2011). Indeed, the competitive landscape for cities arises not just because of the changing needs of MNEs but also because competitor cities are continually evolving their offering (Metaxas, 2010). The idea of city attractiveness has been around for decades (Todd, 1977). According to Todd (1977), it is about conditions in a city, conditions that are amenable to change and improvement such that they become better places to invest in, and for people to work and live. While quantifying cities and ranking them in terms of 'better' and 'worse' is one task of these measurements, it is widely acknowledged that there is a subjective aspect too (Todd, 1977). Socio-economic development has a role to play in attracting migrant workers that can see benefit in job opportunities provided by FDI (Serikzhanova & Aldangarkyzy, 2021). Socio-economic factors can be interpreted in different ways by different MNEs, and even by different managers within the same MNE, adding to the sense of competition between cities.

This intense competition between cities means investors often find it difficult to decide which location to choose, especially when incentives in different cities are difficult to compare. Not only do cities have different spatial, cultural, and economic characteristics, which impact whether the MNE will be able to achieve strategic goals by investing, they also have different branding too (Anttiroiko, 2015). The business promotion activities at the heart of this branding and inward attraction need to be able to absorb investment such that benefits, including spillovers and growth, are sustained. Differences in branding come with differences in value propositions for investing MNEs. Similarities in branding make it difficult for MNEs to 'split the hairs' between two or three locations when deciding on a final location for a given investment. Cities may come with reputational risks that may make it hard for decision-makers to settle on a given location. Reputations may be justified, but they also may be entirely unfounded and based on stereotypical impressions of a place from a bygone era. It also may be difficult to decide whether proximity to neighbouring cities in each country is problematic or not. Such spatial factors may be difficult to assess in advance, especially when there are multiple other cities within reach (Poelhekke & Van Der Ploeg, 2009). In sum, the difficulties facing MNEs when deciding on a city location for investment can be immense, especially as investment promotion agents persist in their respective sales pitches and persuasive arguments.

Both cities and MNEs considering FDI projects in cities are confronted with a highly complex landscape. Complexity occurs in various ways. Firstly, there are many different types of actors involved in investment promotion and facilitating FDI into cities. These include the investors (MNEs) themselves, investment promotion agencies at city and national level, local and national governments, regional blocs (such as the EU), inter-governmental organizations (IGOs) (such as the OECD and UN), non-governmental organizations (NGOs), various types of consultants (local and international), and even local actors in the business ecosystem in the city such as universities, science labs, and business schools. How each of these actors gets involved in FDI at city level will differ from city to city and project to project. The point is there are many different actors potentially involved, and, in most cases (China may be an exception), no one central coordinating authority with the power to bring them together and control them. Secondly, each of these actors brings with them different levels of uncertainty because of the different stakeholder roles they play. As stakeholders in any given investment project, they will have different levels of interest and different levels of influence over outcomes. This raises uncertainty because it is not known in advance exactly how these different actors can help assuage concerns facing investors and how they will act to deal with problems arising both before and after the investment is made. Finally, just as MNEs differ widely in their characteristics and goals, no two cities are the same.

Different types of cities

Cities vary widely in their histories, capabilities and what they offer to foreign investors. On the one hand, a focus on global cities forms a large part of the literature (Beaverstock et al., 1999; Belderbos et al., 2020; Kola-Bezka & Kuzel, 2023). Global cities are '... metropolitan centres of interregional, intercontinental or even global importance' (Kola-Bezka & Kuzel, 2023, p. 102) and are the dominant cultural, political, economic, and social centres of the world. According to Beaverstock et al. (1999), they possess 'advanced producer services' such as accounting, advertising, banking, and law (p. 446). Examples are London, Paris, New York, and Tokyo. Investing in global cities is seen as beneficial for MNEs because it reduces the liability of foreignness (i.e., the costs of doing business abroad that domestic firms in the host country do not face) that the MNE faces entering the country (Belderbos et al., 2020). On the other hand, cities have been characterized in numerous other ways in literature. It is not just about London, Paris, New York, and Tokyo. Smaller, Tier 2, and Tier 3 cities have been discussed, and many others are still considered world cities, possessing specialized producer services (Beaverstock et al., 1999). Examples are Amsterdam, Manchester, and Vancouver. These tend to be smaller and may have slightly lower-income levels than the true global cities, although they can account for a large percentage of a country's GDP and human capital (Rogoff & Yang, 2024). Increasingly, global cities have appeared in developing and transition economies; examples include Jakarta, Shanghai, Istanbul, and Mexico City (Shatkin, 2007). They also are highly diverse, containing a corporate and business centre, as well as many 'sub-cities' with distinct features, determined by the cultural and social make-up of those urban areas (Sassen, 1993).

Other characterizations of cities have been made in the literature. These include gateway cities (Scholvin et al., 2019), open cities (Zheng et al., 2010), and peripheral cities (McDonald et al., 2018). Gateway cities are ones that connect global flows of trade and investment to their 'hinterlands' within their country (Scholvin et al., 2019). They help develop networks and act as important nodes in the FDI flows into other cities within a country. Open cities receive favourable tax status or other government incentives, often positioned in special economic zones, and they attract (and can lose) a fluid migrant workforce (Zheng et al., 2010). Peripheral cities are spatially distinct from core (global or Tier 1) cities, as well as from core cities within their regions. This spatial distance can be a disadvantage as far as FDI is concerned. However, their proximity to core cities can make them more attractive locations for FDI

(McDonald et al., 2018). Overall, these different types of cities, with their different characteristics, incentives, and evolution, can add uncertainty to inward investors seeking to select an ideal location. The fact that no two cities are alike also presents a challenge to theory of FDI at city level.

The importance of cases to understand FDI and cities

FDI at city level is a domain for economic and social activity in our world that is continually changing and adapting to circumstances. There is intense competition between cities, and there is considerable uncertainty facing investors too. Some cities grow, while others decline. Some become more expensive to live in, while others transition with the times. The wide range of actors involved adds to the complexity of the phenomenon, and emerging trends in technology and sustainability add to the pressures facing all actors involved in attracting and retaining FDI in cities. In some situations, such as in warzones and countries where there is violent conflict, FDI into cities is not altogether undeterred (Williams & Steriu, 2022; Fingar, in this book). In these extreme situations, the rules of the game will be completely different compared to the situation where FDI flows into cities in safe, advanced economies.

Understanding the evolving phenomenon is vitally important for leaders, managers, and consultants involved in FDI at city level. It is also important for the academic community, including students of international business and urban development, as well as more established academics and researchers. There are many theories out there to help learners grapple with the phenomenon of FDI and cities. Examples include institutional theory (Blevins et al., 2016), which can be used to explain entry decisions from the perspective of institutional contexts, the capabilities-based approach (Prime, 2012), which can be used to explain why FDI is attracted to cities and how it contributes to growth and development, social exchange theory (Williams & Du, 2014), which can help explain innovative dynamics between subsidiaries and partners in cities after they have been set up, the knowledge-based view of the MNF (Du & Colovic, 2024), which can explain how MNEs profit from global cities, and various tenets of theory from economic geography (Du & Colovic, 2024; Glaeser & Resseger, 2010; McDonald et al., 2018), which can explain agglomeration effects. These are just a few selected examples of theories that have been used in analysing FDI and cities.

The approach we take in this book is different. It does not assume or rest on any specific theory. It does not take for granted any assumptions about how actors behave. And it does not use a specific lens to frame behaviours, investment patterns, and outcomes. Rather, it asserts that our heuristics relating to the phenomenon can be developed by examining case data, in other words, paying attention to storytellers who have detailed knowledge and insight on the evolving relationship between FDI and cities over time.

This approach is not new, as anyone familiar with case writing or teaching with cases will confirm. Indeed, cases of cities used as a primary focus are not uncommon in the academic literature on FDI, as well as in teaching cases. Table 0.1 shows selected examples, illustrating how case data on FDI and cities spans the economically rich to the economically poor locations.

TABLE 0.1 Selected examples of case studies on FDI at city level

City	*City GDP per capita PPP (2020–2023) (est.)*	*Author(s)*	*Emphasis*
Singapore	\$80k–\$90k	Prime (2012)	Documenting the evolution of social capabilities in Singapore from the 1960s through to 2010 and their role in attracting and retaining FDI
Barcelona	\$30k–\$40k	Metaxas (2010)	Strategic development process of the city over a 20-year period; the role of developing a competitive business image to outside investors
Krakow	\$20k–\$30k	Williams et al. (2012)	Revealing the decision-making process and early integration of a new (greenfield) investment by a US/Canadian software company in Poland
Ho Chi Minh City and Hanoi	\$5k–\$15k	Kim (2024)	Differential long-term effects of FDI in Vietnam's two leading cities between 1988 and 2017, including inflow of foreign nationals
Vientiane	<\$3k	Vongpraseuth and Choi (2015)	Documenting the conflicts that arose between FDI projects and urban land management and planning between 1995 and 2010

There are some interesting features with cases of FDI and cities. Firstly, they show an evolution of activity, behaviour and patterns of investment and change *over time*. The time periods in some cases are measured in weeks and months, such as with the case on Infusion's greenfield subsidiary in Krakow (Williams et al., 2012). This type of case is firm-level, managerial in nature, and reveals strategic considerations before and after the investment as portrayed by the leaders of the firm. In other cases, the story spans many years, sometimes decades. These cases tend to be more macro in nature, such as Kim's (2024) analysis of FDI into Ho Chi Minh City and Hanoi over a 30-year period. But they are essentially stories, unfolding over time. Secondly, they all show some kind of *outcome or effect*, mostly positive (growth and development in the case of Singapore), but not exclusively so (Infusion had to previously pull-out of India, prior to considering Krakow (Williams et al., 2012), while Vientiane experienced conflicts between urban land management the demand of FDI).

All the cases in this book follow in this tradition. They all tell a story, showing patterns of behaviour, organizational and institutional change, and investment over time. And they all show effects or outcomes. They differ markedly in their level of analysis – some are macro, some are micro. Some are highly quantitative, with the narrative provided by the authors. And some are highly qualitative, revealing the micro-dynamics and perceptions of individuals involved in specific situations. Importantly, they differ in terms of their storylines. This was largely determined by the interests and access of the respective authors. We worked closely with the authors during the case selection phase to ensure that we did not have any redundancy, such as two cases on the same city or the same company. Our intention is that, by combining this set of cases together in one place, we can provide a new platform for the diversity and scope of stories of FDI and cities to be explored. This will develop a holistic sense of the phenomenon in the reader who reads all the cases. Theoretical interpretation is in the hands of the reader, and we do not attempt to frame the cases individually by any given theory. In the concluding remarks to this book, we will return to the question of theory, which is still an important consideration given that the cases presented all show changes in behaviour and investment over time and some kind of outcome or effect.

Structure of this book

The book is divided into four Parts, each addressing a critical dimension of the relationship between FDI and cities. There are 18 cases in total and they are not presented in a particular order within each Part. In our view, it did not make sense to structure them chronologically, alphabetically or in some kind of order of size or importance. They are each equally important and all contain learning points. But we do structure them according to over-arching themes in the case. This does not mean to say that each case is only about a single theme. Any reader will soon see how a multitude of themes are present in each case. By structuring the book into four Parts, we aim to guide readers to cases sharing a dominant context.

Part 1: Cities in advanced economies as locations for FDI

The first part of the book focuses on the location choices that MNEs make when investing in cities in advanced economies. We examine cities such as Cambridge, New York, Helsinki, cities in Flanders and London, in this section, places, which have long established themselves as attractive destinations for foreign investment. These cities serve as critical 'shop windows' for global business, showcasing innovation, financial and institutional stability, and access to markets and a skilled labour force.

This section delves into the factors that make these cities competitive and the models they use to attract and sustain FDI. The cases illustrate various concepts, such as that of a 'home MNE,' where MNEs have established their headquarters or key operations, and how cities need to develop a unified 'shop window' for global investors. Additionally, we will discuss instances of resistance to FDI, including local opposition to foreign-owned firms, as well as the risks of failed development projects in advanced urban settings. The cases in this part illustrate the successes and challenges these cities face in maintaining their competitive edge in a globalized economy, and the changes they need to go through to compete. They also show the challenges facing MNEs entering advanced locations; just because economic and institutional conditions seem stable and strong, there is no guarantee of success.

Part 2: Cities in transitioning and developing countries

This part looks at cities in less advanced, transitioning and developing countries, where the dynamics of FDI take on a different form. Cities like Johannesburg, Ho Chi Minh City, Bagamoyo, and Katowice offer unique opportunities but also present significant challenges for foreign investors. These cities are often characterized by political instability, underdeveloped infrastructure, and complex institutional environments. However, they also represent high-growth markets, the strong desire for change and development, and considerable potential for returns.

The cases in this section explore the initiative and institutional changes required to attract FDI in these regions and how cities can leverage FDI to spur economic growth and development. The theme of institutional change in facilitating FDI growth (positive and negative) is central to the discussion, particularly when examining cities on the periphery of major economic centres.

Part 3: Technology, FDI and cities

Part three investigates the role played by technology in shaping the relationship between FDI and cities. With cities like Paris, Tel Aviv, Hamburg, Shenzhen, and Suzhou at the forefront of technological innovation and FDI, this section examines how FDI drives – and is driven by – technological advancements. The impact of technology on urban economies is profound, influencing not only economic productivity but also the ways cities operate and compete for foreign capital.

These cases illustrate long-term spillover effects of FDI in terms of IP and technological development, human capital formation and utilization, and the creation and maintenance of innovation ecosystems. Cities that successfully integrate technological innovation into their economies tend to attract more FDI, fostering a cycle of growth and development. The cases provide insight into the challenges cities face in managing rapid technological change, including the shifting nature of FDI types – from manufacturing-based investment to technology-driven capital flows.

Part 4: Sustainable development and resilience in cities through FDI

The final part addresses the pressing issues of sustainability and resilience in urban development. As cities increasingly confront environmental challenges, from climate change to resource scarcity to war and conflict, the role of FDI in promoting sustainable growth has come to the forefront of urban policy discussions. This section examines how cities can balance the economic benefits of FDI with the need for long-term environmental and social resilience.

Focusing on cities like Chennai, Lviv, Redcar, and Lappeenranta, this section explores how FDI can be a catalyst for green innovation and the transfer of sustainable practices, while also showing that practice transfer can be difficult to achieve in reality. Themes of re-purposing and green innovation are central, highlighting how cities facing economic decline or environmental degradation can reinvent themselves through strategic FDI initiatives. The cases speak to the challenges cities face in attracting investment for sustainable development and how knowledge barriers and limited incentives can hinder practice transfer for sustainable development. The cases illustrate the role FDI plays in helping cities recover from economic shocks and external crises, offering a blueprint for fostering resilience in an increasingly volatile global economy.

Note

1 https://www.worldbank.org/en/topic/urbandevelopment/overview

References

Agnew, K., & Lyons, R. C. (2018). The impact of employment on housing prices: Detailed evidence from FDI in Ireland. *Regional Science and Urban Economics, 70*, 174–189.

ALshubiri, F. (2024). Do foreign direct investment inflows affect tax revenue in developed and developing countries? *Asian Review of Accounting, 32*(5), 781–810.

Anttiroiko, A. V. (2015). City branding as a response to global intercity competition. *Growth and Change, 46*(2), 233–252.

Basu, P., & Guariglia, A. (2007). Foreign direct investment, inequality, and growth. *Journal of Macroeconomics, 29*(4), 824–839.

Beaverstock, J. V., Smith, R. G., & Taylor, P. J. (1999). A roster of world cities. *Cities, 16*(6), 445–458.

Belderbos, R., Du, H. S., & Slangen, A. (2020). When do firms choose global cities as foreign investment locations within countries? The roles of contextual distance, knowledge intensity, and target-country experience. *Journal of World Business, 55*(1), 101022.

Blevins, D. P., Moschieri, C., Pinkham, B. C., & Ragozzino, R. (2016). Institutional changes within the European Union: How global cities and regional integration affect MNE entry decisions. *Journal of World Business, 51*(2), 319–330.

Bono, P. H., David, Q., & Desbordes, R. (2024). International attractiveness of cities: The drivers of urban FDI. *Review of International Economics, 32*(5), 2319–2343.

Chintrakarn, P., Herzer, D., & Nunnenkamp, P. (2012). FDI and income inequality: Evidence from a panel of US states. *Economic Inquiry, 50*(3), 788–801.

Demena, B. A., & Afesorgbor, S. K. (2020). The effect of FDI on environmental emissions: Evidence from a meta-analysis. *Energy Policy, 138*, 111192.

Glaeser, E. L., & Resseger, M. G. (2010). The complementarity between cities and skills. *Journal of Regional Science, 50*(1), 221–244.

Iammarino, S., McCann, P., & Ortega-Argilés, R. (2018). International business, cities and competitiveness: Recent trends and future challenges. *Competitiveness Review: An International Business Journal, 28*(3), 236–251.

Kim, H. M. (2024). Foreign direct investment and urban growth in Vietnam: Spatial, economic, and demographic perspectives. *Asian Geographer, 41*(2), 167–184.

Kola-Bezka, M., & Kuzel, M. (2023). global cities and multinational enterprises: Integrating the existing concepts for future research studies. *Bulletin of Geography*. Socio-economic Series, *60*, 101–125.

McDonald, C., Buckley, P. J., Voss, H., Cross, A. R., & Chen, L. (2018). Place, space, and foreign direct investment into peripheral cities. *International Business Review, 27*(4), 803–813.

Metaxas, T. (2010). Cities competition, place marketing and economic development in South Europe: The Barcelona case as FDI destination. *Theoretical and Empirical Researches in Urban Management, 5*(14), 5–19.

Ning, L., Wang, F., & Li, J. (2016). Urban innovation, regional externalities of foreign direct investment and industrial agglomeration: Evidence from Chinese cities. *Research Policy, 45*(4), 830–843.

Poelhekke, S., & Van Der Ploeg, F. (2009). Foreign direct investment and urban concentrations: Unbundling spatial lags. *Journal of Regional Science, 49*(4), 749–775.

Prime, P. B. (2012). Utilizing FDI to stay ahead: The case of Singapore. *Studies in Comparative International Development, 47*, 139–160.
Reckien, D., & Martinez-Fernandez, C. (2011). Why do cities shrink? *European Planning Studies, 19*(8), 1375–1397.
Rogoff, K. S., & Yang, Y. (2024). A tale of tier 3 cities. *Journal of International Economics, 152*, 103989.
Sassen, S. (1993). Rebuilding the global city: Economy, ethnicity and space. *Social Justice, 20*(3/4 (53–54), Fall–Winter 1993, Global Crises, Local Struggles), 32–50.
Scholvin, S., Breul, M., & Diez, J. R. (2019). Revisiting gateway cities: Connecting hubs in global networks to their hinterlands. *Urban Geography, 40*(9), 1291–1309.
Serikzhanova, S. S., & Aldangarkyzy, A (2021). Migration attractiveness as a factor in the development of Kazakhstan cities. *Вестник КазНУ. Серия психологии и социологии, 78*(3), 148–156.
Shatkin, G. (2007). Global cities of the South: Emerging perspectives on growth and inequality. *Cities, 24*(1), 1–15.
Todd, R. H. (1977). A city index: Measurement of a city's attractiveness. *Review of Applied Urban Research, 5*(7), 1–16.
Vongpraseuth, T., & Choi, C. G. (2015). Globalization, foreign direct investment, and urban growth management: Policies and conflicts in Vientiane, Laos. *Land Use Policy, 42*, 790–799.
Wang, D. T., Gu, F. F., David, K. T., & Yim, C. K. B. (2013). When does FDI matter? The roles of local institutions and ethnic origins of FDI. *International Business Review, 22*(2), 450–465.
Williams, C., & Du, J. (2014). The impact of trust and local learning on the innovative performance of MNE subsidiaries in China. *Asia Pacific Journal of Management, 31*, 973–996.
Williams, C., & Steriu, R. (2022). MNE market entry and social investment in battle-weary countries: Evidence from Heineken. *Journal of World Business, 57*(4), 101342.
Williams, C., Van Eerde, W., & Thé, D. (2012) *Infusion's Greenfield subsidiary in Poland*. Ivey Publishing (product ID: 9B12M076).
Zheng, S., Kahn, M. E., & Liu, H. (2010). Towards a system of open cities in China: Home prices, FDI flows and air quality in 35 major cities. *Regional Science and Urban Economics, 40*(1), 1–10.

PART I

Cities in Advanced Economies as Locations for FDI

Abstract

Many factors influence Foreign Direct Investment (FDI) location choices in cities in advanced economies. These cities are advanced in an economic and institutional sense, and they are also geographically and culturally diverse, with different historical roots. This allows us to examine heterogeneity in the strategies they employ – and the outcomes these strategies lead to – when trying to attract and retain foreign investors. By analysing the successes and challenges faced in and by these cities, the cases presented offer a nuanced understanding of how FDI interacts with local economies and institutional frameworks in advanced city environments. The collection of cases in Part I offers insights into the complex relationship between FDI and economic outcomes in advanced economies. Both academics and business leaders will find lessons on how advanced economy cities can sustain growth and adapt to an ever-changing global economic landscape, while also appreciating how investing multinational enterprises can grasp opportunities and manage risks in this type of city.

Intense competition amidst institutional advancement

Advanced economy cities are first-world cities, normally positioned in capitalist and democratic countries. They tend to be aligned with the economically rich Western Bloc and are associated with highly developed institutions and strong governance norms. Foreign Direct Investment (FDI) has become a cornerstone of economic growth and urban development within advanced economies. In an era marked by intensified urbanization, advanced economy cities have emerged as pivotal hubs for multinational enterprises (MNEs) seeking to expand their operations, access new markets, and tap into strategic resources. This is not to say all cities in advanced economies are pivotal

DOI: 10.4324/9781003483410-2

hubs, many have fallen into decline.[1] Nevertheless, advanced economies traditionally played host to the world's most advanced cities, especially in terms of human capital, innovation and financial markets and knowledge-intensive industries.

The competition for FDI among advanced economy cities is fierce. These cities work hard to position themselves as attractive locations for global capital flows – and maintain their positions. The incentives that appeal to investing MNEs tend to be high-value-added – advanced producer – services (Anttiroiko, 2015; Beaverstock et al., 1999). Such cities need to be able to keep abreast of investors' needs in the evolving global economy, as investors have many choices available to them. They also face competition from cheaper – albeit increasingly promising – cities in transition and developing countries.

A multitude of agencies are involved in advanced economy cities to facilitate investment promotion. In some cases, these agencies go back many decades. Empire State Development, the agency responsible for inward investment in New York, traces its roots back to 1941.[2] Others are more recent – London and Partners (L&P) was formed in 2011 but had its roots in the Greater London Authority which could trace its origins back to 1835.[3]

Investment promotion includes both a pre-investment 'selling' phase and an 'aftercare' phase once an investment has been made. Advanced economy cities tend to have established capabilities in both phases, with keen interest from government bodies, and a depth of learning and knowledge about how to bring investors in and keep them in. However, as shown in the case of Cambridge, United Kingdom (Fear et al., in this book), bringing these agencies together to create a united 'shop window' for potential investors is sometimes a challenge, even in advanced economies. It takes institutional leadership and convening skills to make this happen. The institutional leadership surrounding investment promotion strengthens the competitive prowess of advanced economy cities and the nations to which they belong.

Human capital and strategic assets

Cities in advanced economies traditionally were more associated with valuable human capital and strategic assets, as well as access to finance and networks, compared to cities in developing economies. Human capital relates to the stock of educated and skilled workers available in a city, the exact nature of this human capital being city-specific (Simon & Nardinelli, 2002). The presence of tertiary educational institutions and research universities creates a supply of graduates and the production of cutting-edge research that can be useful to an investing MNE. It has been noted that skilled people tend to live in big cities where they will find career opportunities and ways of seeking rewards for their talents (Glaeser & Resseger, 2010), including from foreign MNEs. The levels of human capital in a city can be a determinant of its subsequent growth over many decades (Simon & Nardinelli, 2002), also offering a long-term incentive to foreign investors. There is a recognized interplay between FDI and human capital at the city level. Su and Liu (2016), for instance, find that the positive link between FDI and economic growth at the city level is positively moderated by human capital within the city. Focusing on US city data, Glaeser and Resseger (2010) find that bigger metropolitan areas have larger amounts of skilled workers. They also note that skilled workers experience faster learning in big cities, where the rate of technological change is faster.

Other forms of strategic assets in cities in advanced economies include physical capital and infrastructure that an investing MNE can benefit from. Again, there is large variation across advanced economy cities in this respect, although overall, these types of strategic assets will be more established and reliable as sources of value compared to developing economies. The ability of a city to move its workforce and its goods around is just as important as the skills and abilities of that workforce. Bono et al. (2024) show that transport infrastructure in cities is a main determinant of attractiveness for FDI in cities. Cities in advanced economies tend to have the best urban transport infrastructure, and capital cities in OECD countries have high-quality rail and road networks concentrated in them, despite some of them being far from the geographic centre of the country (OECD, 2006).

From the perspective of the investing MNE, advanced economy cities are also attractive because of the presence of other competing firms and established ecosystems that can support the effective functioning of the firm within the location (Chakravarty et al., 2021). In Porterian terms, these are factor conditions, and related and supportive industries help to make the city attractive (Porter, 1990). Visnjic et al. (2016) conduct an analysis of Vienna, London, and Chicago and argue that cities such as these can be governed either as an extended enterprise or as an 'ecosystem of ecosystems'. They highlight the complexity and diversity of relationships and ties between multiple types of actors in these types of cities, arguing that they can provide a role as either an integrator or a platform hub. As an integrator, the city is responsible for providing one part of a final product and integrating into the value chain of a wider enterprise, such as an MNE. As a platform hub, the city provides the foundation and architecture for enterprises to innovate, such as subsidiaries of MNEs (Visnjic et al., 2016).

Diversity in informal institutions and social environments

While global cities in advanced economies provide concentrations of human capital, innovation capacities and advanced factor markets, as well as strong formal institutions that attract FDI, they are by no means a homogeneous whole as far as informal institutions and local cultures are concerned.

Consider the case of Chinese investments in the West. The EU maintained a generally open FDI policy, as reflected in the OECD FDI Restrictiveness Index. This is indicative of a strong and reliable formal institutional environment that is favourable towards FDI. However, growing political concerns have emerged regarding Chinese state-owned firms acquiring European technology and infrastructural companies (Zhang & Van Den Bulcke, 2014), this following changes in political sentiment and public opinion in the United States towards Chinese investment. Public opinion influences Chinese investments, especially from state-owned Chinese enterprises, although larger institutional differences between China and many host countries have been shown to reduce these positive effects (De Beule & Zhang, 2022). In addition to formal government policies, historical connections can play a role in shaping FDI patterns for Chinese companies investing in the West (Zhang and De Beule, 2024). Liu (2021) developed an expanded model for understanding Chinese MNE investment in the advanced economies of the West, highlighting how bilateral relations and the media environment in the host country have a role to play on top of the traditional factors such as market size and strategic asset endowments. In this case the country-of-origin matters, as cities in the West may have no choice but to follow national level public opinion on highly sensitive Chinese FDI at a time of geo-political tension, despite an openness to FDI at a national or regional (e.g., EU) level (Liu, 2021).

Cities in advanced countries are also highly culturally diverse. One indicator of city culture that matters for FDI is the level of entrepreneurial culture. This can be measured in terms of the rate at which new firms are created in an urban agglomeration (Majocchi & Presutti, 2009). A city with an entrepreneurial culture may be attractive for MNEs wishing to tap into innovative start-ups and cutting-edge knowledge. MNEs seek to be a part of new and emerging ecosystems. Despite the uncertainty surrounding entrepreneurial ventures and their high failure rates, MNEs seeking new learning and early-stage technologies may be attracted because of city-level entrepreneurial culture, which varies across advanced economies. Scholars have pointed out that the social environment of cities in advanced economies matters to FDI (Majocchi & Presutti, 2009); but it is highly heterogeneous. Majocchi and Presutti (2009) show that crime against property (which correlates with city size and income levels) is weakly connected to lower levels of foreign investments. Daniele and Marani (2011) examine the effects of organized crime (extortion, bomb attacks, arson and criminal association) on FDI in regions in Italy, an advanced, OECD country. Many of these issues occur in cities, the target locations for FDI. Their study shows organized crime to have consistent negative effects on FDI inflows, even after controlling for the presence of incentives for FDI.

While we know that strong institutions, human capital and market sizes are prominent in advanced economy cities, there are still informal institutions (including public opinion), cultural attributes (including enterprise culture) and the social environment (including crime levels) that differ substantially across cities and that have been shown to deter investors.

Vulnerability to crisis events and shocks

Despite the level of economic development of cities in advanced economies, they are not immune to disruptive events and shocks that can hinder the operations of international companies located in those cities. The vulnerability to such disruptions can be a deterring force for MNEs considering investments in these cities, despite numerous other factors that make them attractive. To this end, the capability of the city – rather than the MNE – to anticipate, mitigate or prevent the effects of disruptions and shocks affecting the city is an area of concern for investors. Similarly, the city's ability to respond in a coordinated way to shocks – and to recover over the longer term – is something that MNEs may be interested in learning about prior to investment. This resilience in cities – their ability to respond to crisis events in the short term and recover in the longer term – is as important at a collective civic level as it is within individual organizations (Williams & You, 2021).

Shocks that affect the functioning of investments in cities in advanced countries include natural disasters, such as earthquakes, volcanoes, typhoons and hurricanes, as well as man-made ones such as the global financial crisis and the Covid-19 pandemic. Japan is an advanced economy that is highly vulnerable to natural disasters. The San Andreas Fault runs through California in proximity to many clusters of innovation and investment. Iceland's volcanoes can produce ash clouds that last for months, disrupting airborne and other logistical operations of international companies. In these examples, governments, local economic actors, and communities are severely affected, putting pressure on MNE investments. In recent times, major natural disasters in advanced economies have borne a high economic cost, in addition to human tragedy and social costs. Japan's Fukushima nuclear incident was in 2011, costing in the region of $200 billion at the time of writing. Iceland's, Eyjafjallajökull erupted in 2010 causing airlines to lose around $170 million per day. The Ridgecrest earthquakes in California in 2019 caused $5.3 billion of damage.

Another form of crisis is the man-made one. Economic shocks can impact advanced economies more quickly and more severely than developing economies, especially when the shock originates in developed countries. This was evident during the global financial crisis of 2007–2009, which emerged in the credit markets in advanced economies (Edey, 2009). Although developing economies were also affected, the global contagion lagged. Developing countries faced portfolio withdrawals, and FDI was affected, but this varied from country to country (Te Velde et al., 2008). Meanwhile, in advanced economies, business and consumer confidence was hit hard from the outset (Edey, 2009) affecting property prices, investment intentions and confidence in most of the world's global cities. Advanced economy cities were also not immune to the Covid-19 pandemic, despite high levels of health infrastructure. With lockdown enforcement came fundamental shifts in working behaviours, especially in white-collar jobs; many industries needed to grapple with the remote working phenomenon, including the challenge of how to optimize the usage of costly offices in cities and to keep key workers' productivity high when working remotely from non-city locations (Hensher et al., 2023).

The cases in Part I

The collection of cases in Part I aims to explore the phenomenon of FDI in cities within advanced economies. We present five cases from a mix of cities. These include two global cities: London and New York, and other prime cities, including Cambridge and Helsinki. Finally, we have a case relating to small cities in the Flanders region of Northern Belgium, including Ghent, Leuven and Antwerp. These cases offer insights into how urban areas in advanced economies act as 'shop windows' for global investment, showcasing their business models, strategic assets, human capital, and markets to attract foreign investors. The cases also show how cities can put up obstacles and deter investment, sometimes long after initial interest in making an investment has been identified. The cases provide insight into FDI attraction and location choices in advanced economies while highlighting institutional diversity, and the vulnerabilities that cities experience despite their advanced status. Key themes include the complexities of institutional environments, the intensity of competition between cities and the risks associated with business and economic shocks.

- London: A Post-Brexit Landscape

London is a prime example of a global city, with an economy deeply integrated into global financial markets. However, London faced a unique set of challenges in the wake of Brexit, which raised questions about the city's future as a leading financial centre. The concept of institutional change is particularly relevant here, as London sought to navigate an uncertain political and economic landscape. This case illustrates how London adapted to the post-financial crisis and post-Brexit environment with a global openness, and how it attracted FDI bids from China. A key theme in this initiative was a focus on the 'occupier's strategy', although the outcome of this strategy was far from ideal when the investor itself went bust.

- New York: A Global Powerhouse

New York is often cited as a quintessential example of a global city. Its role as a global financial centre, combined with its diverse economy and highly developed infrastructure, makes it a prime location for FDI. The city's business model is built around its position as a centre for finance, media and technology, and it attracts MNEs seeking access to its vast consumer base, skilled workforce and cultural capital. However, the case presented here of a small German company seeking to set up its business model in Manhattan highlights issues associated with entering a fast-paced and highly competitive global city.

- Cambridge: A Hub for Research and Innovation

The city of Cambridge provides an example of how smaller, specialized cities can compete in the global FDI market by leveraging their strengths in innovation and human capital. Cambridge had become a hub for high-tech industries, particularly in software, electronics, and life sciences and healthcare. Its world-renowned university serves as a focal point for attracting research-based FDI, and the city has cultivated an ecosystem that supports innovation through strong links between academia and industry. The concept of the knowledge economy is particularly relevant here, as Cambridge exemplifies how cities can harness intellectual capital to drive economic growth. However, there was a time when Cambridge also faced challenges orchestrating its activities in attracting FDI. Some local communities expressed concerns about the social impact of rapid urban growth, leading to debates about how best to balance economic development with sustainability and quality of life. This case explores how the city navigated these tensions and puts a spotlight on the leadership that was required. Lessons can be drawn for other small and medium-sized cities that have a research-intensive university at their core and how they can seek to attract relevant FDI in knowledge-intensive sectors.

- Helsinki: Leveraging Institutional Strengths

Helsinki, the capital of Finland, offers an interesting contrast to larger global cities like London and New York. As a smaller city in a relatively small – but nevertheless advanced – country, Helsinki has focused on leveraging its institutional strengths to attract FDI into a reliable and innovative environment. Helsinki emphasizes the quality of its institutions and the ease of doing business as key selling points. The case study explores how Helsinki's institutional framework shaped its performance as a recipient of quality FDI in the years following the downfall of Nokia. It highlights how, in the shadow of such a corporate collapse, opportunities for utilizing the human capital in the city continued to exist, and how this can be exploited by new investors.

- Flanders: Regional Cities and Global Competition

Flanders, a region in Belgium, provides an example of how sub-national regions within advanced economies compete for FDI. The region had developed a strong industrial base, with strengths in sectors such as automotive manufacturing and logistics. Flanders had positioned itself as a location for MNEs looking to establish a presence in Europe, offering access to key markets through a well-developed infrastructure and central location. The case shows how FDI is seen as a way of developing infrastructure in regions, including infrastructure in energy that is consumed by inhabitants in regional cities. FDI can be used to revitalize energy infrastructure as well as seek new markets. However, as the case reveals, there can be opposition and obstacles at city level that act to prevent the successful competition of FDI deals in sensitive sectors such as infrastructure and energy.

Notes

1 In this book, the cases of Katowice (author: Irwin-Hunt) and Redcar (author: Wokke) illustrate transitions from industrial decline towards knowledge-intensive economies at city level.
2 https://esd.ny.gov/about-us
3 https://en.wikipedia.org/wiki/History_of_local_government_in_London

1

CASE 1: LONDON'S ROYAL ALBERT DOCK REDEVELOPMENT

A Chinese dream turned nightmare

Jacopo Dettoni

Abstract

They are only five years old, but the empty buildings by Chinese developer Advanced Business Parks (ABP) rising on the shores of the Royal Albert Docks (RAD) in London are already a relic from another geopolitical season. They were meant to usher in a new golden era of Sino-British relationships; to replicate Canary Wharf's success in giving London another business district rising from the ashes of its once fabled docklands; to regenerate one of the city's poorest areas by creating more than 20,000 jobs. Today, they are gathering dust, 21 lego-like blocks waiting to find any use and purpose after ABP went bust and the political consensus that hailed them as the 'most exciting development opportunity in London,' to put it in the words of the then London's mayor Boris Johnson, is long over. The trajectory of ABP's RAD redevelopment, which at face value is the largest non-oil investment ever announced by a Chinese company in the United Kingdom, is a telling story for any city looking for international capital to foster urban regeneration. It speaks volumes about the dos and don'ts of FDI attraction and investment landing.

It was meant to epitomise the new golden era of Sino-British relationship; to replicate Canary Wharf's success in giving London another business district rising from the ashes of its once fabled docklands; to regenerate one of the city's poorest areas by creating more than 20,000 jobs.

About two dozen empty buildings are what is left of the ambitious redevelopment of the Royal Albert Docks (RAD). The buildings form an isolated cluster along the RAD waterfront. Barren land separates it from East London University to the east and the Newham Council building to the west.

On paper, the project should have populated the waterfront with a vibrant business district providing companies from China and elsewhere with

DOI: 10.4324/9781003483410-3

headquarters in London. In reality, only phase 1 saw the light – and it was enough to seal the fate of the project.

It's been five years since the buildings have been completed. Not a single tenant has moved in. In fact, it's Advanced Business Parks (ABP) that moved out. The Chinese developer went officially into administration in 2022 when the GLA took back control of the land, which ultimately led it to find a new developer pursuing a new vision for the area.

If today the project is a celebrated failure, only a few years ago it received the blessing of the very top of the two countries' political elite. In a postcard from another geopolitical era, then British prime minister David Cameron and Chinese president Xi Jinping together witnessed the signing of the general contractor agreement between ABP and Chinese Citic Construction in October 2015.

'Designated to become London's next business district following the City of London and Canary Wharf, the project expects to provide an ideal platform for Asian companies seeking to establish a presence in the UK and the European markets,' wrote real estate firm Savills, which at the time acted as ABP's global partner for the project. 'It is highly anticipated by UK politicians and companies alike to promote China-UK business and trade.'[1]

However, despite the hype and the political backing, the project failed to get buy-in from the local communities from the outset.

The government and the City hall then led by Boris Johnson saw a chance to push its vision for a new golden era of Sino-British relations; China an opportunity to build a vital node at the heart of Europe's financial capital for its 'Go global' platform, which made available generous credit lines for companies to grow overseas (that platform would evolve into the Belt and Road Initiative from 2014 onwards); ABP a unique chance to gain an international profile.

Little mattered that the surrounding Newham borough is one of the city's poorest. Once a nestle for London dock and factory workers, the area went through a slow, challenging requalification as the docks and the factories moved out of town. Although it never lost its blue-collar vocation, waves of migration from South Asia and the Caribbean started turning this part of East London into today's melting pot. Similarly to the adjacent London City Airport, ABP's RAD vision appeared disjointed from its urban surroundings from the outset. More of a new district to fill with companies and workers from the outside than one crowning in local businesses and talent. Once the Sino-British tide turned, and the Covid-19 pandemic limited the engagement with prospective investors, this shortcoming would come back to haunt the project and contribute to seal its fate.

The national opinion was not impressed either. The whole tendering process fell under heavy national scrutiny following a Channel 4 investigation that raised doubts over the track record of ABP, a company that had never built anything outside China, and its real capacity to deliver a development of that magnitude. The network's investigation also called into question the role of London & Partners, the city's investment promotion agency (IPA), and the nature of its engagement with ABP ahead of the tendering process. The Greater London Authority launched its own investigation into the whole process, which ultimately cleared all the parties involved in any misconduct.

Despite its rocky start, ABP did break ground in 2017 and delivered phase 1 in April 2019. By then, though, a number of other issues would inevitably compromise its capacity to attract any tenant.

ABP's RAD promised to grant its occupiers access to London and the European market as a whole.

As regards the former, a long-awaited crossrail connection, which was vital in connecting the otherwise relatively isolated RAD to London's other centres of business in Canary Wharf, the City and West London, was running years behind schedule.

For the latter, Brexit changed the whole calculus. The area had been marketed as a gateway to Europe for Chinese and other businesses. Suddenly that was no more. Even worse, the government was even struggling to articulate a coherent foreign trade and investment vision for post-Brexit Britain.

The geopolitical environment shifted equally dramatically. Just a few months after the Brexit referendum in June 2016, Donald Trump won the US presidency. That marked a watershed moment in the relationship between China and the West.

The Covid-19 pandemic was the nail in the coffin. Not only because it halted any effort by ABP to find tenants; but also, because it questioned the whole need of new business districts with the rise of remote working.

Diving deep into some of these factors can provide valuable insight into those factors that determine the success or failure of such foreign direct investment projects in complex urban areas like London. In the long run, the ABP cluster will likely become the first piece in a decade-long regeneration of the whole area. The GLA has already appointed a new developer to take the project forward.

In this perspective, learning from its mistakes can not only guide any future development in the area but also teach lessons about the factors of success, or rather failure in this case, of major FDI projects like ABP's RAD.

The golden age of Sino-British relationship

The Global Financial Crisis (GFC) sent European governments scrambling for fresh injections of external capital that could shore up investment in times of austerity.

In the United Kingdom, the coalition government led by David Cameron came into office in 2010, putting an end to 13 years of Labour rule.

The new government, particularly its chancellor of the exchequer, George Osborne, became assertive in its efforts to strengthen diplomatic and economic relationships with China, whose potential as an economic and political powerhouse was starting to manifest after the years of tremendous growth that followed its WTO membership in 2001.

'There was a consensus among witnesses that the UK's China policy at the time was focused on the economic benefits of a relationship with China, and as such driven by the Treasury,' writes a parliamentary report on the UK and China's security and trade relationship published in September 2021. 'George Osborne told us that as Chancellor he led on this policy, as a lot of the "positives" of the UK-China relationship were economic, and "the Treasury leads on economic diplomacy".'[2]

Former Commercial Secretary to the Treasury Lord Sassoon is quoted in the report as saying:

> In 2010 we were seeing Chinese policy moving from an economy that was investment-led to much more of a consumer-driven economy ... That clearly played to the UK's strengths in consumer goods of all kinds. China was starting to actively internationalise its currency, the renminbi, which presented significant opportunities for us in financial services. There were many other issues relating to Chinese policy to improve services in healthcare, the environment and education, which played to the strengths of Britain.

Suddenly, national and local authorities around the countries found themselves at work to attract Chinese investors in anything from telecommunications to energy, from transport infrastructure to urban redevelopment.

In the meantime, China's strategic investment with the rest of the world was also evolving. Beijing started encouraging Chinese conglomerates to go global to raise their profile, influence, as well as find markets to absorb some of the overcapacity built at home. Representatives of the GLA listened to first-hand testimony on this in September 2011, when they met with a company called China Security & Surveillance International in Chongqing to scope out their interest in the RAD project. An unnamed representative told them:

> The Chinese Government is encouraging a "Walk Out Policy", encouraging each number 1 entrepreneur in each industry sector to tap into circa $4bn of credit from the Chinese National Credit Bank to invest in international projects.[3]

With political backing on both sides, FDI from China into the United Kingdom went through the roof during Cameron's six-year stint at 10 Downing Street (Figure 1.1).

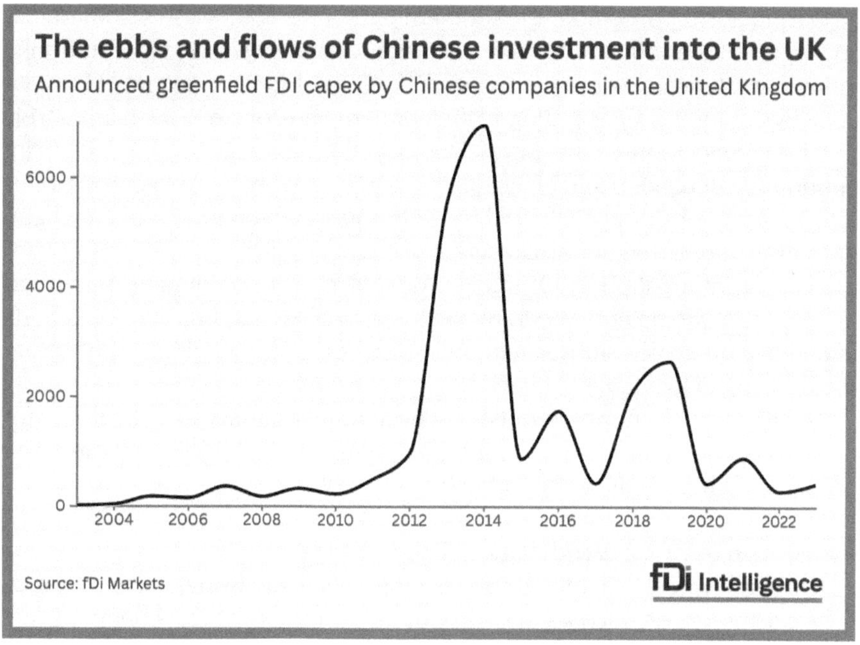

FIGURE 1.1 The ebbs and flows of Chinese investment into the United Kingdom

Overall, they announced 148 projects worth over $15.3bn in between 2010 and June 2016. Real estate was one of their main focus areas, with the $1.6bn project by ABP in RAD standing out as the biggest Chinese FDI project ever announced in the country other than a $1.75bn offshore oilfield development developed by a consortium led by China-based China National Offshore Oil Corporation announced in 2014.

Reaching out to China

The docklands in East London hold a unique value in the city's cultural and economic heritage. They used to handle most of the trade in and out of the East and West Indies and the rest of the world, providing jobs for thousands of dockworkers. As such, they paced life in East London for decades. With the end of the empire and the arrival of containerised trade, the docklands lost their competitiveness and strategic value to downstream ports like Tilbury, which unlike them was able to accommodate the new container vessels.

A protracted fight with the union and dockers ensued. That delayed the closure of the likes of the RAD and the adjacent Victoria dock until the mid-1970s. Once they were shut down for good, an equally slow regeneration process started.

Despite local opposition, the southern part of the RAD was converted into an airport, the London City Airport, which opened in 1987. It would take more than 20 years before the then London Development Agency (LDA) put out a tender for the regeneration of the northern bank of the RAD in July 2011.

'The regeneration of the Royal Docks is the most exciting development opportunity in London and an absolute priority for us both,' wrote Boris Johnson, then mayor of the GLA, and Sir Robin Wales, then mayor of Newham, in the forward of the Royal Docks Development partner selection's memorandum of information (MOI) for pre-qualification questionnaire published in 2011. 'We are determined to make this happen and to put our joint efforts into taking quick decisions, streamlining processes and working with private sector partners to enable delivery.'[4]

The LDA sought from the outset a development partner to deliver an employment-generating scheme on the 34.5-acres site that addresses a few key principles, which include the following:

- It seeks to create a world-class business destination.
- It is employment-led, mixed-use development capitalising on the presence of existing assets, such as City Airport, the University of East London, Excel and the waterfront aspect, as well as the area's excellent highways and public transport access.
- It is centred upon delivering high-tech, knowledge-driven, research and development activities, or similar, as opposed to traditional industrial/warehouse uses.
- It integrates complementary alternative uses, which may include education, transport, health, leisure, retail and ICT in order to provide convenient local amenities for residents and employees.
- It generates a critical mass of development early on in the development scheme.
- It is connected to, and integrated with the surrounding area.
- It aspires to high-quality design and environmental sustainability principles.

Embracing the spirit of the time, London authorities went out of their way to engage with Chinese inventors to redevelop the RAD site. A few months after the MOI was published, the GLA reported several expressions of interest, including three from Chinese companies. At that time, the GLA sent out a memo proposing an engagement trip to China to familiarise interested Chinese investors with the project and the procedures. It read:

> Interest from India, Australia and the US (and certain other geographies) will be relatively familiar with the process of investment within the UK – culturally, legally (particularly from a procurement perspective), economically and in the context of the planning/political background to creating

> value from land here. However, interest from within the People's Republic of China (PRC) – from where the greatest percentage of overseas interest is currently emanating – is on a steep learning curve with regard to investing in/buying land in the UK, particularly from the public sector via the OJEU process. They will need a greater degree of resource applied to engagement/hand-holding about the procurement process, but which on the flip side has the added benefit from a due diligence perspective of allowing us to gauge (a) ability and commitment to delivery, and (b) delivery of an acceptable product in an acceptable way.[5]

The document emphasised the need to put Chinese investors on 'equal footing' with other interested investors from different geographies.

> Whilst difficult to quantify and confirm with certainty, the desired outcome is securing interest from Chinese investors/developers for this key site and the new inward investment to London, and to ensure that they are on an equal footing with the other organisations participating in the procurement process in terms of their familiarity with the procurement process.[6]

The document concluded that such an engagement trip would mitigate the risk that interested Chinese parties 'will not engage seriously.'

> Visiting these potential investors on their home territory will be seen by them as a very positive move that could create a fruitful and potentially profitable relationship with prospective investors. Should the LDA not lead this initiative, there is a risk that these developers will not engage seriously. Whilst the property agents fulfil a key role in managing and administering the response from the property market it is not uncommon for the owner of a property development to be at the heart of a projects promotion – in this case of what is widely regarded as one of the most important regeneration projects in London. We believe there is also an expectation overseas, in business-culture terms, to meet with the 'principal' (vendor) direct – face to face – in order for the 'principal' (purchaser) to take a project/opportunity seriously. The role of 'an agent' is not as established or familiar in as many countries as it is here, hence purchaser/vendor contact direct is important in building and cementing trust/commitment.[7]

The delegation visited China between 19 and 27 September 2011. They met ABP twice on September 20 and 21. In those meetings, an undisclosed company manager said that 'he had been talking to the LDA since late 2008 on RAD; through his proposals RAD will become the central location for emerging Chinese businesses investing in the UK – businesses/ABP clients with assets of at least £1bn each.' In other words, ABP's concept was to leverage the client base of its existing business parks in China – 'about 500/600 buildings/occupiers' – to find occupiers for RAD. The company went as far as saying 'that we continue to receive serious interest from potential end users/occupiers, and that a database of those potential end users/occupiers will be made available in due course to shortlisted parties.'

Another key feature of ABP's interest was its collaboration with established British names and global names. Sensing doubts over its lack of international experience, the company hired British Stanhope as its development manager and Pinsent Mason as lawyers, as well as Australian WT Partnership as quantity surveyors.

The occupier's strategy

The procurement process that commenced in July 2011 has the main objective for the RAD project is to appoint a developer to deliver an employment-led, mixed-use development. However, it somewhat started off on a weak footing as the UK market for business occupiers generating employment opportunities is 'weak' and the procurement process for RAD 'acknowledges its relative market weakness and is designed accordingly,'[8] according to an internal paper by GLA's Housing Investment Group published in May 2012.

The outlook on office space demand is well documented in the market intelligence published at the time. At the end of 2011, real estate firm Savills wrote:

> Rising concerns about sovereign debt and weak economic recovery in Europe and the USA are affecting tenant demand across the country. The lack of economic recovery this year has led to most regional office markets seeing lower occupational demand, with many occupiers looking to either re-gear existing leases at break options, or taking short extensions at expiry in an attempt to avoid relocating and therefore any capital expenditure or staff loss. [...] Is the outlook bright for 2012 and beyond? We believe that the recovery will come, but it's not going to be as strong or as soon as previously anticipated.[9]

Questioned by members of the London Assembly during the GLA Oversight Committee, deputy mayor Sir Edward Lister was reported as saying in March 2015: 'This wasn't a site that everyone was rushing for. There was very little interest – that was part of the problem.'[10]

This detail would play a key role in tilting the procurement process in favour of ABP.

The procurement process commenced in the summer of 2011 using the 'competitive dialogue' procurement process, which allows for the award of particularly complex contracts through a dialogue process where the technical, legal and financial details of a project can be defined with reference to the market. The process enables dialogue with each bidder to determine a commercial solution that best meets the GLA's stated requirements for the site.

In December 2011, eight developers were selected to participate in the outline solutions stage of the procurement process. The developers were asked to provide an outline of their proposed scheme and an indicative financial method for a land offer, together with comments on the contractual terms proposed by the LDA. Six submissions were received by the LDA on 12 March 2012. Three of them were shortlisted: ABP's, as well as two undisclosed proposals by UK firms Muse and Wrenbridge.

According to the GLA document, ABP was proposing an office-based scheme focusing on occupiers from China and the Far East; the undisclosed 'bidder B' a commercial district, knowledge campus, education village, leisure and incubator units; the undisclosed 'bidder C' a ski leisure centre/ snow dome.

> ABP propose 2.7 million square feet by 2020, being more ambitious than in scale and delivery. The estimated number of jobs created is 20,400, approximately 60%–80% of which are expected to be recruited locally. Grant Thornton estimates a slightly higher figure of 21,512 jobs. The present value of the GVA (over 25 years, discounted at 3.5%) is approximately £6,365m if delivered as forecast.[11]

At this stage, an 'early development' criterion (otherwise known as the ability to deliver a viable occupation strategy) became a pass/fail test. 'It was this change in criteria that resulted in ABP becoming the sole contender during the last phase of the process. It was the only bid that could provide adequate assurance of being able to attract enough occupiers quickly.'[12]

Against this backdrop, and the strong emphasis on the occupier's strategy, the bid by ABP was certainly a standout. First, ABP's vision of developing at RAD a new business hub was consistent with the GLA's vision. Besides, ABP was the only one of the three shortlisted companies that was willing to build the development speculatively. In other words, they were willing to commit without pre-lets and go to market once the development was ready. More specifically, they were proposing to break ground in April 2015, with the first of six phases being completed in February 2017. The GLA put the overall development cost at £1.7bn.

David Lunts, then GLA's executive director for housing and land, said to the GLA's oversight committee in March 2015:

> It is worth adding as well that on a scheme like this which is a commercial scheme, it is not a residential scheme, it is pretty unusual to see developers committing to build speculatively without a pre-let. It is extremely unusual outside of the core commercial markets of London, and even more

> unusual coming out of a very deep and difficult recession. Those were some of the reasons why actually – speaking personally and I do not think I was the only one – I was pretty impressed in a way that the LDA and subsequently the GLA managed to get three pretty serious bids. That was pretty good going actually for a site like this that was looking for a large element of speculative investment.[13]

To validate its bid and provide the required 'viable occupiers strategy,' ABP claimed 47 companies originating from its tenants base in China were interested in moving in. London & Partners, which supported the GLA marketing efforts in China, proceeded to validate those claims in a telephone survey. Interestingly, only 10 of 47 companies said they would be interested in moving to London; only eight were even aware of the RAD project by ABP. The Housing Investment Group characterised this outcome as 'mixed response' in September 2012:

> Their submission includes 47 expressions of interest from businesses based in China, and whilst it is not possible to fully verify the extent of this interest at this stage, an initial review was conducted by London & Partners. The review provided a mixed response, which was explained by ABP to relate to the nature of their relationship with a number of the businesses and various cultural differences. However it is clear there is interest from Chinese companies in locating to the UK and working with ABP together with a commitment to building 600,000sq ft of first phase of development.[14]

At that point, with ABP remaining as the only bidder still engaging with the procurement process, the GLA could either terminate the bid or go ahead with ABP. It decided on the latter, and eventually, it was appointed as the preferred bidder in May 2013.

Ultimately, these two main factors secured ABP the project: its vision was consistent with that of the GLA for an employment-led business hub; it guaranteed a relatively rapid speculative development regardless of the challenging market conditions, with the list of interested occupiers suggesting the company had a viable occupier's strategy in place.

Place-making struggle

In November 2014, Channel 4 released an investigation that raised doubts over the human rights track record of ABP in China, as well as over the transparency of the whole procurement process and whether the Chinese company was given preferential treatment.[15] Eventually, a GLA Oversight Committee internal audit and an Oversight Committee meeting found no evidence of any wrongdoing by the GLA and London & Partners in the tendering process.

Finally, ABP broke ground in August 2017. Two years later, in April 2019, the first 21 buildings of phase 1 were completed, which is approximately 500,000 square feet of development. ABP managed to secure only two tenants since the completion of phase 1 before the GLA gained back control of the whole development in March 2022 before the Chinese company went into liquidation.

> Occupation at Phase 1 of the Royal Albert Docks has been disappointing [...] With any large scheme such as this, the first phase is always the most challenging as the first part of establishing a place, and place-making. It is very often the most difficult phase to deliver and develop.[16]

If the mantra of any property development is 'location, location, location,' the place-making of ABP's RAD vision was built on the following pillars: access to London and the wider European market for a business community formed in large part by Chinese and Asian companies. One by one, these pillars crumbled down, crushed by a combination of factors that proved lethal to its business outlook.

Access to London

Those familiar with the London transport system know that zones matter in London. Transport for London classifies central London as 'Zone 1.' As commuters move further away from the city centre, they travel through all the other five zones until they get to Zone 6, which marks the outer edge of the urban area and its transport system.

RAD is in zone 3 in East London – not dramatically far from the city centre, but not that close either. ABP believed the planned upgrade in urban transport infrastructure was capable of shortening distances and bringing RAD closer to the city centre. Similarly to what the DLR had been for Canary Wharf, it pinned hopes on the upcoming Crossrail to shore up the site's strategic value.

A SkyNews calculation estimated the new line would save passengers travelling to Custom House, the closest Crossrail station to RAD, 34 minutes when compared to existing transport alternatives. Unfortunately for ABP, though, the whole endeavour ran over time and budget. First scheduled to open in late 2018, it would end up launching in late 2022 instead, after the Covid-19 pandemic.

'The opening of Crossrail has been delayed, and this was an important part of ABP's decision on timing for Phase 1,' confirms the GLA's retrospective published in July 2022. 'ABP was hoping that Crossrail would have opened by 2019, and that has had an impact on some occupiers' decision-making about whether to locate there.'[17]

If their transport options were limited at the time of launch in 2019, their access to local incentives was limited.

The Royal Docks was awarded Enterprise Zone (EZ) status by the UK government in March, which will mean businesses locating to the area will benefit from business rates relief over five years as well as a simplified planning approach to development within the zone.

The key benefits of EZ status included a 100% business rate discount over five years for businesses moving into the EZ. With a caveat though: occupancy should have started in April 2015, when ABP had not even broken ground, notes an insider. Besides, the EZ also promised 'government support to bring for roll out of superfast broadband in the zone.'[18] There was no follow-up on that, the insider adds.

Access to the European market

Another key pillar of ABP's vision was its efforts to leverage London's role as a gateway to the wider European market. Up until June 2016, the city was unchallenged in its role as Europe's financial capital thanks to its rule of law, hard infrastructure, and its deep pool of capital and talent.

Things took an abrupt turn that year on June 23, when the majority of those who took part in the Brexit referendum chose to leave the European Union, lifting the lid on a pandora box that would throw the country's political agenda into utter chaos.

The new arrangements between the country and the EU would remain uncertain for the years to come, with the two parties signing a final Brexit withdrawal agreement only in January 2020. Despite the frantic years of those years, it always appeared likely that the United Kingdom would lose its passporting rights to sell financial products to the EU market.

History would prove many doomsayers wrong as the end of passporting rights didn't seal the fate of the London financial industry altogether, which continues to evolve and adapt. However, it's equally true that many financial institutions moved teams elsewhere to retain a footprint in the European market, which had an impact on the city's financial ecosystem as desks moved to the likes of Amsterdam, Paris, Dublin and Frankfurt.

In those years, any company looking at office space in London was facing the uncertainty that Brexit engendered as regards future arrangements with the EU. The same perception of that uncertainty was augmented by the political chaos that ensued in those years. When ABP completed RAD's phase 1 in April 2019, the government led by then prime minister Theresa May had been struggling to win parliament support for its proposed 'soft Brexit' agreement, which would ultimately lead her to give way to Boris Johnson and his 'Get Brexit done' mandate.

Inevitably, the country's investment appeal took a hit from the Brexit uncertainty and the political volatility it caused. According to Unctad figures, overall FDI in the country peaked at $258bn in 2016 at the sudden drop of the British pound paved the way for much opportunistic inward investment; it then started a steady decline, to the extent that it reported net negative values in both 2021 and 2023, when foreign investors extracted more capital from the United Kingdom in the form of dividends and other contributions than the amount of capital they injected into the country. In this context, ABP's failure to follow up on its original plan to lure Chinese and Asian investors to open office in London appears as another proof of the weakening investment environment that followed the Brexit referendum.

The end of the 'golden era'

The 'golden era' of Sino-Chinese relations reached its climax in the mid-2010s. With China evolving its foreign policy platform into the Belt and Road Initiative, which Xi Jinping first mentioned in September 2014, dozens of countries around the world rushed to sign up for the initiative.

Although the United Kingdom has never formally joined the BRI, the country became a founding member of the Beijing-sponsored Asia Infrastructure Investment Bank, which stemmed from China's same effort to increase its international sphere of influence through trade and investment.

A train service connecting London to Yiwu in East China was even opened in January 2017. In this context, the ABP project became even more strategic as a node for BRI finance in the European financial capital. However, by the time the first buildings were completed, the mood had already changed.

If Brexit was a shocker, the election of Donald Trump just a few months later was an even bigger one. Trump de facto ended the honeymoon between China and the West that followed its WTO membership in 2001. Suddenly, the United States and Europe woke up to the threat that critical infrastructure fell into the hands of Chinese companies with direct or indirect ties to the politburo in China.

The United Kingdom has been somewhat ambiguous on its stance on Chinese FDI in this evolving geopolitical environment. Dr Alessio Patalano, Senior Fellow at Policy Exchange and Reader in East Asian Warfare and Security at King's College London's Centre for Grand Strategy, told the parliamentary report:

> For the UK government a strong and close relationship with the United States remains a primary security interest. The Trump and Biden administrations have approached policy towards China in more competitive terms. This has, in turn, put pressure on the UK government to maintain policies that are compatible with changes in Washington.[19]

A new National Security and Investment Act was passed to trigger tighter scrutiny of inbound investment deals from China and elsewhere; in the meantime, the government cut out companies like Huawei and China General Nuclear (CGN) from major new infrastructure developments.

However, Chinese state firms still feature among the largest shareholders of other critical infrastructure like water (Thames Water), transport (Heathrow and Manchester Airport) and energy (CGN still has a minority stake in another nuclear plant development, Hinkley Point C).

Besides, whole cities like Manchester had placed big bets in strengthening trade and investment relationships with China, which resulted, among other things, in soaring capital and student inflows into the city.

It's not just the West that reduced the level of engagement with Chinese investment. After supporting the internationalisation of its companies in the wake of the GFC, Beijing changed its course of action and introduced tighter capital controls to stem capital outflows. Even in this case, Chinese outbound FDI peaked in 2016, at over $196bn, to then stabilise around the $150bn mark in the following years until 2023, Unctad data show.

These dynamics affected ABP both directly and indirectly. The project was almost entirely financed via debt by Citic, a state bank. 'In 2019, they didn't see any more value in putting more money into a project in a country they were not that comfortable any longer, with a man [ABP's president, Xu Weiping] they didn't trust any more,' an insider said.

Besides, it constrained the appetite of Chinese companies willing to set up operations in London, narrowing further the pool of prospective tenants for RAD.

The Covid-19 disruption

With all these factors making it hard for ABP to sign up any occupier, the Covid-19 pandemic proved the nail in the coffin. It killed any outreach activity in the short term. It disrupted the whole raison d'etre of central business districts in the long term.

The hybrid models of work that the pandemic years unlocked have been testing demand offices in London and elsewhere. Both the City and Canary Wharf have been dealing with low occupancy rates since the pandemic, which has prompted local authorities and owners to diversify their offerings and adjust them to the new models of work.

Londoners have been slower to return to the office than other global cities, found research by the Centre for Cities published in September. According to the research, Londoners currently spend 2.7 days at the office, versus 3.5 in Paris, 3.2 in Singapore and 3.1 in New York, and a pre-pandemic Lonon average of 3.9.[20]

New hybrid models of work, combined with rising interest rates in the wake of the pandemic lockdown proved a hard one to swallow for London's commercial property market.

Even in 2024, 'large London office buildings are proving almost impossible to sell as high interest rates and investor nerves over hybrid working thwart efforts to kick-start dealmaking,' the FT reported in July. 'Investors who bought central London offices since 2014 would probably have to stomach a loss to sell today, according to an MSCI index. At current prices, 64 per cent of London offices would sell for less than what they were bought for, the MSCI index shows.'[21]

With its more illustrious neighbours in the City or Canary Wharf struggling to fill office space, ABP's offering felt even more compromised. Besides, its options were also limited as the adjacent airport constrained the residential density that any pivot could have added to ABP's master plan.

Conclusion

The investor's long-term commitment typically features among the biggest perks of greenfield FDI. Arguably, it's also one of its main perils. Geopolitics, market conditions, and even a pandemic can disrupt any long-term plan, as ABP has come to know to its own expense. While the combination of exogenous factors discussed here has inevitably compromised the outcome of ABP's RAD project, indigenous elements played a key role too in sinking the whole endeavour.

- *Policy stability remains a key factor for the success of FDI projects*. The United Kingdom had lived through a turbulent political cycle. The Tory government sent mixed signals as regards foreign trade – Brexit anyone? – and foreign engagement, with the twists and turns of the Sino-British 'golden era' being just one of the victims of this volatility.
- *Market timing is key*. The GLA vision, from which the ABP project stemmed, hoped to tap into a weak market for new office space from the very beginning. The delays in the Crossrail didn't help in raising the profile of the area. With several other areas currently up for redevelopment, developers are facing a similar gamble as regards the post-Covid-19 recovery of office demand. Building speculatively in this market remains a high risks/high rewards type of strategy.
- *Alignment with the local ecosystem*. The ABP project was a heavily top-down endeavour, which limited its capacity to pivot its offer to local prospective tenants when external factors limited the interest from China and abroad. Some level of engagement with local communities, perhaps in the form of residential units too, would have secured some local occupants,

proved the development could generate cash flow and avoid the current white elephant scenario. The new RAD developers are reportedly stepping up their stakeholders' engagement efforts to limit these risks.

- *The devil is in the detail.* In hindsight, procurement rules favoured a convenient, but still weak bidder. Another set of rules, the enterprise zones rules, failed to make a dent. The UK's bureaucracy is generally perceived as a major hindering factor for new developments. In this case, poor regulation led to a poor outcome.

Notes

1 Savills News, (2015), "President Xi witnesses the signing of the General Contractor Agreement for ABP", accessed 15.01.2025.
2 House of Lords, (2021), "The UK and China's security and trade relationship: A strategic void", 1st Report of Session 2021–22 by International Relations and Defence Committee – p. 13, https://committees.parliament.uk/publications/7214/documents/75842/default/, accessed 15.01.2025.
3 Greater London Authority, (2022), "MGLA231121-8461" by GLA Information Governance Officer – p. 23, https://www.london.gov.uk/sites/default/files/mgla231121-8461_-_eir_response_redacted.pdf, accessed 15.01.2025.
4 Greater London Authority, (2022), "MGLA231121-8461" by GLA Information Governance Officer – p. 50, https://www.london.gov.uk/sites/default/files/mgla231121-8461_-_eir_response_redacted.pdf, accessed 15.01.2025.
5 Greater London Authority, (2022). MGLA231121-8461" by GLA Information Governance Officer – p. 7, https://www.london.gov.uk/sites/default/files/mgla231121-8461_-_eir_response_redacted.pdf, accessed 15.01.2025.
6 Greater London Authority, (2022), "MGLA231121-8461" by GLA Information Governance Officer – p. 8, https://www.london.gov.uk/sites/default/files/mgla231121-8461_-_eir_response_redacted.pdf, accessed 15.01.2025.
7 Greater London Authority, (2022), "MGLA231121-8461" by GLA Information Governance Officer – p. 9, https://www.london.gov.uk/sites/default/files/mgla231121-8461_-_eir_response_redacted.pdf, accessed 15.01.2025.
8 Greater London Authority, (2022), "MGLA231121-8461" by GLA Information Governance Officer – p. 38, https://www.london.gov.uk/sites/default/files/mgla231121-8461_-_eir_response_redacted.pdf, accessed 15.01.2025.
9 Savills, (2011), "UK Office Market Report Winter 2011" – p. 2, https://pdf.euro.savills.co.uk/uk/office-reports/uk-office-market-report---winter-2011.pdf, accessed 15.01.2025.
10 EGI, (2015), "ABP was 'only appointable' Docks bidder", https://www.egi.co.uk/news/abp-was-only-appointable-docks-bidder/, accessed 15.01.2025.
11 Greater London Authority, (2022), "MGLA231121-8461" by GLA Information Governance Officer – p. 90, https://www.london.gov.uk/sites/default/files/mgla231121-8461_-_eir_response_redacted.pdf, accessed 15.01.2025.
12 GLA Procurement. (2022). GLA Oversight Committee – LONDON ASSEMBLY" – p. 28, https://www.london.gov.uk/sites/default/files/gla_procurementvfinal2.pdf, accessed 15.01.2025.
13 GLA, (2015), "GLA Oversight Committee, 24 March 2015 – Transcript of Item 12: Royal Albert Dock Appendix 2" – p. 32, https://gla.moderngov.co.uk/documents/s47493/Minutes%20-%20Appendix%202%20-%20Transcript.pdf, accessed 15.01.2025.

14 Greater London Authority, (2022), "MGLA231121-8461" by GLA Information Governance Officer – p. 91, https://www.london.gov.uk/sites/default/files/mgla231121-8461_-_eir_response_redacted.pdf, accessed 15.01.2025.
15 Channel 4 News, (2015), "Serious questions for Boris Johnson over property deal", https://www.youtube.com/watch?v=YOMrq1oX-mc, accessed 15.01.2025.
16 GLA, (2015). GLA Oversight Committee, 24 March 2015 – Transcript of Item 12: Royal Albert Dock Appendix 2" – p. 31, https://gla.moderngov.co.uk/documents/s47493/Minutes%20-%20Appendix%202%20-%20Transcript.pdf, accessed 15.01.2025.
17 GLA, (2015), "GLA Oversight Committee, 24 March 2015 – Transcript of Item 12: Royal Albert Dock Appendix 2" – p. 31, https://gla.moderngov.co.uk/documents/s47493/Minutes%20-%20Appendix%202%20-%20Transcript.pdf, accessed 15.01.2025.
18 Greater London Authority, (2022), "MGLA231121-8461" by GLA Information Governance Officer – p. 59, https://www.london.gov.uk/sites/default/files/mgla231121-8461_-_eir_response_redacted.pdf, accessed 15.01.2025.
19 House of Lords, (2021), "The UK and China's security and trade relationship: A strategic void", 1st Report of Session 2021–22 by International Relations and Defence Committee – p. 18, https://committees.parliament.uk/publications/7214/documents/75842/default/, accessed 15.01.2025.
20 Centre for Cities, (2024), "Return to the office: How London compares to other global cities, and why this matters", https://www.centreforcities.org/publication/return-to-the-office/, accessed 15.01.2025.
21 FT, (2024), "Large London office buildings proving almost impossible to sell", https://www.ft.com/content/d1ffb476-601c-485e-a020-388631ed7064, accessed 15.01.2025.

2

CASE 2: GORILLAS IN NEW YORK

The role of Foreign Direct Investment (FDI) in the expansion of delivery services

Petra Smith

Abstract

Gorillas in New York describes the early days of the meteoric rise of the rapid food delivery service firm Gorillas (a Berlin-based startup) and its attempt to establish a presence in New York City via a greenfield Foreign Direct Investment (FDI) project. The case looks at the first steps in the market, the strategic choices and challenges faced, and the eventual outcome of the project. FDI plays a pivotal role in the international expansion strategies of companies in growth industries. With the global market for rapid delivery services witnessing exponential growth, a logical step for growth-oriented firms is to pursue opportunities beyond their home market. We examine how Gorillas, a Berlin-based startup, attempted to establish a significant presence in New York City's competitive market via a greenfield FDI project, looking in turn at the wider market context, strategic choices and the eventual outcome of the project.

Gorillas – a company profile

Gorillas was a German 'on-demand grocery delivery' start-up, which was founded in May 2020 by Kağan Sümer and Jörg Kattner in Berlin. Kağan Sümer, originally from Turkey, moved to Germany to complete his studies at the RWTH Aachen. Before founding Gorillas, Sümer worked – among other things – as a consultant at Bain & Company, and – was an influential figure in the European start-up scene in the 2010s and 2020s. Jörg Kattner had, prior to Gorillas, already extensive experience in corporate management. His role at Rocket Internet, working on the HelloFresh project (a meal-kit provider active across Europe and the US, stock-listed at the Frankfurt stock exchange), was crucial for the Gorilla`s venture.

DOI: 10.4324/9781003483410-4

The startup scene in Berlin was one of the most dynamic in Europe and attracted entrepreneurs from all over the continent, due to access to international capital and a strong start-up network. Co-working spaces, incubators, mentors and investors were the reasons why ventures such as Zalando, Delivery Hero and N26 had their starting point in Berlin.

The underlying idea for Gorillas was to make shopping much easier and less hassle. The company's Unique Selling Point (USP) was the promise to deliver groceries within ten minutes, based on a network of micro-fulfilment centres or so-called 'dark stores,' setting it apart from traditional grocery delivery services.

Early success and rapid expansion

By December 2020, within months of its launch, Gorillas had secured $44 million in a Series A funding. This infusion of capital enabled Gorillas to expand rapidly within Germany and across Europe. Within its first year, the company established subsidiaries in several major German cities, including Hamburg, Munich and Cologne. Gorillas' value proposition clearly resonated with city dwellers. Encouraged by its domestic success, Gorillas embarked on an ambitious internationalisation strategy. With significant additional funding, Gorillas decided to rapidly scale its operations not only back home in Berlin but also internationally. In March 2021, Gorillas announced its entry into the Netherlands, setting up operations in Amsterdam. This was followed by launches in London and Paris in April 2021. Gorillas established a presence in over 30 cities across Europe, including Amsterdam, Manchester and Milan. The selection criteria for cities to set up in were based on a combination of population density, and a highly young, urban, digitally connected population.

To expand, Gorillas typically used a greenfield strategy (i.e. set-up new operations from scratch rather than acquiring existing companies). This allowed them to maintain full control over their operations.

The step across the pond – New York

Encouraged by its European triumphs, Gorillas turned its attention to the United States, identifying New York City as the prime market for its rapid delivery service. New York City's unique demographic and consumer behaviour made it seemingly the ideal location choice for hyper-localised on-demand rapid delivery services. With an estimated population of 8.3 million people (according to the US Census Bureau, n.d.), New York was one of the most densely populated urban landscapes in the United States. Add to this the fast-paced lifestyle and the preference for convenience as well as the sheer economic weight of the city. All the boxes of location choice factors were seemingly ticked. Additionally, the impact of the COVID-19 pandemic further accelerated the demand for contactless food delivery, creating a conducive environment for entering the market. In May 2021, Gorillas officially launched in New York.

Kağan Sümer, at that time Gorillas' CEO, led the efforts to establish the foothold in the city. A local team was assembled to manage operations, marketing and logistics, while dark stores were strategically placed across Manhattan. In its initial months, Gorillas saw a promising uptake from New York consumers, attracted by the convenience and speed of its delivery service. The company expanded its network of dark stores across multiple boroughs, including Brooklyn, and Queens, aiming to cover a broad customer base.

In selecting the locations for their dark stores, Gorillas focussed heavily on optimising delivery speed and efficiency. They went into areas with dense urban populations and residential neighbourhoods, in order to achieve their promise of delivering within minutes. Inner city areas are however traditionally not meant to be warehouse locations, which in some locations led to difficulties with regulators.

To build brand awareness, Gorillas focused heavily on digital marketing, particularly on social media platforms, where they sought to engage young, tech-savvy customers. They created a series of social media ads, designed to resonate with affluent young adults. Additionally, Gorillas invested in 'analog' marketing such as billboards to increase visibility in the market.

Challenges and competition

However, the rapid expansion came at a cost. Apart from the high cost of real estate and labour in New York, the operational expenses quickly mounted, and the company struggled to achieve the same level of efficiency it had in European cities. Delivery times occasionally exceeded the promised ten minutes, and logistical hiccups became more frequent. High turnover rates among delivery riders and warehouse staff, coupled with labour disputes over working conditions, further complicated matters. Some employees staged protests demanding better pay and safer working conditions, drawing negative attention to the company.

When looking for US locations and picking New York, Gorillas had unfortunately failed to notice the intense competition in New York City's delivery market. This quickly turned out to be a problem. The market was already fiercely competitive when Gorillas entered, with established players (e.g. Uber Eats, Amazon Fresh, Instacart, FreshDirect) and further market entrants (such as GoPuff and Grubhub) vying for market share.

It had been observed that delivery companies pursued different strategies, and that Gorillas might have been out-competed on operational terms.

Uber Eats, DoorDash and Grubhub were food delivery platforms, whose core business model was a pick-up service from local restaurants. Typically, customers could browse menus, place orders and track their deliveries through their proprietary apps or websites. While the technical infrastructure was relatively similar, these companies weren´t direct competitors to Gorillas due to focussing on the prepared food market. Instacart, an online grocery delivery service, was much closer to Gorillas' business model but did pick up goods from local grocery stores, thereby being able to offer a more diverse range of grocery items, giving customers more flexibility and choice. FreshDirect and Amazon Fresh, commanding extensive logistics networks, sourced products directly from local farms or producers. While Gorillas sought to differentiate themselves through ultra-fast delivery, its competitors emphasised a wider selection of products. The most immediate and direct competitors though were GoPuff and Getir. Getir attacked Gorillas head on, as a super-fast delivery service (10 min), delivering groceries, fresh produce, household goods and ready-to-eat meals within minutes. Gorillas found it difficult to carve out a distinctive and profitable niche.

Also, regulatory complexities arose from New York City imposing stringent regulations on food delivery and transportation services. This included health and safety standards set by the New York City Department of Health and Mental Hygiene, and labour laws on minimum wage, overtime pay and employee classification. All of this made navigating the regulatory landscape unexpectedly difficult and added layers of complexity to Gorillas' operations.

The logistical demands of operating in a densely populated urban environment like New York City were also problematic. Gorillas had to re-stock inventory of their dark stores and deliver goods while grappling with traffic congestion, limited parking and supply chain disruptions. According to insiders, Gorillas already struggled with similar problems in Berlin, only to encounter them more ferociously in New York.

Many accomplishments were made in a short space of time – such as the purchasing organisation being set up and negotiating supplier contracts within 3 months. This was something classical food retail structures typically complete in 2 to 2.5 years. However, there were rapid changes in acting managers and a high staff turnover.

Internal challenges and decision to exit

By late 2021, it became increasingly clear that Gorillas' New York operations were not meeting financial expectations. With regular reports about mounting operational challenges, high labour turnover and growing dissatisfaction within the local management team, the company faced increased scrutiny from investors. Gorillas' hallmark, the rapid expansion strategy, became a liability. When investors lost trust in the over-stretched management, so did their willingness to bankroll the losses of the New York operations. Faced with these mounting pressures, Gorillas announced in January 2022, just eight months after its launch, that it would cease operations in New York City. This was part of a broader strategic shift, which included consolidating its European activities, aiming for profitability rather than rapid expansion.

Reference

U.S. Census Bureau. (n.d.). *QuickFacts New York city,* New York. https://www.census.gov/quickfacts/newyorkcitynewyork.

3

CASE 3: BUILDING THE SHOP WINDOW FOR INWARD INVESTMENT INTO CAMBRIDGE, UK

Harriet Fear, Duncan McCunn and Christopher Williams

Abstract

Cambridge, UK, was a city 90 km north of London with a population of 145,000 people in 2021. It hosted the world leading University of Cambridge, founded in 1209, as well as Anglia Ruskin University, a former college granted University status in 1992. There were over 50,000 students in Cambridge at these two institutions. Cambridge was one of the UK's most successful science and high-tech hubs, the centre of an R&D cluster that had become known as 'Silicon Fen'[1] and which was Europe's largest in 2020 (Citystay, 2020). The Cambridge Cluster, as it was also known, hosted many knowledge intensive businesses in software, electronics and life sciences and healthcare. Science parks included Cambridge Science Park (the oldest, established in 1970), Cambridge Business Park, St John's Innovation Centre, Peterhouse Technology Park, Melbourn Science Park, Granta Park and many others. University related tech centres included the Cambridge Judge Business School and ideaSpace Enterprise Accelerator. The cluster employed over 61,000 people working in over 5,000 technology related businesses. From an inward investment perspective, the city was in need of one shop window.

Keywords

Inward FDI; Ecosystem; University; Cambridge; Shop Window

In need of one shop window

The economic development that had occurred since the 1970s to reach this position had come with a dilemma as far as inward investment was concerned. While it was unquestionably world leading in its focus areas, the ecosystem had been perceived as being 'messy', with many agencies involved

DOI: 10.4324/9781003483410-5

in supporting, managing or engaging with all forms of international interest and investment into the cluster. Foreign companies interested in investing in Cambridge would be confronted with an array of possible contact points, messages and impressions.

There were various regional membership organisations representing industries such as life sciences, technology and cleantech all based in Cambridge with a level of international focus. The University had its Strategic Partnerships Office and there were many science parks, incubators and innovation centres all focused on working with companies. In addition, the Mayoral Combined Authority[2] had a remit for inward investment (run by Growth Works[3] from 2021 to the end of 2023). It was not entirely clear who the most appropriate organisation was to support foreign investors and help them understand and navigate the evolving Cambridge ecosystem. The membership organisations did not have specific Foreign Direct Investment (FDI) attraction in their mandates as their principal focus was supporting their member bases. By 2017 it became increasingly clear that the problem of having one compelling story about what Cambridge could offer in terms of hosting inward FDI had not been solved. Where was the agreed one story about Cambridge to the world?

In 2017, the leadership of the University of Cambridge had become very aware, after feedback from global pharmaceutical companies, that Cambridge needed to organise itself better. The leadership teams at international firms were struggling to find where the one source of accurate data was about the leading sectors in Cambridge and Cambridge's message about investment potential was confusing to them. The ecosystem was perceived as hard to navigate.

In 2017, Sir Leszek Borysiewicz (Vice Chancellor of the University of Cambridge) tasked Edward Benthall and Michael Anstey at Cambridge Innovation Capital (CIC) to undertake a community-wide project which become known as 'Project Spring' (based on the season the work took place but around the concept of the Cambridge ecosystem 'springing' forward).

Mike interviewed over 50 stakeholders in the ecosystem to identify the challenges and opportunities Cambridge was facing. The findings led to three broad recommendations:

- Focusing the ecosystem's resources on supporting scale-ups.
- Strengthening connections with other innovation hubs in the UK and spreading the prosperity of Cambridge further afield locally.
- Establishing a 'front door' for the ecosystem, and driving a coordinated effort promote Cambridge globally.

The first two recommendations were being addressed by other existing organisations within the ecosystem. The third recommendation led to the creation of Cambridge& in 2020, with Harriet Fear as the founding Director and Andy Neely as the Chair, with the mission to work with stakeholders across the ecosystem to attract the highest quality individuals and organisations in the knowledge intensive industries from around the globe into Greater Cambridge.

But how did we get to that?

A series of dinners with leading stakeholders was then convened with Professor Andy Neely, the then Pro Vice Chancellor for Enterprise and Business Relations at the University of Cambridge chairing them.

Each Dinner had 20–25 guests drawn from academia, industry, finance, the local community and, importantly, civic leadership. And it was widely concluded that the 'front door' and co-ordinated effort was the one to focus on.

Neely proceeded by establishing a working group of 18 key representatives from across the ecosystem, including Fear who had worked across the public, private and not for profit sectors. It included representatives from University colleges and departments, the investment community, science parks, serial entrepreneurs and the Greater Cambridge Partnership (GCP, 2025). The working group became known as 'Project Spring'. Its remit was to flesh out the third of the three identified issues – the lack of one agreed story about Cambridge and the 'shop window' requirement. The rationale being that the issue of scaling was being addressed by others (and was to some extent a national issue) and the other – that of spreading the wealth of the city region was being considered at the time by the CPIER (the Cambridgeshire and Peterborough Independent Economic Review) – www.cpier.org.uk.

Project Spring

The working group soon developed a narrative about what Cambridge was, what made it vibrant and culturally, innovatively and historically distinctive. This included the type of innovation being conducted in Cambridge as a way of delimiting the scope of the ecosystem; there was a recognition that the shop window could not be so huge as to make it even more confusing. The three areas of focus were Cambridge's CORE strengths: life sciences and healthcare, technology and advanced manufacturing. It was not going to be about tourism, or creative industries or broader sectors. There was a recognition that what was needed was a razor-sharp focus on handholding large companies to support them as they started to consider Cambridge as an investment location.

The project was structured into four separate sub-working groups consisting of 4–5 participants each: branding, science parks and incubators, networks and vibrant Cambridge (the latter addressing what Cambridge might mean for individuals and families). The branding group was headed by Fear and supported by Bob Driver (then at Cambridge Wireless) and David Secher (of Gonville and Caius College). The overarching narrative was originally drafted by David Gill (then Head of St. John's Innovation Centre) and Sabine Jaccauld (then Head of Communications and PR at AstraZeneca). Collectively the full group developed a clear narrative which was distilled into what the group described as 'One Source of Truth'.

The four sub-working groups all delivered against their defined mandates. There were regular bi-monthly meetings and contact points between the sub-working groups and it was recognised that high level content was being produced to address the first of the three problem areas that arose from the Spring dinners.

The content that the groups provided was then channelled to the branding group for consideration and planning next steps. The content and narratives eventually became the main sections of the Cambridge& website: A Unique Ecosystem, Why Cambridge and Vibrant Cambridge.

However, by the end of 2018, an elephant in the room had been identified. As Fear recalled: 'What were we going to do with this as Project Spring?'

From informal initiative to a dedicated company: the creation of Cambridge&

While Project Spring had started to deliver a compelling narrative, it remained unclear what the project would mean organisationally, what should happen with the content and how would the issue of a 'front door' for Cambridge be addressed and funded? And where would its ownership reside? There was a widely held view that the informal nature of Project Spring needed to become more formalised. While these governance questions were being discussed, Fear became more involved in the project as 2019 dawned, now devoting two days a week from her consultancy business to Project Spring over a period of 8 months. This allowed her to build on the outputs from the four sub-working groups to (a) write a formal Business Case for the creation of an organisation, (b) deliver a new online portal that encapsulated the essence of the offering and how Cambridge could attract and handhold large companies as they considered the city for investment and (c) start to work on raising funds from across academia, business and the civic community to enable plans to take shape.

Fear drew on a local company called KISS Communications for website development and branding work, having secured funding from the University and the Greater Cambridge Partnership. Subcontracting to KISS resulted in a detailed engagement process with the ecosystem and included brand articulation workshops, focus groups and interviews, including with former UK government Science Minister Lord Willetts, and from large companies down to micro businesses and entrepreneurs. The logo, messaging and brand articulation were all developed.

Towards the end of 2019, with the Business Case agreed by the Project Spring Working Group, the portal being ready and funding starting to be attracted, Fear advised Neely and Anstey that working on the recommendations of the Business Case and engaging with companies would be a full-time role. It wasn't going to be viable to 'rely' on a part-time consultancy, so she recommended putting her other clients to one side to focus fully on the new company in a leadership rather than a consulting capacity. Neely agreed and a private company limited by guarantee was created in February 2020 with Fear as its Director on a full-time basis. The company was called Cambridge&. By that time the website was ready to be publicly launched, the narrative was clear, and some funding was in place.

The mandate for Cambridge& was to identify global and scaling companies around the world who may be interested in physically setting up in Greater Cambridge. Research had shown that many innovative companies around the world were either not aware that Cambridge was an innovation hotbed or Cambridge was not even on their radar. Fear and colleagues worked on a three-tier approach to identifying potential inward investment companies:

- A list of global organisations.
- A series of deep dive research projects by Ph.D. and Post Doc students out of the University of Cambridge who would analyse who the Unicorns of the Future were in areas where Cambridge was world class and
- Supporting the work of the Mayoral Combined Authority (CPCA) with large scale inward investment opportunities that the latter received from national Government.

Fear conducted due diligence on those international companies before engaging in any serious dialogue. For years there had been huge interest from international delegations in doing business with Cambridge but there had been no mechanism for the ecosystem working out whether there was benefit both ways from engaging together. A triaging and sifting function was seen as essential to make the investment facilitation process more efficient. Cambridge& did not pretend to be experts in any of the sectors of interest; its main purpose was to be the shop window or concierge service that had been missing. When Cambridge& engaged with companies proactively or reactively on specialist subjects, e.g. AI, quantum computing, genomics or other, it would draw on the leading expertise of the Universities, member organisations and/or other experts from the large pool of local tech experts and entrepreneurs. This helped to create the best experience in terms of meetings, workshops and dialogue for the international company. Cambridge& also decided not to be a membership organisation; it was funded by the University, a small number of renowned Commercial Service Providers and the Greater Cambridge Partnership. It could legitimately call on the membership organisations to meet with the companies as Cambridge& had already undertaken some due diligence and was charging no fee to anyone.

Lockdown activity and the digital strategy

Cambridge& was incorporated in February 2020. In March 2020 the Covid-19 pandemic struck. The business model was premised on putting high level and customised visit programmes together for foreign investors. This suddenly was not possible. As Director of the newly formed entity, and having been involved in every stage since 2017, Fear felt a weight of responsibility. The business case had been extremely well received across A, B and C of the ecosystem: academia, business and the civic community. But now potential funders for Cambridge& (Commercial entities) had financial, strategic and operational pressures with the pandemic and so several possible funders had to put their interest on hold.

She turned to developing a digital strategy and contacted key individuals in her Cambridge network to seek their input on how to go about this: they included Dr David Cleevely CBE (a telecoms expert, serial entrepreneur and co-founder of biotech company Abcam), Dr Soraya Jones (former CEO of Cambridge Wireless and consultant) and others. The digital strategy focused on how to engage with potential inward investors virtually and created smaller working groups of leading figures in Cambridge who already had relations with some of the companies Cambridge& was seeking to attract. The idea was that the compelling offer could be used by them to gauge interest from the company itself.

She also engaged with the local Mayoral Combined Authority for Cambridgeshire and Peterborough which at that point had very limited resources to work on large scale inward investment opportunities that came into the national Department for International Trade in London (later becoming Department for Business and Trade). Fear secured a contract with the Mayoral Combined Authority for Cambridge& to handle enquiries from large companies that they received during the lockdown period. The contract extended to almost 3 years, finishing in December 2023.

Cambridge& also worked very intently on the identification of unicorns[4] of the future around the world. For this Cambridge& engaged with post-graduate students at the University of Cambridge in the field of biotech and engineering. Their deep dive primary and secondary research against a robust set of criteria identified companies that were scaling quickly and that aligned with the knowledge-intensive sectors at Cambridge. Fear had run projects with previous cohorts of these students when she worked for the national Government. She selected key sub-sectors within life sciences and healthcare and the students worked on them. The first, during lockdown, was genomics, given the world class status Cambridge enjoys in the field of genomics. Future projects then included gene and cell therapy, and data analytics in healthcare. She oversaw the project as it established criteria for long- and short-listing unicorns of the future that Cambridge& would then target virtually.

As Fear recalled: 'The unicorns of the future piece came about *because* of lockdown'.

She also took the opportunity during lockdown to review Cambridge&'s website, taking a critical look at what had been done and asking the question: does it address what international companies need to know about us? She pulled together a new group of experts who had little to no prior experience of the website to critically evaluate it. It was a very healthy debate and useful activity. The group concluded that changes were needed as the website, while being good in many ways, told the audience what it wanted to, rather than very clearly addressing the key questions any inward investor would have. This culminated in Cambridge& returning to KISS Communications for a reconfiguration of the website during 2020. This involved bringing the website to life with case studies of companies investing in Cambridge in each of the target sectors, as well as having smooth links to content and 'Talking Head' personal videos from Cambridge 'Champions' within a 20-mile radius of the city centre.

With funding in place from the University of Cambridge and the three Councils via the Greater Cambridge Partnership, Cambridge& started to enjoy strong relations with leading Service Providers who became Supporting Organisations. These were intentionally not blue blood R&D companies (who already paid fees to membership organisations). These were strategic partnerships with companies that had a common interest in Cambridge being seen as easy to navigate, understand and welcoming. They included Deloitte, Barclays, CIC, London Stansted Airport and leading property developers including Brockton Everlast and Bruntwood SciTech. Fear made sure all funders were kept informed about developments as lockdown continued by having virtual calls with them every 4–6 weeks and the funding model was to sign up for 3-year periods.

Status in 2023 and decisions needed

As the end of 2023 drew closer, Cambridge& had successfully negotiated its launch, the pandemic, and had secured funding until 2025. It achieved its objectives of establishing a single shop window for Cambridge, presenting a clear and differentiated message to the outside world, as well as cementing its own additive position within the ecosystem. It made sure it supported and did not obstruct other agencies involved in nurturing relationships with potential investors.

At this point Fear found herself spending at least 50% of her time on stakeholder relationships and the profile of Cambridge& locally, nationally and internationally (the latter virtually). She had plans to have a career change to create some space for writing a book, charitable and pro bono work and to return to consulting. She stepped down at the end of 2023 but not until she had worked with the Board to secure her successor, Duncan McCunn who had been her key contact at Barclays. The Board suggested she remain as a Special Adviser to the organisation, albeit one day a week on a consulting basis for a period.

What happened next?

It took McCunn about 3 seconds to say 'yes' when Harriet floated the idea of him taking over at the helm of Cambridge&. A year later, in late 2024, the next stage of the journey had begun.

What would that journey look like?

In 2024 Cambridge& joined forces with Innovate Cambridge and became an integral part of the Innovate Cambridge organisation.

Its mission to attract new companies to Cambridge continued to be supported by an Innovation Ecosystem firing on all cylinders.

Notes

1 The Fens was the name given to the region in the East Anglia region north and west of Cambridge; a flat and marshy area of land.
2 The MCA included Cambridge City, plus Cambridgeshire and Peterborough.
3 The service provided by Growth Works later became part of remit of the Mayoral Combined Authority's Growth Hub: https://cpcagrowthhub.co.uk/ (Accessed 4 September 2024).
4 A start-up company valued at over $1 billion (USD).

References

Citystay. (2020). *The Cambridge Cluster – The UK's answer to Silicon Valley?* Available at: https://citystayuk.com/the-cambridge-cluster/

GCP. (2025). *Welcome to the greater Cambridge partnership.* https://www.greater-cambridge.org.uk/

4

CASE 4: FROM NOKIA TO UNICORNS

The evolution of FDI in the Helsinki region

Michel Lemagnen

Abstract

This chapter case provides evidence of how foreign direct investment (FDI) into Helsinki region, and more widely in Finland, has grown strongly since 2010, especially greenfield investments in the technology sector. Multiple, high-impact, greenfield FDI projects landed in Finland since 2010 in key technology sectors where ex-Nokia and Microsoft Mobile employees had specialist expertise. Had the talent not been made available from the layoffs, these investments would almost certainly never have happened. It also shows how foreign venture capital investment has been critical in the funding of the start-up boom – many founders, staff and investors are Nokia alumni. One of Finland's new generation of Unicorn companies – HMD Global (Human Mobile Device) – established in 2016, markets Nokia mobile handsets – from relaunched 'retro' classics to new Android models – under licence, with great success internationally.

The end of Nokia's dominance in the mobile telephone handset market and the subsequent failure of Microsoft windows mobile business were seismic events in Helsinki region, Finland as a whole and its impact was felt across the country (and internationally). However, this situation gave rise to new opportunities which would most likely never have happened had Nokia mobile retained its dominance.

The investment promotion agencies, notably Helsinki Business Hub (now Helsinki Partners) and Business Finland, responded proactively to the post-Nokia challenges through a range of initiatives. The KAATO network, formed by Nokia alumni, was a pioneering initiative whereby former Nokia executives, or those in the process of being laid off, became an active investment attraction 'sales force', leveraging their personal networks to

DOI: 10.4324/9781003483410-6

bring foreign companies into Finland, becoming either the country manager or key executives in the new Finnish entity. Nokia remains a major employer in Finland today although the mobile phone business is now confined to history.

Introduction

The launch of the iPhone in 2007 was a pivotal moment in the history of mobile handsets and one which ultimately triggered the downfall of Nokia's mobile phone business. In terms of its impact on jobs at Nokia, this started to be felt most significantly in 2010, followed by its initial partnership, sale to and eventual closure of Microsoft Mobile. The economic and societal impact of the end of Nokia Mobile have been well documented; the consequences of which were felt throughout Finland and internationally, wherever there had been significant operations.

This case chapter focuses on how FDI into the Helsinki-Uusimaa region has been 'enabled' and stimulated by these changes. There are three dimensions to this: firstly, direct investment by international companies seeking expert talent; secondly, indirect investment though M&A and; thirdly, by international growth capital investors (angel and venture capital) in Finnish start-ups, many of which have either been invested in, founded, co-founded or staffed by Nokia Mobile 'alumni'.

Through a combination of interviews with key stakeholders and companies, empirical research from official data, supplementary desk research and interviews with key stakeholders, this case chapter explores how the impact of FDI in Helsinki region has evolved in the years since.

The direct impact of foreign affiliates in the Helsinki region following Nokia's downfall

Changes to the data collection and reporting methodology of official Finnish FDI statistics mean that it is impossible to provide a 'like-for-like' comparison of the footprint of foreign affiliates in Finland since 2010. Special data analysis has been commissioned from Statistics Finland by MCJ Lemagnen Associates Ltd from Statistics Finland for the purposes of this case, building on previous data originally commissioned by Greater Helsinki Promotion/ Helsinki Business Hub.

Foreign affiliates had an increasingly critical impact in Helsinki region

Table 4.1 shows the evolution of the economic 'footprint' of foreign affiliates in the Helsinki region in 2013, 2017 and 2022. In December 2022, there were 3,064 foreign owned enterprises with 6,307 establishments. These

TABLE 4.1 Direct impact of foreign affiliates in Helsinki region 2013, 2017 and 2022

	2013	*2017*	*2022*	*Growth 2013–2022*
Establishments				
Total number	4,357	5,155	6,307	45%
Personnel	112,869	123,524	144,086	28%
Turnover EUR M	39,753	49,173	61,413	54%
Enterprises				
Total number	2,027	2,538	3,064	51%
Personnel	171,621	175,981	220,462	28%
Turnover EUR M	55,281	65,595	90,003	63%
Value added EUR M	13,947	17,627	22,821	64%
Profits	2,568	4,311	5,092	98%
Gross investments in tangible goods	2,738	4,525	3,792	38%

Source: Special analysis from Statistics Finland data, commissioned by MCJ Lemagnen Associates Ltd.

enterprises employed 220,462 people although the figure associated with the establishments is lower at 144,086.

Although these foreign affiliates accounted for only less than 2% of enterprises in the region, they accounted for 29% of their personnel, 26% of turnover, 28% of value added, 30% of profits and 29% of income taxes.

Foreign affiliates an essential component of research and development (R&D)

Table 4.2 and Figure 4.1 show the development of foreign enterprises undertaking R&D in the Helsinki region.

Table 4.2 shows that, in 2022, there were 189 foreign enterprises doing R&D, investing EUR 892 million in R&D and employing 6,307 R&D

TABLE 4.2 Foreign enterprises doing R&D in Helsinki region 2013, 2017 and 2022

	2013	*2017*	*2022*	*Growth 2013–2022*
Total number	162	168	189	17%
R&D expenditure EUR M	613	662	892	45%
R&D personnel	4,892	5,473	6,307	29%

Source: Special analysis from Statistics Finland data, commissioned by MCJ Lemagnen Associates Ltd.

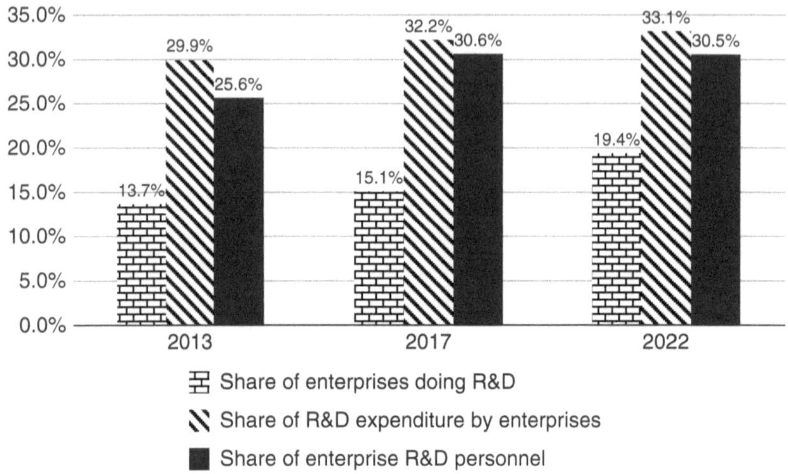

FIGURE 4.1 Foreign enterprises in Helsinki region doing R&D – direct impact

Source: Special analysis from Statistics Finland data, commissioned by MCJ Lemagnen Associates Ltd.

personnel. They accounted for 19% of enterprises doing R&D, 31% of R&D personnel and 33% of R&D expenditure.

Figure 4.1 shows that whilst the share of foreign enterprises doing R&D increased from 14% in 2013 to 19% in 2022, the share of R&D expenditure rose by 3% to 33% and the share of R&D personnel increased from 26% in 2013 to 31% in 2022. The data shows how critical foreign companies were in relation to total corporate R&D spend and employment in the Helsinki region.

Strong growth since 2013

Figure 4.2 shows the growth of foreign affiliates between 2013 and 2022.

Between December 2013 and December 2022, the number of foreign controlled establishments in Helsinki region increased by 45% and accounted for 42% of the total number of foreign affiliates across Finland, compared with 43% in 2013. The growth in the total number of enterprises in Helsinki region is even higher than for establishments with a 51% increase between 2013 and 2022.

However, share of income tax from enterprises fell relative to enterprises as a whole

In 2014, foreign enterprises in Helsinki region paid EUR 684 million in income taxes which was 53% of all income taxes paid by enterprises in the region in that year. Between 2014 and 2022, income taxes paid by foreign enterprises in

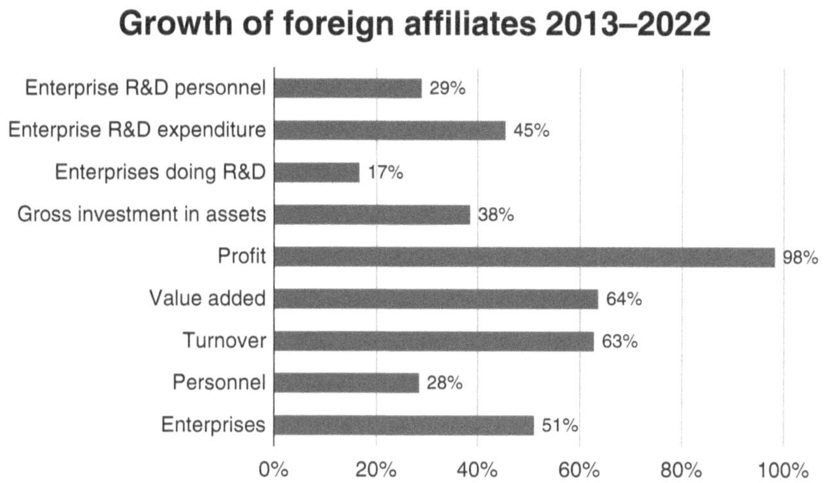

FIGURE 4.2 Growth of foreign affiliates in Helsinki region 2013–2022

Source: Special analysis from Statistics Finland data, commissioned by MCJ Lemagnen Associates Ltd.

Helsinki region increased by 29%. However, as a share of income tax from all enterprises, this fell steadily from 53% in 2014 to 25% in 2022.

In a national context, the importance of FDI spread more widely across Finland but Helsinki region remains the key hub

Since 2013, the number of foreign affiliated establishments across Finland increased by 48%. Analysis of other indicators – turnover, value added and profits – suggests that foreign investment's impact has become more widely felt beyond the capital region.

One of the most noteworthy organic FDI projects was Google's investments in its data centre in Hamina, southeastern Finland. This was a brownfield investment in an old paper mill, using seawater to cool the building. Huawei was another important investor in Finland – one which was very much driven by the Nokia/Windows mobile expert talent becoming available. It invested initially in the Helsinki region and then made subsequent investments in Tampere.

Helsinki region remained the epicentre of FDI in Finland

In 2022, foreign affiliates in the Helsinki region accounted for circa 70% of both turnover and personnel of all foreign affiliates in Finland but only 58% of enterprises and 42% of establishments (which would include all sites and branches). The importance of Helsinki region based foreign affiliates in an R&D context slightly reduced over time, noticeably since 2017 when it

TABLE 4.3 Helsinki region as a share of foreign affiliates in Finland 2013–2022

	2013	*2017*	*2022*
Establishments	43%	43%	42%
Enterprises	58%	59%	58%
Personnel – enterprises	75%	69%	71%
Turnover – enterprises	75%	71%	69%
Value-added	72%	68%	66%
Profits	64%	62%	57%
Gross investment in tangible assets	75%	71%	62%
Income tax[a]	69%	59%	62%
Enterprises doing R&D	40%	38%	38%
R&D expenditure by foreign enterprises	51%	55%	50%
R&D personnel of foreign enterprises	51%	52%	49%

Source: Special analysis from Statistics Finland data, commissioned by MCJ Lemagnen Associates Ltd.

Note:

[a] 2014, no data available for 2013.

accounted for 55% of R&D expenditure and 52% of R&D personnel of all foreign enterprises doing R&D in Finland. This suggests that foreign companies have been growing their R&D outside the capital region (Table 4.3) – between 2017 and 2022:

- R&D expenditure by foreign enterprises across Finland as a whole increased by 47% compared to 35% for those in the Helsinki region.
- The number of R&D personnel employed by foreign enterprises across Finland increased by 24% compared to 15% for those in Helsinki region.

Greenfield FDI trends

Table 4.4, kindly provided by the Financial Times, shows data from its fDi markets greenfield foreign investments database for the Helsinki region and Finland between 2010 and 2022. These cover 'announced' projects (new, co-locations and expansions). The data for both capital expenditure and jobs include modelled estimates, so are indicative. There was a strong growth in projects between 2010 and 2015, especially from 2010 to 2013, the period when the Nokia/Microsoft Mobile layoffs were at their highest levels.

In Helsinki region, the volume of projects increased fourfold between 2010 and 2013. Helsinki region's share of FDI projects in Finland increased from 58% in 2009 to 88% in 2014 (the highest it has been between 2010 and 2022).

TABLE 4.4 Greenfield foreign direct investment projects in Helsinki-Uusimaa 2010–2022

	No of FDI projects			*Capital investment (US$mn) (includes estimates)*			*No of jobs created (includes estimates)*		
	Helsinki-Uusimaa	*Finland*	*Helsinki-Uusimaa % share*	*Helsinki-Uusimaa*	*Finland*	*Helsinki-Uusimaa % share*	*Helsinki-Uusimaa*	*Finland*	*Helsinki-Uusimaa % share*
2010	26	39	67%	588	1,133	52%	670	2,252	30%
2011	59	75	79%	1,001	1,590	63%	2,285	4,228	54%
2012	88	105	84%	822	1,341	61%	1,587	2,201	72%
2013	95	120	79%	748	1,690	44%	1,971	3,534	56%
2014	92	105	88%	933	1,143	82%	1,566	1,955	80%
2015	106	127	83%	1,520	1,897	80%	2,708	3,319	82%
2016	74	117	63%	1,031	4,303	24%	1,789	5,615	32%
2017	112	133	84%	1,520	2,268	67%	2,256	3,953	57%
2018	105	143	73%	621	1,863	33%	1,991	5,210	38%
2019	155	184	84%	1,309	2,302	57%	2,571	4,263	60%
2020	106	136	78%	1,127	2,486	45%	2,432	3,764	65%
2021	86	116	74%	1,119	2,568	44%	1,898	3,761	50%
2022	56	92	61%	1,034	2,982	35%	1,576	3,163	50%

Source: © fDi Markets, from the Financial Times Ltd 2024. Data subject to terms and conditions of use.

Notes:

[a] All Capex figures shown in the table are in United States Dollar millions.

[b] Capex data includes estimated values. Financial Times Ltd takes no responsibility for the accuracy or otherwise of this data.

[c] Jobs data includes estimated values. Financial Times Ltd takes no responsibility for the accuracy or otherwise of this data.

Post-Nokia/Microsoft mobile greenfield FDI investments

One of the almost immediate consequences of Nokia's troubles was the round of closures of facilities and large-scale redundancies, both in Finland and around the world. For example, Nokia closed its handset factory in Bochum (Germany) in 2008, relocating production to a new factory in Cluj Romania in the same year, which then closed in 2011. In Finland, the closures were particularly hard for the cities of Salo in southwest Finland and Oulu in Northern Ostrobothnia. Subsequently, when the business was sold to become Microsoft Mobile, the company eventually closed its operations entirely.

Nokia and Microsoft redundancy support programmes

Both Nokia and Microsoft provided major support programmes to help employees being made redundant. These programmes were not specifically linked to FDI. The two main 'umbrella' initiatives in Finland were:

- Nokia – Bridge, established in 2011.
- Microsoft – Polku, established in 2015, which included start-up coaching schemes and potential grants of up to EURO 60,000 per person or EURO 240,000 per company.

Table 4.5 provides more information about greenfield FDI investments which had either direct or indirect linkages to the Nokia/Microsoft mobile changes and redundancies.

Cross-border M&A

Data for mergers and acquisitions was kindly provided by Bureau Van Dijk – a Moody's Analytics Company – from its ORBIS cross-border investor and Zephyr databases.

Tables 4.6 and 4.7 focus on the M&A data between 2010 and 2022. The number of deals averaged 32 deals between 2010 and 2012. Since then, the number of deals per year ranged from 51 (in 2013) to 75 in 2021.

Target companies headquartered in Helsinki region accounted for over 85% of all cross-border M&A target deals in Finland. Note: most companies founded outside the Helsinki region tended to eventually have their HQ in the capital region, often with a very small direct presence. Likewise, almost all larger companies had multiple sites and branches around the country – the very largest often with international subsidiaries.

Table 4.7 provides a list of the largest M&A deals ranked by value. The two largest deals concern Supercell (mobile games developer) and Wolt (online food ordering and delivery platform), two of the most celebrated Finnish tech start-ups. Supercell was founded in 2010, Wolt was founded in 2015.

TABLE 4.5 Examples of cases with linkages to post Nokia/Microsoft Mobile

Company, country	*Timing*	*Project details*
Huawei Technologies Co. Ltd, China	2011–2023	Multiple investments, first announced in 2011. These investments focused on multiple aspects of mobile phone device and technologies R&D. The company eventually hired teams in Otaniemi (Espoo), Helsinki, Tampere as well as a satellite office in Salo.
Intel Corporation, USA	2011	Expansion of R&D centre in Espoo relating to mobile devices, components and software. This project was announced following the end of Intel's partnership with Nokia for the development of the MeeGo, Linux-based software platform.
Fiksu Inc. USA	2013	US mobile marketing optimization startup opening office in Helsinki. This was an outcome from the Kaato initiative, the initial goal was to establish an HQ and R&D unit with 15 staff.
Samsung Electronics	2013	Korean technology giant Samsung established an R&D centre in Otaniemi (Espoo), the initial goal being to hire 50 staff.
Tech Mahindra	2014–2023	Indian IT services company Tech Mahindra established a new office. In 2023, it opened an innovation centre in Espoo. The company now employs more than 50 staff in Finland.
Zalando	2015	German ecommerce company Zalando established a technology centre in Helsinki, initially hiring 50 experts, which reached 155 personnel at the end of 2022.

Examples of M&A cases with strong linkages to Nokia

The most notable M&A deal, linked directly to Nokia, was by Renesas Electronics, details of these are provided in Table 4.8.

Yasushi Akao, President of Renesas Electronics Corporation summed up the rationale for the acquirors in 2010:

> In line with our ongoing efforts to strengthen our business structure, the transferring wireless modem technology and the innovation power and expertise of Nokia's employees will perfectly complement our core competences and serve as the key driving forces in growing our mobile business in the global market.
>
> *(Nokia, 2010)*

TABLE 4.6 Foreign acquisitions of Helsinki-Uusimaa target companies 2010–2022

	Number of deals (completed and completed/assumed)
2010	29
2011	34
2012	34
2013	51
2014	67
2015	69
2016	66
2017	68
2018	55
2019	54
2020	53
2021	75
2022	54

Source: ORBIS Crossborder Investment, Bureau van Dijk – a Moody's Analytics Company.

TABLE 4.7 Largest foreign acquisition deals of Helsinki-Uusimaa target companies 2010–2222

Year	*Target*	*Acquiror*	*Value EURO m*
2016	TENCENT HOLDINGS LTD	SUPERCELL OY	*7,191*
2022	DOORDASH INC.	WOLT ENTERPRISES OY	*7,000*
2017	POLAR BIDCO SARL	SPONDA OYJ	*3,700*
2018	Consortium led by CVC	MEHILAINEN OY	*1,800*
2021	PPG INDUSTRIES INC.	TIKKURILA OYJ	*1,520*
2019/2020	TELENOR ASA	DNA OYJ	*2,765*
2018	BRACKET GLOBAL HOLDINGS LLC	CRF BOX OY	*1,200*
2014	SSAB AB	RAUTARUUKKI OYJ	1,089
2015	GEBERIT AG	SANITEC OYJ	1,035
2019	LOXAM SAS	RAMIRENT OYJ	978
2015	CVC CAPITAL PARTNERS LTD	Paroc Group	*700*
2021	HOLOGIC INC.	MOBIDIAG OY	673
2020	ARDIAN INFRASTRUCTURE	NEVEL OY	*656*

Source: ORBIS Crossborder Investment, Bureau van Dijk – a Moody's Analytics Company.

Note: Italics are estimated values.

TABLE 4.8 Examples of cases with strong linkages to Nokia

Company, country	*Timing*	*Project details*
Renesas Mobile, Japan	2010	In April 2010 Japan's Renesas Electronics Corporation (created from the integration of NEC Electronics Corporation and Renesas Technology Corp), established Renaissance Mobile Europe Oy with its headquarters in Helsinki. Renesas paid $200 million to acquire Nokia's wireless modem business and certain patents. Approximately 1,100 Nokia employees altogether transferred to Renesas, including approximately 640 in Finland (Oulu 460, Salo 90, Tampere 60, remainder, about 30 people, in Greater Helsinki area/support functions. Rising to 70–80 people altogether in Greater Helsinki area (Espoo and Ruoholahti).
Broadcom Corporation, USA	2013	Sadly, the Renesas deal proved short-lived: in June 2013, the company announced it would close down all its sites in Finland and make all 800 staff redundant. In September 2013, Renesas Mobile Europe (and also its unit in India) was sold to Broadcom Corporation in 2013 for USD 164 million – at the time, Renesas had 760 staff in Finland of which 530 on Oulu. In July 2014, Broadcom announced it would close its chip business in Finland, leading to 600 layoffs.
Audi, BMW, Daimler	2015	In August 2015, Nokia sold its HERE maps business to a consortium of Audi, BMW and Daimler for EURO 2.8 billion.

Source: MCJ Lemagnen Associates Ltd.

Excluded from this table is the creation of Microsoft Mobile in November 2013 through the EURO 5.44 billion sale of Nokia's mobile phone business and related patents. The ill-fated deal involved the transfer of 32,000 Nokia staff to Microsoft, of which 4,700 were based in Finland.

Cross-border growth capital

It was mainly foreign growth capital which enabled and fuelled Finland's start-up 'boom'. This was not just in terms of the volume and capital invested but, also the 'quality' of the international VCs taking part in the funding rounds. This growth in venture capital investment only really started to take off following the layoffs, firstly by Nokia itself (from 2010) and the later closure of Microsoft Mobile operations in 2014.

TABLE 4.9 Venture capital investments in startup companies in Helsinki-Uusimaa 2012–2022

	Investment value EUR (thousands)				*Number of companies receiving investments*	
	Domestic	*Foreign*	*Total*	*Foreign share %*	*Domestic*	*Foreign*
2012	30,312	31,434	61,746	51%	59	10
2013	31,413	33,296	64,709	51%	69	15
2014	40,903	30,895	71,798	43%	79	18
2015	61,676	15,955	77,631	21%	81	11
2016	48,009	37,591	85,600	44%	88	16
2017	49,939	52,112	102,051	51%	66	20
2018	83,322	110,748	194,070	57%	92	26
2019	81,773	308,611	390,384	79%	114	22
2020	164,760	256,337	421,097	61%	113	33
2021	167,303	568,115	735,418	77%	111	30
2022	191,020	688,568	879,588	78%	118	35

Source: Finnish Venture Capital Association (FVCA).

According to data from the Finnish Venture Capital Association (FVCA), the cumulative value of foreign venture capital (VC) investment into Finnish start-ups and scale-ups between 2012 and 2022 was EURO 2.13 billion – 69% of all VC investment.

Table 4.9 shows the development of the value of VC investments and the number of Helsinki region start-ups receiving these investments between 2012 and 2022. This data was collected by FVCA. In 2022, foreign VC investment reached a record high of EURO 688.6 million in 35 companies. The average investment value per company increased from EURO 3.14 million in 2012 to 19.7 million in 2022. Two important factors contributed to this growth in average investment values:

- Firstly, Finnish start-ups established in (and before) the earlier years of the analysis period received larger, follow-on funding rounds – Series, B, C, D, even E, e.g. satellite technology company, Iceye, based in Espoo, raised a Series D round of USD 136 million in February 2022 (Iceye, 2022).
- Secondly, in addition to Iceye, there have been several other 'mega-deals' which are not representative of average deal values, e.g. in June 2022, AlphaSense became another Finnish Unicorn when it raised a further USD 225 million in a Series D round (AlphaSense, 2022).

The value of foreign VC investments in 2022 was almost 22 times greater than in 2012. By comparison, the value of domestic VC investments was only 6.3 times higher.

Table 4.10 provides examples of 14 Finnish 'unicorn' companies, 13 of which had their registered head-office in Helsinki region, either (in descending order) in Helsinki, Espoo or Vantaa. All of these companies were recipients of critical venture capital investments. These ranged from relatively early-stage investments to late-stage financing. For example, Accel, Initial Capital and London venture partners invested in Supercell's USD 12 million Series A round in 2011, only one year after the company was founded.

TABLE 4.10 Finnish unicorn companies

Founding year	*Unicorn year*	*Company name*	*Sector*	*Key international investors*
1995	2008	**MySQL**	Enterprise software	IVP, Intel Capital, Red Hat, Sapphire Ventures, Balderton Capital, Holtron Ventures
2010	2013	**Supercell**	Gaming	Accel, Atomico, Initial Capital, Index Ventures, London venture Partners
2003	2017	**Rovio Entertainment**	Gaming	Quantum Venture Partners, Atomico, Felicis, Accel
2000	2018	**CRF Health**	Healthcare & medtech	Vitruvian Partners, Nordic Venture Partners, 3i Group, SMAC Partners, Canada Pension Plan Investment Board
2016	2018	**HMD Global**	Consumer goods	Qualcomm, Google, DMJ Asia, Ginko Ventures, FIH Mobile
2013	2021	**Small Giant Games**	Gaming	EQT Ventures, Spintop Ventures, Creandum, PROfounders Capital
2016	2021	**Aiven**	Enterprise software	IVP, BlackRock, Earlybird Ventures, Atomico, Eurazeo, Salesforce Ventures

(*Continued*)

TABLE 4.10 (Continued)

Founding year	*Unicorn year*	*Company name*	*Sector*	*Key international investors*
2014	2021	**Wolt Enterprises**	Retail & distribution	Tiger Global Management, 83North, Vintage Investment Partners, DST Global, EQT Ventures, Highland Europe, Prosus Ventures, ICONIQ Growth
2013	2022	**Oura Health**	Healthcare & medtech	MSD Capital, Forerunner Ventures, Jazz Venture Partners, Roosh Ventures, Elysian Park Ventures, One Capital, True Capital Management
2014	2022	**Iceye**	Enterprise software	Seraphim Space, True Ventures, Promus Ventures, BAE Systems, Space Ventures
2008	2022	**AlphaSense**	Enterprise software	BlackRock, CapitalG, Goldman Sachs Asset Management, Viking Global Investors, GrowthX Accelerator, Wells Fargo Strategic Capital, Bank of America, Citi
2005	2022	**Relex**	Enterprise software	Blackstone Growth, TCV, Summit Partners
2008		**Applifier**	Gaming	PROfounders Capital, MHS Capital, LVP, Webb Investment Network
2013		**Smartly.io**	Enterprise software	ConsenSys Mesh, Highland Europe

Source: Finnish Venture Capital Association (FVCA).

Note: Companies in bold text have/had registered head office in Helsinki-Uusimaa region.

Rovio Entertainment is probably the most globally famous Finnish start-up thanks to its Angry Birds series of mobile games. Rovio went to IPO in 2017 and was acquired by Sega Corporation in 2023 (for USD 775 million – therefore less than Unicorn value).

HMD Global (now called Human Mobile Devices), headquartered in Espoo, was the company established by former Nokia executives in 2016 which continued the Nokia mobile phone brand, developing and marketing its products under licence. HMD and FIH Mobile (Foxconn) acquired Microsoft Mobile's feature phones business in May 2016. Since 2023, the company announced it would be selling phones under its own HMD brand and its licence with Nokia runs until 2026.

FDI governance and support initiatives relating to Nokia and Microsoft redundancies

National and regional agencies

Attraction and support for FDI saw several significant changes since 2006 both at the national level and specifically for the Helsinki region.

Business Finland

At the national level, Invest in Finland was subsumed by FinPro (the export trade support agency) in 2014, which was in-turn merged with Tekes (the Finnish funding agency for technology and innovation) to become Business Finland in 2018. Invest in Finland remained as a unit within Business Finland as Finland's official investment promotion agency, helping foreign companies to establish and expand operations in Finland.

Helsinki region investment promotion agencies

At the city and regional level, Greater Helsinki Promotion (GHP) was established in 2006 as a limited company, funded by the main cities in the capital region – Espoo, Helsinki, Kauniainen and Vantaa. GHP's trading brand was Helsinki Business Hub (HBH) and the company's legal name was changed to the latter in 2014. Helsinki-Uusimaa regional council was a key stakeholder in GHP/HBH.

GHP/HBH had a number of dedicated long-term programmes such as China Golden Bridge, MOCT (aimed at Russian start-ups) and International VC Zone (focusing on international angel and venture capital investors). The Huawei investments in Finland were largely facilitated by the China Golden Bridge programme. International VC Zone played a significant role in the targeting and attraction of international VC companies to invest in Helsinki region start-ups and deepening relationships with Finnish venture and angel investors. At the end of 2022, HBH was closed, and its activities became a part of the new company, Helsinki Partners, which was a merger of three different entities in and owned by the City of Helsinki.

The city of Espoo always had its own agency, firstly called Otaniemi Marketing which, following changes in branding and governance, became Enter Espoo. Otaniemi Marketing was an important player for FDI attraction during the period of the Nokia/Microsoft Mobile closures, working closely with GHP/HBH and Invest in Finland. Espoo's Otaniemi district is the home of Aalto University and major research facilities of VTT Technical Research Centre of Finland, one of Europe's leading multi-disciplinary research institutions. Otaniemi Marketing was directly and indirectly involved in landing some of the key FDI success stories in Finland.

The city of Vantaa was somewhat less active in terms of its having staff dedicate to FDI attraction, other than during the time of the Vantaa Innovation Institute (VII) and its Airport Cluster Finland programme. Two of its team joined GHP/HBH.

Outside of the capital area, ten Uusimaa municipalities established a joint marketing brand called Helsinki Ring of Industry (HRI), although this brand was created after the Nokia/Windows Mobile closure period. Helsinki-Uusimaa regional council was a key stakeholder in HRI. HRI's municipalities stretched round from the southeast, over the north and to the southwest of the capital region. It was a very important hub for manufacturing and logistics facilities. One of these municipalities, Hyvinkää, was home to the headquarters of Kone Oyj, one the global market leaders in elevator engineering and one of Finland's flagship companies.

Kaato – a greenfield FDI initiative related specifically to former Nokia professionals

Kaato was a Nokia alumni initiative established by ex-Nokia professionals (notably by Markku Huotari) in 2012, which established a networking community of tech professionals. One of its original core aims was to support ex-Nokia personnel in leveraging their international work to establish companies in Finland with the aim of hiring these alumni as the country management team and taking on other personnel. Kaato means 'strike' in English, in the sense of a ten-pin bowling 'strike'.

According to Kaato (n.d.): 'Nokia demonstrated great corporate responsibility by supporting employees to start new companies or careers. As a result, about 1,000 startups were formed, many of them classified as deep tech'.

It was supported by Nokia and by the Ministry of Economic Affairs and Employment (TEM). It was facilitated and supported through the Team Finland initiative involving the Finnish embassies, FinPro, Invest in Finland and with further support from the regional investment promotion agencies, including HBH. After 2014, Kaato was integrated within Invest in Finland's ICT team.

According to Business Finland, between 2012 and 2014, there were nine greenfield investments created which resulted from the Kaato programme. Of these nine companies, three created employment in the Helsinki region.

One successful example was Nordic Semiconductor Finland Oy, established in 2014 in Oulu (Northern Finland), initially with plans to set up a 20–25 person R&D unit, expanding to up to 100. The company was a subsidiary of Nordic Semiconductor ASA, headquartered in Trondheim, Norway. At the end of 2023, the business in Finland employed 338 staff, mostly in Oulu but with additional branch offices in Tampere, Turku and in Espoo, Helsinki region. In September 2024, there were 13 employees (of which 11 in R&D jobs) with LinkedIn profiles based in the Espoo office.

Conclusions and key learnings

- Foreign investment into Helsinki-Uusimaa (and Finland as whole) grew strongly since 2010. This is supported by evidence from multiple data sources:
  - official government statistics,
  - economic development and investment promotion agencies: Invest in Finland, Helsinki Partners,
  - trade associations: Finnish Venture Capital Association (FVCA),
  - private sector databases.
- Multiple, high-impact, greenfield FDI projects landed in Finland since 2010 in key technology sectors where ex-Nokia and Microsoft Mobile employees had specialist expertise. Had the talent not been made available from the layoffs, these investments would almost certainly never have happened.
- The Ministry of Economic Affairs and Employment, Invest in Finland, HBH, Otaniemi Marketing as well as Finnish regional investment promotion agencies (e.g. TREDEA/Business Tampere and Business Oulu) played a proactive role in supporting the ex-Nokia/Microsoft Mobile employees through a range of programmes and instruments.
- Both Nokia and Microsoft provided highly successful support programmes, Bridge and Polku respectively, to help former employees to retrain, start companies and to find new jobs.
- The Kaato network developed an innovative initiative to leverage former Nokia personnel's networks to attract new greenfield FDIs. Nine affiliates of foreign entities were created around Finland, thee of which had operations and hired staff in Helsinki region.

- The Finnish start-up boom has been both directly and indirectly enabled by Nokia alumni, as founders, co-founders, key staff and, increasingly, as investors in Finnish start-ups and scale-ups.

Acknowledgements

Michel would like to say 'kiitos paljon' to the following people for sharing their thoughts and insights about the development of FDI in the Helsinki region and Finland. Micah Gland, Tatu Laurila and Marja-Liisa Niinikoski (former CEOs of Greater Helsinki Promotion and Helsinki Business Hub), Marja-Leena Rinkineva (Director of Economic Development, City of Helsinki), Johanna Huurre (Senior Director Marketing and Offering, Business Finland), Ilona Kuusi (Manager, Research and Customer Insight, Helsinki Partners), Kaija Laitinen (Senior Advisor Market Intelligence Invest in Finland, Business Finland), Janne Kari (Head if Industry, ICT & Digitalisation Invest in Finland, Business Finland and Kaato Programme Coordinator), Arto Pussinen (Senior Director Ecosystems Digitalisation Invest in Finland, Business Finland), Jonne Kuitinnen (Deputy Chief Executive, Finnish Venture Capital Association, FVCA), Miika Mähönen (Analyst Intern, Finnish Venture Capital Association, FVCA), Ari Huczkowski (Founder & CEO, Lumintel Oy), Fernando M. Gutierrez (Director Government Industry Practice Lead, Head of Trade and Investments Moody's Analytics Inc.) and David East (Senior Director, Global Head of Sales, Data Solutions, Moody's Analytics Inc.), Carmel Ferris (Head of Data, fDi Intelligence, Financial Times Business Intelligence), Anna-Maija Laakko (Statistics Finland), Matti Saarinen (Senior Partner and Chairman of the Helsinki Board, KREAB) and Eero Holstila (former Director of Economic Development, City of Helsinki)

References

AlphaSense. (2022). *Announcing our $225M series D led by Goldman Sachs & Viking Global.* Company news report. Available at: https://www.alpha-sense.com/blog/news/series-d-announcement/

Iceye. (2022). *ICEYE raises USD 136M in series D funding round.* Iceye Press Release. Available at: https://www.iceye.com/press/press-releases/iceye-raises-usd-136m-in-series-d-funding-round

Kaato. (n.d.). *Once upon a time in Finland.* https://www.kaato.org/story-of-kaato/

Nokia. (2010). *Renesas Electronics to acquire Nokia's wireless modem business; companies to form strategic business alliance for modem technology development.* Nokia Press Release. Available at: https://www.nokia.com/about-us/news/releases/2010/07/06/renesas-electronics-to-acquire-nokias-wireless-modem-business-companies-to-form-strategic-business-alliance-for-modem-technology-development/

5

CASE 5: THE FAILURE OF CHINA STATE GRID IN ACQUIRING EANDIS IN FLANDERS

A marriage takes more than two

Haiyan Zhang and Zhiping Zhu

Abstract

This chapter analyzes the unsuccessful acquisition of Eandis by China State Grid Corporation (SGCC) in Flanders, focusing on the challenges posed by foreign direct investment (FDI) in critical infrastructure. The 2016 failure was shaped by national security concerns, political opposition, and public sentiment, highlighting the necessity for effective stakeholder management. It explores the challenging balance city governments face in attracting FDI while ensuring local control over strategic assets. The study emphasizes the need for transparent regulatory frameworks, cooperation between federal and local authorities, and active citizen engagement to address the complexities of FDI and foster sustainable economic growth.

Introduction

Foreign direct investment (FDI) can play a vital role in developing and enhancing infrastructure, which is essential for a city's economic growth and sustainability. However, foreign involvement in infrastructure projects can lead to tensions between economic interests and national security concerns. Striking a balance between the interests of foreign investors and host countries necessitates robust regulatory frameworks, transparent stakeholder engagement, and strategic safeguards at both the national and local government levels. This case study highlights the dilemma faced by city governments in needing FDI to revitalize utility infrastructure while wanting to maintain local ownership and control over strategic assets.

DOI: 10.4324/9781003483410-7

The collapse of the Eandis-SGCC deal in 2016 serves as a compelling example of how national security concerns, political and public opposition, and broader geopolitical tensions can drive local governments to intervene in international business transactions. This incident underscored the critical need for effective stakeholder management to navigate the complexities and mitigate the risks associated with international mergers and acquisitions, especially in strategic sectors like energy infrastructure. It also highlighted the growing importance of local governments in scrutinizing and regulating foreign investment in critical infrastructure to safeguard national security, protect public interests, and preserve long-term competitiveness and economic growth.

Eandis-SGCC deal

Eandis was the largest energy distribution network consortium in Belgium, of which the shareholders were uniquely local municipality and provincial governments of the Flemish region. Consisting of seven intercity power and natural gas distribution network operating companies in Flanders, it was responsible for electricity and gas supply for 229 towns in Flanders (accounting for about 78% of all cities in Flanders) and provided approximately 2.7 million electricity and 1.8 million natural gas access points. Its revenue and pre-tax profit in 2016 amounted to 2.8 billion and 429 million euros respectively, with more than 4,000 employees (Eandis, 2016, 2017).

In December 2014, Electrabel – a Belgian based electricity supplier of Électricité de France (EDF), withdrew from Eandis according to the Third Energy Package adopted by the EU in 2009, which was purposed to separate energy supply and generation from the operation of transmission networks to improve the functioning of the EU internal energy market. The total amount of divestment and dividends of Electrabel was nearly 1 billion euros, equal to 1/3 of Eandis's operating income for that year. From then on, Eandis failed to recover from its financial losses and slumped into a deep debt crisis. Moreover, this capital outlay coincided with an increasing need for investments to convert the natural gas network from low to high-calorific gas (i.e., high calorific has a higher calorific value, providing more energy per unit volume or mass when used as a fuel), because of the reduced supply of low-calorific natural gas from the Netherlands. All this caused Eandis' debt ratio to rise, endangering the favorable credit rating (A1) from the rating agency Moody's (Verbeek, 2016).

In order to leverage the balance sheet and establish a viable international financing entity, Eandis management proposed "two action plans" in 2015 to its shareholders, of which the first one consisted of fully integrating the seven intercity infrastructure companies in Flanders Region (i.e., Gazelwest,

IMEA, Imewo, Intergem, Iveka, Iverlek, and Sibelgas) to establish Eandis Assets, while the second plan was to look for new investment in the international market for Eandis Assets, i.e., about 400 million euros. To this end, the Flemish Government had amended the decree of July 6, 2001 (known as "Flemish Energy Decree") on inter-municipal cooperation in April 2016, allowing private capital to be contributed to a missionary association in the waste and energy distribution sectors, i.e., assigned association with private participation. This amendment introduced frameworks for public-private partnerships (PPPs) in the energy sector, aiming to leverage private sector efficiency and capital in the development of large-scale energy infrastructure, particularly in renewable energy and smart grid technologies (Deruytter et al., 2022).

These two action plans were collectively referred to as the "Volta Action" by Eandis management. They were closely intertwined and essential to one another. The plan was implemented step-by-step under the supervision of the Company's Strategy Committee, which included four prominent figures from Flanders' political circles at that time: Mr. Louis Tobback, Minister of State and mayor of Leuven (former interior minister and former leader of the Socialist Party); Mr. Geert Versnick, vice-mayor of Ghent (Open-Flanders Liberal Democratic Party); Mr. Piet Buysse, municipal councilman of Ghent (Flanders Christian Democratic Party); and Mr. Koen Kennis, former Chairman of the Cabinet of the Flanders Region and vice-mayor of Antwerp. This composition was clearly intended to obtain a consensus from leading Belgian political parties for the long-term strategic development of the company.

From 2015, Eandis collected information about over 70 investors who were interested in acquiring 14% of the shares in the Company, and finally determined a shortlist of 21 companies. After preliminary data exchange, five candidate companies submitted their non-binding quotations in early February 2016. These potential investors were allowed to enter the second stage of the selection process. On May 27, 2016, Eandis received three binding quotations from Dutch pension fund APG, Australian pension fund and infrastructure investment company Australian Super/IFM and State Grid Corporation of China. In early June 2016, SGCC Europe (SGEL) was selected as the "preferred bidder" through a comprehensive analysis of the bidding documents (Vanlerberghe, 2016).

SGCC agreed to invest 830 million euros for a 14% stake in Eandis Assets, while the net asset value of that share package was evaluated at 484.4 million euro. Eandis therefore stated that the offer yielded a "commercial premium" (capital gain) of 345.6 million euros, i.e., 71% higher than the net asset value. On June 29, 2016, SGCC successfully signed the subscription agreement and the shareholder agreement. Eandis emphasized in its communication that SGCC was an interesting partner because of its technological capabilities in the field of ultra-high voltage (UHV) power lines and its extensive experience with smart electricity grids. Also SGCC strived for long-term strategic investments abroad, which could provide Eandis with the stable partnership for future growth (Verbeek, 2016).

SGCC is the largest state-owned utility company in China and plays a vital role in the country's energy infrastructure. It drives innovations in grid technology and supports the transition to a more sustainable energy future. SGCC is also the largest power production and supply company in the world and ranked the third largest company on the Fortune Global 500 in 2023. It has been actively expanding its overseas investments since it obtained 25 years of franchise rights on Philippines National Transmission Network in 2010. Aligning with China's broader strategy of internationalization and the Belt and Road Initiative, it successfully achieved several key overseas investment projects in Brazil, Portugal, Philippines, Australia, Italy, and Greece. The company leverages its advanced technologies, particularly in UHV transmission, to improve the efficiency and reliability of power grids in the countries where it invests. From a strategic viewpoint, SGCC aims to expand its footprint in key international markets and focuses on strategic acquisitions and partnerships that enhance its global reach and influence. SGCC's investments often focus on integrating renewable energy sources and enhancing grid stability, contributing to the sustainability goals of the host countries. SGCC's overseas investments demonstrate its commitment to become a global leader in the energy sector and contribute to the development of robust, sustainable, and technologically advanced power grids worldwide (Wang, 2017).

Yet, SGCC's overseas investments have been sometimes viewed through the lens of geopolitical considerations, particularly in regions where there is significant strategic interest. In 2014, SGCC's bid to acquire a 51% stake in the Austrian electricity utility, E-Control, was blocked by the Austrian government. In 2016, SGCC's acquisition of a 50.4% stake in Ausgrid, an electricity distribution company in Australia, was rejected by the Australian government. These failures highlighted the growing scrutiny and regulatory barriers Chinese state-owned enterprises have faced in expanding their global footprint, especially in sensitive industries (Kratz et al., 2023).

Reaction of key stakeholders to the deal

Before the summer vacation began, Eandis management briefed over 200 shareholder representatives from various municipal governments on the proposed deal with SGCC. They issued two detailed 100-page documents outlining SGCC's shareholding responsibilities and conditions. According to Eandis management's plan, they intended to introduce the "Volta Action" to councilors from provincial and municipal governments in the Flanders Region between September 6 and 13, following the summer break. After these discussions, local governments could deliberate on the project, with the plan set to be finalized through a vote at the extraordinary general meeting on October 3, 2016.

Civil society

During the summer vacation, a group of activists focused on rights protection, along with social and environmental organizations, calling themselves "Macharius", closely examined the documents regarding SGCC's acquisition of Eandis shares. By the end of August, they had alerted 2,100 council members in Flanders to their concerns about the project, urging them, "Ladies and Gentlemen, Council Members, we recommend that you do not approve the Volta Plan" (Vanlerberghe, 2016). Their objections were primarily twofold.

First, the distribution and supply of electricity and gas are public services, which hold a monopoly in the market and are governed by society, with oversight by the public. If the municipal government or state agency cannot guarantee investment or capital increases, citizens should have the right to be invited to become new shareholders, and the government should participate in ownership through cooperative means. This principle aims to defend local interests and protect national heritage or vital strategic resources. The activists also emphasized that the statutory annual return on investment for this project would be nearly 5%, while bank savings accounts offered zero interest at that time. They questioned, "Why deny local citizens such lucrative investment opportunities while offering them to foreign investors?"

Second, the shareholder agreement between Eandis management and SGCC was seen as undermining the decision-making power of Eandis's primary shareholders, the municipal governments. The agreement granted new shareholders the right to invoke a special "deadlock" mechanism or withdraw from the company over 11 types of decisions, including budgeting, investment plans, return on investment, the appointment of the CEO, and other significant strategic issues. If the new shareholder disagreed with a company decision, it could request a 28-day postponement of the decision's implementation. If consensus was still not reached, the shareholder could withdraw its capital from the company. Activists viewed this provision as a true Sword of Damocles, threatening Eandis's decision-making process (Vanlerberghe, 2016).

Media and public opinion

During their lobbying efforts, the activists of "Macharius" focused on direct dialogue with elected town council members, carefully avoiding significant media attention. However, on September 1, some council members leaked their analysis report to the press, sparking a sudden surge of interest in both local and social media. De Morgen, a left-leaning Flemish newspaper, soon published a petition from Transitienetwerk Middenveld – a civil association advocating for climate and social justice in support of the transition to renewable energy – strongly condemning the share transaction between Eandis and SGCC (Holslag et al., 2016). With this media exposure, the controversy surrounding SGCC's acquisition of shares in Eandis intensified, transforming the previously quiet equity transfer plan into a heated public debate, described as a "tsunami" (Vanlerberghe, 2016).

After the "Volta Action" project was leaked to the media in early September 2016, the acquisition quickly became a trending topic on Twitter, garnering significant attention within just a month. The platform amplified the debate by bringing diverse viewpoints and attitudes directly to the public, prompting various parties to voice their opinions. When the letter from the National Security Agency was disclosed (see further details below), discussions around the case surged, accounting for over 0.16% of all Twitter traffic, and this activity persisted for several days (Figure 5.1). A detailed analysis of 702 tweets revealed that more than 84% were posted by adults over the age of 25. Of these, 8.7% supported the acquisition, 71.7% opposed it, and 19.6% were neutral (Machteld Ryckaert, 2017).

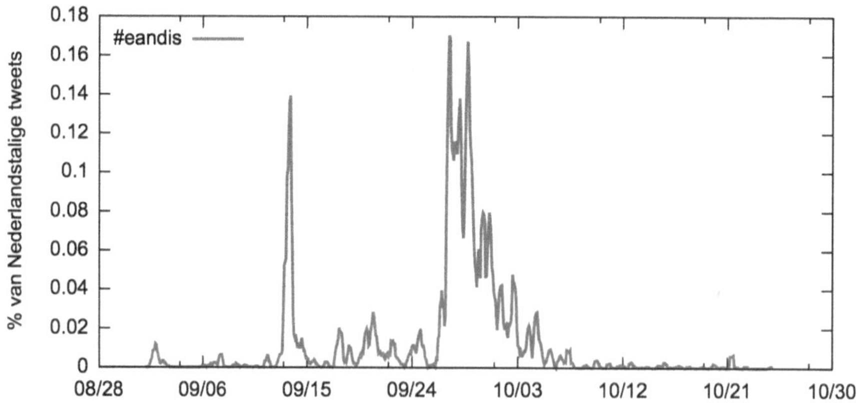

FIGURE 5.1 Period with higher Tweet frequency (% of total Dutch speaking Tweets)

Source: Ryckaert (2017).

Political parties

The media exposure shattered the consensus among political parties and created significant social upheaval. The Green Party was the first to unanimously oppose SGCC's entry into Eandis, arguing that the energy distribution network should uphold the principle of public service. They emphasized the need to prioritize locally produced energy and shift power distribution to lower levels. For the Green Party, decentralizing decision-making was seen as crucial for effectively implementing the energy transformation strategy in the Flanders Region.

The four major political parties in Flanders, which were central to forming Eandis's Four-Member Strategy Committee, played a crucial role in driving the acquisition project, alongside the Vice Chairmen of Eandis's board of directors. Despite the evolving situation, these parties remained steadfast in their support for the acquisition plan. However, internal disagreements emerged within these parties. For example, Socialist Party leaders such as Louis Tobback, mayor of Leuven, and Johan Vande Lanotte, mayor of Ostend, pushed the motion through by majority vote with minimal discussion before Eandis had presented the relevant information. Meanwhile, grassroots members of the Socialist Party held differing views from those of the party leaders involved in the energy transformation project.

In Ghent, which is governed by a coalition of the Green Party and the Socialist Party, the city council requested more detailed information from Eandis, threatening to abstain from voting at the general meeting on October 3 if their request was not met. Councils in other smaller cities either voted against the proposal or chose to abstain. In Antwerp, the Socialist Party, Green Party, and Labor Party (PVDA, extreme left) united in their opposition to the project. The Open-Flanders Liberal Democratic Party initially supported the "Volta Action" but shifted its stance as public dissent grew, ultimately expressing support for Eandis's public listing and encouraging public shareholding (Vanlerberghe, 2016).

Governments

One week before the vote at the extraordinary general meeting, on September 26, De Standaard, Belgium's leading newspaper, published an anonymous letter sent to several ministers of the Federal Government and the Flanders Region. The letter raised concerns that SGCC, led by the Communist Party of China, had close ties with Chinese intelligence agencies and military forces. It urged increased scrutiny of SGCC's proposal to acquire shares in Eandis for national security reasons, noting that similar acquisitions had been rejected by Australian authorities on security grounds. Another local newspaper,

Het Laatste Nieuws, criticized the investment, suggesting that the Chinese company's interest in Eandis was not purely altruistic. They likened the investor to a Trojan horse, warning, "China aspires to build a global power company, envisioning a future where Beijing could control when and where the lights are turned on across the world" (Kniebs, 2016).

The State Security Agency of the Belgian Federal Government later confirmed that they had sent the anonymous letter to Belgian Prime Minister Charles Michel, Flanders Energy Minister Bart Tommelein, and Minister of the Interior Liesbeth Homans (N-VA) five days earlier. Minister Homans also indicated that the letter was forwarded to the Flanders VVSG (the alliance of towns and communities). She emphasized that she was not involved in the Eandis acquisition process at that time and would not have a role until the competent municipal authority made a decision at Eandis' general meeting. She confirmed that the local authority would determine whether to use the document when the general meeting occurred. Although she had oversight responsibilities for regional security, the decision on the matter would not come to her desk until after the motion was voted on.

After the letter's release, Flanders Energy Minister Bart Tommelein (VLD Party), who had previously supported the project, reversed his stance. He expressed concern that the public did not fully understand the implications of selling the strategic energy distribution network to a foreign investor and raised issues about private data protection. Two days later, Tommelein indicated that he had received "new sensitive information" about SGCC, which validated his concerns. Conversely, Piet Buyse, chairman of Eandis's board of directors (from the CD&V Party and mayor of Dendermonde), dismissed these concerns, arguing that the issue was purely financial.

Ghent was the first major municipality to seek a postponement of the deal with SGCC, thus delaying its scheduled approval by the 230 municipal representatives at the Eandis general meeting on October 3. The city requested more time to conduct a thorough review of the deal. This move was particularly noteworthy since Leuven, represented by Louis Tobback (Socialist Party) major of the city and Vice-Chairman of Eandis, had already approved the agreement (Vandaele, 2016).

Facing the growing public debates on the national security of the deal, Mr. Louis Tobback joined the opposition faction and issued a warning: "When we have to admit that we could not properly evaluate a EUR 830 million project in such a short time, we must conclude that we cannot handle this project". He also blurted out that several municipal governments had already rejected the equity transfer agreement (Vanlerberghe, 2016).

Mr. Geert Bourgeois from N-VA, chairman of Flanders Region tried to downplay this warning. He considered the letter as "a piece of wastepaper" in a dismissive manner (Vanlerberghe, 2016). His statement caused uproar in Belgian politic circles. Two days later, the case was included as a special topic by the Judicial Committee of the House of Representatives of Belgium.

The media uproar over SGCC's identity and the deal's complexity caused municipalities to hesitate. Ultimately, the city of Antwerp vetoed SGCC's acquisition of a 14% stake in Eandis. While Antwerp was not opposed to privatization in principle, it objected to a key condition of the deal: the merger of its own distribution network company, i.e., Imea into Eandis Assets. This merger would lead to the standardization of all distribution tariffs, which would have resulted in a tariff increase for Antwerp just before municipal elections (Deruytter et al., 2022). On September 26, the Energy Regulation Commission of Flanders (VREG) announced that the Antwerp-based energy distribution company Imea could not unilaterally set prices or implement a special pricing system. Early in the "Volta Action" plan, Imea had proposed that its condition for merging with other intercity distribution companies was to maintain its right to set independent and preferential pricing. However, the Energy Regulation Commission's notice made it clear that Imea's request was untenable, leading to its withdrawal from the "Volta Action" plan.

Failure of the deal and follow-ups

On October 3, 2016, Eandis held its extraordinary board of directors meeting as planned. The meeting, attended by 250 municipal representatives, focused on voting to amend the meeting schedule rather than discussing SGCC's proposed share subscription in Eandis. SGCC's subscription was contingent upon the merger of seven Flanders intercity infrastructure companies (Gazelwest, Imea, Imewo, Intergem, Iveka, Iverlek, and Sibelgas) into Eandis Assets. However, Imea's withdrawal from the merger led to the suspension of this plan, and as a result, the SGCC subscription proposal could not be addressed. The meeting concluded after just 13 minutes with a unanimous decision to "not proceed with the original agenda of the extraordinary meeting".

Facing its failure to acquire external financial resources, in 2018 Eandis had to merge with Infrax which was another utility company in Flanders to create Fluvius – a cooperative company for 11 intermunicipal companies active in energy distribution in the Flemish region. In addition to this corporate restructuring, there was also a plan to integrate seven intermunicipal companies that had a participation in a renewable energy project into a municipal renewable energy holding company, in which citizen participation in shares was made possible. As a result, all shares of Fluvius were kept in "the Flemish hands", explicitly stated by Flemish Regulator for Electricity and Gaz (VREG, 2020).

As compared to the "localization" of Eandis, SGCC actively pursued international expansion through various strategic projects and acquisitions. Notable initiatives included acquiring CPFL Energia in Brazil for $3.4 billion in

2017 and constructing a 2,000 km UHV power line, purchasing Chilquinta Energía, Tecnored SA, and Compañia General de Electricidad in Chile in 2020, and making substantial investments in Australia by acquiring a 41% stake in ElectraNet, a 19.9% stake in AusNet Services, and a 60% stake in Jemena. In Ethiopia, SGCC financed the construction of 700 kilometers of transmission lines connecting the Grand Ethiopian Renaissance Dam to the national grid. SGCC's recent international expansion underscores its strategic global focus and commitment to acquiring assets in politically stable and regulated markets, while also investing in greenfield projects in emerging markets. This dual approach is designed to optimize its investment portfolio, manage risk, and contribute to the development of global energy infrastructure (Lee, 2019).

In the political debates about the acquisition of Eandis by SGCC in the Belgian federal and Flemish regional parliaments, the issue of national security concerns about FDI in critical infrastructure was brought into sharp focus (Chambre des Représentants de Belgique, 2016; VERG, 2020). Given the limited power of the government in decision-making process of foreign investors due to the lack of related regulations, the Flemish government included a special regulation in its Administrative Decree in 2019 to safeguard the strategic interests of Flanders. It provided an "emergency brake" for the Flemish Government to annul or declare inapplicable for the projects which allow foreign investors to control over public institutions or agencies in case there is a risk to the strategic interests of Flanders (SERV, 2020). The Belgian federal government also aligned to most of other European members states and issued its FDI screening regulation, the so-called "Interfederal foreign investment screening mechanism", came into effect in 2023. The increase of European governments in scrutiny of Chinese investment and applying an extended scope of national security resulted in a continuous decline of Chinese FDI in Europe (Kratz et al., 2023).

Conclusion

The collapse of the Eandis-SGCC deal highlights the complex challenges of FDI in critical infrastructure sectors. Despite initial agreements and the potential benefits of SGCC's investment, the deal was ultimately derailed by a combination of factors, including stakeholder opposition, political disagreements, public outcry, national security concerns, and widespread negative sentiment. This case underscores the delicate balance needed in managing foreign investment in strategic sectors, emphasizing the importance of transparent regulatory frameworks, effective stakeholder engagement, and safeguards to promote local economic development while protecting strategic assets. City governments, in particular, can learn valuable lessons from the Eandis-SGCC case when managing FDI.

First, because utility companies are often deeply rooted in the local socio-economic environment, subnational governments – such as regional or city authorities – may have interests and perspectives on FDI projects that differ from those of the central government. Therefore, creating FDI policies and regulations necessitates collaboration between federal and subnational institutions and stakeholders to avoid fragmented control, which could deter potential investors.

Second, given the unique nature of utility companies – especially their purpose-driven goals and ownership by multiple municipalities – transparent corporate governance, along with the professionalization and autonomy of management, is crucial to prevent the politicization of FDI projects and conflicts among political parties during policymaking. Engaging in FDI through privatization exposes local public companies to the global corporate networks of multinational enterprises, which can profoundly alter their management autonomy and decision-making processes. As a result, their existing connections to local institutions may evolve and function differently.

Third, strategic alignment with multinational enterprises is crucial for local governments to achieve their long-term goals when collaborating on FDI. The Eandis-SGCC case highlighted that the shareholders of these two companies had differing perspectives on the future of energy networks. SGCC envisions a global electricity grid connecting large-scale installations (renewable or otherwise), while Eandis supports maximizing energy savings and promoting decentralized renewable electricity production under local community control. These opposing visions could lead to divergent strategic approaches and potential managerial conflicts among different types of shareholders.

Fourth, effective stakeholder management during the M&A process is essential for the success of any deal. It is important to keep citizens and civil society groups informed, especially when projects involve public services and impact the economic interests of local communities. A lack of political and social debate on the long-term strategic direction of public services and companies could lead to public outcry over a specific FDI project, which may fail to offer viable alternatives for local development.

References

Chambre des Représentants de Belgique. (2016). Compte Rendu Analytique: Document parlementaire de la 54e législature. Commission de la Justice.

Deruytter, L., Juwet, G., & Bassens, D. (2022). Why do state-owned utilities become subject to financial logics? The case of energy distribution in Flanders. *Competition & Change*, *26*, 266–288.

Eandis. (2016). *Activity report 2016*. Activity report.

Eandis. (2017). *Economic group Eandis: Condensed consolidated interim IFRS financial statements 2017*.

Holslag, J., Vandaele, J., & Poel, D. V. D. (2016). *Eandis belongs to you and me (and not to the Chinese)*. *De Morgen*, 01/09/2016.
Kniebs, A. (2016). *China = Trojanisches Pferd? Die Presseschau von Mittwoch, dem 28. September 2016*. http://brf.be/meinung/presseschau/1025917/
Kratz, A., Zenglein, M. J., Sebastian, G., & Witzke, M. (2023). *EV battery investments cushion drop to decade low: Chinese FDI in Europe: 2022 Update*. Merics Report. Merics and Rhodium Group.
Lee, A. C. (2019). *Sustainable energy and the State Grid Corporation of China*. Cornell SC Johnson College of Business. https://business.cornell.edu/hub/2019/06/20/sustainable-energy-state-grid-corporation-of-china/
Ryckaert, M. (2017). *Welche Emotionen kamen am häufigsten bei der Eandis-Unternehmenskrise vor? Eine korpusbasierte Studie anhand von Twitter-Daten*. Master, Universiteit Gent.
SERV. (2020). *Screening buitenlandse directe investeringen*. Sociaal-Economische Raad van Vlaanderen.
Vandaele, J. (2016). *Eandis deal with Chinese state-owned company: 'Never seen in 25 years of experience', says acquisition specialist Schrans*. MO. https://www.mo.be/analyse/nooit-gezien-25-jaar-ervaring-zegt-overnamespecialist-schrans-over-eandisdeal.
Vanlerberghe, P. (2016). Eandis chinois? Chronique d'une privatisation avortée. *Ensemble*, 56–59.
Verbeek, P. (2016). *Everything you ever wanted to know about Eandis and the Chinese*. https://abvv-experten.be/milieu-energie/alles-wat-je-ooit-wilde-weten-over-eandis-en-de-chinezen/
VERG. (2020). *Fluvius – Financing – Establishment of municipal renewable energy holding company: Answer to the Flemish Parliament's questions*. Vlaamse Regulator voor de Elektriciteits- en Gasmarkt.
Wang, X. (2017). 历时九年, 细数国家电网的海外布局战绩. *新浪财金*, 08/05/2017.

PART II

Cities in Transition and Emerging Economies as Locations for FDI

Abstract

As globalization reshapes economic landscapes across the world, cities in developing and emerging economies have become increasingly important targets for Foreign Direct Investment (FDI). While cities in advanced economies often dominate the narrative around global investment flows, urban centres in less advanced countries are rising as significant players in the competition for FDI. These cities present a mixture of opportunities and risks, access to natural resources, and low-cost labour but can be associated with political instability, underdeveloped infrastructure, and institutional weaknesses. Part II explores how cities in transition and emerging economies navigate the complexities of attracting FDI. These cities face distinctive challenges compared to their counterparts in advanced economies, often characterized by periods of change in industrial policy, rapid urbanization, institutional transformation, and socio-political shifts. The cases presented in this section examine the ways in which these cities and foreign investors engage with each other, how they adapt to global market pressures, and how they attempt to foster economic growth through new types of FDI, starting from a lower-income position.

The catch-up context

Transition and emerging economies are ones that are effectively in a state of catch-up. A transition economy is one that is transitioning from a centrally planned economy to a liberal market one. Examples include the Eastern Bloc of countries in Europe following the fall of the Soviet Union. Emerging economies do not fully meet the standards of advanced economies but aspire to hold those standards through policy reform and strategic investment. They aspire

DOI: 10.4324/9781003483410-8

to reach the levels of economic development of more advanced economies, and they undertake policy reforms and programmes of economic and social change to reach this goal. The extent to which they have been successful in this has varied dramatically across the world; some (e.g., China or Poland) have been more successful than others (e.g., Russia or Bulgaria). The convergence theorem dictates that lower-income countries will have a faster growth rate than their richer country counterparts, as they attempt to raise their levels of GDP per capita to be on par.

According to Mazzoleni and Nelson (2007), there have been three common reasons for successful catch-up in the 19th and 20th centuries. Firstly, catch-up economies accumulate new technologies and technological capabilities through the flows of human capital into their countries. This involves both outward flows of people who gain new knowledge in other (advanced) economies before returning, as well as inward immigrants and visitors who bring knowledge. Allard and Williams (2020) note that the economic integration of countries in Africa (which includes cross-border transfer of human capital) is a determinant of national-level innovation in African countries. People are the conduits for the knowledge required for technological advancement, and this is then linked with subsequent economic development. Secondly, there has been official government support for industrial development, including subsidies, and some of this has been protectionist in nature (Mazzoleni & Nelson, 2007). Thirdly, successful catch-up economies had intellectual property (IP) regimes that allowed a degree of imitation and permitted the companies in the country to replicate technology developed in the advanced nations (Mazzoleni & Nelson, 2007).

Correspondingly, Foreign Direct Investment (FDI) has been linked with these changes to industrial policy in catch-up contexts. Some have noted how FDI in low-tech and medium-tech manufacturing industries was common during the early phases of catch-up, with investing companies using the catch-up context as an export platform (Buckley & Meng, 2005). This proceeded to more advanced forms and motives for FDI – including R&D – as investors understood the value of human capital available in these countries and were comfortable with improvements to IP regimes.

In this context, the cities of catch-up economies have had a critical role to play. Many of these cities are home to high-level research-intensive universities that can provide talent. Some countries – notably China – have prioritized cities (including coastal cities) as part of an industrial policy to attract FDI as part of its development. This prioritization included the establishment of economic development zones (EDZs) around cities, prompting an influx of FDI and a mass migration of workers from rural areas into cities (Tao, 2005). In some catch-up economies, the nation's own MNEs have embarked on FDI into advanced countries' cities. Wu et al. (2023) show how Chinese MNEs have targeted cities with research-intensive clusters for their own R&D through FDI. This strategic asset-seeking can then have benefits for enterprises and business groups in the home country, further advancing the catch-up phenomenon over time. This has included the acquisition of IP – especially patents – developed and possessed in Western companies through acquisitive strategies of those companies (Shi et al., 2022). As Wu et al. (2023) note, much of Chinese firms' attention for strategic assets has focused on cities.

Political instability and corruption

The context for FDI in transition and emerging economies has been characterized by institutional weaknesses in many cases, and institutional change in others. This has been a concern to inward investors, especially where there has been political instability and corruption. This adds volatility and creates uncertainty for potential investors who initially may lack the managerial skills to operate in these environments (Hoskisson et al., 2000). Political instability refers to environments in which the political system does not run smoothly, where there is a greater likelihood of violence (through war or terrorism, for instance), and where governments can be destabilized and overthrown undemocratically and sometimes without warning. Corruption – which is highly correlated with political instability (Campos & Giovannoni, 2007; Kaufmann et al., 2009) – relates to the extent to which public power is used for private gain (Kaufmann et al., 2009). Allard et al. (2012) show that political instability is negatively correlated with different aspects of a country's national innovation system, including the quality of its scientific institutions and the availability of scientists and engineers. These components of a national innovation system are usually found in cities and are features that attract inward FDI into cities under normal circumstances. Allard and Williams (2020) report a positive and significant correlation between control of corruption (which negatively correlates to corruption itself) and FDI stock in African countries.

One way in which MNEs can deal with issues of institutional voids, political instability, and corruption when entering a transition or emerging economy is to reflect on the nature and level of risk involved and then choose an appropriate entry mode. A wholly owned investment (whether by acquisition or greenfield) will carry greater risk, although it provides for full control over the investment. This in turn may make it easier to manage and conduct efficient knowledge and practice transfer from other parts of the corporation. Williams and Steriu (2022) analysed how Dutch MNE Heineken made strategic investments in violent contexts between 2002 and 2019, violence in host countries is normally related to political instability. Their study showed that the trend towards violence (worsening vs. improving) in the 5 years prior to entry impacted the company's choice of ownership mode. In worsening contexts, the company would be more likely to choose joint ventures over full ownership. Brewing investments are normally in and around cities to be close to markets (Meyer & Tran, 2006). Joint ventures allow investors to share risk in city locations where political instability and corruption are high; they allow investors to learn about the host country context in detail, to monitor it for signs of improvement before committing greater levels of resources (Tsang, 2002; Meyer & Tran, 2006).

Continuing this theme of managing risk through the mode of entry, Meyer and Tran (2006) highlight a range of options used by international brewer Carlsberg when entering emerging markets. These included staged acquisition (opting for a lower stake initially, and increasing this over time as learning and confidence in the location are gained); multiple acquisition (acquiring different businesses at more or less the same time, with an intention to merge them together); indirect acquisition (acquiring a business outside of the target emerging economy that has a subsidiary business in the city of interest); brownfield acquisition (investing subsequent resources and upgrading the initial investment); and joint venture (sharing the acquisition with another international partner) (Meyer & Tran, 2006).

In addition to these strategic choices that MNEs can make at entry, there is a managerial side to coping and relating to issues on the ground when MNEs set up in cities in emerging economies. Managerial psyches are likely to be very different to those among managers in investing firms from advanced economies (Luo & Peng, 1998). Hoskisson et al. (2000) explored this in terms of the resource-based view of the firm: there are essential capabilities that play a role in creating sustainable competitive advantage for investors operating in emerging economies. These managerial competencies can help firms gain first-mover advantages and gain positive reputations. As Hoskisson et al. (2000) point out, these managerial skills need to be applied in the social context of the emerging economy, i.e., the social context of the specific city. They include the ability to build and maintain good relationships with governments and government agencies. Hoskisson et al. (2000) also highlight the importance of building early relationships (in order, for instance, to secure licenses), understanding the changing nature of institutions and what this may mean for networking and maintaining relationships. Such managerial capabilities will help the MNE learn and gain knowledge of impending changes at the city level, and to be able to manage risk as the nature of the institutional environment changes.

Boosting transition through FDI

FDI can play an important role in helping cities in transition and emerging countries to restructure and re-purpose their industrial landscapes. But there are important risks and difficult choices facing investors too. Cities that were once powerhouses for the Soviet Union in sectors such as coal, steel, and manufacturing soon realized the need to diversify their economies following the fall of the iron curtain. New industries in the services and IT sectors have been emphasized, with cities being major hubs for these new sectors (Tsenkova, 2006). Their ability to attract FDI and use FDI as part of an economic transformation and diversification has varied. In the first decade following the collapse of the Soviet Union, the Czech Republic, and Hungary attracted the largest share of FDI, with Balkan countries receiving the least (this was a decade of political and violent turmoil for the Balkan states), and former CIS countries of Azerbaijan and Kazakhstan receiving investment in oil and gas sectors (Tsenkova, 2006). FDI has a role to play in shaping the fortunes of these cities, harnessing new pools of human capital (Williams, Van Eerde, & Thé, 2012).

Notwithstanding the new opportunities provided to inward investors from transitioning cities, additional sources of risk have also been at play over and above those related to instability and corruption. For instance, in many of these cities, there has been an out-migration phenomenon, particularly of young people (Mykhnenko & Turok, 2008), leading to population decline and urban shrinkage that in some cases has endured for over 30 years (Eva et al., 2021). This has a negative effect on the economic output of a city and can dampen its attractiveness, particularly for MNEs seeking human capital or access to new markets. Predicting the nature and speed of urban shrinkage, and whether it will plateau and potentially reverse, is not an easy feat. Timing of entry into cities in transition economies is also a tricky decision to make for investors. Early entry can lead to first mover advantages, including early access to resources, and a lack of competition. However, there can be downsides too, such as government restrictions on the number of foreign investors at the early stages of a newly transitioning country (Luo & Peng, 1998). Late entry – i.e., a 'wait and see' strategy – can benefit from experience effects, including learning from the experiences of earlier investors. It can also be beneficial because governments themselves are learning to adapt to free-market economy logic, a process of regulatory stabilization that can take time. However, competition can be more intense by the time the investment is made, and the MNE can miss out on market share opportunities (Luo & Peng, 1998).

Beneficial effects of FDI in economic transformation of emerging economy cities have been observed by scholars. For instance, much of the innovation performance in these economies is driven by foreign investment and in the subsidiaries set up by foreign MNEs (Ženka et al., 2017). MNEs investing in emerging economies with an innovative goal will inevitably form relationships and encourage learning from local companies (Williams & Du, 2014). In China, when foreign investors have taken partial ownership (i.e., through equity joint ventures), their investments can lead to higher levels of patenting over time (Choi et al., 2011). MNEs source local human capital and spur local suppliers into action. In effect, they become central to emerging technological ecosystems where there were previously none.

On the other hand, scholars have noted the downsides of FDI in cities, particularly in non-knowledge-intensive sectors. In some instances, in emerging economies, FDI has been associated with mismanaged urban expansion that challenges sustainable development norms (Vongpraseuth & Choi, 2015). Another area of concern has been environmental damage and the link between FDI and pollution. Xie and Sun (2020) report this to be an S-curve relationship based on an empirical analysis of 11 emerging countries between 2010 and 2016; at low levels of FDI, it has a negative effect on pollutants, but as levels of FDI increase, this relationship becomes positive (i.e., FDI contributes to raising pollution levels) before flattening out. These pollution effects are concentrated in cities. What is interesting about Xie and Sun's (2020) discussion is the tension between two competing theories. The 'pollution haven' theory argues that tighter emissions regulations in developed countries lead MNEs from those countries to seek emerging countries with weaker regulations, leading to FDI contributing to pollution in emerging economy cities. The 'pollution halo' theory argues that the presence of MNEs in emerging economies will promote environmental consciousness and regulatory change, especially as MNEs will bring environmentally advanced technologies as part of their FDI. Williams and Steriu (2022) found evidence of a positive role of FDI in environmentally friendly construction in Heineken's FDI in Ethiopia when the company built a new greenfield brewery. Overall, there was a negative effect in Xie and Sun's (2020) study, providing support for the 'pollution halo' effect. This negative effect of FDI on environmental emissions has also been supported by a meta-analysis conducted by Demena and Afesorgbor (2020).

The cases in Part II

The collection of four cases in Part II explores the phenomenon of FDI in cities within the catch-up contexts of transition and emerging economies. The cases are set in the cities of Johannesburg, Ho Chi Minh City, Bagamoyo, and Katowice. They represent different stages of transition and development in cities in very different parts of the world. The cases show how cities in these contexts face their own unique sets of challenges in attracting and sustaining foreign investment, and how they are not always successful in overcoming these challenges. The cases in Part II highlight a diverse range of experiences of urban centres in transition and emerging economies as they compete for FDI, manage local conditions, and attempt to become part of broader global economic trends.

- Johannesburg: Progressing while Navigating Political and Economic Complexity

Johannesburg, South Africa's largest city, has long been a key player in attracting FDI to the African continent. With its deep historical ties to the mining industry and a growing financial sector, Johannesburg is a focal point for investors looking to tap into Africa's rich natural resources and emerging consumer markets. However, the city's complex socio-political environment, marked by issues such as corruption, inequality, and political instability, makes Johannesburg a challenging location for sustained foreign investment. The case of Johannesburg illustrates how the city was able to change the nature of the FDI that it attracted despite these issues. There was a slow but steady rise in FDI in business services and R&D, offsetting a fall in FDI in manufacturing. Despite the difficulties of the context, the city was able to progress along the value chain in a concerted way over a two-decade period.

- Ho Chi Minh City: An Emerging Hub for Manufacturing and Innovation

Ho Chi Minh City (HCMC) is one of Southeast Asia's fastest-growing urban centres and a key destination for FDI in Vietnam. The city has experienced rapid industrialization and urbanization over the past few decades, transforming from a predominantly agricultural economy into a major hub for manufacturing, technology, and services. HCMC's growth has been driven by its favourable location, low-cost labour, and an open-door policy towards foreign investors. However, the city also faced significant challenges, including poor infrastructure, environmental degradation, and uneven economic development. The case shows how FDI has impacted the city's labour market, productivity, and geospatial development as it progressively shifted into higher value-added sectors.

- Bagamoyo: The Promise and Perils of a Mega-Development Project

Bagamoyo, a small coastal city in Tanzania with a population of 82,000 inhabitants, represents one of the most ambitious FDI projects in Africa: The Bagamoyo Port and Special Economic Zone (SEZ). Initially envisioned as the largest port in East Africa, the Bagamoyo project was designed to transform Tanzania into a key logistics hub for trade between Africa, Asia, and Europe. However, ambitious projects in contexts such as this can be plagued by delays, political controversy, and concerns about economic feasibility. While the potential for FDI-driven growth in Bagamoyo remains significant, the case highlights the risks associated with large-scale foreign investment in developing countries, especially where there are state interests at stake.

- Katowice: Reindustrialization of a City amidst European Integration

Katowice, located in the Silesian region of Poland, provides an example of how cities in post-industrial regions can leverage FDI to drive transition through reindustrialization and economic transformation. Once known primarily for its coal mining and heavy industry, Katowice has undergone a significant transformation in recent decades, attracting FDI in sectors such as automotive manufacturing, technology, and services. The case shows how the city was able to attract a major pro gaming event and how this catapulted the city into the eyes of new investors who began to see the city in a new light.

6

CASE 6: THE EVOLUTION OF FDI ACROSS THE VALUE CHAIN – JOHANNESBURG (SOUTH AFRICA)

Davide Castellani, Katiuscia Lavoratori and Frans Van der Colff

Abstract

This chapter provides a view of Foreign Direct Investment (FDI) in Johannesburg, focussing on the evolution in volume and nature of investments from 2003 to 2021, using Nairobi, Lagos, and the broader Africa as benchmarks. Johannesburg emerged as a prime FDI destination in Africa. Comparing FDI dynamics over time, a steady increase in investments was noted, characterised by a dominance of investors from Europe and North America. Most notably, the nature of FDI in Johannesburg changed significantly over the past two decades (2003–2021): we observed a shift in FDI along the value chain, with a decline in manufacturing and a rise in activities like business services, headquarters, and research and development. This case study underscores the ability of the city to attract FDI in knowledge-intensive activities, shaping Johannesburg's economic landscape and highlighting opportunities for further growth.

Introduction

Foreign direct investment (FDI) plays an important role in shaping the economies of countries worldwide and Africa is no exception. Africa has multiple economic powerhouses, notably Johannesburg (South Africa), Nairobi (Kenya), and Lagos (Nigeria) (Contractor et al., 2020). These three stand out as major players, as they have attracted significant FDI, which has assisted in driving economic growth and development in each country. The United Nations Human Settlements Programme (2018) identified Johannesburg, Nairobi, and Lagos as the leading FDI attractions in sub-Saharan Africa.

DOI: 10.4324/9781003483410-9

This chapter aimed to provide a comprehensive case study of FDI in Johannesburg spanning from 2003 to 2021, utilising Nairobi, Lagos, and the rest of Africa as comparative benchmarks. Specifically, our analysis delved into the characteristics of FDI projects directed towards Johannesburg, examining their evolution over time, key investors, sectors involved, and value chain activities. To achieve this, we relied on data on greenfield investment projects sourced from Orbis Cross-border Investment (CBI) and fDi Markets and covered the 2003–2021 period.

By analysing a dataset comprising 8,010 greenfield projects across the African region (4,839 projects spanning 2013–2021 sourced from CBI, and 3,171 projects from the 2003 to 2012 period sourced from fDi Markets), we underscored an upward trajectory in the number of FDI projects directed towards the African continent. Notably, Johannesburg, Lagos, and Nairobi represent approximately 18% of the total FDI in Africa. Within this context, Johannesburg emerged as the primary beneficiary of FDI, with a relatively greater proportion of projects in high knowledge-intensive (value-added) activities, as opposed to lower value-added activities, in particular manufacturing.

When examining the evolution of FDI in Johannesburg over time, a notable trend emerged: the number of FDI projects exhibited significant growth from the initial period (2003–2012) to the subsequent period (2013–2021), peaking in 2018. This upward trajectory underscored the increasing attractiveness of the city to international investors. Europe and North America were the major sources of FDI, while we observed a relatively lower presence of investors from other African countries. Moreover, a shift in FDI patterns along the value chain was discernible, with a decline in manufacturing projects and a rise in activities such as business services, headquarters, and research and development (R&D). This highlighted the increasing competitiveness in attracting high value-added investments, indicative of Johannesburg's evolving economic structure and global strategic positioning.

The rest of the chapter is organised as follows. The next section discusses the history of Johannesburg, while 'Comparing Johannesburg with Nairobi and Lagos' section discusses the factors influencing FDI in the city. 'Foreign direct investment in the African context' section describes the data employed in the empirical analysis. 'Foreign direct investment in Johannesburg' section discusses the empirical results, while the final section concludes with some recommendations.

History of Johannesburg

Johannesburg is a city with a population of approximately six million people, home to the largest artificial forest in the world, with about six million trees (City of Johannesburg, 2018), where you could listen to Amapiano, the unique subgenre of house music that originated in South Africa, and was also the city where most of the occupants were denied dignity and a voice for a very long time (Conteh, 2021).

Often dubbed the 'City of Gold', Johannesburg has been a prominent economic hub on the continent for many years. As the largest city in South Africa and the country's economic powerhouse, Johannesburg has been characterised by a diverse economic environment and a vibrant business sector. Being in a strategic location and having a well-developed infrastructure played a key role in making Johannesburg an essential player in connecting global markets within the fast-growing African continent (City of Johannesburg, 2018; Kollamparambil & Jogee, 2018).

The economic trajectory has been shaped by FDI since 1886, when the city started as a shanty town following the discovery of gold. The city is home to the largest stock exchange in Africa (Johannesburg Stock Exchange) and contributed to 16.5% of South Africa's wealth, while employing over 12% of the country's workforce in 2018. In addition, in 2018, 70% of South African companies had their headquarters in Johannesburg (City of Johannesburg, 2018).

However, for most of the 20th century (from 1948 to the early 1990s), Johannesburg evolved as a city under the apartheid system of institutionalised racism. Prime areas were designated for white people only, which were provided with all the necessary services and amenities; while in the outlying areas, or townships, that were allocated to black people, services and amenities were non-existent. Furthermore, these people had limited opportunities for employment and education, which, when available, was inferior. The foreign mining companies adhered to the system of apartheid and exacerbated it by only placing white males in positions of authority. The laws of apartheid allowed these companies complete control over black workers and to keep their wages low, which contributed to increased profitability for the companies and their shareholders. This resulted in the city becoming, and still being, one of the most unequal places in the world.

The 1960s saw the start of economic sanctions against South Africa. Companies were asked to disinvest, but none of the Western-based companies, often with diverse shareholder bases, held significant influence over operations in various industries heeded the call, as they were too profitable. In the 1980s, the calls started gaining momentum and sanctions were imposed by major trading partners, such as the United States (US), the European Commission, and Japan. This led to significant disinvestment (Manby, 1992). After the withdrawal of short-term credits in 1985 by international banks, immediate loan repayments took a heavy toll on the economy. It is estimated that 350 foreign-owned companies, mostly US-owned, sold their South African investments (Manby, 1992). The post-apartheid era, beginning in 1994, saw a shift towards a more inclusive and democratic political environment, aiming to attract more foreign investment. Despite an increase in FDI post-1993, reaching around 1.5% of the gross domestic product, Johannesburg's historical challenges have left a lasting impact on its economic landscape and social dynamics (Arvanitis, 2005).

The biggest transformation of the city in the 1990s happened in the inner city, the central business district, where big businesses – including many multinationals – fled the area due to increasing decay and crime and the arrival of slumlords who illegally occupied buildings and accommodated the increasing number of migrants, this trend has continued into the 21st century, contributing to ongoing challenges the city faces today. Businesses moved to the suburb of Sandton, often referred to as the richest 'square mile' in Africa. Other significant changes were the emergence of the black-owned minibus taxi industry as well as an increase in informal settlements (Harrison et al., 2014). The city's economy transitioned from a mining economy to a manufacturing economy and later to a service economy, which occurred before 1990 and the age of democracy (Harrison et al., 2014).

FDI has played a role in job creation across the different sectors, which has been beneficial to other sectors as well. The diverse FDI portfolio has ensured a broader spectrum of job opportunities, ranging from skilled positions to labour-intensive positions (Saurav et al., 2020). Lately, Johannesburg has been known as a financial hub, which can largely be attributed to the FDI in the financial sector. International financial institutions have significantly invested in the city, building and enhancing the financial infrastructure and services. This growth has created several high-skilled job opportunities, which has made the city a hub for financial expertise (Kollamparambil & Jogee, 2018). In recent years, the FDI in the technology sectors has also become increasingly significant. Johannesburg has managed to attract global tech companies, fostering innovation and employment opportunities in exciting fields. These advancements have not only contributed to job creation in the city but have also increased the flow of money within the economy (Asafo-Adjei, 2007).

The goals outlined in Gauteng's Growth and Development Strategy (GDS) 2025 form the basis for aligning an investment incentive policy for the City of Johannesburg. Gauteng, one of South Africa's nine provinces, aims to position itself as a competitive region in the global economy. Johannesburg played a central role in the planning and success of the Gauteng City Region initiative. To promote Gauteng as a globally competitive city region, the provincial government has identified specific economic sectors with the potential to drive economic growth and job creation. These sectors include value-added manufacturing, competitive sports, creative industries, tourism, and information and communications technology infrastructure and services (City of Johannesburg, 2018).

A study by Kollamparambil and Jogee (2018) – based on interviews with foreign firms based in Johannesburg – found that a 'new generation' of policy frameworks that better facilitate foreign investment, while allowing investment regulation in line with the public policies of the host nation and responsible investor behaviour is needed. The companies surveyed in the study expressed cautious optimism over their future in South Africa. Uncertainty in politics and policy is their primary worry. Numerous companies declared that they would not be making any more investments until there was more certainty, particularly concerning the Mining Charter and the nation's political leadership. The fairly recent collapse in commodity prices, which was fuelled by the slowdown in China's economy, had a significant impact on a large number of domestic and international businesses that supply mining companies, which highlighted the requirement to lessen reliance and diversify South Africa's economic structure (Kollamparambil & Jogee, 2018).

Comparing Johannesburg with Nairobi and Lagos

Nairobi, Kenya's capital and largest city, was established in the late 1890s as a colonial settlement and stood as a dynamic regional hub for trade and finance in East Africa owning to its strategic location. The name 'Nairobi' came from the Maasai phrase Enkare Nyrobi, which means 'cool water' (Mundia, 2017).

FDI has played a significant role in the economic development of Kenya and Nairobi, with the city also acting as the regional hub for East Africa. As a gateway to the East African market, Nairobi offered access to more than 150 million people. The city has emerged as a technology and innovation hub and the vibrant tech ecosystem, often referred to as 'Silicon Savannah', attracting global investors seeking opportunities in Africa's digital economy. Renewable energy was another area attracting investors. Multinationals located their regional headquarters here due to the strategic position of the city within East Africa. Organisations, such as Coca-Cola, IBA, Microsoft, Standard Chartered, and Unilever, established their headquarters in Nairobi (Gachigo et al., 2019).

The challenges of FDI in Nairobi included regulatory hurdles, infrastructure gaps, and political uncertainties. Simultaneously, opportunities from the city's strategic positioning, increasing consumer market, and innovation give policymakers and investors valuable considerations for strategic decision-making (Ndagijimana, 2022).

Lagos has been the economic heartbeat of Nigeria and West Africa. In the 15th century, it was known as Oko and was the home of Yoruba fishermen and hunters. The Portuguese arrived in 1472 and Lagos came under British control in 1861. Nigeria obtained its independence in 1960 (Britannica, 2024). Lagos is the biggest city in Nigeria and the biggest recipient of FDI, although, as in other regions, FDI has declined since 2020. In 2022, Lagos received approximately 47% of Nigeria's FDI, playing a pivotal role in shaping the city's community and economy (National Bureau of Statistics, 2023). Historically, the main obstacles facing Lagos were corruption (in 2023 Nigeria ranked 143 out of 180 countries in Transparency International's Corruption Perceptions Index), the underdeveloped power sector, and security. Multinationals in Lagos include Accenture, British American Tobacco, Chevron, DHL, Cadbury, and Coca-Cola (Blair, 2023; U.S. Department of State, 2021).

Foreign direct investment in the African context

The chapter aimed to understand the evolution of FDI in Johannesburg. To do so, the analysis relied on data from two databases on new greenfield FDI. First, the *Orbis Cross Border Investment* (CBI) database, provided by Moody's, details greenfield investments worldwide from 2013, including information on parent companies, home and destination countries, cities, and value chain activities (e.g., HQ, R&D, manufacturing, business services, logistics, and marketing and sales). To cover years before 2013, we used *fDi Markets*, developed by fDi Intelligence (Financial Times Ltd.), which tracked greenfield investments across various industries and countries since 2003. This database has been widely used by international organisations (e.g., UNCTAD, OECD) and scholars (Belderbos et al., 2020; Castellani & Lavoratori, 2020). Both datasets provide comparable information, allowing us to analyse investments from 2003 to 2021. Our sample included 8,010 greenfield projects in Africa: 4,839 from 2013 to 2021 (CBI) and 3,171 from 2003 to 2012 (fDi Markets). Projects lacking essential data were excluded. The number of projects increased steadily, peaking at 809 in 2019 (Figure 6.1).

A marked decrease was observed in 2020 and 2021, likely influenced by the COVID-19 pandemic. South Africa consistently emerged as the largest recipient of FDI, accounting for an increasing share of investments over the period, rising from 17.2% to 18.9%.

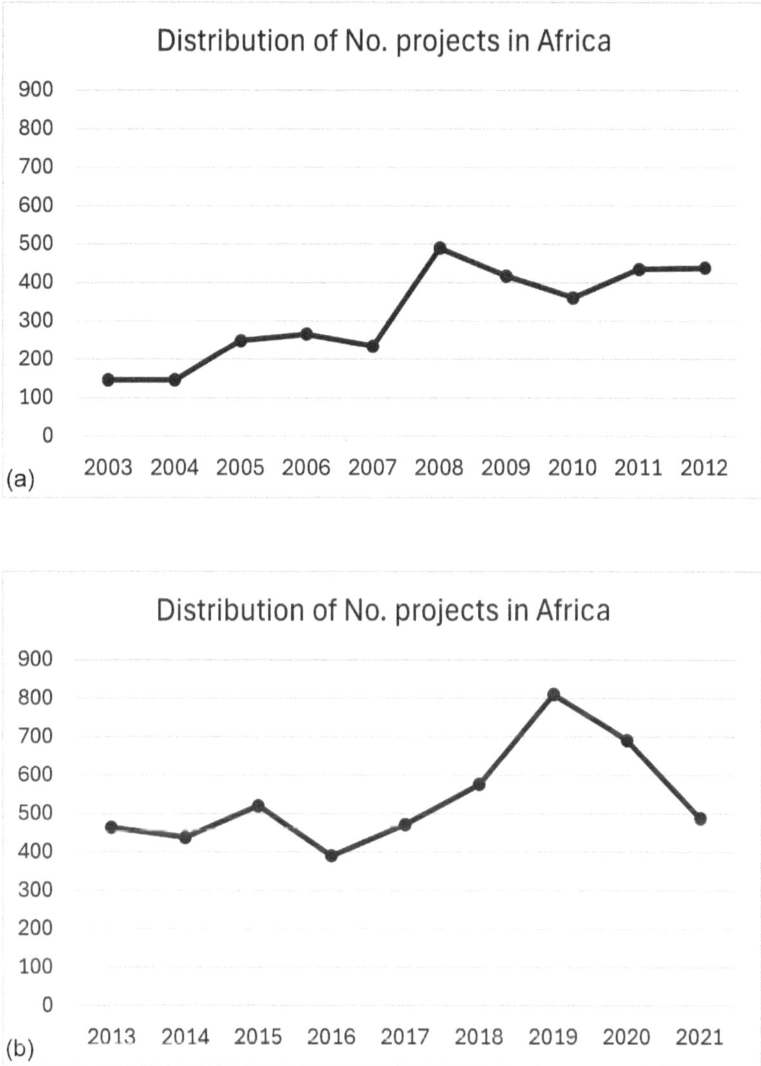

FIGURE 6.1 Distribution of FDI projects over years, 2003–2021

Source: Authors' elaboration from fDi Markets and CBI.

Over the period, more than 50 African countries received inward FDI projects. In more recent years, the top five recipients were South Africa (19%), Morocco (17%), Egypt (8.8%), Kenya (8.6%), and Nigeria (6.6%). The top 10 destination countries are reported in Table 6.1.

TABLE 6.1 Distribution of inward FDI in Africa by country (top 10)

	2003–2012			*2013–2021*	
Destination country	*Freq.*	*%*	*Destination country*	*Freq.*	*%*
South Africa	660	20.81	South Africa	917	18.95
Egypt	401	12.65	Morocco	836	17.28
Morocco	334	10.53	Egypt	428	8.84
Nigeria	191	6.02	Kenya	418	8.64
Tunisia	185	5.83	Nigeria	321	6.63
Algeria	183	5.77	Tunisia	182	3.76
Angola	169	5.33	Ghana	177	3.66
Kenya	149	4.7	Algeria	161	3.33
Ghana	128	4.04	Cote d'Ivoire	154	3.18
Tanzania	80	2.52	Ethiopia	125	2.58

Source: Authors' elaboration from fDi Markets and CBI.

Foreign direct investment in Johannesburg

Zooming in, we found that projects involved over 800 different cities. Johannesburg had the highest number of inward FDI projects (9.2% in 2003–2012 and 7.6% in 2013–2021). In the more recent period, Nairobi caught up, becoming the second most important African city for foreign investors (6.6%). Other major recipients of FDI were Casablanca (6%), Cairo (4.9%), Cape Town (4.2%), and Lagos (3.9%). Johannesburg accounted for over 40% of investment projects in South Africa. Nairobi and Lagos, which share similarities with Johannesburg, accounted for 11% of total investment in Africa, as illustrated in Table 6.2 showing the distribution of inward FDI in the top 10 destination cities.

TABLE 6.2 Distribution of inward FDI in Africa by city (top 10)

	2003–2012			*2013–2021*	
Destination city	*Freq.*	*%*	*Destination city*	*Freq.*	*%*
Johannesburg	292	9.21	Johannesburg	369	7.63
Cairo	207	6.53	Nairobi	319	6.59
Casablanca	182	5.74	Casablanca	291	6.01
Nairobi	146	4.6	Cairo	237	4.9
Cape Town	142	4.48	Cape Town	202	4.17
Lagos	108	3.41	Lagos	190	3.93
Tunis	106	3.34	Abidjan	127	2.62
Luanda	103	3.25	Tangier	122	2.52
Algiers	79	2.49	Accra	117	2.42
Accra	69	2.18	Rabat	87	1.8

Source: Authors' elaboration from fDi Markets and CBI.

Source countries

Africa received investment projects from over 100 different countries, with nearly half originating from Europe, approximately 20% from the United States, and 19% from Asia, as shown in Table 6.3. The top investors were the United States (15.9%), France (12.6%), the United Kingdom (6.6%), Germany (5.6%), and Spain (4.9%). China ranked sixth, accounting for 4.5% of the total projects.

When comparing the distribution of total projects by source continent with the distribution among the three cities under investigation, Johannesburg stood out due to its greater relevance of investments from multinational companies based in Western economies across Europe, North America, and Oceania (Australia), and its significantly lower propensity to attract investments from other African countries compared to the rest of the continent and other major African cities such as Nairobi and Lagos, underscoring Johannesburg's role as the gateway to Africa for multinationals from advanced economies.

FDI projects going into Africa during the period 2003–2012 originated from 92 different countries, with 48% from Europe, 17% from North America, and 19% from Asia, as shown in Table 6.3. The top investors were the United States (14.9%), the United Kingdom (11%), France (11%), Germany (5.2%), and the

TABLE 6.3 Distribution of FDI projects in Africa and its major cities by source continent, 2003–2021

Source continent name	*Total*		*Johannesburg*		*Lagos*		*Nairobi*	
	Freq.	*%*	*Freq.*	*%*	*Freq.*	*%*	*Freq.*	*%*
2003–2012								
Africa	395	12.46	8	2.74	14	12.96	22	15.07
Asia	625	19.71	56	19.18	24	22.22	43	29.45
Europe	1544	48.69	136	46.58	46	42.59	55	37.67
North America	549	17.31	84	28.77	24	22.22	25	17.12
Oceania	37	1.17	8	2.74				
South America	21	0.66					1	0.68
Total	3171	100	292	100	108	100	146	100
2013–2021								
Africa	534	11.04	10	2.71	20	10.53	48	15.05
Asia	926	19.14	61	16.53	35	18.42	72	22.57
Europe	2341	47.47	173	47.15	79	41.58	125	39.28
North America	965	19.94	111	30.08	55	28.95	71	22.26
Oceania	32	0.66	10	2.71	1	0.53	2	0.63
South America	14	0.29	3	0.81				0
Other	27	0.56					1	0.31
Total	4839	100	369	100	190	100	319	100

Source: Authors' elaboration from fDi Markets and CBI.

United Arab Emirates (4.6%). China ranked 15th, accounting for less than 2% of the total projects. An increased role of China was observed as a key investor, doubling its share in the second period (2013–2021).

Similar patterns were observed in the 2013–2021 period: Johannesburg showed a relatively greater presence of investments from multinational companies from Europe and North America, and a lower propensity to attract investments from other African countries. The top five investors were the United States, the United Kingdom, India, France, and Germany, followed by Japan.

Sectors

As revealed in Table 6.4, the majority of projects were related to services industries, followed by construction and manufacturing. Johannesburg attracted a relatively higher proportion of investment projects in services and a lower proportion in manufacturing compared to the rest of Africa, aligning with Lagos and Nairobi in this regard. This trend intensified in recent years, with the share of manufacturing dropping, while services saw a slight increase. Most notably, construction experienced a remarkable increase in investments over the years (especially in the second half of the period, 2013–2021), for this reason, we kept it as a separate class.

Business functions

When comparing the distribution of total projects by business function with the distribution among the three cities under investigation, we found that Johannesburg attracted a higher proportion of investments involving high

TABLE 6.4 Distribution of FDI projects by sector, 2003–2021

	Total		*Johannesburg*		*Lagos*		*Nairobi*	
Sector	*Freq.*	*%*	*Freq.*	*%*	*Freq.*	*%*	*Freq.*	*%*
2003–2012								
Manufacturing	1,228	38.73	101	34.59	36	33.33	59	40.41
Construction	126	3.97	6	2.05	1	0.93	1	0.68
Primary	181	5.71	7	2.4	4	3.7	2	1.37
Services	1,636	51.59	178	60.96	67	62.04	84	57.53
Total	3,171	100	292	100	108	100	146	100
2013–2021								
Manufacturing	1,025	21.18	41	11.11	24	12.63	43	13.48
Construction	1,229	25.40	75	20.33	41	21.58	88	27.59
Primary	50	1.03	2	0.54				
Services	2,535	52.39	251	68.02	125	65.79	188	58.93
Total	4,839	100	369	100	190	100	319	100

Source: Authors' elaboration from fDi Markets and CBI.

knowledge-intensive activities (e.g., Marketing and Sales, R&D, and Regional Headquarters) compared to Africa as a whole, while it was relatively less attractive for manufacturing investment. In the period 2003–2012, manufacturing accounted for 22.3% of foreign investments in Africa, but only 9.2% in Johannesburg. Interestingly, in the more recent period, the proportion of foreign investment projects aimed at creating manufacturing capacity in Africa dropped to 13.6%, and 2.7% in Johannesburg. However, changes in categorisation between datasets may have affected this shift. Specifically, CBI identified Hotels and Retail in the more recent period, which were not specified by fDi Markets in 2003–2012, potentially distorting the comparison over time. Nevertheless, Johannesburg, along with Lagos and Nairobi, exhibited a higher attractiveness for knowledge-intensive activities. Johannesburg particularly stood out for its increased propensity to attract R&D centres, which grew from 3% to 5%, whereas in Africa overall and in Lagos and Nairobi, these figures remained constant or decreased (Table 6.5).

Johannesburg's ability to attract FDI into knowledge-intensive activities has been driven by strategic policy reforms, institutional developments, and the city's inherent advantages. Post-apartheid economic liberalisation in the 1990s, including the Growth, Employment, and Redistribution (GEAR) strategy, laid the foundation for a more attractive investment climate by promoting fiscal discipline and trade liberalisation (South African Government, 1996).

The establishment of the Johannesburg Development Agency (JDA) in the year 2001 spearheaded the city's proactive approach to facilitating and supporting foreign investments through comprehensive services and incentives (OECD, 2010). As the JDA noted, 'Johannesburg is open for business, and we are committed to making it easier for investors to enter our market and thrive' (OECD, 2010).

Additionally, in 2009, the establishment of Special Economic Zones (SEZs), such as the OR Tambo International Airport SEZ, has provided attractive environments for high-tech industries (GGDA, 2021). According to the Gauteng Growth and Development Agency, 'The OR Tambo International Airport SEZ is a significant development in our efforts to attract high-tech industries' (Gauteng Growth and Development Agency, 2021).

Educational institutions have also played a vital role. Several strong national and international higher education institutions, including the University of the Witwatersrand, the University of Johannesburg, the Gordon Institute of Business Science – University of Pretoria, and Henley Business School Africa, established in Johannesburg, contributing to a skilled workforce essential for knowledge-intensive sectors. Professor Zeblon Vilakazi, Vice-Chancellor of the University of the Witwatersrand, emphasised, 'Our commitment to research and innovation is central to Wits' mission' (University of the Witwatersrand, 2023). Similarly, Professor Tshilidzi Marwala, Former Vice-Chancellor of the University of Johannesburg, stated, '[the University of Johannesburg] is at the forefront of fostering an entrepreneurial spirit and

TABLE 6.5 Distribution of FDI projects by business function, 2003–2021

Project business function	*Total*		*Johannesburg*		*Lagos*		*Nairobi*	
	Freq.	*%*	*Freq.*	*%*	*Freq.*	*%*	*Freq.*	*%*
2003–2012								
R&D (including Design, Development, and Testing)	95	3.00	9	3.08	4	3.71	5	3.42
(Regional) Headquarters	80	2.52	13	4.45	2	1.85	11	7.53
Manufacturing	707	22.3	27	9.25	15	13.89	15	10.27
Technical Support	21	0.66	4	1.37	2	1.85		
Sales, Marketing, and Support	693	21.85	112	38.36	26	24.07	56	38.36
ICT and Internet Infrastructure	42	1.32	7	2.4	3	2.78	1	0.68
Logistics, Distribution, and Transportation	124	3.91	13	4.45	8	7.41	6	4.11
Maintenance and Servicing	65	2.05	2	0.68	6	5.56	6	4.11
Others[a]	1344	42.38	105	35.96	42	38.89	46	31.51
Total	3171	100	292	100	108	100	146	100
2013–2021								
R&D (including Testing Centres)	121	2.5	19	5.15	6	3.16	11	3.45
(Regional) Headquarters	119	2.46	20	5.42	11	5.79	14	4.39
Manufacturing	658	13.6	10	2.71	11	5.79	14	4.39
Technical Support	60	1.24	9	2.44	3	1.58	6	1.88
Sales Office	756	15.62	113	30.62	49	25.79	98	30.72
ICT Infrastructure	53	1.1	10	2.71	5	2.63	2	0.63
Logistics, Distribution, and Transportation	226	4.67	17	4.61	4	2.11	15	4.7
Maintenance and Repair	47	0.97	4	1.08	3	1.58	5	1.57
Others[a]	2799	57.84	167	45.26	98	51.58	154	48.28
Total	4839	100	369	100	190	100	319	100

Source: Authors' elaboration from fDi Markets and CBI.

Note:

[a] fDi Markets and CBI use slightly different classifications of business functions. While some a broadly comparable, some are not. To avoid confusion, we have created a category 'Others' that includes all business functions that are not exactly comparable. This category includes Business Services, Construction, Customer Contact Centre, Education and Training, Electricity, Extraction, Recycling, Shared Services Centre in fDi Markets (2003–2012) and Agriculture, Banking and Finance, Business Services, Commercial Real Estate, Construction, Customer Contact Centre, Data Centre, Education and Training, Electricity, Entertainment, Health, Hotels, Mining, Recycling Residential Real Estate, Retail, Software Development Centre, and Utilities in CBI (2013–2021).

innovative thinking' (University of Johannesburg, 2023). Jon Foster-Pedley, Dean of Henley Business School Africa, highlighted that Henley Africa 'build the people who will do the businesses that will build Africa' and trains 'students in the fourth industrial revolution competencies so that they can go out there and build new industries'.[1] These insights illustrate the collaborative efforts between government, educational institutions, and industry to foster an environment conducive to knowledge-intensive FDI.

Finally, investments in ICT infrastructure and public-private partnerships have further enhanced the city's appeal (Broadband Commission, 2020). Despite challenges such as regulatory complexity and infrastructural deficiencies, ongoing efforts to streamline business processes and improve policy stability have continued to support Johannesburg's position as a hub for knowledge-intensive FDI (IMF, 2021). The city's strategic location on the continent and connectedness to the rest of the World have further enhanced the attraction (Kollamparambil & Jogee, 2018).

The South African government's commitment to attracting foreign investment to foster economic development was confirmed by President Ramaphosa himself on 6 May 2024:

> We will continue to build on the gains that we made towards creating an enabling business and investment climate that promotes economic growth and creates jobs. It is only through attracting higher levels of investment, both foreign and domestic, that a swift, sustainable economic environment can be assured.[2]

Conclusions

This chapter provided a case study of FDI in Johannesburg offering a historical overview of the development of the city and FDI, and a detailed analysis of CBI projects in the city spanning the last two decades (2003–2021), along with comparisons with Nairobi, Lagos, and broader Africa. Our examination of 8,010 greenfield projects underscored Johannesburg's emergence as a pivotal FDI hub within the continent, particularly notable for its dominance in service sectors. The steady increase in FDI projects over time, largely driven by investors from Europe and North America, reflected the city's potential for economic growth and FDI attraction. Moreover, the observed shift in FDI patterns towards knowledge-intensive activities such as headquarters, and R&D, underscored the economic trajectory of the city.

Johannesburg's pursuit of knowledge-intensive FDI has continued to face significant hurdles despite progress made over the past decades. While the city has improved its regulatory environment and infrastructure, persistent challenges include bureaucratic inefficiencies, intermittent power supply issues, and a skills mismatch between the local workforce and the needs of knowledge-intensive industries. These factors, combined with broader economic uncertainties and increasing competition from other emerging markets, create a complex landscape for potential investors. According to the World Bank's Global Investment Competitiveness Report 2023–2024, while South Africa remained a key FDI destination in Africa, regulatory unpredictability and complex business environments continue to be cited as major obstacles by international investors, suggesting that Johannesburg still has work to do in streamlining processes to enhance its attractiveness for knowledge-intensive FDI (World Bank Group, 2023). For example, foreign ICT companies have encountered difficulties with data protection laws, such as compliance with the Protection of Personal Information Act, which requires significant adjustments in data handling practices (Broadband Commission, 2020). The telecommunications sector has also faced challenges with licensing and spectrum allocation, with delays in spectrum auctions hindering the expansion plans of companies like MTN and Vodacom (International Monetary Fund, 2021). Additionally, General Motors exited South Africa in 2017, citing the need to optimise global operations amid declining sales and economic instability, which underscores the broader issues of economic volatility and regulatory challenges (Reuters, 2017). High levels of crime and concerns about personal and business security add to the operational costs and risks for investors (Broadband Commission, 2020).

Addressing these regulatory, economic, and security challenges will be crucial for Johannesburg to maintain its attractiveness as a hub for knowledge-intensive FDI. Therefore, for policymakers, will be important to recognise the role of political stability, favourable regulatory environments, and robust infrastructure in attracting FDI.

To foster a more conducive environment for FDI, policymakers could prioritise ongoing regulatory reforms, address infrastructural gaps, and enhance political stability. Developing and promoting the unique strengths of the city. Collaboration between governments, businesses, and local communities is essential for creating an environment that not only attracts but also sustains foreign investment.

The potential for FDI in Johannesburg is significant, and strategic measures are needed to overcome challenges and fully unlock its economic potential. The dynamic nature of this city requires adaptive and forward-thinking approaches from all stakeholders to ensure sustainable growth, economic development, and shared prosperity.

Notes

1 https://africalive.net/interview/1125/
2 https://www.stateofthenation.gov.za/newsletter/south-africa-is-an-increasingly-attractive-investment-destination

References

Arvanitis, A. (2005). Foreign direct investment in South Africa: Why has it been so low? In M. Nowak & L. A. Ricci (Eds.), *Post-apartheid South Africa: The first ten years* (pp. 64–79). International Monetary Fund.

Asafo-Adjei, A. (2007). *Foreign direct investment and its importance to the economy of South Africa*. Master's dissertation. University of South Africa.

Belderbos, R., Du, H. S., & Slangen, A. (2020). When do firms choose global cities as foreign investment locations within countries? The roles of contextual distance, knowledge intensity, and target-country experience. *Journal of World Business, 55*(1), 101022.

Blair, A. (2023). *The FDI landscape in Nigeria in 2023*. https://www.investmentmonitor.ai/features/fdi-nigeria-investment-africa-oil-gas-diversification/?cf-view

Britannica. (2024). 'Lagos', in *Encyclopædia Britannica*. Available at: https://www.britannica.com/place/Lagos-Nigeria

Broadband Commission. (2020). *State of broadband: Tackling digital inequalities*. https://www.broadbandcommission.org/state-of-broadband-report-2020/

Castellani, D., & Lavoratori, K. (2020). The lab and the plant. Offshore R&D and co-location with production activities. *Journal of International Business Studies, 51*, 121–137.

City of Johannesburg. (2018). *Work in Joburg: A brief history*. https://joburg.org.za/work_/Pages/Work%20in%20Joburg/General%20Advice/Links/A%20Brief%20History.aspx

Conteh, M. (2021). Inside the rise of Amapiano, the genre that's taking over South Africa and coming to a dance floor near you. *Rolling Stone*, 2 July. https://www.rollingstone.com/music/music-features/amapiano-genre-house-south-africa-1191523/

Contractor, F. J., Dangol, R., Nuruzzaman, N., & Raghunath, S. (2020). How do country regulations and business environment impact foreign direct investment (FDI) inflows? *International Business Review, 29*(2), 101640. https://doi.org/10.1016/j.ibusrev.2019.101640

Gachigo, S. M., Kahuthia, J., & Muraguri, C. (2019). Exploration innovative strategy and performance of the telecommunication industry in Kenya: A case of Safaricom PLC in Nairobi metropolis. *International Academic Journal of Human Resource and Business Administration, 3*(6), 299–319.

Gauteng Growth and Development Agency (GGDA). (2021). *Special economic zones (SEZs)*. https://www.ggda.co.za/special-economic-zones-sez/

Harrison, P., Gotz, G., Todes, A., & Wray, C. (2014). Materialities, subjectivities and spatial transformation in Johannesburg. In P. Harrison, G. Gotz, A. Todes, & C. Wray (Eds.), *Changing space, changing city: Johannesburg after apartheid* (pp. 2–39). Wits University Press.

International Monetary Fund (IMF). (2021). *South Africa: 2021 Article IV Consultation-Press Release; Staff Report; and Statement by the Executive Director for South Africa*. https://www.imf.org/en/Publications/CR/Issues/2021/07/19/South-Africa-2021-Article-IV-Consultation-Press-Release-Staff-Report-and-Statement-by-the-462376

Kollamparambil, U., & Jogee, R. (2018). Johannesburg: interlinked narratives and investment by foreign firms, in UN-Habitat (2018) The state of African cities 2018, pp. 232–251, United Nations Human Settlements Programme, https://unhabitat.org/the-state-of-african-cities-2018-the-geography-of-african-investment.

Manby, B. (1992). South Africa: The impact of sanctions. *Journal of International Affairs, 46*(1), 193–217.

Mundia, C. N. (2017). Nairobi Metropolitan area. In Y. Murayama, C. Kamusoko, A. Yamashita, & R. C. Estoque (Eds.), *Urban development in Asia and Africa: Geospatial analysis of metropolises* (pp. 293–317). Springer.

National Bureau of Statistics. (2023). *Nigerian capital importation (Q4 2022)*. https://nigerianstat.gov.ng/elibrary/read/1241434

Ndagijimana, E. (2022). *Opportunities and obstacles to foreign direct investment in Kenya's energy sector*. Project report. United States International University – Africa.

OECD. (2010). *Organising local economic development: The role of development agencies and companies*. OECD Publishing. https://doi.org/10.1787/9789264083530-21-en

Reuters. (2017). *General Motors to exit South Africa, sell plant to Isuzu*. https://www.reuters.com/article/us-gm-safrica-idUSKCN18D0FJ

Saurav, A., Liu, Y., & Sinha, A. (2020). *Foreign direct investment and employment outcomes in developing countries: A literature review of the effects of FDI on job creation and wages*. https://documents1.worldbank.org/curated/en/956231593150550672/pdf/Foreign-Direct-Investment-and-Employment-Outcomes-in-Developing-Countries-A-Literature-Review-of-the-Effects-of-FDI-on-Job-Creation-and-Wages.pdf

South African Government. (1996). *Growth, employment and redistribution: A macroeconomic strategy*. https://www.gov.za/documents/growth-employment-and-redistribution-macro-economic-strategy-south-africa

U.S. Department of State. (2021). *2021 investment climate statements: Nigeria*. https://www.state.gov/reports/2021-investment-climate-statements/nigeria/

United Nations Human Settlements Programme. (2018). *The state of African cities 2018: The geography of African investment*. https://unhabitat.org/sites/default/files/download-manager-files/The%20State%20of%20African%20Cities.pdf

University of Johannesburg. (2023). *Research and innovation*.

University of the Witwatersrand. (2023). *Research and innovation at wits*. https://www.wits.ac.za/research/

World Bank Group. (2023). *Global investment competitiveness report 2023–2024: Rebuilding investor confidence in times of uncertainty*. World Bank.

7

CASE 7: FDI-LED DEVELOPMENT IN HO CHI MINH CITY

Tom Becker

ABSTRACT

Ho Chi Minh City (HCMC) is increasingly becoming an international economic hub and – while long a favourite for tourists, travellers and traders from around the globe – its attractiveness for foreign investors and companies is no longer to be underestimated and assuming global relevance. Foreign Direct Investment (FDI) has played a prominent role in the city's development since Viet Nam's accelerated integration into the world economy post-Doi Moi and left its mark on the city. The chapter offers a glimpse into the impact FDI has had on HCMC's labour market, productivity and geospatial development. High inflows of FDI did not only contribute to economic growth but also to the city's changing urban geography, i.e. spatial growth and urban sprawl. FDI contributed to positioning the HCMC as one of Southeast Asia's economic powerhouses in the 2020s and did have positive effects on the productivity of domestic firms. By 2024, the city had, since first opening-up to foreign investment in 1987, moved towards attracting largely FDI in the services sector. The jobs FDI contributed to create in and around the city were to a large extend in higher value added activities by the mid-2020s. However, high levels of FDI do not come without challenges; those related to urban sprawl, inefficient infrastructure and the environment are only some.

Introduction

Ho Chi Minh City (HCMC), formerly known as Saigon, did increasingly become an international economic hub and by the early 2020s – while long a favourite for tourists, travellers and traders from around the globe – its attractiveness for foreign investors and global businesses could no longer be underestimated and had assumed global relevance, having ranked 85th in the 2023 rendition of Euromonitor's Leading Cities of the World Ranking (Ngyuen, 2023). Foreign Direct Investment (FDI) played a prominent role in the city's development since

DOI: 10.4324/9781003483410-10

Viet Nam's accelerated integration into the world economy post-*Doi Moi* and left its mark on the city. The chapter offers a glimpse into the impact FDI has had on HCMC's labour market, productivity and geospatial development.

Due to the city's impact on the overall development of Viet Nam (see Du & Fukushima, 2010) and its attractiveness for foreign investors, it makes for an interesting case of FDI's contribution to development.

As of summer 2024, HCMC was the most powerful economic region in Viet Nam, considerably driving economic development and advancing the sectoral transition of the country, having contributed more than a fifth to Viet Nam's overall GDP in 2022, 22 per cent (Huong, 2023). In fact, Viet Nam's economic boom and increasing relevance for regional and global supply and value chains since the mid-2000s has led to the emergence of phrases such as 'Rising Dragon' (Hayton, 2020).

The city emerged as one of Asia's economic hubs and one of the Association of Southeast Asian Nations' (ASEAN) leading greenfield FDI destinations, second only to Singapore, with 1,140 foreign greenfield investment projects recorded in the 2004–2023 period. While the Lion City recorded 6,805 projects in the same period, HCMC forms part of the quadrumvirate of FDI hubs in ASEAN, with the remaining spots claimed by Bangkok, Thailand (1,030) and Kuala Lumpur, Malaysia (1,005).

The metropolis attracted foreign companies from around the word. Between 2004 and 2023, 53 per cent of companies investing in HCMC were based all over the vast Asia-Pacific region, 26 per cent in Western Europe and 18 per cent in North America. In fact, Japan (18 per cent), the United States (16 per cent), Singapore (9 per cent), South Korea (8 per cent), Germany (6 per cent) and the United Kingdom (5 per cent) were the largest source countries of investors settling, expanding or co-locating in the Viet Namese city.[1]

Ho Chi Minh City's FDI-led development and economic growth over time

FDI focus under Doi Moi and onwards

FDI featured prominently in Viet Nam's export-led development strategy and thereby contributed considerably to the country's impressive growth over the past decades (Arif-Ur-Rahman & Inaba, 2021).

This foundations of this were laid with the *Doi Moi* ('renovation' or 'innovation') paradigmatic shift in policy, introduced in 1986 at the 6th National Congress of the Communist Party of Viet Nam (Vu et al., 2022). Doi Moi saw a range of liberalising measures enacted in Viet Nam, from deregulation to lower rates of investment in SOEs, all while placing great emphasis on FDI (Arif-Ur-Rahman & Inaba, 2021; Kim, 2023). HCMC was positioned – and de facto acting – as the main gateway for FDI and foreign companies into Viet

Nam from the outset and issuance of the corresponding 1987 Foreign Investment Law (Du & Fukushima, 2010; Kim, 2023) and Decree No. 322/HDBT first regulating the establishment of export processing zones in 1991 (Phi, 2011). A range of revisions and new laws continued to change the environment for foreign investment in the country and city – for an indicative list of key policies since 1987, see Table 7.1.

TABLE 7.1 Key policies impacting foreign direct investment in Viet Nam 1987–2024[a]

Year	*Policy*	*Description*
1987	Foreign Investment Law	First opening-up Viet Nam to foreign direct investment and ruled out nationalisation (Kim, 2023; OECD, 2018)
1990	Law on Private Enterprises and Law on Companies	Further established a liberal corporate regime.
1991	Decree No. 322/HDBT	First regulating the establishment of export processing zones in 1991 (Phi, 2011).
1992	Constitution 1992	Officially recognised the role of the private sector. The economic chapter affirmed its willingness to increase the inflow of foreign investment and specifically encouraged foreign organisations and individuals to invest capital and technology in Viet Nam (Article 25). In return, it promised to 'guarantee the right of ownership of the legitimate capital, property and other interests of foreign organisations and individuals.'
1995	ASEAN membership	Commitment to standards and regulations as part of the ASEAN Economic Community.
2005	Unified law on investment: Enterprise Law, Intellectual Property Rights Act	The new Investment Law draws on the reform initiated in the 2001 Enterprise Law and moves further away from the previous 'positive list' approach to a 'negative list.' It also abrogates the evaluation procedure and provides for a single registration process.
2007	World Trade Organisation membership	Commitment to broad investment and trade related aspects under the WTO regime.
2010	Commercial Arbitration Law and of the Law on Administrative Procedures	Brought the legal system more in line with international standards.

(Continued)

TABLE 7.1 (Continued)

Year	*Policy*	*Description*
2013–2015	Revision of various laws fundamental to the investment climate, such as the Enterprise Law, the Investment Law, the Housing Law, the Real Estate Business Law and the Land Law.	Further liberalisation, facilitation and move towards international standards.
2020	Law on Investment	The introduction of a 'negative list' for foreign investment and increases in ownership thresholds for treatment as a national investor, a 'national security' provision, yet also new investment incentives, and additional measures to streamline investment procedures (White & Case, 2020).

Source: Adapted and expanded from OECD (2018), unless otherwise stated.

Note: This list is indicative only. It is highlighting some of the key policies impacting and increasing foreign investment in Viet Nam. A full list can be found on the website of the Foreign Investment Agency, Ministry of Planning and Investment of the Socialist Republic of Vietnam and UNCTAD Investment Policy Hub, for instance. The descriptions are taken from OECD (2018), unless otherwise stated.

[a] September.

The government of HCMC contributed to render the principles of Doi Moi effective in its jurisdiction. For instance, it designed export processing and industrial zones (IZs) from the early 1990s onwards, specifically to attract foreign investors to the city. In 2002, 12 IZs had been developed in HCMC (Du & Fukushima, 2010), a number that had increased to 19 by 2024, totalling just over 4,500 hectares (Sai Gon Vrg, 2021). The greater HCMC area already featured 84 industrial – export processing – and special economic zones by the late 2000s (Phi, 2011).

Over time, HCMC came to act as attractive force for FDI in itself, concentrating FDI in and around it, due to its industrial infrastructure, industrial estates, market friendliness and urban services that developed (Du & Fukushima, 2010), rather than the existence of IZs and Doi Moi style policies. However, FDI did contribute to enhance the very factors that came to improve the city's attractiveness to foreign investors.

Hence, FDI has played a prominent role in the economic development of southern cities and most notably HCMC – an increasing share of FDI in Gross Regional Domestic Product (GRDP) was found to lead to considerable growth of the local economy, contrasting starkly with the moderate effects of public investments (Huy, 2021). In fact, with the onset of Doi Moi and through to mid-2007, HCMC and surrounding areas had attracted more than half of all FDI into the country (Dapice et al., 2010). In 2015, FDI contributed a 30 per cent of the GRDP in HCMC and adjacent areas, while the rest of the country (excluding Ha Noi and surrounding areas) enjoyed a mere 2.1 per cent (Kim, 2023). Due to the static and limited nature of the GRDP metric (see Viet, 2010), FDI's de facto contribution is expected to be much larger, if 'indirect effects are taken into account,' i.e. its impact on fostering supplier ecosystems, for example (Arif-Ur-Rahman & Inaba, 2021).

FDI is increasingly concentrated in higher value-added sectors

Supported by FDI in associated sectors, manufacturing was driving much of the growth in HCMC in the 1990s – the industrial sector had been growing at above 17 per cent for most of the decade (Du & Fukushima, 2010). However, this began to change in the mid-2000s, when HCMC and surrounding areas' above-average GRDP growth rate was already fuelled in large parts by the trade and services sector – and ever increasingly so – established HCMC as 'a center for regional business and consumption' (Du & Fukushima, 2010).

Comparing the 2004–2013 period with the 2014–2023 period, greenfield FDI has targeted certain sectors in a more concentrated manner; projects into business services and software and IT services increased notably (Figure 7.1).

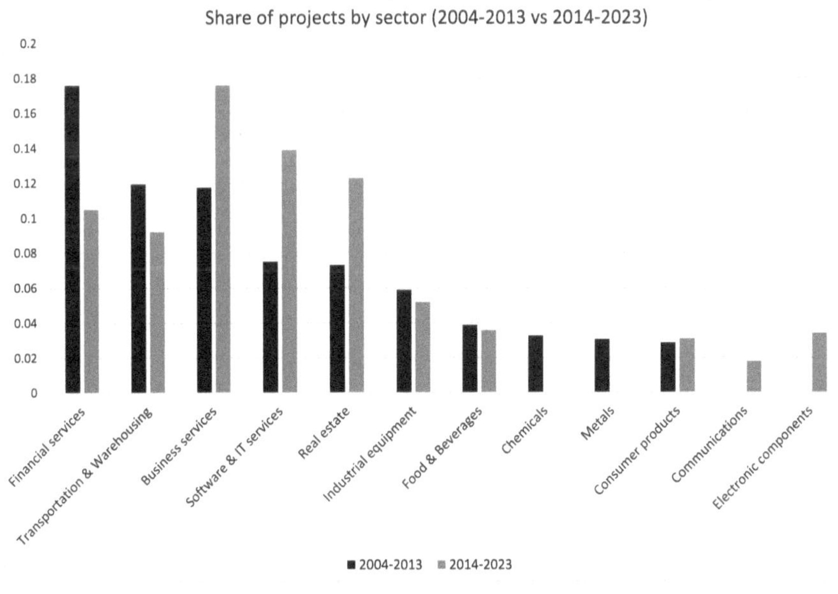

FIGURE 7.1 Sectoral changes of inward FDI in HCMC: 2004–2013 vs 2014–2023[3]

In the 2004–2013 period financial services came out top, with 87 projects recorded, followed by transportation and warehousing (59), business services (58), software & IT services (37), real estate (36) and industrial equipment (29). In the following ten-year period, 2014–2023, business services were the top target sector of foreign investors in the city (109), followed by software & IT services (86), real estate (76), financial services (65), transportation and warehousing (57) and industrial equipment (32).

Thus, those sectors lower down the value chain (transportation and warehousing and industrial equipment) have remained rather stagnant, while sectors towards the upper end of the value chain (business services, software & IT services, for instance) have attracted significantly more investment projects.[2]

Impact analysis

Labour market development

Towards better skill and labour supply

FDI businesses were a major source of employment in HCMC and have impacted the development of the labour market. Just considering the period after the turn of the century (2001–2007), employment growth rates in HCMC for private and FDI enterprises, 168 per cent and 130 per cent to 1,020,452 and 446,717 respectively, have far exceeded that of total employment growth at 83.3 per cent to 1,695,681 – all while SOE employment has notably gone down by 18.9 per cent to 288,512 (Phi, 2011).

Up until the mid-2000s, evidence suggested limited skill upgrading of the local labour force. This issue was largely confined to manufacturing, the then dominant sector. Research has shown that electronics manufacturing had been largely of 'reproductive' nature with low impact on the skill upgrading of the local labour force. Production line upgrading was often related to innovations in the home country, which were trialled and tested there and only in the maturity stage installed in HCMC with home country experts leading and supervising the set up (Vind, 2008).

While companies expressed concern finding skilled labour – locally issued certificates and training courses were not deemed sufficient – the training they provided for the local workforce was mostly targeted at labour management rather than technical fields to improve the general skill level of the workers (Vind, 2008).

Neither did evidence suggest that highly skilled local engineers trained in foreign companies became domestic entrepreneurs building an innovative supplier base or that workers in higher level or managerial positions had moved from foreign to local companies, transferring skill and knowledge (Vind, 2008).

However, at the same time, factories and businesses operating beyond simple assembly were indeed contributing noticeably to skill upgrading and invested in appropriate training for workers. While those operations were still few in the early 2000s (Vind, 2008), they had proliferated by the mid-2020s (see section below).

Foreign companies are locating more sophisticated business activities in the city

By the mid-2020s foreign companies were increasingly launching and conducting operations higher up the value chain in HCMC.

A comparison of the 2004–2013 with the 2014–2023 period shows that projects have been more concentrated in a select few business activities higher up the value chain, such as sales, marketing and support, business services and research and development, with growth rates of 35 per cent, 48 per cent and 52 per cent respectively, outpacing the negative growth of manufacturing projects of −14 per cent (Figure 7.2). Hence, FDI followed the sectoral transition trajectory from manufacturing towards a service-based urban economy.

In fact, according to estimates from the Financial Times (2024a, 2024b), FDI projects with sales, marketing and support business function have created approximately 16,500 jobs between 2004 and 2023, projects in business services

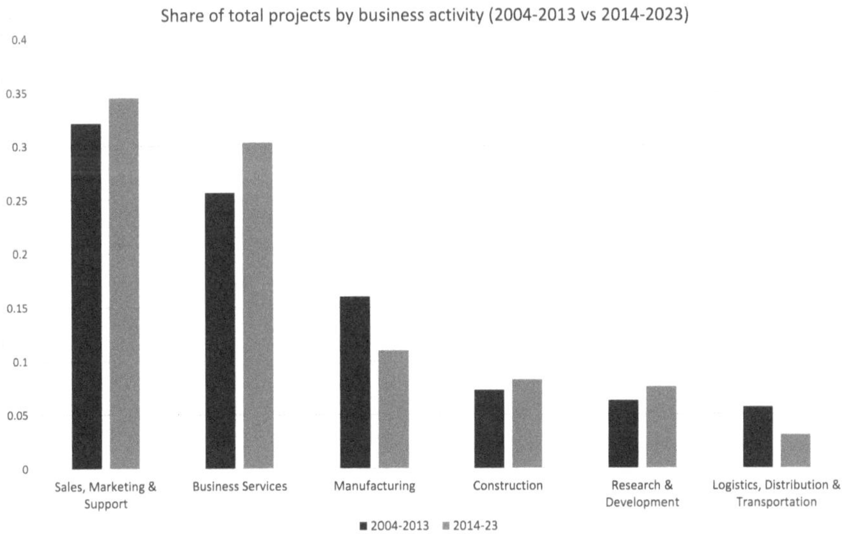

FIGURE 7.2 Change in business activities of inward FDI in HCMC: 2004–2013 vs 2014–2023[4]

saw 18,800 jobs created and those in research and development 15,000 – a significant portion of overall employment in private enterprises in HCMC.

The motives and determining factors that were driving decisions to invest in HCMC by foreign companies support this. While domestic market growth and proximity to markets or customers were still key factors for investments in HCMC in 2014–2023, lower cost notably dropped from fifth to eighth place among the top 10 motives vis-à-vis the 2004–2013 period. Qualitative factors, such as technology and innovation and university and research hub existence entered the top ten motives cited, coming in at sixth and tenth place, respectively. Similarly, skilled workforce availability and the regulatory environment had also been cited more frequently (authors calculations based on data from the Financial Times, 2024a).

For example, in November 2022, the managing director of Eastvantage, Joeri Timp, complimented the 'large pool of skilled professionals and growing investment in infrastructure and education from both the government and the private sector,' when asked about the company's decision to invest in the city. He added 'Ho Chi Minh City's talent pool is fed by 80 universities and colleges with over 400,000 students' (fDi markets, 2024). Thus, FDI was increasingly appreciative of HCMC's dynamic qualitative attributes, which in turn also meant that FDI projects were increasingly moving in that direction, creating more higher value-added jobs in the city. Foreign companies were no longer struggling – as they used to – to acquire the skilled labour needed to perform their operations successfully.

Productivity impact

The presence of foreign firms has raised productivity in their proximity

The presence of foreign companies had resulted in productivity improvements of domestic firms operating in their proximity in and around HCMC. Research supports positive spillover effects on the total factor productivity of domestic firms in the wider Mekong Delta region around HCMC (Vu et al., 2022). In fact, productivity in the region had been found highest in local businesses with a close geographical proximity to FDI hotspots, and particularly within a 100 km range of FDI company agglomerations, such as HCMC (Vu et al., 2022, see also Thang et al., 2016). Conversely, the spatial impact on productivity also decreased considerably with increasing distance to foreign companies.

While there is limited data and studies for HCMC, in Viet Nam as a whole, firms struggled to increase productivity when connected to FDI companies in the same industry (horizontal linkages), only vertical linkages seemed to support local productivity improvements. In fact, competitive enterprises had benefitted from the presence of FDI companies, while those with low productivity faced disadvantages competing with foreign business and risked crowding out (Vu et al., 2022).

The export participation of domestic manufacturing companies was found to be negatively impacted by a high concentration of FDI businesses in Viet Nam (Troung & Dong, 2021), the opposite could be observed in HCMC, however, where FDI played an enabling role for many domestic businesses. As export participation strongly depends on the quality of infrastructure, labour force and administrative procedures in the host country (Troung & Dong, 2021), FDI's role in not only strengthening the aforementioned, but also legal frameworks and predictability, improved infrastructure and burgeoning business ecosystems, had benefitted domestic and foreign firms in HCMC in their export participation (Huy, 2021). The strong pressure exerted by foreign invested companies and business associations on the central government – which, in turn, was facing strong fiscal and budget constraints in the 2010s – to increase arbitration standards, intellectual property protection and transparency contributed to these developments (East Asia Forum, 2020).

Moreover, HCMC began to experience a change in the nature of its export structure; a reduced share of manufacturing and an increasing share of services. By the mid-2020s, FDI in HCMC already increasingly targeted the services sector, catering to domestic or regional markets – an evolution away from low-cost production for export-led development. In fact, the city started to actively promote its digital economy sectors to increase to 40 per cent of its GRDP by 2030 (OpenGov Asia, 2024).

HCMC's immediate surroundings were inseparable from the core city's development and increasingly encroached upon, with productivity, project numbers and growth strongly impacted by the proximity to HCMC. Thus, the next section will outline the geospatial changes of HCMC city and its surroundings.

Geospatial development

FDI has contributed to a geospatial reorganisation of the city

FDI contributed significantly to spatial urban growth as well as changes in the geospatial layout of HCMC and its surrounding provinces. As of summer 2024, HCMC had assumed the role of economic core, with an increasing proliferation of the services cluster, while the suburbs – or fringes – of the mega city increasingly hosted associated manufacturing activities and companies catering the core businesses in the city. This outcome related to the phenomenon is called 'Global City-Region' (Kim, 2023).

Larger manufacturing FDI projects, shifted to the outskirts and neighbouring provinces since the mid-2000s (Du & Fukushima, 2010), advancing urban expansion, and population growth/expansion there. FDI attraction policies had sped up peri-urbanisation – rapid and fragment urban growth – and urban sprawl with approximately 30 per cent of new urban expansion through to the 2010s taking place around >40 km from the old centre (Kontgis et al., 2014). Similarly, 50 per cent of population expansion had occurred in the associated peri-urban communes (Kontgis et al., 2014).

Data from the Atlas of Urban Expansion (2016) helps to visualise the development towards a global city-region (Figure 7.3).

The provinces bordering HCMC had experienced much higher FDI project and employment numbers than other regions in Viet Nam. In 2015, over half a million workers were employed in FDI sectors in neighbouring Dong Nai and 178,000 in Bac Ninh – equivalent to 61.8 per cent and 67.2 per cent of total employment in the respective provinces (Kim, 2023). Similarly, in Ba Ria-Vung Tau 56,700 jobs in FDI businesses contributed around a third of total employment (Kim, 2023). In the same manner, FDI sectors accounted for just under 50 per cent of GRDP in Ba Ria-Vung Tau and Dong Nai (Kim, 2023).

With HCMC as the services and financial hub, surrounding provinces assumed complementary functions, supported by decrees to foster the wider development of HCMC via FDI; Binh Doung and Dong Nai, for instance, saw their investment environments improved significantly (Phi, 2011). Ba Ria-Vung Tau province had emerged as a logistics hub due to its maritime

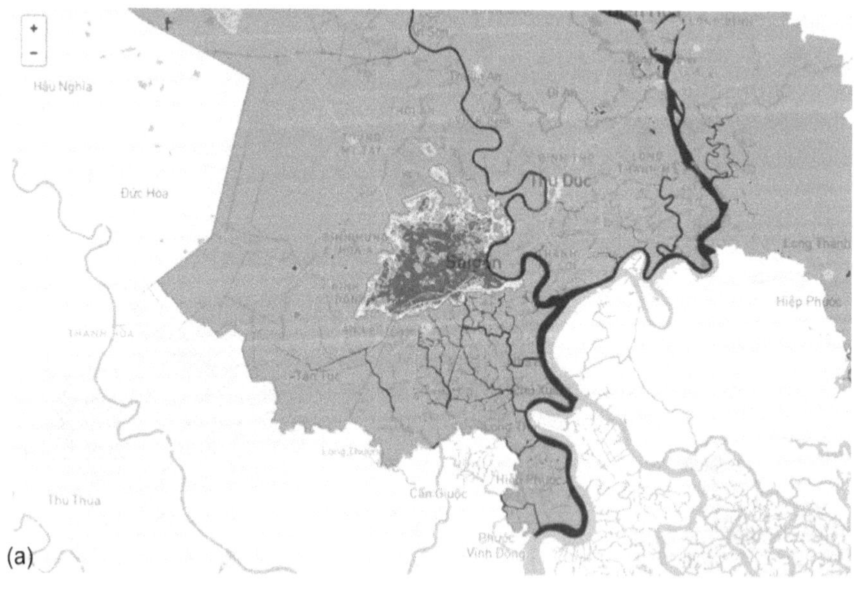

FIGURE 7.3 Urban expansion of HCMC: 1989, 1999 and 2015 *(Continued)*

Source: Data from the Atlas of Urban Expansion (2016).

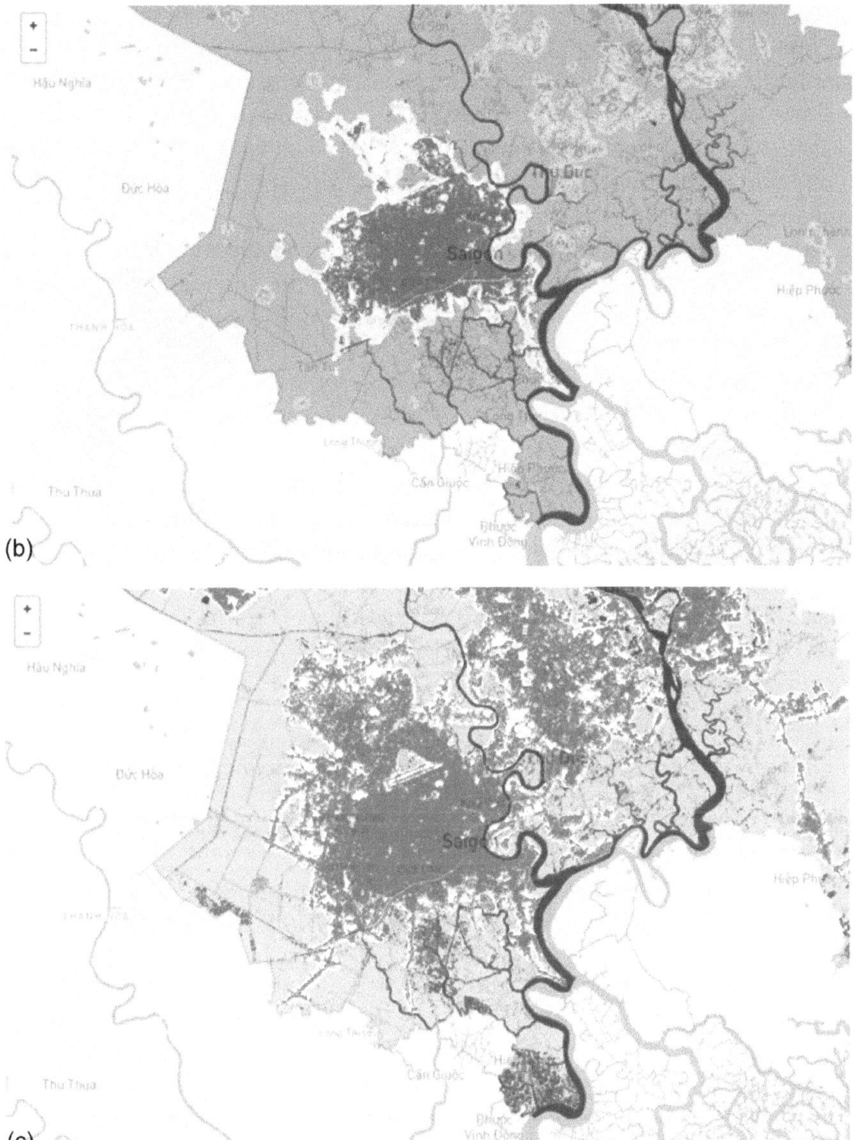

FIGURE 7.3 *(Continued)*

location, Dong Nai continued to host related manufacturing activities, and Binh Doung functioned as human resource provider due to its obtained manufacturing experience (Phi, 2011). The latter, located just north of the city's boundaries, had undergone an evolution from agriculture – to industry – and even service-based (Kim, 2023).

The town of Ben Cat, for example, just 50 km north of HCMC, is located on one of the main arterial roads leading out of HCMC to the border with Cambodia and other key infrastructure axis in the southern region such as the My Phuoc–Tan Van expressway leading into the northern periphery of HCMC. Numerous industrial parks and workforce availability had slowly but surely turned the town into a city, which was also supported by government initiatives (Binh Doung News, 2023).

In fact, most incentive deals in Viet Nam were awarded under economic zone and industrial park acts, and those in proximity and with good connections to HCMC had been a hotspot of incentive deal awards. This underpins the hub and fringes argument with larger manufacturing settling around HCMC urban area with good access to the city, such as Ben Cat. 17 out of 18 deals awarded in its province, Binh Doung, supported projects with a manufacturing business activity across sectors, such as consumer goods or textiles. However, incentive deals in around HCMC have declined in recent years[5] – generally, business environment factors are assuming increasing importance for investors, with governments often overestimating the power of tax incentives to sway investor perception in their favour (Kronfol, 2020; UNCTAD, 2023). As even HCMC's surroundings became increasingly service-based, traditional fiscal incentives played a lesser role in investment location decision making.

High levels of FDI are exacerbating the challenges of rapid urban growth

Due to HCMC's unprecedented growth – population, urban build up and density – another development began to emerge in the late 2010s. The core city's investment attraction success rate had begun to slow and new investors – even in the services realm – were deliberately considering setting up shop near HCMC, rather than the core city. Two key factors can explain this. Firstly, neighbouring provinces and towns had built up their ecosystems, also thanks to FDI, as described above. Secondly, and more importantly, HCMC had compromised some of its attractiveness due to the challenges it faced associated with tremendous unplanned growth, such as congestion and wider infrastructure problems, 'housing area below the national average,' pollution and flooding (Tri & Hoa, 2023) as well as scarcity of central and representative sites due to the high concentration of businesses in the core area (Dapice et al., 2010).

This trend was common among megacities in developing countries and among one of the 'new security challenges' in international relations scholarship. Demographic change (including the provision of sanitary and other public goods) and (related) environmental challenges emerged to become foundational concerns for foreign investors when deciding on a location to invest in. While FDI from innovative companies in green sectors – those that tangibly contribute to the United Nations Sustainable Development Goals – can help mitigate some of these challenges, in practice, the key issue for policy makers and investment promotion officials is less about how to attract this type of FDI but rather a political one. The rejection of proposed FDI projects with no impact on the SDGs or those that are even harmful the environment – while providing financial resources, jobs and potentially infrastructure to the host economy – is oftentimes politically challenging. The perceived clash and trade-off between economic growth and sustainable development remains one of the key policy challenges to advance the SDGs in the 21st century.

Conclusion

The chapter has provided an insight on some of the more prominent effects FDI can have on host cities, namely labour market, productivity and geospatial development.

Overall, FDI did contribute significantly to the development of HCMC and its economy. It has not only contributed to economic growth but also contributed to its changing urban geography, i.e. spatial growth and urban sprawl. By 2024, the city had, since first opening-up to foreign investment in 1987, moved towards largely attracting FDI in the services sector. While it is difficult to assess the impact of FDI on the labour market, the jobs FDI contributed to create in and around the city were to a large extend in higher value-added activities. While direct spillovers of FDI may not have been extensive, it has contributed to positioning HCMC of the 2020s as one of Southeast Asia's economic powerhouses and did have positive effects on the productivity of domestic firms. However, high levels of FDI do not come without challenges; those related to urban sprawl, inefficient infrastructure and the environment are only some.

To this end, in early 2024, the Planning and Investment Department of the People's Committee of HCMC initiated a project to harness and attract FDI projects with a special focus on new technologies, high value-added activities, increasing spillover effects and integration into global supply chains (Voice of Vietnam, 2023).

Acknowledgements

With thanks to the Ho Chi Minh City People's Committee Investment and Trade Promotion Centre (ITPC) for their support in providing the author with relevant materials and information and to Eva-Maria Nag, Executive Editor of the *Global Policy Journal* based at the School of Government and International Affairs, Durham University as well as Heather Taylor-Strauss, Economic Affairs Officer at the United Nations Economic and Social Commission for Asia and the Pacific for their valuable comments.

Notes

1 Author's calculations based on data from fDi Markets, Financial Times. Accessed February 2024.
2 For a discussion of value chain activities, see Warwick (2013).
3 Author's calculations based on data from fDi markets, Financial Times. Accessed February 2024.
4 Author's calculations based on data from fDi markets, Financial Times. Accessed February 2024.
5 Author's calculations, based on data from IncentivesFlow, Financial Times. Accessed February 2024.

References

Arif-Ur-Rahman, M., & Inaba, K. (2021). Foreign direct investment and productivity spillovers: A firm-level analysis of Bangladesh in comparison with Vietnam. *Journal of Economic Structures, 10*(17), 1–23.

Atlas of Urban Expansion. (2016). *Ho Chi Minh City*. http://atlasofurbanexpansion.org/cities/view/Ho_Chi_Minh_City

Binh Doung News. (2023). *Ben Cat develops strongly to become a city*. https://baobinhduong.vn/en/ben-cat-develops-strongly-to-become-a-city-a290623.html

Dapice, D., Gomez-Ibanez, J. A., & Thanh, N. X. (2010). *Ho Chi Minh City: The challenges of growth* (Policy dialogue paper number 2). UNDP – Harvard Policy Dialogue Papers.

Du, P. T., & Fukushima, S. (2010). Transformation of socio-economic structure of Ho Chi Minh City under the Doi-Moi policy and the accompanying globalization process. *Meijo Asian Research Journal, 1*(1), 33–45.

East Asia Forum. (2020). *The paradoxes of private sector development in Vietnam*. https://eastasiaforum.org/2020/06/04/the-paradoxes-of-private-sector-development-in-vietnam/

Financial Times. (2024a). *fDi Markets database*. www.fdimarkets.com

Financial Times. (2024b). *IncentivesFlow database*. www.incentivesflow.fdiintelligence.com

Hayton, B. (2020). *Vietnam: Rising dragon*. Yale University Press.

Huong, N. T. L. (2023). Ho Chi Minh City's economy: Overview, statistics and future prospects. *American Research Journal of Humanities & Social Science*, 6(4), 35–38.

Huy, D. N. M. (2021). FDI and growth: Evidence from provinces and cities in South East region of Vietnam. *Journal of Science and Technology, 19*(6.1), 54–57.

Kim, H. M. (2023). Foreign direct investment and urban growth in Vietnam: Spatial, economic, and demographic perspectives. *Asian Geographer, 41*(2), 167–184.

Kontgis, C., Schneider, A., Fox, J., Saksena, S., Spencer, J. H., & Castrence, M. (2014). Monitoring peri-urbanization in the greater Ho Chi Minh City metropolitan area. *Applied Geography, 53*(September), 377–388.

Kronfol, H. (2020). *Leveraging corporate tax incentives to attract FDI: Design and implementation considerations*. Columbia FDI Perspectives, no. 279: 1–4.

Ngyuen, T. (2023). Hanoi and Ho Chi Minh City make top 100 leading cities in the world for 2023. *Vietnam Insider*.

OpenGov Asia. (2024). *Ho Chi Minh City's digital economy ambitions*. https://opengovasia.com/2024/05/07/ho-chi-minh-citys-digital-economy-ambitions/

Organisation for Economic Cooperation and Development (OECD). (2018). OECD investment policy reviews: Viet Nam 2018. In *OECD investment policy reviews*. OECD Publishing. https://www.oecd-ilibrary.org/docserver/9789264282957-8-en.

pdf?expires=1727583410&id=id&accname=guest&checksum=860E9EC027A00A2EDB975EDB8ACFC883

Phi, V. T. (2011). Development of special economic zones, industrial estates, ports, metropolis and alternative roads in the greater Ho Chi Minh City area. In M. Ishida (Ed.), *Intra and inter-city connectivity in the Mekong region* (pp. 322–376). IDE-JETRO Research Center.

Sai Gon Vrg. (2021). *List of Industrial Zones/Industrial Parks in Ho Chi Minh Vietnam*. https://saigonvrg.com.vn/en/list-of-industrial-zones-industrial-parks-in-ho-chi-minh-vietnam

Thang, T. T., Pham, T. S. H., & Barnes, B. R. (2016). Spatial spillover effects from foreign direct investment in Vietnam. *Journal of Development Studies, 52*(10), 1431–1445.

Tri, N. M., & Hoa, L. T. (2023). Science technology development: A case of Ho Chi Minh City, Vietnam. *Journal of Law and Sustainable Development, 11*(1), 1–18.

Troung, Q. H., & Dong, V. C. (2021). Spillover effects of foreign and domestic exporting firms on export decisions of local manufacturing firms: Evidence from Viet Nam. *ERIA Discussion Paper Series*, no. 410.

United Nations Conference on Trade and Development (UNCTAD). (2023). *The impact of international tax reforms on special economic zones*. UNCTAD.

Viet, V. Q. (2010). *Gross regional product (GRP): An introduction. International workshop regional products and income accounts 15–17 March*. United Nations Department of Economic and Social Affairs and National Bureau of Statistics of China. Available at: https://unstats.un.org/unsd/economic_stat/China/background_paper_on_GRP.pdf

Vind, I. (2008). Transnational companies as a source of skill upgrading: The electronics industry in Ho Chi Minh City. *Geoforum, 39*, 1480–1493.

Voice of Vietnam. (2023). *Ho Chi Minh City changes strategy to attract FDI*. https://vovworld.vn/en-US/economy/ho-chi-minh-city-changes-strategy-to-attract-fdi-1205262.vov

Vu, H. Q., Ngoc, P. T. B., & Quyen, N. L. H. T. T. (2022). The effect of institutions on productivity spillovers from FDI to domestic firms: Evidence in Vietnam. *Global Business and Finance Review, 27*(3), 28–40.

Warwick, K. (2013). Beyond industrial policy: Emerging issues and new trends. *OECD science, technology and industry policy papers* (pp. 1–57). OECD Publishing.

White and Case. (2020). *Key outcomes for foreign investors in Vietnam's new law on investment*. https://www.whitecase.com/insight-alert/key-outcomes-foreign-investors-vietnams-new-law-investment

8

CASE 8: INTERNATIONAL CAPITAL, NATIONAL POLITICS AND INVESTMENT IN SECONDARY CITIES IN AFRICA

The case of the stalled Bagamoyo Port Project in Tanzania

Kristian Hoelscher

Abstract

This case study examines the Bagamoyo Port Project (BPP), a large-scale port and SEZ project by China Merchant Holdings International in Bagamoyo, Tanzania. This case offers a perspective on how state-based Foreign Direct Investment (FDI) intersects with strategic political influence and economic return for foreign investors and host countries, offering two main insights. First, 'local' investments in secondary cities may be tied to and face opposition from larger national or regional interests or national elites that may complicate ostensibly 'local' inward FDI. Second, even large state-directed investments tied to geopolitical goals can still suffer from similar problems faced by traditional for-profit investors, and may not be more astute at navigating domestic political challenges to otherwise promising investment opportunities. I conclude by offering insights on how this case reiterates the importance of mutually beneficial investment terms that deliver a return for investors, support national economic strategic priorities and support the development of emerging urban areas.

Keywords

FDI; Tanzania; China; Africa; Shipping; Infrastructure; State-owned Enterprises; Bagamoyo Secondary Cities; Urbanisation

Introduction

Africa is rapidly urbanising, representing a transformational demographic and socioeconomic shift. About 1.5 billion people are projected to live in the continent's towns and cities by 2050 and the vast majority of the largest cities in the world will be African by the end of this century (Hoornweg &

DOI: 10.4324/9781003483410-11

Pope, 2017). As the number of urban residents grow, so too are the demands for urban services. Foreign Direct Investment (FDI) has become an important tool to help deliver on these needs, and is contributing to further urbanisation across the continent (Grekou & Owoundi, 2020). UNHABITAT has stated that 'foreign firms and investors in African cities can play a catalytic role in the development of the continent' with promises to 'help alleviate urban poverty and unemployment by supporting Africa's transition towards growth', in investments that vary from industrial parks and manufacturing, to technology and retail development (United Nations Human Settlements Programme, 2018).

The majority of inward investments in urban areas in Africa are directed at large cities, primarily national capitals. Thus far, smaller secondary cities have generally failed to attract investment that may be needed to spur development (Roberts, 2014). Yet secondary cities in Africa of between 100,000 and 1m inhabitants are becoming increasingly important for managing sustainable urbanisation in Africa (The Economist, 2023) and are overwhelmingly where the majority of Africa's urban population reside (Galtier, 2023).

Secondary cities are also becoming more attractive places to invest: while FDI has tended to flow to larger African cities, returns on investment may be declining in these places compared with the opportunities offered by smaller cities (Thomson, 2023). Yet where greater returns are presented, so too are there often also greater risks. Smaller urban centres tend to lack the infrastructural or institutional development of larger cities, face higher start-up costs and fewer agglomerative benefits. Moreover, large scale inward investment in frontier urban areas often must contend with local or national political dynamics that may be opposed to the economic interests of investors or to the interests of those in larger or capital cities.

This case study examines the Bagamoyo Port Project (BPP), a large-scale port and SEZ project in Bagamoyo, a town of approximately 100,000 people that lies around 70 km north of Tanzania's capital Dar Es Salaam. The case study primarily examines the period 2008 to 2020, outlining the promising yet ultimately failed process of investment of the Chinese state-owned firm China Merchant Holdings International (CMHI)[1] to develop the port and SEZ in Bagamoyo.

This case offers a perspective on how state-based FDI intersects with strategic political influence and economic return for foreign investors and host countries. Through BPP, I show how FDI and growth 'for good' can intersect in intended and unintended ways vis-à-vis investment in secondary cities in Africa. This case offers three main insights. First, that 'local' investments in secondary cities may face opposition from larger national or regional interests or national elites that complicates ostensibly 'local' inward FDI. Second, it shows that even large state-directed investments from Chinese firms tied to broader geopolitical goals can still suffer from the same problems faced by

Western firms, and such actors may not be more astute at navigating domestic political challenges to otherwise promising investment opportunities. And third, despite the relative failure of the BPP thus far, the financial and strategic returns to developing large scale investments in smaller African cities may still be worth taking on additional risk given the potential future returns.

The case of the Bagamoyo Port Project

Background

With a population of 65 million, the East African country of Tanzania is urbanising rapidly. It is characterised by relative political stability and a growing and diversified economy including natural resources, agriculture and tourism. Under the remit of the Export Processing Zone Authority established in 2006, Tanzania has pursued the development of Special Economic Zones (SEZs) to attract FDI and boost growth and employment through export-led economic activity (Kinyondo et al., 2016) Such conditions have contributed to making the country an increasingly attractive location for foreign investment, climbing from 400 million USD in 2006 to 1.1 billion USD in 2022 and with greenfield projects rising by 60% in the same year (UNCTAD, 2023; World Bank, 2024). Chinese firms and state-owned enterprises (SOEs) have played a central role. Tied to China's Belt and Road Initiative (BRI) and Maritime Silk Road Initiative (MRSI), China has become the largest investor in African infrastructure and represents the single largest provider of inward investment to Tanzania.

Within this dynamic of export-oriented growth through SEZs, shipping plays an important role in Tanzania's economy. Shipping capacity in Tanzania has been predominantly served by the Dar Es Salaam port as a key trade gateway for both Tanzania and neighbouring interior countries. However, the Dar Es Salaam port lacks sufficient deepwater facilities to handle larger freight ships. In seeking to serve growing import and export markets in the interior and link with neighbouring landlocked countries (Rwanda, Zambia, Uganda) a new deepwater port facility was proposed in Bagamoyo.

Prior to the proposed redevelopment, Bagamoyo was – and broadly remains – a small yet rapidly growing coastal town. As the former German colonial capital of Tanganyika, Bagamoyo has a rich cultural heritage and is a UNESCO listed world heritage site. Economic activity is primarily concentrated in the agricultural and fisheries sectors, in addition to informal sector trading. Despite its rapid population growth, local government capacity has been limited, exacerbating urban service delivery and employment challenges as poverty remains prevalent (United Nations Human Settlements Programme, 2009). Moreover, 'in the context of Bagamoyo's top-down transformation, authorities situated at the city and district levels struggle to expand services and infrastructure to accommodate a growing population and expanded urban area' (Schindler et al., 2021), hampering large-scale investment and highlighting common disconnects between global financial capital and everyday lives of citizens and governments in secondary cities across Africa.

The Tanzanian and Chinese governments and Chinese investors began to explore the development of the Bagamoyo port and SEZ in the mid-2000s. The concept was first officially raised in 2008, following Tanzanian President Jakaya Kikwete visiting Chinese President Hu Jintao in Beijing. Born in Bagamoyo district, Kikwete was an ardent supporter, which also had the backing of the World Bank, who recognised the inefficiencies and shipping capacity constraints at the Dar es Salaam port (Morisset, 2013). This led to the development of a proposal for Mbegani-Bagamoyo SEZ (Jansson et al., 2009) that would establish Bagamoyo as the largest shipping and logistics port in East Africa. The project would mold Bagamoyo into a modern urban centre that would benefit local development, principally through skilled and unskilled employment creation during construction phases, and spillover benefits for the local economy once operational (COWI, 2013). In being imagined as Tanzania's new gateway to the world (Kanai & Schindler, 2019), Bagamoyo would be transformed from an underdeveloped small town to what the Chinese Ambassador to Tanzania termed a 'city of prosperity' (Schindler et al., 2021).

The project was slated to be led by CMHI, a subsidiary of the China Merchants Group (CMG), the largest SOE in China that operates under the direction of the Ministry of Transport. Established over 140 years ago, CMG has been a leader in Chinese industrial development since the 1980s and has taken a key role in furthering China's BRI through major international infrastructure projects. Yet they have also faced criticism for their role in what has been termed 'debt-trap diplomacy', where the Chinese government and its SOEs and subsidiaries have been accused of offering excessive credit, or predatory lending and investment terms, to smaller nations and then leveraging the subsequent debt burden for economic or geopolitical concessions when creditor countries are unable to fulfil repayment obligations (Chellaney, 2017).

The BPP was confirmed when new Chinese President Xi Jinping met with Tanzanian President Kikwete on a state visit to Tanzania in March 2013. CMHI signed a framework agreement between the Tanzanian government, CMHI and the State General Reserve Fund (SGRF) of Oman to develop the BPP, totalling a USD 10 billion investment that would include development of a new deepwater shipping port, SEZ and integrated rail infrastructure. Following President Xi's visit, CMHI Chairman Hu Jinhua returned to Tanzania in January 2014 to sign contracts with the Tanzanian government. The economic and geopolitical returns to Chinese investors were to be significant; for both the construction and operation of port facilities and in securing a strategic access to East African markets. For an 80% investment, CMHI would lead construction and port management under a 99-year leased Build-Operate-Transfer contract. They would also receive beneficial terms including: significant tax holidays; below market rate water and electricity concessions; freedom to establish further businesses in the port and SEZ without Tanzanian government regulation; and a guarantee the Tanzanian government would not develop other ports facilities along its coastline (Mishra, 2019). Ceremonial groundbreaking commenced in October 2015, attended by President Kikwete and China's Ambassador to Tanzania Lu Youqing. CMHI Chairman Jinhua called it 'the most significant event in Tanzania-China relations over the past four decades' (Ng'wanakilala, 2015, p. np)

Contention: 2015–2019

These events were set against the backdrop of a national election in Tanzania, where President Kikwete was to finish his term in October 2015. The election campaign was characterised by contention over the role of foreign investment's use of land in Tanzania. Opposition voices criticised FDI that led to productive agricultural land controlled by foreign interests, while the government argued that this was central to economic development. The issue of foreign versus national ownership of large land tracts and the contested role of foreign investment in development became central to the election discourse, in the 'failed development plans, broken promises made to local communities and illegal land procedures' of foreign interests in Tanzania (Schlimmer, 2018). Partially for these reasons, the election was won by the incoming leader of the ruling party, John Magafuli, who had been critical of foreign economic interests in the country. He took office in leader November 2015 with a reputation as an uncompromising and frugal reformist with the nickname 'the Bulldozer' (Paget, 2017). While China expressed its desire to continue warm economic relations with Tanzania, this change created challenging political conditions for inward FDI.

Magafuli sought to shore up his electoral status by pursuing populist and nationalist policy positions that expressed an aversion to excessive foreign ownership and pushed for greater national control over Tanzania's resources and strategic infrastructure (Barton, 2023; Nkobou & Ainslie, 2021). Magufuli's 'resource nationalism' (Barton, 2023; Lange & Kinyondo, 2016) saw him take aggressive actions against foreign companies. This included demanding 300 million in back taxes, revoking licenses and banning exports for mining firm Acacia (Pedersen et al., 2019). After threatening re-appropriation of the gold and copper mines of Acacia and Barrick Gold, Magafuli renegotiated a greater stake in Barrick's Tanzanian mining interests (Roder, 2019). Successfully standing up to the interests of foreign multinationals where his predecessors had not emboldened Magafuli to pursue economic nationalism more widely (Barton, 2023).

Magafuli then moved to challenge the onerous terms set by CMHI for the BPP. Magafuli called the terms akin to 'selling Tanzania to China' and halted construction for 6 months pending a review of the framework agreement (Barton, 2023). In January 2016, conflicting reports emerged that both the project had been suspended in favour of upgrading the Dar es Salaam port (The Citizen, 2016) and conversely that 'construction of the (Bagamoyo) port will start in July ... upon conclusion of financing negotiations with key partners' (Mooney, 2016).

In 2017, following CMHI revising its investment terms, the Government of Tanzanian government subsequently announced the recommencement of the BPP, with a slated date for the SEZ and port to be operational by 2021. Details on the concessions granted by CMHI remain unclear, with negotiations remained complex and somewhat secretive, although Chinese interests were clearly in opposition to Tanzania establishing new port facilities other than the existing Dar Es Salaam port. These renegotiations may have also been a bargaining tactic from Magafuli; reports suggest the Tanzanian government struggled to raise the 28m USD required to compensate relocated landowners, with Chinese investors offering to provide necessary funds in exchange for alternative investment terms (Tairo, 2017).

Yet progress remained mired in protracted negotiations over investment terms that continued throughout 2018, with an impasse reached in 2019. In May, according to Reuters (2019, p. np), the Director General of the Tanzania Ports Authority (TPA) stated that:

> the conditions that they have given us are commercially unviable. We said no, let's meet halfway ... they shouldn't treat us like schoolkids and act like our teachers. We are waiting for them to begin new talks. When they are ready, we will resume the negotiations.

In response, CMHI stated that (the BPP) 'is a purely commercial, investment project and China Merchants Port has in its overseas investments always followed the principles of commercial feasibility and win-win cooperation'. The Tanzanian ambassador to China suggested in July that the deal was not off the table, and that both parties remained willing to engage (South China Morning Post, 2019).

However, in October 2019, negotiations reached a breaking point. Magafuli presented CMHI with a five-point agenda if the project was to proceed. Barton summarises these as:

> The offer of granting CMHI a 33-year lease to the port, not the 99-year lease it was seeking; the demand that other port facilities (from Mtwara to Tanga) be developed in parallel without CMHI's legal avail being required; the Tanzanian Revenue Authority should be granted the right to collect tax

> in the port's SEZ; CMHI should not be charged any special rates with regards to utilities such as water and electricity; The government also denied CMHI the ability to open and operate other businesses it deemed necessary within the port without government approval.
>
> *(Barton, 2023, p 346)*

Such demands from Magafuli included both reasonable negotiating points (e.g. reducing the length of the lease), but also unreasonable demands or poison pills (the right for Tanzania to open competing ports). Magafuli – emboldened by his victories over Barrick Gold – decried to the public that Chinese investors were trying to rob Tanzania saying that 'only a drunkard' would accept the original terms. This may suggest that Magafuli's primary intent during negotiations may have been to bolster his own domestic political capital by standing up to foreign interests rather than to broker a deal that would forward the development of Bagamoyo. Ultimately though, the inflammatory remarks and ultimatums laid down by Magafuli led to the extended sidelining of the project, with CMHI effectively walking away from negotiations.

Lessons and implications

The BPP case has implications for foreign investors in strategically important infrastructural investments in secondary cities in Africa. Beyond the costs to investors, there was significant loss of previously warm political capital and diplomatic relationships between Chinese and Tanzanian interests that came with these protracted negotiations. Provocatively, just days following his ultimatum to CMHI, Magafuli ordered the arrest of four Chinese nationals in Dar es Salaam in 2019 for 'delays' related to separate investment projects. From late 2019, it appeared that the BPP was indefinitely halted, with neither Tanzanian nor Chinese parties appearing willing to offer concession on their respective positions. The assumed continuation of Magafuli's uncompromising approach to foreign investors was cemented by his reelection in November 2020.

Yet this abruptly changed with Magafuli's unexpected death in March 2021, which saw Vice President (Ms.) Samia Hassan assume presidential office. In June 2021 Hassan moved to distance the government from Magafuli's position, stating that the project should proceed for the 'benefit of the country' and announcing the reopening of negotiations around the BPP with Chinese investors (The Citizen, 2021). Yet in 2024 the situation still remains unclear as to if or how the investment will proceed. Reports have variously suggested the Tanzanian government may take a greater role in the construction of the port, explore investments from non-Chinese investors, and scale down the scope of the BPP.

For Bagamoyo, the BPP created expectations for transformational local development, which provided few benefits. Local populations have been relocated from the port and SEZ area, and Bagamoyo continues to grow at a rapid pace – partly in anticipation of the economic opportunities afforded by the BPP construction – without meaningful investment in urban planning and development. While the terms offered by Chinese investors may have offered limited meaningful development for Bagamoyo, local interests and political consultation were largely ignored, superseded by national level political interests that ultimately led to its 10 year and counting delay. As a result, Chinese investors, the government of Tanzania and local authorities and populations in Bagamoyo have all been left seemingly worse off, the promised returns, growth and development as yet to materialise.

Two main lessons emerge for managers and investors seeking to operate in Africa's secondary cities. First, while secondary cities often lack the mature institutions and markets that characterise larger urban area, they are also not 'ungoverned' spaces that can simply have investment conditions imposed upon them. In responding to the domestic enthusiasm for the BPP, the CMHI and Chinese interests may have taken for granted that they could push through an agenda that underprioritised how benefits would be shared with local communities and contribute to Bagamoyo's development. In pressing what were deemed to be onerous investment from the outset, China may have misjudged the potential pushback that they faced from Tanzanian authorities.

Second, rapid changes in the domestic political context can dramatically impact investments in secondary cities in Africa. CMHI's aggressive stance may have contributed to bringing Magafuli to power, compromising what was otherwise a mutually desired project. Outside investors should understand that African leaders – both local and national – are likely to place growing demands that foreign investments align with African development or political interests, and that these deliver results locally (Hursh, 2019). In this case, despite the importance of the BPP to the development goals of both Bagamoyo and as an urban centre and Tanzania's overall economic growth, the government walked away from negotiations where they deemed terms unsatisfactory or unjustifiable. While this may reflect Magafuli's principled negotiating stance, it also may simply be that he was caught in a bluff that Chinese investors called him on, ultimately resulting in both parties reaching a negotiation point that neither could back down from, ultimately dooming the deal.

This underscores the need for investors to be attuned to the domestic political context – and how their *own* actions may shape it – and the various ways that they may derail inward investments. While pursuing a utility maximising position may be sound negotiating practice when brokering investment terms, such actions can have an unintended agency that may provoke host country stakeholders into unanticipated actions that are detrimental to the investment. Simply, there may be consequences to being 'too good at dealmaking', particularly in institutionally fluid operating contexts.

Conclusion

The demand for investment in secondary cities in Africa will continue to increase as the continent continues to urbanise. But major investments in secondary cities face their own challenges for investors. This case reiterates the importance of mutually beneficial investment terms – both ones which deliver a return for investors, support national economic strategic priorities in host countries, and support the development of emerging urban areas. But it also underscores the challenges related to host country political dynamics and how there are limits to the terms which host countries may accept even related to mutually appealing investments.

Moreover, while the BPP was to be situated in and contribute substantially the development of a strategically important secondary city, this subsequently became overridden by the national and regional significance of the BPP. Fundamentally, for large-scale investments in secondary African cities, foreign investors will increasingly need to consider both local institutional dynamics, but also align their investment conditions with the host country's political economic and development goals. While potentially more complex than inward investments in larger cities in Africa, such investments in smaller cities are likely to continue and justify the additional risk given the potentially outsize financial and strategic returns.

Note

1 China Merchant Holdings International (later renamed to China Merchant Ports) is a publicly listed company on the Hong Kong stock exchange with the Chinese state as majority shareholder.

References

Barton, B. (2023). Infrastructure nationalism and political vulnerability—Examining the stalled negotiations over the Bagamoyo Port Project during Magufuli's Reign. *Journal of Asian and African Studies, 58*, 338–353.

Chellaney, B. (2017). *China's debt-trap diplomacy*. Project Syndicate. https://www.project-syndicate.org/commentary/china-one-belt-one-road-loans-debt-by-brahma-chellaney-2017-01.

COWI. (2013). *Bagamoyo SEZ master plan, final report*. Report for the Export. Processing Zones Authority. COWI, Kongens Lyngby.

Galtier, M. (2023). *From Cape Coast to Ibadan, Africa's future is in its second cities*. The Africa Report. https://www.theafricareport.com/328928/from-cape-coast-to-ibadan-africas-future-is-in-its-second-cities/

Grekou, C., & Owoundi, F. (2020). Understanding how foreign direct investment inflows impact urbanization in Africa. *International Economics, 164*, 48–68.
Hoornweg, D., & Pope, K. (2017). Population predictions for the world's largest cities in the 21st century. *Environment and Urbanization, 29*, 195–216.
Hursh, J. (2019). *A bump in the belt and road: Tanzania pushes back against Chinese Port Project*. Center for International Maritime Security.
Jansson, J., Burke, C., & Hon, T. (2009). *Patterns of Chinese investment, aid and trade in Tanzania*. Briefing paper by the Centre for Chinese Studies Prepared for World Wide Fund for Nature (WWF), October 2009. https://wwfint.awsassets.panda.org/downloads/ccs_tanzania_briefing_paper__october_2009.pdf
Kanai, J. M., & Schindler, S. (2019). Peri-urban promises of connectivity: Linking project-led polycentrism to the infrastructure scramble. *Environment and Planning A: Economy and Space, 51*, 302–322.
Kinyondo, A., Newman, C., & Tarp, F. (2016). *The role and effectiveness of Special Economic Zones in Tanzania* (WIDER working paper No. 9292561669). EconStor.
Lange, S., & Kinyondo, A. (2016). Resource nationalism and local content in Tanzania: Experiences from mining and consequences for the petroleum sector. *The Extractive Industries and Society, 3*, 1095–1104.
Mishra, A. (2019). *Tough conditions and unfavorable demands: Does China risk losing Tanzania's Bagamoyo Port Project?* ORF.
Mooney, T. (2016). Tanzania says mega-port project will start in July. *Journal of Commerce*. https://www.joc.com/article/tanzania-says-mega-port-project-will-start-in-july-5233358
Morisset, J. (2013). *Opening the gates: How the port of Dar es Salaam can transform Tanzania* (Working paper No. 77729). World Bank.
Ng'wanakilala, F. (2015). *Tanzania starts work on $10 bln port project backed by China and Oman*. Reuters.
Nkobou, A. T., & Ainslie, A. (2021). 'Developmental nationalism?' Political trust and the politics of large-scale land investment in Magufuli's Tanzania. *Journal of Eastern African Studies, 15*, 378–399.
Paget, D. (2017). *2 years on: Tanzania's Magufuli isn't a bulldozer. He's a magician*. African Arguments.
Pedersen, R. H., Mutagwaba, W., Jønsson, J. B., Schoneveld, G., Jacob, T., Chacha, M., Weng, X., & Njau, M. G. (2019). Mining-sector dynamics in an era of resurgent resource nationalism: Changing relations between large-scale mining and artisanal and small-scale mining in Tanzania. *Resources Policy, 62*, 339–346.
Reuters. (2019). *Tanzania's China-backed $10 bln port plan stalls over terms – official*. https://www.reuters.com/article/business/finance/tanzanias-china-backed-10-bln-port-plan-stalls-over-terms-official-idUSKCN1ST084/
Roberts, B. H. (2014). *Managing systems of secondary cities: Policy responses in international development*. Cities Alliance/UNOPS, Brussels.
Roder, K. (2019). "Bulldozer politics", state-making and (neo-) extractive industries in Tanzania's gold mining sector. *The Extractive Industries and Society, 6*, 407–412.
Schindler, S., Nguyen, N. D., & Barongo, D. G. (2021). Transformative top-down planning in a small African city: How residents in Bagamoyo, Tanzania connect with a city in motion. *Environment and Planning C: Politics and Space, 39*, 336–353.
Schlimmer, S. (2018). Talking 'land grabs' is talking politics: Land as politicised rhetoric during Tanzania's 2015 elections. *Journal of Eastern African Studies, 12*, 83–101.
South China Morning Post. (2019). *China, Tanzania in talks to get US$10 billion Bagamoyo Port project back on track, ambassador says*. https://www.scmp.com/news/china/diplomacy/article/3018217/china-tanzania-talks-get-us10-billion-bagamoyo-port-project

Tairo, A. (2017). *Tanzania surrenders Bagamoyo Port Project to Chinese firm*. The East African.
The Citizen. (2016). *Govt halts building of Bagamoyo Port*. https://www.thecitizen.co.tz/tanzania/news/national/govt-halts-building-of-bagamoyo-port-2543780
The Citizen. (2021). *Analysts: Why Samia is right on proposed Bagamoyo Port*. https://www.thecitizen.co.tz/tanzania/news/national/-analysts-why-samia-is-right-on-proposed-bagamoyo-port-3455944
The Economist. (2023). *The growth of Africa's towns and small cities is transforming the continent*. https://www.thecitizen.co.tz/tanzania/news/national/-analysts-why-samia-is-right-on-proposed-bagamoyo-port-3455944
Thomson, T. Y. (2023). *Secondary cities are Africa's next big investment opportunity*. Investment Monitor.
United Nations Human Settlements Programme. (2009). *Tanzania: Bagamoyo urban sector profile*. UN-Habitat, Nairobi.
United Nations Human Settlements Programme. (2018). *The State of African cities, 2018: The geography of African investment*. United Nations Human Settlements Programme.
United Nations Conference on Trade and Development. (2023). *World investment report 2023: Investing in sustainable energy for all*. United Nations.
World Bank. (2024). *Foreign direct investment: Tanzania*. https://data.worldbank.org/indicator/BX.KLT.DINV.CD.WD?locations=TZ

9

CASE 9: FROM COAL TOWN TO ESPORTS HUB*

Katowice's path to post-industrial revival

Alex Irwin-Hunt

Abstract

Katowice exemplifies how attracting a major event and foreign direct investment (FDI) related to emerging industries, namely competitive gaming, can reinvigorate a city's image and economic development. This case study explores the story behind how Katowice has changed since Intel Extreme Masters (IEM), one of the longest-running global pro gaming events, moved to the city in 2013. From a simple speculative Facebook message, a city Councillor in Katowice was able to convince Germany-based ESL to relocate IEM to the city. The annual Esports event has since given Katowice global notoriety and attracted thousands of tourists and their spending. It has also redefined how prospective investors view the city, helping to magnetise FDI from companies in gaming, Esports and ancillary services like production studios. Esports has become a key part of Katowice's image branding, as the city redevelops a former mining district into a gaming and technology hub.

Case study

Promoting new foreign direct investment (FDI) in cities is an inherently global endeavour. Local economic development professionals and political leaders recruiting foreign businesses must convince them why their city is better than a growing number of urban centres. In 2020, there were 14,000 cities worldwide, a figure expected to reach 17,000 by 2070.[1] Business

* Exploring the impact of a competitive gaming event on a Polish city's global image and its ability to attract FDI.

DOI: 10.4324/9781003483410-12

fundamentals like favourable regulations, operating costs, availability of skilled workers and quality of infrastructure will always be important to attract FDI. But, in a crowded field, so too is place-branding to increase investor awareness and positive perception of a city and distinguish it from competitors. Branding influences how both consumers and business leaders make decisions.[2]

Katowice, the capital city of the Silesian Voivodeship in southern Poland, exemplifies how a city can rejuvenate its image on the global stage by attracting an annual event for Esports – or organised, professional competitive video gaming. Intel Extreme Masters (IEM), a global Esports event that has run since 2006, debuted its first event at Katowice's Spodek arena in 2013. Since then, the historic coal town has become associated with an industry that has grown rapidly. Newzoo estimates the global Esports audience doubled from 260m in 2015[3] to 532m in 2022, helped by the growth of free streaming platforms like Twitch. Just under half of these global fans in 2022 were Esports enthusiasts, with the remainder occasional viewers.

Academic studies suggest that hosting sporting events can be a means to improve a city's image.[4] But evidence of how hosting major sporting events, such as the Olympic Games and Football World Cup, impact future FDI inflows is mixed. Some studies find countries that host major sporting events can experience an increase in FDI inflows,[5] while others suggest a mixed, nuanced legacy[6] depending on factors like country size, geographical region and levels of economic development. There is little evidence into how Esports events impact FDI flows.

But other research indicates that Katowice's branding and economy has benefited from the event. IEM Katowice attracts thousands of visitors from abroad each year, filling hotel rooms, restaurants and providing a boost to local businesses. The last IEM Major event hosted before the pandemic in 2019 contributed €12.7m to Katowice's economy, according to estimates in an economic impact study by consultancy BCW.

The hosting of the large event has helped Katowice's branding. "The city has created a visibility in our industry that is unheard of in probably any other discipline on such a global scale," said Sebastian Weishaar, president of Esports at ESL FACEIT Group, the organiser of IEM Katowice. "If people from China, America, Brazil and all over the world have an affiliation with our industry, Katowice really means something to them."

Katowice's image as an Esports hub could not be further from the historical stereotype of the city as a polluted, industrial town run on coal.

Bogumił Sobula, Katowice's first deputy mayor who oversees investment, said that the city has tried to host "a few big symbolic events" to break this stereotype and "gain some advantage in comparison" to other competing cities. Major conferences hosted in the city include the UN's annual climate conference COP24 in 2018; the UN's World Urban Forum in 2022; and the European Economic Congress in May 2024.

Coal mining and tragic history

For generations, Katowice was synonymous with coal. Development of mines for hard coal and metal ores started in the 17th century[7] and fuelled its growth from a small village into an industrial metropolis.[8] As the largest urban area of the Upper Silesia Coal region, Katowice's prosperity was wedded to the world's dirtiest fossil fuel.

The Silesian Voivodeship, as well as Katowice as its capital city, has a complex history chequered by conflict and tragedy. The first Silesian Voivodeship, or province, was formed as an autonomous province in the Second Polish Republic between 1918 and 1939.

After Germany's invasion of Poland in 1939 during the Second World War, the territory was temporarily incorporated into the German province of Silesia. Under Nazi Germany's annexation, the region was used as a base for *Polenlager* forced labour camps and prisons. This included the Auschwitz concentration camp, where at least 1.1 million people,[9] the majority of which were Jews, were killed in the gas chambers immediately or soon after being transported there.

After the tragic war period, newly formed regions in 1950 were divided into the Opole and Katowice Voivodeships, the latter of which held borders similar to the region today. The modern Silesian Voivodeship was created on 1 January 1999 after local government reforms in 1998.[10]

Throughout its chequered history, Katowice has been Poland's coal capital, with 11 mines in operation at the end of the 1980s. At the time, coal was central to Poland's economy, accounting for 78% of all total energy consumption, supporting livelihoods and used to fuel critical energy-intensive industries like steelmaking. Katowice was the largest industrial district in Central Europe, according to city authorities.

When communist rule over Poland ended in 1989, the country's mining industry employed more than 415,000 people and had an output of 177.5 million metric tons. Many of these jobs and industrial activities were concentrated around Katowice in the historic Upper Silesia region. But Poland's transition to democracy and a free market economy would bring fundamental change to Katowice.

Generations of dust from the coal mines and smoke from local coal-fired power plants made the city one of the most polluted in Europe. The entire city of Katowice "was a dark grey, black colour from the smoke" in 1991, according to an account[11] by Jean Christophe-Adrian, the UN Habitat's head of sustainable cities at the time.

Progressive decarbonisation efforts and reduction of public assistance for coal mines would lead many in Poland to be decommissioned, including the closure of Kleofas mine in Katowice in 2004. That same year Poland joined the European Union, which has in recent years put pressure on the central government to close down unprofitable mines and transition to cleaner energy sources. Today just two mines still operate in Katowice: Staszic-Wujek and Mysłowice-Wesoła, the latter of which is in both Katowice and the neighbouring city of Mysłowice.

A brazen Facebook message

It was within this context of transition away from coal that Michał Jędrzejek, a former Katowice city councillor who is now in his 40s, tried to change his city's image. He intimately understood Katowice's industrial heritage; both his father and grandfather were miners. When Mr Jędrzejek was growing up in Katowice as a young child up to the age of 10, mining was viewed as an honourable and respectable job. But over the next 20 years, this began to slowly change in the city, he said. Neither Mr Jędrzejek nor his brother ever considered taking the same career path as their father and grandfather. While Katowice "did not lose its miner's ethos overnight," over 30 years it "lost the foundation of its previous development and narrative," said Mr Jędrzejek.

After becoming a city councillor in 2006, Mr Jędrzejek wanted to play his part to change this narrative; by introducing the rapidly growing Esports and video gaming industry to Katowice. This came in 2012, a moment when new tech start-ups were disrupting industries worldwide. Due to his time playing games like *StarCraft and Quake* during his childhood, Mr Jędrzejek was aware of Esports and saw an opportunity for Katowice's citizens, who were like "orphans" after the mine closures, he said. The timing was fortuitous: the number of global viewing hours of Esports would grow from 1.3 billion in 2012 to 2.4 billion in 2013.[12]

An interview in *Forbes*[13] about the world finals of IEM, which were held on the sidelines of the CeBIT computer expo held in Hannover, caught the councillor's eye. The interviewee was Poland-born Michael "Carmac" Blicharz, an Esports player and promoter with whom he had mutual friends.[14] As the director of pro gaming ESL, the Cologne, German-based company that organised IEM's events, Mr Blicharz oversaw the coordination and preparation of the major Esports competition in video games like *StarCraft II, League of Legends* and *Counter-Strike*.

In a Facebook message to Mr Blicharz, the councillor asked "is there a chance to organise an IEM in Katowice?". The response from Mr Blicharz was searching: "There is always a chance. What about 2012 and how do you know [our mutual friend] Pieca?".

At the time, IEM events were held in well-known cities like New York, the United States, Brazil's commercial capital São Paulo and the Chinese city of Guangzhou. "Katowice is not the most obvious city to find itself among those cities," remarked Mr Blicharz.

So, why then did a city as unlikely as Katowice end up attracting the Esports event? For one, it was good timing. The finals of IEM, organised by ESL, had outgrown its hall on the side of the CeBIT expo at Hannover's Fairground. Katowice also showed active support and willingness to take a risk on something that had never been done before in Europe. "The city was very serious about [IEM] immediately," recalled Mr Blicharz, who noted the city offered its Spodek sporting arena for the event and a marketing budget to promote the Katowice event in Polish cities like Warsaw and Krakow.

"It was a big decision because nobody knew at the time how it [would turn out]," said Mr Sobula, Katowice's vice mayor who oversees investment and other policy areas in the city.

The first event hosted in January 2013 instantly filled Spodek arena's 11,000 capacity, the highest attendance at a Western Esports event at the time and way ahead of the 1,000 ticket sales at ESL's previously most successful event. The 2013 event was a test of what was possible in Katowice. By 2014, ESL hosted the IEM finals there as the Spodek arena allowed them to gain "a magnitude and scale that we couldn't replicate elsewhere," said Mr Blicharz.

The event would progressively grow in the years that followed, with an IT trade fair added to its offerings in 2014. Five years after its debut, IEM Katowice would attract 175,000 different fans to the arena over the 2018 finals weekend, with trade magazine *PC World* calling it the largest Esports themed expo in the world.[15]

For Mr Jędrzejek, the success of the event has injected confidence into the local population. "People in Katowice started to believe they live and work in a city that can attract the attention of people from all over the world," he said.

Some 230 million people viewed broadcasts of the IEM Katowice tournaments worldwide in 2019, according to BCW. An estimated €5.78m of tourism impact was generated by visitors from outside Katowice that same year. City leaders stress that IEM has benefitted local residents due to visitors spending money with hotels, restaurants, taxi drivers and entrepreneurs servicing the event.

"IEM has stimulated growth in the hotel and conference industry market. This event has been so successful that its implementation and costs are never questioned by either the residents or the opposition in the city council," said Marcin Krupa, the mayor of Katowice. The success of IEM has led the city to recast its efforts to encourage investment and visitors from abroad. "It is an important part of Katowice promotion strategy on the domestic and international markets," said Mr Krupa.

The FDI benefits

As ESL's annual Esports event grew in Katowice, so did their presence in the city. The Germany-based company first opened an office in Katowice, later launching in 2020 their production hub[16] for the Europe, Middle East and Africa region in the city. "We have a number of people there that provide graphics and video services for the entire ESL FaceIT Group globally," said Mr Blicharz, who describes their base in Katowice as the "creative assets hub" for the company. "We've got a wonderful relationship with the city," he added.

Since the event, visitors to Katowice include industry leaders and those managing large companies, said Mr Jędrzejek. "They know Katowice; it's no longer just a strange name in a country on the fringes of Europe," he explained. After Katowice "achieved something from nothing" by attracting IEM, Mr Jędrzejek argued this has made it "credible" when the city tries to attract companies in the Esports or gaming industries as well as technology and global business services.

To build on this success, the city of Katowice has put technology and gaming at the centre of its strategy to promote investment and change their brand image. This is evident in Nikiszowiec, a former mining worker housing estate in the southeast of the city next to the now closed Wieczorek mine. The distinctive neighbourhood, with its redbrick apartments, is being redeveloped into a technology and gaming hub,[17] with plans to attract more companies and talent for the gaming and tech industries. In November 2023, the EU approved[18] state aid totalling PLN309m (€72m) for the construction of the strategic project for the city. "The Katowice Gaming and Technological Hub (KGTH) is to become not only an attractor for high-tech staff, contributing to successive regional development, but also a laboratory for the next generations," reads a promotional brochure for the project distributed at international FDI events like Mipim, an annual real estate conference hosted in the south of France.

Its global notoriety as an Esports hub has helped boost Katowice's image among other gaming companies, both foreign and local. In July 2018, Ireland-based Keywords Studios opened[19] a new player support studio in Katowice. Marek Niszkiewicz, then the company's project manager, said at the time of the announcement that the Irish company sought a location that would enable them to recruit a large number of passionate gamers. "We are certain that the Katowice metropolitan area, with a population of more than two million and a well-known reputation as a successful Esports events host, will be able to provide that," he said.

At least 23 video game development companies have a base in Katowice, with a total of 70 across the Silesian Voivodeship. Those in the city include virtual reality game development companies like Incuvo, Spectral Games,

Artifex Mundi and Anshar Studios. "If you have a city that is now synonymous in the whole world and in all of Poland with Esports, it only makes sense to double down and bring the video game industry at large to that city," said Mr Blicharz.

Keywords Studios has continuously expanded its presence in Katowice. Since opening its studio, it has grown from less than 50 to over 1,100 people of over 50 nationalities[20] in the city.

The success of Katowice in attracting tech companies transcends beyond just IEM. The city has experienced a "snowball effect" after IBM set up an office there in 2012,[21] according to Katowice's mayor, who argues this helped encourage other companies to set up in the city like consultancy PwC and Japan-based Fujitsu. IBM's office in Katowice was set up to serve clients in the mining industry, but also to expand access to cloud computing services in the Silesia region.

The city's strategy to build its image around top-tier investors in their respective industries has helped in its efforts to attract more FDI. Data from fDi Markets shows that sub-sectors in Katowice that have attracted the most greenfield FDI projects since 2003 have been software publishers and custom computer programming services (Table 9.1).

TABLE 9.1 Greenfield foreign direct investment in Katowice by sub-sector (2003–2023)

Industry sub sector	*FDI projects*	*Capex ($m)*	*Avg. capex*	*Jobs created*	*Avg. jobs*	*Companies*
Software publishers, except video games	15	98.7	6.6	1,424	94	11
Custom computer programming services	14	118.5	8.5	1,387	99	11
Commercial and institutional building construction	9	1,118.2	124.2	8,541	949	7
General purpose machinery	9	58.0	6.4	310	34	9
Freight/Distribution Services	7	227.0	32.4	576	82	7
Retail banking	7	53.8	7.7	1,246	178	6
Accounting, tax preparation, bookkeeping and payroll services	6	17.7	2.9	1,312	218	3
Accommodation	5	291.0	58.2	792	158	5
Industrial building construction	5	364.4	72.9	2,638	527	4
Other motor vehicle parts	5	153.2	30.6	988	197	5
Air transportation	4	178.5	44.6	649	162	4
Measuring and control instruments	4	33.0	8.3	378	94	3

(Continued)

TABLE 9.1 (Continued)

Industry sub sector	*FDI projects*	*Capex ($m)*	*Avg. capex*	*Jobs created*	*Avg. jobs*	*Companies*
Metalworking machinery	4	26.9	6.7	543	135	4
Rental and leasing services	4	7.6	1.9	32	8	3
Steel products	4	30.8	7.7	173	43	4
Business support services	3	18.4	6.1	863	287	3
Data processing, hosting and related services	3	495.0	165.0	391	130	3
Motor vehicle gasoline engines and engine parts	3	284.1	94.7	750	250	3
Other (Software and IT services)	3	13.2	4.4	524	174	2
Video games, applications and digital content	3	12.6	4.2	499	166	1
Wireless telecommunication carriers	3	56.9	19.0	559	186	3
All other industrial machinery	2	7.1	3.5	142	71	2
Cement and concrete products	2	65.7	32.9	311	155	2
Converted paper products	2	66.6	33.3	192	96	2
Corporate and investment banking	2	8.9	4.5	176	88	2
Employment services	2	3.0	1.5	210	105	2
Motor vehicle steering and suspension components	2	413.4	206.7	1,500	750	2
Power transmission equipment	2	29.6	14.8	258	129	1
Real estate services	2	59.1	29.6	387	193	2
Architectural and structured metals	1	42.5	42.5	123	123	1
Architectural, engineering and related services	1	1.5	1.5	113	113	1
Automobiles	1	21.2	21.2	37	37	1
Basic chemicals	1	3.8	3.8	35	35	1
Building material and garden equipment and supplies dealers (Building materials)	1	25.5	25.5	120	120	1
Coating, engraving, heat treating and allied activities	1	26.5	26.5	110	110	1
Coffee and tea	1	19.0	19.0	71	71	1
Commercial and service industry machinery	1	6.2	6.2	100	100	1
Communications equipment	1	4.6	4.6	115	115	1
Computer and peripheral equipment	1	45.1	45.1	400	400	1

(Continued)

TABLE 9.1 (Continued)

Industry sub sector	*FDI projects*	*Capex ($m)*	*Avg. capex*	*Jobs created*	*Avg. jobs*	*Companies*
Engines and Turbines	1	19.0	19.0	200	200	1
Furniture, homeware and related products (Consumer Products)	1	64.2	64.2	579	579	1
Furniture, homeware and related products (Wood Products)	1	6.0	6.0	27	27	1
General medical and surgical hospitals	1	35.2	35.2	209	209	1
Household appliances	1	3.5	3.5	38	38	1
Insurance	1	4.3	4.3	100	100	1
Internet publishing and broadcasting and web search	1	.5	0.5	20	20	1
Iron and steel mills and ferroalloy	1	1.3	1.3	8	8	1
Laminated plastics plates, sheets and shapes	1	5.5	5.5	70	70	1
Medical equipment and supplies	1	16.0	16.0	157	157	1
Motor vehicle electrical and electronic equipment	1	4.2	4.2	245	245	1
Natural, liquefied and compressed gas	1	463.5	463.5	237	237	1
Other (Building materials)	1	10.5	10.5	29	29	1
Other (Business machines and equipment)	1	6.4	6.4	50	50	1
Other electric power generation (Renewable Energy)	1	20.5	20.5	28	28	1
Other non-metallic mineral products	1	2.3	2.3	7	7	1
Performing arts, spectator sports and related	1	255.0	255.0	989	989	1
Plastic bottles	1	18.4	18.4	103	103	1
Plastics packaging materials and unlaminated film and sheets	1	12.9	12.9	87	87	1
Postal service	1	14.9	14.9	108	108	1
Printing and related activities	1	12.0	12.0	100	100	1
Rail transportation	1	24.2	24.2	12	12	1
Travel arrangement and reservation services	1	1.3	1.3	18	18	1

(Continued)

TABLE 9.1 (Continued)

Industry sub sector	*FDI projects*	*Capex ($m)*	*Avg. capex*	*Jobs created*	*Avg. jobs*	*Companies*
Truck transportation	1	20.6	20.6	21	21	1
Warehousing and storage	1	4.2	4.2	10	10	1
Waste management and remediation services	1	1.5	1.5	97	97	1
Wood products	1	11.8	11.8	104	104	1
Total greenfield FDI (2003–2023)	173	5,546.3	32.1	32,628	188	149

Source: © fDi Markets, from the Financial Times Ltd 2024.

Notes:
All Capex figures shown in the table are in United States Dollar millions.
Capex data includes estimated values Financial Times Ltd takes no responsibility for the accuracy or otherwise of this data.
Jobs data includes estimated values Financial Times Ltd takes no responsibility for the accuracy or otherwise of this data.

While IEM has given the city a new image on the world stage, Katowice still attracts FDI in industrial areas including machinery, automotive and metals. The Katowice special economic zone (KSSE), set up in 1996, has an ecosystem of multinationals across sectors, including carmakers US-based General Motors and Stellantis as well as Capgemini, the French multinational IT and consulting company.

Marcin Nowak, vice president of the city's planned gaming and technology hub, said that the entry of Capgemini to Katowice is another example of how city authorities have been open to new industries and companies. Capgemini was the first global business services provider to set up in the city. "Katowice authorities have always been prepared to take a risk, to do something which is out of the box," said Mr Nowak, who also helped set up Capgemini's office in Katowice back in 2007.

He argued the gaming hub is the same. An example of the city willing to take a risk to build a new community and invest money to promote the city to another level on the international stage. And so too has the story been with IEM. As with any conference, Katowice must still continuously negotiate its terms with ESL Group to continue hosting the event. While this presents some risks for the future, the event has still put the previously unknown city on the map.

By attracting IEM to its city, Katowice has made itself synonymous with the Esports industry and made this a critical part of their promotional strategy. "Katowice has become the Mecca of Esports and gaming," said Mr Weishaar of ESL. Since attracting IEM, Katowice is trying to shake off its stereotype as an industrial city and attract further FDI in emerging industries. This is epitomised by its plans to redevelop the site of the former coal mine Wieczorek into a hub for gaming and technology. Only time will tell if it proves as successful as the IEM event itself.

References

1. UN-Habitat. (2022). World cities report 2022: Envisaging the future of cities. UN. https://unhabitat.org/sites/default/files/2022/06/wcr_2022.pdf
2. O'Doherty, J. (2024). *Does place branding really count in FDI attraction?* Financial Times Ltd. https://www.fdiintelligence.com/content/news/opinion-does-place-branding-really-count-in-fdi-attraction-84101
3. Newzoo. (2011). *The eSports industry to date: The drivers behind current and future growth*. Newzoo BV. https://newzoo.com/wp-content/uploads/2011/06/Newzoo-eSports-Conference-Slides-2015.pdf
4. Yu, H. Y., Lee, D., Ahn, J., Lee, M., & Foreman, J. J. (2023). City Branding's impact on cities hosting sporting events: Top-down and bottom-up effects in a pre-post study. *Tourism Management Perspectives, 46*, 101098. https://www.sciencedirect.com/science/article/abs/pii/S2211973623000260
5. Lertwachara, K., Tongurai, J., & Boonchoo, P. (2021). Mega sporting events and inward foreign direct investment: An investigation of the differences among the types of sporting events and host countries. *Journal of Sport Management. 36*(1), 9–24 https://journals.humankinetics.com/view/journals/jsm/36/1/article-p9.xml
6. Jakobsen, J., et al. (2012). Fool's gold: Major sport events and foreign direct investment. *International Journal of Sport Policy and Politics. 5*(3), 363–380.https://www.tandfonline.com/doi/abs/10.1080/19406940.2012.717099
7. Łukaszczyk, J., & Popczyk, M. (2018). Changing the mining industry in the heart of Silesia. *IOP Conference Series Earth and Environmental Science. 174*(1), 1–9 https://doi.org/10.1088/1755-1315/174/1/012006
8. InYourPocket. (2024). *A brief history of Katowice*. https://web.archive.org/web/20170316024836/https://www.inyourpocket.com/katowice/history
9. Jews in Auschwitz. https://www.auschwitz.org/en/history/categories-of-prisoners/jews-in-auschwitz/
10. Silesian Voivodeship. https://local-government-history.fandom.com/wiki/Silesian_Voivodeship
11. Puttkamer, L. (2022). *How Katowice, Poland, went from coal city to culture and conference hub*. UN. https://unhabitat.org/news/18-jul-2022/how-katowice-poland-went-from-coal-city-to-culture-and-conference-hub
12. Dredge, S. (2014). *eSports viewing nearly doubled in 2013 as games-watching fanbase grew*. Guardian. https://www.theguardian.com/technology/2014/jun/02/esports-viewing-2013-league-of-legends
13. Gaudiosi, J. (2012). Michal "Carmac" Blicharz discusses the rise of intel extreme masters pro gaming around the globe. *Forbes*. https://www.forbes.com/sites/johngaudiosi/2012/02/01/michal-carmac-blicharz-discusses-the-rise-of-intel-extreme-masters-pro-gaming-around-the-globe/
14. ESL Group. (2023). *10 year anniversary of IEM Katowice*. ESL Group. https://pro.eslgaming.com/tour/csgo/10th-anniversary/foundations/#first
15. Gaudiosi, J. (2017). *Inside IEM Katowice: How a small Polish city became an e-sports goliath*. PC World/IDG. https://www.pcworld.com/article/412279/inside-iem-katowice-how-a-small-polish-city-became-an-e-sports-goliath.html
16. ESL Group. (2020, August 26). *Jak wygląda produkcja turniejów esportowych w ESL Gaming Polska?* [Video]. YouTube. https://www.youtube.com/watch?v=dWXKwAGk2cE

17. Katowice City Council. (2023). *New technologies district: Katowice gaming and technology hub*. https://invest.katowice.eu/wp-content/uploads/2024/03/folder-hub-tech-2023_eng.pdf
18. Katowice City Council. (2023). *Katowice gaming and technology HUB*. https://invest.katowice.eu/en/support-and-incentives-for-investors/katowice-gaming-and-technology-hub/
19. O'Brien, C. (2019). Keywords Studios to expand operations in Poland and Mexico. *The Irish Times*. https://www.irishtimes.com/business/technology/keywords-studios-to-expand-operations-in-poland-mexico-1.4001056
20. Keywords Studios. (2022). *Discover our new office space in Katowice*. Keywords Studios. https://www.keywordsstudios.com/en/about-us/news-events/news/discover-our-new-office-space-in-katowice/
21. IBM. (2012). *IBM increases presence in Poland with new branch offices*. IBM. https://www.prnewswire.com/news-releases/ibm-increases-presence-in-poland-with-new-branch-offices-144654165.html

PART III

Technology, FDI and Cities

ABSTRACT

Globalization has led to the spread of technological capabilities and R&D around the world. Companies have been at the forefront of this, seeking human capital and knowledge-intensive environments to locate aspects of their R&D activities and support their innovation efforts. Companies do not stay in their home country for all their explorative R&D activities. They benefit by having a presence close to intellectually capable and creative actors that allow them to advance their own products and services to compete globally. Cities provide a basis for this proximity, and many cities have become important hubs for technological creativity and innovation. These locations are not only in advanced economies (Part I of this book) but also increasingly in transition and emerging economies (Part II of this book), such as China. Part III now explores this phenomenon through four diverse cases in Europe, the Middle East, and East Asia. There is no one single city or place in the world that has a monopoly on technological innovation and the creation of intellectual property (IP). While IP regimes can vary between cities, and levels of available human capital and supporting infrastructure too, global connectedness has brought with it new geographical opportunities for technological advancement in distant cities that companies can pursue. From the point of view of cities, they cannot stand still as far as attracting Foreign Direct Investment (FDI) in technological sectors is concerned. The policies and practices adopted by cities will determine the extent to which tech FDI flows in, what kind of tech FDI flows in, and how this then has an impact on city development and prosperity.

Technological FDI, knowledge spillovers, and IP

Arguably, the most important dimension to consider in tech Foreign Direct Investment (FDI) into cities is the motives for companies to invest, and to stay invested in the location. Simply put, they are tech-related motives.

DOI: 10.4324/9781003483410-13

Multinational Enterprises (MNEs) making investments will be looking to explore new ideas, breakthroughs, innovations, and technologies that could be then exploited by the company in its global market. To do this, they need access to strategic assets, including researchers, scientists, and engineers, as well as a supportive environment with tech suppliers, partners, and other actors such as universities and research labs. This mainly comes through proximity to these types of actors, which cities provide a natural basis for (Belderbos et al., 2014; Castellani & Lavoratori, 2019). MNEs engage in innovative projects with other actors on a local, and city basis and their learning in urban clusters is a basis of innovative performance (Williams & Du, 2014). The state of development of clustering – including university-industry collaborations – can influence an MNE's decision to choose tech joint ventures in a tech-intensive industry (Williams & Vrabie, 2018). These R&D-related factors can be more relevant to location choice and mode of entry than many of the traditionally accepted factors used in international business research, such as market size and cultural distance. Belderbos et al. (2014) find the importance of R&D-related factors in host cities to attract R&D investment from abroad. These include the technological strength of a city, the extent of its international knowledge connectivity, and the strength of its universities. Du et al. (2022) extend this to differentiate more clearly between the 'R' (research) and the 'D' (development) in R&D, i.e., between early stage (more explorative and science based) and late stage (more commercial market-driven) innovation activity. The number of top universities per capita in a city matters for FDI in 'R', but not in 'D'. And intellectual property (IP) rights protection matters for attracting FDI in 'D' but not 'R' (Du et al., 2022). Overall, the physically close nature of the actors in city locations for tech investment means that knowledge spillovers are more likely. Knowledge spillovers occur when there is an exchange of ideas and information between actors such that an innovation occurring in one actor will stimulate an innovation in another actor. This does not imply a direct handing over of technology from the investing MNE to one or more local actors in the city. Rather, it means there will be a range of diffusion channels – some of which are informal in nature – that allow tacit knowledge to flow.

In return, cities can benefit through tech FDI. Again, technological and knowledge spillovers are central to this because they provide a reason for skilled knowledge workers to migrate to a city. Tech FDI helps to reinforce and improve the evolving smart city; providing new technologies and know-how that cities can use to make themselves more digitally connected, environmentally friendly, and liveable (Jayathilaka & Park, 2022; De Jong et al., 2024). Smart cities will not only attract tech FDI but also use tech FDI to improve the standard of living in the city. FDI is part of the total investment that goes into smart cities for new infrastructure and digital technology (De Jong et al., 2024). Tech FDI can also help the overall technological upgrading of cities, particularly when the investing MNE is an established leader at the cutting edge of a field, and the city is in a catch-up mode. Tang et al. (2020) show how tech FDI into a city can spill over into technological upgrading in related industries in neighbouring and nearby cities. These spillover effects form a basis for longer-term economic development of cities, putting the importance of attracting tech FDI sharply into the spotlight.

One concern facing MNEs – and a deterrent to FDI that involves knowledge and IP transfer – is the potential loss of IP or IP rights infringement and the threat of imitation. Cities can have an important role to play in assuaging investors' concerns in this respect. The state of development of the legal system, the availability of legal services and lawyers, especially IP lawyers and international law experts, are important. If the MNE subsidiary that is set up in a city is mandated to create new IP through patenting or trademarking new creations, then the presence of an IP office and institutional system for the registering of patents according to international standards will be necessary. Awokuse and Yin (2010) find that in China, FDI flows into the country increased because of the strengthening of its IP rights system. Dussaux et al. (2022) find that FDI in low-carbon technologies is dependent on having strict IP rights protection in place. Given the potential for Greentech spillovers into cities through inward FDI in low-carbon technologies, this illustrates the importance of strengthening IP rights systems for city development. However, it may put some cities in a difficult situation: unable to attract FDI in Greentech due to IP rights weaknesses, and at the same time unable to innovate for themselves in these areas.

Ecosystems for technology

One interesting role of tech FDI in cities is how it helps to build and strengthen nascent ecosystems (Lorenzen et al., 2020). The presence of tech FDI in a city can contribute to the development of an ecosystem by stimulating local suppliers, partners, and entrepreneurs to enter and operate within the city. Ecosystems emphasize interdependent relationships between multiple actors, and multiple different types of actors, all with a common goal, broadly defined. They emphasize the benefits of networks within the city, although these networks can also be fluid and somewhat porous, not restricted to the geographical limits of a city. This is especially the case with virtual networks and relationships that tech companies build and maintain online as well as in person. It is also particularly relevant in new, emerging industries, which can be highly disruptive in nature. Turkina and Sultana (2023) found there to be an important role for FDI in promoting new ecosystems in the cleantech sector in cities. Through their FDI, MNEs play a brokering role in the formation of these ecosystems, allowing boundary spanning between actors in an emerging industry space that might not otherwise have been connected. Brokering is important in emerging networks; a powerful position that opens pipelines and connections between different nodes. An investing MNE becomes structurally and relationally connected to a broad range of actors as the ecosystem develops. This does not only include local firms and universities; it also extends to actors such as law firms and banks. Foreign firms with advanced cleantech IP need to be connected to local city networks for these effects to occur (Turkina & Sultana, 2023).

According to Bhawe and Zahra (2019), MNEs have a vital role to play in stimulating entrepreneurial ecosystems through their investments. These entrepreneurial ecosystems are characterized by high ratios of tech start-ups, which in turn provide a boost for economic development and growth over the longer term. Bhawe and Zahra (2019) point out that absorptive capacity in a newly forming ecosystem is necessary to allow knowledge from investing MNEs to be transferred and acted upon. Local entrepreneurs can be proactive in seeking to capture and assimilate the knowledge possessed by MNEs through their local operations. These ecosystems often form in and around cities and are supported by entrepreneurial policy and ICT readiness in the city (Audretsch & Belitski, 2017).

City connectivity and technological FDI

FDI is influential in connecting cities together under technology initiatives and investments. Investors do not only engage with local entrepreneurial ecosystems with a view to benefitting from their presence in those ecosystems in the short term; they also allow ecosystems to be developed across borders and between cities over the longer term. One way this happens is through the connections between operations in the home country (and cities) of the MNE, third country (and cities) of the MNE, and newly entered ecosystems in a new city for the MNE. These connections are both person-based (such as family ties and friendships that develop) and organization-based (alliances, partnerships, projects) (Lorenzen et al., 2020). Castellani et al. (2022) show empirically that MNEs make R&D investments in cities that are connected to other countries in the world through their networks of inventors. Global connectivity of cities, therefore, is something that comes about because of MNE investment but is also one of the attractive features of cities as far as the pattern of MNE investment is concerned.

Cities can also proactively develop partnerships with other cities around the world – sometimes officially done as 'twinning' arrangements – cognizant that this can spur multi-way investment and the identification of new business and growth opportunities. They also allow new social connections to form that can boost entrepreneurial investment and the pursuit of newly identified opportunities. Examples exist in many areas of collaboration, not just technological ones, such as promotion of tourism (Gil, 2020) and cultural exchanges (De Villiers, 2009). However, city-city partnerships in the technological space have increased in recent decades. One way these city-city partnerships benefit tech FDI is when they help to establish new technological development zones through the sharing of capital, know-how, and resources (Du & Krusekopf, in this book). This happens in the case of specific investments in new industrial parks (Inkpen and Pien, 2006), as well as in grander terms where governments embark on trans-national initiatives to promote trade, investment, and influence throughout the world, such as with China's Belt and Road Initiative (Song et al., 2021).

FDI motives in tech investments

It was noted above how MNEs' tech investments can be seen in terms of 'R' and/or 'D', and that the characteristics of cities that matter for both motives can either be the same (such as the city's technological strength) or differentiated (such as the IP regime) (Du et al., 2022). Research has shown fundamental differences in terms of the nature of technological innovation conducted by MNE subsidiaries set up in overseas cities. Ecker et al. (2013) describe this in terms of the research nature in MNE subsidiaries: a continuum ranging from basic research and scientific exploration to more applied, late-stage activities closer to market commercialization. Early-stage activity is more explorative, carries higher levels of uncertainty, and may generate IP for which customer application and product market are not yet clearly identified. Ecker et al. (2013) show that, in MNE investments in Austria, these motives for tech activity in the subsidiary will influence how the subsidiary is controlled internally by the MNE; greater decentralization, and autonomy given to early-stage research. This matters for tech FDI in cities because it shows how MNEs need to think beyond the features of the city that are aligned with the FDI motives for tech, but also how they control internally when seeking to generate early-stage IP.

The cases in Part III

The collection of five cases in Part III explores FDI and cities with a strong emphasis on technology and innovation. The cases are set in the cities of: Paris, Tel Aviv, Shenzhen, and Suzhou. These cities have grown to offer valuable opportunities for tech investors. They have developed technological and innovation capacities over many years by having a strong international orientation and openness to inward investors. The cases here highlight diversity in the motives for seeking tech-oriented FDI in cities, the difficulties of land usage and inequality that can be fuelled by tech FDI, how ecosystems can be developed and sustained because of investor friendly policy towards FDI in R&D, and how reforming policy relating to industrial parks can lead to technological and economic development of a city region.

- Paris: Inward Investment into Hi-Tech Industries

Paris, France's capital city, is a major global hub for technological innovation. It hosts a range of leading universities and research labs and attracts inward investment from some of the world's leading tech companies. Its cultural vibrancy, high-quality transport infrastructure, and quality health system attract migrant knowledge workers, including researchers and scientists. The case portrays the city as host to an ecosystem that consists of large and small companies alike, domestic and foreign investments. It shows how tech companies choose Paris for quite different reasons and describes two tech companies – one Finnish and one American – that invested in Paris with differing motives. The case illustrates how established global cities offer different types of opportunities to tech investors.

- Hamburg: A Strategic Port City

Hamburg, Germany's second-largest city, is one of Europe's most important port cities and a key port hub for global trade. Its strategic location on the Elbe River and its highly developed logistics infrastructure make it an attractive destination for FDI in sectors such as shipping, logistics, and manufacturing. Hamburg's attractiveness hinges on its role as a gateway to global markets, and it has attracted significant investment from MNEs looking to establish a foothold in Europe. However, it also offers opportunities for tech FDI and the case presented here explores how the city developed a 'landing pad' strategy for tech-oriented inward investors. The Hamburg landing pad connected potential investors with partners and opportunities to develop and deploy technology in pursuit of learning and market penetration.

- Tel Aviv: Developing a Start-Up Hub through FDI in a Conflict Environment

Tel-Aviv has become an important technology-driven city economy in a region beset by geo-political uncertainty. FDI has had an important role to play in the city's economic development, as well as its social culture. The case presented here shows there was a 'darker side' as well; there was a depletion of land capacity and an increase in inequality. FDI may have had an indirect role to play in this. The case takes a long-time horizon perspective, giving the reader insights into selected key events that affected the city throughout the 20th century. It also poses the question of what policy steps can be taken to retain the city's attractiveness to outside investors in tech fields since the escalation of violence in the region in 2023.

- Shenzhen: Greenfield FDI and the Development of an Innovation Ecosystem

Shenzhen – originally a fishing village – has become an important innovation ecosystem in China. It was able to do this through concerted efforts and incentives to attract inward investment. It created an international orientation and an open economic system for investment. Given a lack of target companies for acquisition, the Greenfield mode of entry for foreign MNEs has been prevalent. This case examines the trends in terms of Greenfield FDI in tech into Shenzhen, and the role this has played in technology transfer to allow upgrading of local companies through spillovers. Key aspects of the policy for developing the ecosystem included tax breaks, financial support for R&D conducted within the ecosystem, and a strengthening of the IP protection regime.

- Suzhou: An Industrial Park with Institutional Links to Cities in Other Countries

Suzhou is an example of a non-hub city in China that embarked on a journey to establish itself as a place of technological and economic importance for China as well as for the firms that invested there. As a Tier 2 city in China, its journey started somewhat differently to major Tier 1 cities such as Shanghai, Beijing, and Guangzhou. Its industrial park started as a collaboration between Singapore and the city of Suzhou. The case illustrates how reputational effects and kudos associated with the linkage with an advanced economy can provide confidence for potential investors. With the passage of time, the local Suzhou government acquired a majority stake in the park, restructuring and re-focusing it as a business service and high-tech location facilitated by FDI. The case also illustrates how attraction capabilities such as a one-stop service model can assist in successful FDI projects.

10

CASE 10: HI-TECH INVESTMENT IN PARIS

Ana Colovic

Abstract

In the 2020s, Paris Region was the top innovation hub in Europe. As a global city, Paris featured high numbers of engineers, scientists, top universities, research institutions and industrial clusters. Leading global companies had numerous activities in Paris. Paris Region received a high volume of Foreign Direct Investment (FDI) in hi-tech sectors. It boasted a vibrant ecosystem made up of start-ups, small-and-medium-sized enterprises, large firms and research and education institutions. A number of companies invested in Paris to serve as suppliers to the 2024 Olympic and Paralympic Games. IQM and Twilio both made hi-tech investments in Paris Region but for different reasons. Both companies had well-defined interest in Paris Region. The stories of these companies highlight various aspects of Paris Region's attractiveness for hi-tech FDI.

WHY INVEST IN HI-TECH SECTORS IN PARIS REGION?

Paris Region is Europe's top innovation hub, leading in R&D workforce, researchers, scientists and engineers. It hosts 40% of France's R&D employees and boasts 34 Nobel Prize winners, 4 Abel prizes and 11 Fields medals. Companies, public and private R&D centres, universities can recruit numerous PhD students, researchers, scientists and engineers to develop their activities in the region.

Paris is the 2nd European city in AI, behind London according to Startup Blink,[1] attracting major tech companies like Google, Meta, Apple and Microsoft. Startups like Mistral AI, Snips and Shift Technology thrive here.

DOI: 10.4324/9781003483410-14

The Choose France Summit in May 2024 highlighted significant hi-tech investments in AI, Quantum and IT in Paris Region: Accenture, Amazon, IBM, Microsoft, Tata Group and ProLogium, underscoring the region's commitment to innovation and technology development.

Other examples of tech companies that have recently chosen the Paris region include AI Redefined, a Canadian artificial intelligence company, Google France AI Center, the British company Mimecast in cyber-security or Samsung Computational Design Lab.

Lionel Grotto, CEO of Choose Paris Region, June 2024

Paris as an investment destination

In 2024, Paris featured among the key cities in the world, the so-called 'global cities' – large metropolitan areas characterized by a vibrant business environment, high-quality infrastructure, a high concentration of researchers and scientists and elite universities and research institutions. The Metropolitan area of Paris, covering Paris and its suburbs, also known as 'Paris Region,' was the top business and innovation hub in 2024 in the European Union (EU). It had the highest GDP in the EU, housed Europe's largest cluster of Fortune Global 500 corporations, corporate headquarters, as well as innovative start-ups and small- and medium-sized enterprises.[2] According to the Paris Region Facts and Figures 2024 coproduced by Choose Paris Region, the Paris Île-de-France Regional Chamber of Commerce and Industry and l'Institut Paris Region,[3] in 2024 the Paris Region was home to 18.8% of France's population, it gathered 23.1% of all jobs in France, employed 34% of all French executives, and was home to 37.9% of R&D workforce and 29.3% of scientists and engineers in France.

In 2024, Paris hosted the Olympic and Paralympic Games, with 15 venues for the Olympic and 11 venues for the Paralympic Games. While some venues had existed before these sports events, many were constructed for the purpose of hosting them. Close to 15,000 athletes took part in the games. A large number of firms, both French and foreign, participated in the preparation of the games in one way or the other. Close to a hundred foreign firms made FDI directly or indirectly linked to the Olympic games. Some made FDI to serve as suppliers to the games, while others wanted to benefit from business opportunities the games offered. Examples included Equinix (USA), the world leader in digital infrastructure specializing in data centres, which opened a data centre in Paris Region in 2022, and Ecocem (Ireland), which supplied its ultra-low carbon technology for the

TABLE 10.1 Global Cities Index 2023 on economic performances

	2021	*2022*	*2023*
New York	1	1	1
London	2	2	2
Paris	**3**	**3**	**3**
Tokyo	4	4	4
Beijing	5	5	5
Brussels	16	11	6
Singapore	9	9	7
Los Angeles	5	6	8
Melbourne	12	8	9
Hong Kong	7	10	10

Source: AT Kearney, 2023.[4]

construction of the Olympic village, Thermo Fisher Scientific (USA), which participated in the analyses of doping controls during the Games by supplying analytical instruments, laboratory equipment and its expertise in identifying forbidden substances.

As a global city, Paris was included in the global attractiveness rankings. Paris ranked third in the world in economic performance and tenth in the world in the ranking combining economic dynamism, excellent universities, transportation infrastructure and forward-thinking environmental policies (see Tables 10.1 and 10.2). It ranked fifth in 2023, behind San Francisco, Copenhagen, London and Luxembourg on the potential to attract and retain global capital, people and ideas in the coming years according

TABLE 10.2 Global Cities Index 2023 (economic dynamism, universities, environmental policies, infrastructure)

	2021	*2022*	*2023*
San Francisco	2	3	1
Boston	3	2	2
London	2	1	3
New York	5	4	4
Melbourne	10	5	5
Toronto	7	6	6
San Jose (USA)	–	12	7
Singapore	11	8	8
Hong Kong	6	9	9
Paris	**4**	**7**	**10**

Source: Schroders.[5]

TABLE 10.3 Global Power City Index 2023 (World's most attractive cities according to their ability to attract people, capital and enterprises from around the World)

	2021	*2022*	*2023*
London	1	1	1
New York	2	2	2
Tokyo	3	3	3
Paris	**4**	**4**	**4**
Singapore	5	5	5
Amsterdam	6	6	6
Seoul	8	7	7
Dubai	14	11	8
Melbourne	10	9	9
Berlin	7	8	10

Source: Mori Memorial's Foundation's Institute for Urban Strategies, 2023.[6]

to AT Kearney, 2023. Besides, it ranked first worldwide in liveability, third in cultural interactions and fifth in accessibility, and fourth overall in the Global Power City Index 2023, which ranked the world's most attractive cities according to their ability to attract people, capital and enterprises from around the world (Table 10.3).

Foreign Direct Investment in Paris Region

Paris Region attracted high volumes of Foreign Direct Investment (FDI) in a number of sectors and industries. After a record year 2022, 2023 showed a slight decrease in FDI in terms of the number of investments, but an increase in jobs created as shown in Table 10.4. While, on average, 16 jobs were created per investment in 2017, 27.34 jobs were created per investment in 2023.

Regarding the geographic zones from which investments originated, Europe scored the highest, followed by North America and Asia (Table 10.5).

TABLE 10.4 Evolution of FDI in Paris Region from 2017 to 2023 in terms of the number of new investments (projects) and number of jobs created

	2017	*2018*	*2019*	*2020*	*2021*	*2022*	*2023*
Number of investments	414	409	415	336	404	431	410
Jobs created	6,626	6,303	9,660	10,797	10,178	10,937	11,212
Average number of jobs created per investment	16.00	15.41	23.27	32.13	25.19	25.37	27.34

Source: Choose Paris Region (2024).[7]

TABLE 10.5 Geographic regions of origin of investments (in numbers of investments)

	2019	*2020*	*2021*	*2022*	*2023*
Europe	215	188	234	219	200
North America	113	78	89	120	122
Asia Oceania	72	54	48	57	55
Africa	10	9	17	15	14
Middle East	3	2	5	7	11
South America	2	5	11	13	8
Total	415	336	404	431	410

Source: Choose Paris Region (2024).

TABLE 10.6 Top ten countries of origin of FDIs to Paris Region (in numbers of investments)

	2019	*2020*	*2021*	*2022*	*2023*	*Total 2019–2023*
United States	98	67	77	107	102	451
United Kingdom	50	37	45	38	40	210
Germany	42	27	46	44	26	185
Italy	38	23	31	32	26	150
China	30	19	25	19	21	114
Netherlands	12	16	22	20	28	98
Spain	13	12	17	15	18	75
Japan	20	22	7	6	8	72
Canada	15	11	12	13	20	71
Switzerland	14	11	18	17	10	70

Source: Choose Paris Region (2024).

FDI originated from a high number of countries, among which top 10 were the United States, the United Kingdom, Germany, Italy, China, the Netherlands, Spain, Japan, Canada and Switzerland, as shown in Table 10.6.

In 2023, the main five countries of origin by the number of jobs created were the United States, the United Kingdom, Germany, Ireland and Canada, as shown in Table 10.7.

When it comes to types of activities that were located in Paris, the greatest number of FDIs concerned the 'decision centres' – places where strategic functions of a firm are located (finance, marketing, communication, R&D, etc.), followed by business services, and R&D, engineering and design centres. Table 10.8 shows the breakdown of FDI activities in the last 5 years.

TABLE 10.7 Main countries of origin by number of jobs in 2023

Countries of origin	*Companies*	*%*	*Jobs created*	*%*
United States	102	24.87	4,003	35.70
United Kingdom	40	9.75	1,121	9.99
Germany	26	6.34	778	6.93
Ireland	7	1.70	592	5.28
Canada	20	4.87	573	5.11

Source: Choose Paris Region (2024).

TABLE 10.8 Breakdown of activities involved in FDI investments in Paris Region and the corresponding jobs

	Investments					*Jobs*				
Type of activity	*2019*	*2020*	*2021*	*2022*	*2023*	*2019*	*2020*	*2021*	*2022*	*2023*
Decision centre	219	162	211	228	167	3,242	2,028	4,062	3,858	2,637
Business services	60	61	42	45	65	2,534	4,073	1,346	2,463	3,771
R&D, engineering, design	42	41	50	61	38	1,353	793	1,367	1,925	590
Consumer services	30	24	33	30	42	1,224	367	1,725	693	1,031
Sales points	43	28	37	27	36	976	879	890	391	665
Manufacturing	18	16	16	21	39	231	476	382	525	1,088
Logistics	3	4	15	19	23	100	2,181	406	1,082	1,430
Total	**415**	**336**	**404**	**431**	**410**	**9,660**	**10,797**	**10,178**	**10,937**	**11,212**

Source: Choose Paris Region (2024).

Hi-tech FDI in Paris Region

Paris was eager to host hi-tech FDI from around the world. Several initiatives demonstrated its interest in attracting such investment. In 2004, France launched the policy of innovation and industry clusters and, within this framework, Paris Region became home to clusters in the hi-tech industries. Such clusters included Systematic Paris Region (European innovation and technology cluster in digital technologies and Deep Tech), Medicen cluster (high-tech healthcare and new therapies cluster), Cap Digital (digital and ecological transformation cluster), ASTech Paris Region (Aeronautics, space and defence), NextMove (Automotive and mobility industry). Systematic Paris Region was the most developed cluster in cutting-edge technologies. It focused on six technological hubs: Data Science & Artificial Intelligence, Cyber & Security, Digital Infrastructure & Internet of Things, Digital Engineering, Optics & Photonics (including Quantum Technologies) and Open Source. In its operations, Systematic

Paris Region relied on the best academic research labs such as CEA List, IRT SystemX and INRIA, and unique infrastructures such as Supercomputers Joliot-Curie (22PetaFlops).

The Paris Saclay area concentrated a large number of educational and research institutions, including Paris Saclay University and the Ecole Polytechnique, the most prestigious school in France whose alumni included three Nobel Prize winners: Jean Tirole (Nobel Prize in Economics, 2014), Maurice Allais (Nobel Prize in Economics, 1988) and Henri Becquerel (Nobel Prize in Physics, 1903), as well as former Presidents of France (Marie François Sadi Carnot, Valéry Giscard d'Estaing and Albert Lebrun). In 2023, in the Shanghai University Ranking, three universities from Paris Region were among the top 10 universities in the world in Mathematics: Paris Saclay University (#2), Sorbonne University (#4) and Paris Cité University (#7).[8] HEC Paris was Europe's number one business school in the Financial Times ranking, and INSEAD's MBA programme ranked second in the world. In 2021, Paris Region's R&D workforce numbered 186,264, including 135,531 researchers.[9] According to Eurostat data for 2022, Paris Region hosted 774,200 scientists and engineers, followed by Greater London (with 619,500).[10] Paris was home to the 'French Tech' since 2013, an ecosystem of hi-tech start-ups and institutions supporting their development. According to the EY report (EY, 2022), starting from 2017, the French Tech ecosystem experienced dazzling growth, placing it among the most dynamic ecosystems on the planet in 2021, according to the World Intellectual Property Organisation. In 2022, French technology companies raised €13.5 billion, putting them in first place in the European Union. Paris was the centre of this vibrant development. In 2017, Station F was created in Paris. Station F was a startup campus, spreading over 34,000 square meters located in the Freyssinet Hall in Paris. Created by Xavier Niel, the founder of Free, Station F, home to 1,000+ start-ups, 30+ international startup programs, 1,500+ total residents since its creation, was the largest startup campus in the world.[11]

It is very difficult to distinguish clearly hi-tech FDI from other FDI. This is because hi-tech investment is not necessarily related to the digital technology industries. There can be hi-tech investment in other industries, such as for example automotive (sensors), or medical equipment industry (digital diagnostics solutions), to name just a few. Nevertheless, an insight into hi-tech investment can be gained by considering investment in some sectors and industries, which are known for the widespread use of cutting-edge technologies. The evolution of the hi-tech foreign investment in the Paris Region from 2017 to 2023 is shown in Table 10.9.

The figures above show that close to a quarter of all investments in Paris Region were hi-tech investments. Two cases – one of a small company and one of a large company are interesting to examine as illustrative cases of hi-tech FDI in Paris Region – IQM, a small quantum computer company

TABLE 10.9 Hi-tech foreign investment in Paris Region, 2017–2023

	Investments					*Jobs*				
	2019	*2020*	*2021*	*2022*	*2023*	*2019*	*2020*	*2021*	*2022*	*2023*
Software and computer services	96	84	65	75	67	1,874	1,942	2,303	1,742	1,404
Electric, electronic and computer equipment	17	15	17	20	12	254	254	205	340	266
Electronic components	4	1	2	2	5	37	50	16	230	130
Telecom operators and Internet access providers	2	4	5	1	3	35	210	452	10	130
Total	119	104	89	98	87	2,200	2,456	2,976	2,322	1,930

Source: Choose Paris Region (2024).

from Finland and Twilio, a large company of more than 5,000 employees from the United States.

IQM's FDI in Paris Region

IQM was founded in 2018 in Finland by a team of scientists, with the desire to build quantum computers that would impact humanity. The company was led by Dr. Jan Goetz and Dr. Mikko Välimäki. IQM started as a spin-out from Aalto University and VTT in Finland. At the time of its foundation, there was an increasing interest in quantum technology in the public and private sectors. The founding team envisioned to build a quantum computer from scratch. The work started with technological breakthroughs that allowed the building of large-scale quantum processors. Then the work progressed to the design of unique hardware and digital-analog quantum computing. There were many companies in the quantum computer domain, including giants such as IBM, Google, Microsoft, AWS (Amazon) and Alibaba, and a high number of smaller players. Although of small size (less than 500 employees), in 2024, IQM was one of the leading companies in quantum computing. It built and supplied full-stack quantum computers and applications for High Power Computers to universities, firms and research institutes. Key products were IQM Radiance, the most advanced superconducting quantum computer and IQM Spark, a superconducting quantum computer tailored for universities and research labs.

The primary focus of IQM was crafting scalable hardware tailored for universal quantum computers, with an emphasis on superconducting technology. IQM was working on the development of next-generation quantum processors, all by using in-house technology. Distinguishing itself from numerous competitors that chose the 'cloud' approach, IQM concentrated on developing computers for research and supercomputing centres.[12]

In addition to its headquarters in Espoo, Finland, IQM had offices in Munich, Germany, Madrid, Spain, Paris, France, Singapore and Palo Alto, USA. The objectives of IQM, as stated by the company were the following:

- To use quantum computing technologies for the well-being of humankind and create a safer world for future generations;
- To retain technology sovereignty and establish Europe as a technology leader in order to create a secure future;
- To create jobs by commercializing quantum hardware and software;
- To reskill the workforce with industrial training and education programs;
- To create networks of decision-makers, policymakers and universities in order to put quantum computing on the European agenda.

In 2021, IQM created IQM France SAS, in Paris, through FDI. IQM France SAS was a subsidiary owned 100% by IQM Finland. This was IQM's fourth European office. With this investment, IQM created 20 jobs. Its activity was R&D, Engineering and Design within the 'Electric, electronic and computer equipment' sector. In Paris Region, IQM was set to collaborate and co-design quantum computers with customers in aviation, space and cybersecurity. It was also to focus on HPC integration and to offer quantum accelerators to supercomputing centres worldwide.

In the first phase of its establishment, IQM France aimed to tap into the large pool of talents in Paris Region. In Paris Region there was a concentration of many players of the French quantum ecosystem in a relatively small geographic area.[13] Starting with a core team of quantum scientists, business developers and product managers, the aim of IQM France was to create a centre of excellence and to create synergies with the French quantum ecosystem made up of leading universities, research institutes, the growing start-up ecosystem and excellent infrastructure.[14]

Twilio's FDI in Paris Region

Twilio Inc. was an American cloud communications company traded on the New York Stock Exchange. In 2024, it had around 5,000 employees. It was founded in 2008 by Jeff Lawson, Evan Cooke and John Wolthuis in Seattle, but its headquarters later moved to Rincon Center, San Francisco, California. Twilio provided programmable communication tools for making and receiving phone calls, sending and receiving text messages, and performing other communication functions using its web service Application Programming Interfaces (APIs). An API is a kind of software interface enabling two or more computer programmes or components to communicate with each other to exchange data, features and functionality.[15] In November 2008 Twilio launched Twilio Voice, an API allowing to make and receive phone calls completely hosted in the cloud.[16] This was followed by text messaging API and SMS shortcodes. Twilio benefited from venture capital funding in several rounds. It then filed for IPO on New York Stock Exchange and started trading in 2016. Twilio acquired several companies, both in the United States and abroad.

Twilio was a cloud communication platform enabling client companies to build, scale and operate their communication experience. It was a customer engagement platform helping client companies to create bonds and engagement with their customers using multiple channels (phone, SMS, email and video). Twilio used Amazon Web Services to host its communication infrastructure via APIs. Twilio supported open source software development. It launched Open VBX, Stashboard, Banker's Bow, Flask Restful and others.[17]

Twilio opened a 'decision centre' type office in the 'software and computer services' sector in the very heart of Paris in 2019 through a greenfield investment. Twilio France SARL was 100% owned by Twilio. It was Twilio's first FDI in France and it involved the creation of seven jobs. To oversee the opening of its office in France, Twilio recruited Jeremy Greenbaum, who had previously been in charge of the South Europe market at Box.com.[18] By recruiting an experienced executive who had previously worked at Google and Microsoft, Twilio was aiming to attract French firms and their developers to use its platform of communication services. Twilio was targeting a variety of French firms such as department stores, financial companies, fast food, distribution and retail firms, to help them strengthen their marketing engagement and client relationships. Soon after the opening of its offices in Paris, Twilio's clients included Galeries Lafayette, Domino's Pizza, Uber and Evaneos. Talking about why Twilio chose Paris Region Jeremy Greenbaum explained:

> The French business environment consists of both a big startup ecosystem and well-established enterprises. Both of these are important to Twilio, as a company that helps digital natives grow and supports digital transformation in large organizations. There are several well-respected educational establishments and also organizations hiring and developing a range of skills and capabilities, which creates a diverse and high-quality talent pool. Within technology, the Paris region is strong and offers a lot of opportunities for both businesses and individuals. A lot of tech companies have established a presence in France, and notably in Paris, and the environment is therefore very dynamic with a lot of potential to find and embrace new challenges.[19]

TABLE 10.10 Comparison between IQM and Twilio cases

	IQM	*Twilio*
Year of FDI to Paris Region	2021	2019
Jobs created	20	7
Headquarters' country	Finland	United States
Headquarters' continent	Europe	North America
Type of investment	R&D, engineering, design	Decision centre
Motives for FDI as indicated by the company	Access a large pool of hi-tech assets in Paris Region (engineers, scientists, ...), create synergies and develop projects in Quantum computing.	Tap into a large client base in the hi-tech sector, made up of start-ups, SMEs and large companies and exploit business opportunities.

Comparison of IQM's and Twilio's investments in Paris Region

As presented above, both IQM and Twilio made high-tech investments in the Paris Region. Although to some extent similar, two investments also exhibited differences. In Table 10.10, the two cases are compared against key points.

From Table 10.10, we see that the motives of IQM and Twilio for investing in Paris Region were very different. This suggests that Paris was offering a range of different opportunities for companies in the hi-tech sectors.

Prospects for the future

In 2024, Paris Region was very vibrant and attractive for hi-tech investment. Along with a well-developed hi-tech ecosystem, the Olympic Games – Paris 2024 – attracted a lot of investment. Paris Region featured high numbers of scientists, research institutions, competitiveness clusters and other important assets in hi-tech industries. It attracted many investments in this area, which chose Paris Region for different reasons, such as the large size of the market, business opportunities and the ability to tap into valuable R&D assets. However, there was also fierce competition between global cities in attracting FDI. Could Paris continue attracting increasing levels of hi-tech FDI after the Olympic Games?

Acknowledgements

The author is grateful to Choose Paris Region, and in particular to Lionel Grotto, Arthur Castel, Florence Humbert and Thomas Fauvel for their help in preparing this chapter.

Notes

1 https://www.startupblink.com/
2 Choose Paris Region, the Paris Île-de-France Regional Chamber of Commerce and Industry and l'Institut Paris Region (2024) Paris Region Facts and Figures 2024, (https://www.chooseparisregion.org/sites/default/files/pdf/Paris-Region-Facts-Figures-2024/Paris-Region-Facts-Figures-2024.pdf).
3 In the Facts and Figures, the names of the sources are indicated below the graphs or tables, particularly for attractiveness studies. Numerous data are extracted from INSEE (by ticking the appropriate theme for the Paris Region (Ile-de-France), Eurostat (in NUTS 2 regions), various ministries (Education, Research, etc.), accessible online as open data or in online publications.
4 https://www.kearney.com/service/global-business-policy-council/gcr/2023-full-report
5 https://www.schroders.com/en-gb/uk/intermediary/spotlight/global-cities/global-cities-index/
6 https://mori-m-foundation.or.jp/english/ius2/gpci2/index.shtml
7 Choose Paris Region (2024). Bilan de l'Attractivité 2023 (https://www.chooseparisregion.org/sites/default/files/pdf/Bilan-IDE-2024/Choose-Paris-Region-Bilan-Attractivite-2023.pdf).
8 Choose Paris Region (2024). Bilan de l'Attractivité 2023, (https://www.chooseparisregion.org/sites/default/files/pdf/Bilan-IDE-2024/Choose-Paris-Region-Bilan-Attractivite-2023.pdf).
9 Choose Paris Region, the Paris Île-de-France Regional Chamber of Commerce and Industry and l'Institut Paris Region (2024). Paris Region Facts and Figures 2024, (https://www.chooseparisregion.org/sites/default/files/pdf/Paris-Region-Facts-Figures-2024/Paris-Region-Facts-Figures-2024.pdf).
10 Data for Greater London refer to 2019, as Greater London has left the EU on 01/01/2021 and is no longer included in Eurostat: Scientists and Engineers in NUTS2 regions.
11 «Avec Station F, Xavier Niel s'impose comme figure incontournable du monde des start-up», *lesechos.fr*, 29 juin 2017.
12 https://thequantuminsider.com/2023/12/29/quantum-computing-companies/
13 https://www.chooseparisregion.org/fr/success-stories/le-groupe-finlandais-iqm-rejoint-l%C3%A9cosyst%C3%A8me-quantique-de-l%C3%AEle-de-france
14 https://www.meetiqm.com/newsroom/press-releases/iqm-expansion-to-france See also: https://www.chooseparisregion.org/success-stories/finnish-group-iqm-joins-paris-regions-quantum-ecosystem
15 https://www.ibm.com/topics/api
16 Kincaid, Jason (February 9, 2010). 'Twilio's Telephony API Now Lets Applications Send And Receive SMS Messages.' TechCrunch.
17 https://en.wikipedia.org/wiki/Twilio
18 https://www.lemondeinformatique.fr/actualites/lire-twilio-specialiste-des-communications%C2%A0cloud-%C2%A0s-installe-a-paris%C2%A0-maj-%C2%A0-77254.html
19 https://www.chooseparisregion.org/success-stories/twilio-expands-its-international-presence-offices-paris

Reference

Choose Paris Region. (2024). *Foreign direct investment in Paris Region 2017–2023*. Choose Paris Region.

11

CASE 11: ATTRACTING CUTTING-EDGE TECHNOLOGIES TO LOCAL ECOSYSTEMS – THE SCALEUP LANDING PAD HAMBURG

Joachim Arnold

Abstract

This chapter explores the strategic shift in Foreign Direct Investment (FDI) promotion towards high-value project attraction, focusing on the emerging role of soft-landing programmes to attract technologies and drive innovation, sustainability and regional development. This case study examines the Scaleup Landing Pad Hamburg (SLPH), a soft-landing programme that evolved from a general business set-up incentive for foreign SMEs to an innovation-focused FDI attraction initiative that partnered with local corporates to address business challenges through technology pilots. Leveraging a 'venture clienting' model together with local corporates the programme attracted scale-ups that advanced Hamburg's technology ecosystem and drove regional economic growth. The programme's emphasis on targeted innovation attraction reflected a broader trend in FDI promotion, prioritising long-term economic benefits over mere investment volume.

Foreign Direct Investment (FDI) promotion was undergoing a strategic shift towards attracting high-value projects in the 2020s. This marked a significant evolution in how countries and regions approached FDI. Traditionally the focus of investment promotion agencies was on maximising the volume of investments projects and jobs, irrespective of the type and quality of them. Now rather than simply seeking any form or size of investment project, governments and agencies increasingly focused on attracting investments that offered significant long-term benefits, such as driving innovative industries and fostering ecosystems, and projects that enhanced sustainability and regional development. High-value investments often lead to the creation of high-skilled jobs, foster knowledge transfer and promote economic diversification. This new strategic focus required innovative and targeted approaches

DOI: 10.4324/9781003483410-15

to investment attraction to identify and embed global industry leaders and emerging scaleups that had developed technologies that support the development of clusters and shaped future industry structures in the region.

Soft-landing programmes as a non-fiscal economic development tool aimed at attracting foreign companies to a region had been around for more than two decades. Offered to primarily small- and medium-sized companies for a limited time by government institutions, the programmes typically provided free dedicated office or co-working spaces and created a supportive environment for businesses to initiate their operations. The main rationale for the programmes was to alleviate costs associated with establishing a physical space and company establishment. In addition, they facilitated access to the network and integration into the local ecosystem. Following the traditional approach in supporting with establishing a local entity, soft landing programmes did not differentiate by company but rather offered the service to any interested company. In line with the shift towards high value investment attraction, soft landing pad programmes were becoming more selective to support companies that advanced technology ecosystems, drove innovation and solved regional economic challenges.

This chapter delves into the Scaleup Landing Pad Hamburg (also referred to as Scaleup Hamburg – a Landing Pad Programme or SLPH), a case study of a soft-landing programme that served as a non-monetary measure in FDI attraction. It illustrates the programme's evolution from a traditional soft-landing pad model aimed at attracting companies in selected industries to an innovation-first model that attracted technology pilot projects in collaboration with local corporate partners to address their business challenges. At its core the programme's main objective was to attract innovative companies to the Hamburg region. For this, it used a highly tailored targeting approach docking into the 'venture clienting' model of local corporates. The concept of venture clienting was the creation of new ventures within a larger, established organisation. This strategy allowed corporations to innovate and diversify their business portfolios without being constrained by the existing corporate structure and processes. Consequently, attracting new technologies in partnership with local corporates benefitted the wider regional ecosystem and the prosperity of the economy.

Origins of the programme

The SLPH was initially set up to integrate foreign GreenTech scaleups into Hamburg's innovation ecosystem and fill a gap in the local value chain. The programme's goal was to recruit companies that would not only establish a presence in Hamburg but also actively engage with local stakeholders, such as research institutions, industry associations, government bodies and potential collaborators, to cultivate business relationships. The programme provided tailored support services to each participating scaleup, acknowledging the difficulties of scaling GreenTech ventures internationally.

The initiative for the SLPH arose from the Regional Innovation Strategy (RIS) introduced by the Senate in 2021, aiming to foster innovative and sustainable solutions across various sectors. With contributions from over 300 regional stakeholders, the RIS emphasised collaboration between science and business, with Hamburg institutions mandated to actively promote this synergy. Launched in the beginning of 2022, the city of Hamburg economic development agency Hamburg Invest Wirtschaftsförderungsgesellschaft mbH (HIW) was selected by the Ministry for Economics and Innovation (BWI) to receive the funding and execute the programme. As a result, a new Scaleup Hamburg Team was established with the Business Services Department of Hamburg Invest.

The programme was aligned with the institutional goal of positioning Hamburg as an internationally leading destination for innovative companies. It was seamlessly integrated into the existing institutional framework, enhancing Hamburg's mission to become a renowned start-up hub by promoting it to global innovation stakeholders. During the initial phase, the Hamburg Invest team dedicated three months to market analysis and stakeholder engagement to assess the programme's potential. Funded for an initial one-year period, the Scaleup Landing Pad's overall objective was to attract new innovative companies and to strengthen the innovation ecosystem of the City of Hamburg.

For the first pilot phase in year one the programme was fully publicly funded but it required additional funding sources to ensure sustained services afterwards. The Hamburg team turned to identify external sources. In 2023, as part of its internationalisation efforts, the Scaleup Landing Pad set itself the goal of initiating its own project entitled 'Norscale' as part of the EU funding programme 'Interreg-Nordsee,' following the recommendation of the BWI to participate in Interreg as a refinancing source due to budget constraints. In preparation for the application, an international consortium was successfully put together to work on an overarching meta-landing pad, building on the inbound and outbound activities of the respective partners, which largely complement each other. In the end, the application was rejected by the responsible committee due to weaknesses in the project intervention logic. However, the efforts undertaken for Norscale initiated the contact with another project consortium which led to a further application for an Interreg project entitled BRAVE. The aim of this project was to develop new financing models for scaling innovative energy solutions. By connecting the SLPH to the next generation of GreenTech investment, Hamburg Invest aimed to create a replicable model that benefited not only the city of Hamburg but also other regions targeting to scale cleantech solutions.

After the first pilot year, the Scaleup Hamburg team had to expand from four to eight staff members to meet the increasing demands for programme management and enhanced service offer. The increased workload mainly resulted from the individual and very close support of the scaleups as they ran through the programme and then move from participants to becoming investor accounts that need management in their process to set up in Hamburg. With a stronger focus on pilot projects and use cases together with local corporates, the time to manage the corporate partner network had significantly increased.

In contrast to other business attraction programmes that provided specific financial support for pilot projects, this programme offered only non-monetary services. The primary reason was that foreign companies without a local entity were not eligible for monetary funding in the federal state of Hamburg. The IFB did provide financial support schemes but only once an entity was set up locally. The SLPH programme closed this gap through indirect financial support by covering costs for professional services.

Scaleup Landing Pad Services

The SLPH played a pivotal role in fostering strategic business partnerships in the region for the participating companies. The services ranged from market analysis, and regulatory compliance to strategic business model refinement and financial resource access. This comprehensive support facilitated a smoother transition for Scaleups into the German market, positioning Hamburg as the gateway. Specifically, the following 4 pillar approach had been provided to the participating companies from which they could choose based on their individual demands (Figure 11.1).

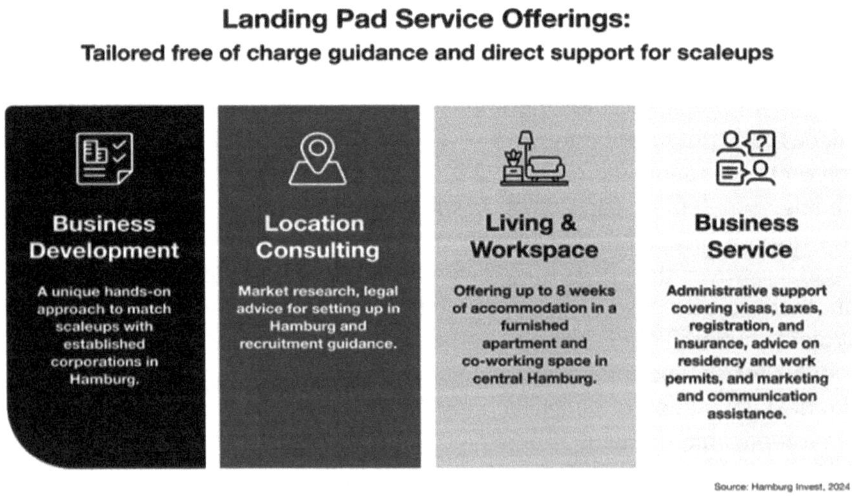

FIGURE 11.1 Landing Pad Service Offerings: Tailored free of charge guidance and direct support for scaleups

Source: Hamburg Invest, 2024.

With the service pillar Business Development, the Scaleup Hamburg team and its selected business development experts provided local market analysis and actively engaged in matchmaking with suitable business partners and potential clients. It also included support for the scaleups in initiating, funding and implementing pilot projects together with the corporate partners. Scaleups were connected with mentors, industry experts and potential collaborators to expand their network and received support in preparing pitches or attending business meetings.

As part of the location consulting offer, scaleups could select a market potential analysis, organisational development advice or recruitment services. The market potential analysis became the most relevant type of service in this pillar, especially as the focus had shifted to the launch of pilot projects that tested the scalability and effectiveness of technology solutions in Hamburg's ecosystem and the broader German market.

These service packages went beyond the traditional support packages of soft-landing pad programmes. Even though many programmes did offer general matchmaking support to facilitate market entry, tailored company specific, proactive business development services for client identification and qualification were usually not included in Landing Pad Programmes offered by government organisations. In Hamburg, however, they had emerged as the most utilised service and, according to the participants' feedback, created the highest value to the scaleups.

Finally, the SLPH offered practical infrastructure support around living and workspace as well as administrative support in establishing a local business. The living and workspace offer was including up to 8 weeks of accommodation in a furnished apartment in central Hamburg and access to co-working spaces or private offices. This support service was also highly valued by the participating companies.

To effectively deliver this wide array of support services with a limited in-house team, the SLPH established an operational model with pre-selected service partners to provide various services on demand.

Promotion and recruitment of applicants

Initially, the industry targeting strategy was focused on the sectors: Mobility and Logistics, Renewable Energy and Advanced Materials in Construction Industry and the Maritime industry. However, feedback after the first year's cohort indicated that a more refined, technology-specific approach would better serve to localise scaleups and contribute to regional economic value. In 2023 the programme positioning expanded to a more holistic theme of Green Technologies covering applications in a variety of key industries that Hamburg Invest was aiming to attract FDI into to grow the regional economy.

The programme's primary goal had been to attract international scaleups interested in expanding into Germany, with a geographic focus on markets such as the Nordics, Netherlands, the United Kingdom, Israel and Singapore. The aim was not to relocate companies within Germany but to introduce new technologies to the German market from abroad. The target markets were in line with the overall FDI attraction strategy of the City of Hamburg. As the programme pivoted towards technology-specific targeting, the geographic focus became less relevant. Instead, selected companies with a specific expertise were approached in a very targeted proposition-based message regardless of the originating market.

With a limited marketing budget, initial efforts to recruit companies required hands-on sales tactics and direct outreach to companies that matched the industry target segments or presented a clear fit for a pilot project. In addition, a network of multipliers comprised of the Hamburg Invest international offices and the German Chambers of Commerce Abroad (AHK) as well as scaleup associations such as SCALE (European network of cities with a vibrant startup ecosystem), Startup Champs Germany (cooperation of Germany's leading start-up cities) and the German Digital Hub Initiative (network of 25 de:hubs that stimulates innovation) was built to promote SLPH. These partners together with specialised professional service firms in investor company recruitment proved to be an effective complementary network to mobilise programme applicants.

With the more tailored approach addressing the technology solution needs of the local ecosystem, the target group definition evolved from industry-specific to use case or pilot project-specific. This shift required the need to develop pilot technology projects with leading local Hamburg corporations and their venture client units, offering scaleups concrete opportunities to develop business cases for the German market in collaboration with prestigious clients. The following venture units within Hamburg's leading corporations became integral partners to the programme:

- HHLA Next, venture builder for Hamburg's Port, fostered innovation in Logistics.
- OTTO DOCK 6 (Venture Client Unit) supported resolving complex corporate challenges via startups and helped to test solutions for the leading e-commerce platform OTTO and other organisation of the Otto Group.
- Jungheinrich Venture Builder within global intralogistics leader Jungheinrich AG sought innovative solutions in intralogistics and material handling equipment.
- The Airbus StartUp Engagement Team engaged in start-ups working on advanced aerospace solutions in a range of areas, from autonomy to industrial efficiency.
- Beiersdorf Venture Capital supported startups through investments and access to the Beiersdorf assets and expertise to jointly drive disruptive technologies, new business models and skin care innovations.

Additionally, GovTecHH, as the city's own venture client unit, served as a vital link between scaleups and Hamburg's government institutions. Acting as the initial point of contact for scaleups seeking collaboration with the local government, it helped identify the challenges and needs of authorities and state organisations.

Building on a strong network of international promotion partners as well as the collaboration with local corporate partners pilot projects were seen as the key ingredients to drive high-quality scaleups into the programme.

Selection of applicants

A tightly managed selection process for the participating scaleups by SLPH ensured that the programme focused only on mature companies with a proven track record. The basic filter criteria for scaleups aligned with the OECD's definition, that a scaleup company is one that grows its employment numbers or turnover by more than 20% per annum over a period of three years, with at least 10 employees at the start of the period.

Further criteria included being active in green technologies applicable to mobility, logistics, energy, construction or advanced materials and a proven product-market fit in the home market. Candidate firms should have not yet been present in Hamburg but ready to enter the German market and confirm readiness to scale in the Hamburg ecosystem within the timeframe of the programme. This required a clear demonstration of dedicated resources for expansion and an initial proof of interest.

The application process consisted of an online form and providing a pitch deck with the proposition to participate in the programme. This was designed to assess the compatibility of the scaleups with Hamburg's business environment and their approach to the local use case.

The applicants then entered a selection process managed by Hamburg Invest and a jury of local industry and technology experts ensuring that only the most promising scaleups were selected, maintaining the quality and potential impact of the programme. The first screening and short-listing of applications was conducted by Hamburg Invest. Following this, first a pre-jury and then a main jury reviewed this group of candidates to take the final selection decision based on a custom rating system. Each jury consisted of ten members from Hamburg Invest, the participating corporations and subject matter experts.

The final selection process ensured that the companies were well-suited for the Hamburg ecosystem and the use cases that were piloted. In addition to the basic criteria which provided evidence of company growth, the concrete fit with solving business challenges with corporate partners emerged as the most important criteria for the application selection.

Results and successes

The SLPH programme established itself as a successful model for enabling market expansion. With 35 companies participating from 4 continents and 14 countries the programme's international reach was impactful. The positive feedback from participants highlighted the effectiveness of the programme's mentorship in market entry, establishment and the creation of valuable business opportunities.

The emphasis of the programme on tailored access to customers and partners was particularly noteworthy, as it aligned with the participants' needs for support that directly contributed to their business objectives. Specifically, the matchmaking and client access through business development and the pilot projects were elements that were well-received.

In total the programme attracted 164 registered applicants, of which 93 completed the application. Out of this group, 35 participants were selected across the 3 cohorts between 2022 and 2024. The total programme KPIs are listed below number of companies participating in the programme (Figure 11.2).

The key performance metric for the programme was not measured on companies which set up, but on the number of scaleups that applied and entered the programme, and specifically the number of pilot projects started. By August 2024, a total of 14 companies initiated a pilot project in the Hamburg region, of which 11 had successfully completed. Four companies had already set up in Hamburg. The wider cumulative effect of the programme went beyond this. With the programme up to August 2024, Hamburg Invest managed to build up a pipeline of 379 companies with innovative technologies that were looking to expand to Germany.

Scaleup Landing Pad Hamburg Key Results 2022-2024

	2022-2024*	2022	2023	2024*
Matchmaking (Contacts)	379	123	190	75
Matchmaking (Meetings)	147	89	46	20
Applicants (Registrations)	164	43	52	69
Applicants (Completed)	93	30	27	36
Programme Participation	35	13	12	10
Pilot Projects (Initiated, ongoing)	16	5	9	2
Pilot Projects (Implemented)	12	4	7	1
Establishment / Representation	5	2	2	1

*until November 2024

Source: Hamburg Invest, 2024

FIGURE 11.2 Scaleup Landing Pad Hamburg Key Results 2022–2024

Source: Hamburg Invest, 2024.

Despite its successes, the programme has encountered challenges. In some cases, participants found greater success conducting business outside of Hamburg, due to an inadequate product-market fit within the city. This was a significant challenge for the SLPH, as it affected the programme's efficacy. This learning accelerated the strategic focus on specific use cases within the region to tie scaleups to local corporate partners through collaborations. Case studies of companies that went through the programme and established their base in Hamburg provided additional insights into how they achieved successful integration into the local business ecosystem.

SunGreenH2 from the 2022 cohort specialised in building high-performance electrolysers for green hydrogen production. Founded in 2020 in Singapore, SunGreenH2 wanted to bring its affordable green hydrogen technology to Europe, specifically the German market. The company was particularly drawn to the Landing Pad as it valued the connections to partners. The owners were very business development oriented and sought opportunities for the greatest potential to launch their technology and grow the business. The Landing Pad programme enabled introductions to the right people and partners in Hamburg and helped the company learn about the market and identify the right partnerships and pilot opportunities.

A successful example for the 2023 cohort, was the Norway-based scaleup Infinite Mobility, a manufacturer of solar-powered cargo bikes. The company was originally spun out of SINTEF, the largest independent research organisation in Scandinavia. Infinite Mobility was able to close a pre-seed financing round of 1.2 million euros in 2020. With this backing, Infinite Mobility wanted to expand into new European Markets when they spotted the Landing Pad Programme and the Future Hamburg Award. The founder successfully applied to the programme which provided support in the search for suitable premises and personnel and, above all, in contacting potential business partners in the region. Since then, Infinite Mobility had seen fast international growth closely linked to Hamburg.

The Italian startup Fybra, founded in 2019, developed a technology to improve air quality in schools while reducing energy waste from ventilation. Building on its success in Italy, Fybra sought to expand internationally, with Germany being a natural choice due to its population size and potential as a gateway to other Northern European markets. The founders attended several events in Germany, and during one in Berlin, Hamburg Invest discovered Fybra and encouraged it to apply for the programme. In 2023, Fybra joined the programme, opening doors to the German education sector. The programme facilitated connections with 87 schools in Hamburg, conducted a detailed assessment of 17, and ultimately launched a pilot project with 7 schools. This foundation helped Fybra expand its business in Germany and made Hamburg the strategic base for entering other international markets.

As part of the 2024 cohort, the SLPH was seeking applications in the field of efficient intralogistics. Four corporate partners from Digital Hub Logistics

Hamburg, who were retailers and fulfilment service providers, were looking for solutions to minimise manual labour in intralogistics with focus on palette handling including real time data (digital twin). This included solutions such as autonomous forklifts, palette trackers, multi-use concepts of spaces, warehouse digital twin solutions and other. The partners from the Digital Hub Logistics teamed up with the Landing Pad to attract foreign companies with technologies that they had not been able to find in the German market.

The SLPH achieved international recognition for its innovative approach. In December 2023, it won the Startup Ecosystem Stars Award from the International Chamber of Commerce and 'Mind the Bridge' in Paris, under the categories 'Startup Programmes' and 'SME Support.'

The next stage of the Scaleup Landing Pad Hamburg

The next phase of the SLPH commenced in 2025. The programme was planned to build upon the success of established venture clienting practices fostering collaborations and piloting projects with local corporates. While the exact scope of these initiatives was still being determined, the primary objective remained to address existing technological gaps in the market. Furthermore, the programme aimed at enhancing the innovative capabilities of local companies while concurrently attracting foreign investments to the region.

By partnering with various stakeholders and service providers within Hamburg's ecosystem, the programme established the location as a hub for innovation and sustainable solutions for external scaleups and local businesses, especially SMEs. The curated use cases, developed in collaboration with key stakeholders, were intended to serve as adaptable frameworks across different sectors and industries. These use cases were aligned with political objectives such as achieving carbon neutrality, potentially unlocking opportunities for local, national or international funding and establishing a foundation for the further growth of participating foreign scaleups in Hamburg.

Acknowledgements

This work was developed in collaboration with the Scaleup Hamburg team from the Business Services division of Hamburg Invest and is based on interviews with Sascha Jacobi, Director of Scaleup Landing Pad Hamburg. I would like to extend my sincere gratitude to the entire Hamburg Invest Team for their invaluable guidance and support during the development of this chapter.

12

CASE 12: TEL AVIV – YAFO

The rise of a start-up powerhouse attracting global FDI

Ruxandra Victoria Steriu

Abstract

This case shows how Foreign Direct Investment (FDI) impacted the city of Tel Aviv, including both positive and negative effects on the Israeli city. The period between 1909 and 1990 will be covered to outline a brief history of Tel Aviv and understand the original situation ahead of the economic boom as a result of FDI. The period between 1990 and 2024 will then be covered to assess the role FDI played in the city's economic and political transformation. The chapter will seek to understand the effects of these investments and the role which the military played to shape the city and attract wider foreign investment. This chapter will mostly cover venture capitalist and foreign acquisitions in Tel Aviv and explore the economic development of Tel Aviv as a result of FDI. The conflicts around the city's borders have been prevalent for many years after 1909, but the growth has been consistent up until 2023. How did FDI shape the Israeli city's economy and its culture, witnessing a remarkable growth despite the ongoing conflicts and how can the city recover in the aftermath of the 2024 conflicts?

A brief history of Tel Aviv – how FDI shaped the city

Tel Aviv was founded by sixty families at the beginning of the twentieth century in 1909. It was previously referred to as 'Ahuzat Bayit' and later changed to Tel Aviv, meaning 'hill of spring'. The city was originally a suburb for the Arab Jaffa city, where middle-class immigrants set to build a European-style suburb to serve as the new Jewish state, which was run by an elected autonomous local council (Razin, 2024a, 2024b). The city and its inhabitants were constantly affected by tumultuous historical events, spanning from when the Jewish inhabitants were banished from the city during World War I by

DOI: 10.4324/9781003483410-16

the Turks, all the way to recent times in 2023, with conflicts at its border (Jewish Virtual Library, 2024). Before 1940, following the defeat of the Ottoman Empire, Britain took control of the city and under the Balfour declaration attempted to provide a home for European Jews fleeing Nazi persecution (BBC, 2023). In 1948, the Jewish military forces took control of the ancient city of Jaffa, which caused the expansion of Tel Aviv beyond its borders. Later on in 1990, the number of immigrants increased significantly, with a majority coming from the former Soviet Union and other European countries. This caused the gentrification of the city, which further enticed a wealth of foreign investors initiating a real estate boom and a proliferation of high-technology start-ups (Razin, 2024a, 2024b).

Despite the political unrest and the violent conflicts surrounding its borders throughout the years, Tel Aviv became Israel's second largest city, after Jerusalem, and the country's business, political and cultural centre (Razin, 2024a, 2024b). The historical tensions and complex hostility between the Arab Muslims and Jewish people have long divided the country of Israel, but Tel Aviv remained a dynamic multicultural city, a modern liberal hub allowing technology and innovation to thrive (Razin, 2024a, 2024b). Following this rapid development after 1990, the amount of Foreign Direct Investment (FDI) and Portfolio Investment increased significantly. This peaked in 2000 at nine billion USD, accounting for nine per cent of the country's GDP and was enabled by the creation of the Tel Aviv stock exchange, free from almost all exchange controls (OECD, 2002). The United States and Canada provided the highest investment, which in 2002 accounted for forty-nine per cent of FDI in Israeli equities traded in Tel Aviv. These investments were followed by European companies with a particular interest in high technology sectors such as software, medical devices and semi-conductors, which attracted the highest amount of FDI (OECD, 2002).

Between 2014 and 2024, Tel Aviv recorded major developments in the manufacturing and service sectors, with a focus on technology and communications (City Monitor, 2021). These industries developed to allow breakthroughs in big data and internet security, agricultural technology, bio and water technology. From 2018, Tel Aviv recorded the highest number of start-ups per capita in the world and the highest investment of GDP in research and development (Sheppard, 2018). Tel Aviv University and Technion University ranked sixty-sixth and seventy-fifth in the world for the number of patents generated in the United States in 2018 (thirty-seven and thirty-two respectively). In the same year, Tel Aviv University registered one hundred and twenty-one patents globally, via its Ramot technology transfer arm (Solomon, 2019). The city ranked third in the world in 2023 for the number of AI powered start-ups (Michaeli, 2023). Israel's powerful military, which was funded majorly by the United States since 1946 (AlJazeera, 2023) also contributed to the rapid developments of the city.

The role of the Israeli military in shaping Tel Aviv's FDI journey

After World War II, the United States considered Israel a powerful ally to advance their strategic interest in the Middle East, supporting the nation with almost two hundred and forty-six billion USD between 1946 and 2023 (AlJazeera, 2023). As indicated in Table 12.1, Israel became the largest beneficiary of US foreign aid, for both economic and military assistance. Between 1946 and 2024, Israel received eighty billion USD in economic aid, but the majority of the US foreign aid contributed to Israel's military (Masters & Merrow, 2024).

The United States agreed through a memorandum of understanding to provide the country with military aid of nearly four billion USD a year from 1980 through to 2028 (Masters & Merrow, 2024). The large investments in Israel's military laid the foundation of Tel Aviv's development of the high-tech industry. This led the city's industries to focus strongly on R&D, with state-of-the-art military technology being re-purposed into brand-new start-up ideas. One company with such technology was PillCam, a re-purposed high-accuracy video-guided missile system into a pill-sized video camera. Through this technology, patients could ingest this micro-camera to have their digestive system inspected by medical professionals (Michaeli, 2023). Since 1986, Israeli law stated that Israeli citizens of all genders between the ages of eighteen and twenty must serve a compulsory conscription in the army (UNHCR, 2013). This experience provided the citizens with not only the technical knowledge of advanced military technology, but also with resilience and leadership skills, an asset for managing any company (Michaeli, 2023). When looking for investment opportunities, Venture capitalists (VC) focused mainly on finding strong leadership and teams with unique experience before looking at novel

TABLE 12.1 US foreign aid since World War II, 2023

US foreign aid 1946–2023 – comparison between countries	
Name of country	*Amount received ($BN)*
Israel	263.6
Egypt	151.9
Afghanistan	147.6
Vietnam	134.6
Iraq	91.7
South Korea	88.1
United Kingdom	81.6
India	76.8
Turkey	74.7
France	73

Source: Foreign Assistance, US. (2023). foreignassitance.gov.

technologies (Richard & Kane, 2019). Tel Aviv fostered the environment for start-up founders to become targets of interest for VCs, by combining mandatory military training with a strong culture of continuous fighting. This culture fuelled the start-up founders' disruptive mindsets and desire to reshape and redefine industries (Mitchel, 2016).

The majority of these founders were members of the Israeli Defense Forces (IDF) and one popular company was Waze, founded by Uri Levine. Applying the information he learned while serving in the IDF, he adapted a powerful GPS tracking software into an application that provided driving directions (IDF, 2023). He later sold his company to Google in 2012 which was attracted by its user engagement, and kept the company's headquarters in Tel Aviv (Cohan, 2013). By 2022 and 2024, Tel Aviv hosted the fifth-highest number of unicorns (start-ups valued at over $1bn) worldwide counting no less than ninety-five as of 2022 (Wrobel, 2023a, 2023b). The city was also ranked third in the EMEA region for attracting foreign venture capital investments in 2023, twenty per cent of which were in the cybersecurity industry (Wrobel, 2023a, 2023b).

The government's role in attracting MNEs to invest in Tel Aviv through incentives

VCs played a crucial role in the development of the many start-ups in Tel Aviv. In 2022, Tel Aviv-based start-ups raised nearly seven billion USD in venture capital funding (All Israel News, 2023). The foreign investors took a great interest in these start-ups, which placed Tel Aviv amongst the biggest cities to receive foreign investment in the EMEA region, as shown in Table 12.2.

Table 12.2 also highlighted that between 2020 and 2022, Tel Aviv received more foreign investment than London or Paris. Similarly, large multinationals engaged in various strategic acquisitions, such as the acquisition of Anobit

TABLE 12.2 Total VC investment in selected EMEA hubs 2020–2022

	Investment by investor location 2020–2022				
Investment source	*Tel Aviv*	*Berlin*	*London*	*Paris*	*EMEA average*
Domestic	29%	19%	27%	42%	29%
European	11%	30%	13%	22%	20%
United States	44%	34%	31%	22%	29%
Rest of the World	7%	12%	16%	6%	11%
Undisclosed	9%	5%	13%	8%	11%

Source: Michaeli (2023).

by Apple in 2012 for nearly four hundred million USD (Solomon, 2012), the acquisition of Waze by Google in 2013 for over one billion USD$1.3bn (Rushe, 2013) or the acquisition of CyActive by PayPal in 2015 for sixty million USD (Solomon, 2016).

These companies were also attracted by the various incentives and benefits of conducting business in Tel Aviv, to invest in the city's business ecosystem. Tel Aviv's economic landscape was majorly supported by the Israeli government which provided investment incentives via tax breaks and subsidised workplaces (FDI Intelligence, 2015). The government played a key role in shaping the FDI environment, by creating the Yozma Programme in 1993. This programme was created as a state-owned investment company which fuelled the venture capital sector (Sheppard, 2018). Yozma was initiated to incentivise private capital investment in Israeli ventures, where the government provided tax breaks for foreign VCs and matched any investments with equal government funding (Garbi & Garzik, 2021). The programme proved to be a success immediately after its inception in 1993, as it supplied risk sharing to large MNEs which in turn boosted Tel Aviv's private sector (Bar-El, 2019). The inflow of foreign capital was well received by the Israeli government, who created a special promotion agency called 'Invest in Israel'. This agency offered guidance for foreign investors on regulations and incentives and even provided local business connections with industry leaders for a more seamless local integration (US Department of State, 2023). The government also created the 'Start up Visa' project, financed by the Ministry of Economy which aimed to provide two-year visas for foreign entrepreneurs who wished to open a start-up in Israel. This initiative raised the profile of Tel Aviv as a city for international business collaboration. The city also signed multiple 'city-to-city collaborations', such as the partnership with Berlin. This programme was designed as a start-up exchange of ideas and talent, to promote innovation between the two cities (Israel21c, 2015).

The government also offered tax cuts for tech companies (ranging from six to twenty-five per cent) and eased bureaucratic processes (Sheppard, 2018). This sparked the interest of the worlds' tech giants in the Tel Aviv tech-oriented culture. Google took advantage of the country's visa programme to send engineers in Tel Aviv and launched Google Insights for Search (FDI Intelligence, 2015). Microsoft created the 'Ventures Accelerator Tel Aviv' which supported the start-ups' incubation process and gained visibility of Microsoft customers and partners (FDI Intelligence, 2015). Moreover, IBM invested almost one billion USD in four Tel Aviv-based Israeli companies to collaborate on big data storage solutions (Kalman, 2013). Another global giant investing in Tel Aviv was Coca Cola, who created 'The Bridge' project which connected worldwide start-ups to solve the firm's strategic issues and foster innovation. This exposed the city to a wide base of international entrepreneurs and global markets (Woods, 2016). The number of R&D hubs which were created in the city increased from seventy in 2017 to one hundred and seven by 2020 and continued to grow. Major tech players such as Visa, Google, Ford, Bosch, AOL, Salesforce, PayPal, SAP, eBay, and Amazon developed R&D centres in Tel Aviv to encourage innovation (Leichman, 2020). In 2024, US research firm Start-up Genome ranked Tel Aviv in fourth place in its annual survey on the world most attractive ecosystems (Wrobel, 2024a, 2024b).

Tel Aviv also demonstrated a strong performance in Intellectual Property (IP) generation, especially in creating patents. This was due to the IP legislation and enforcement in Israel, protected through a system of common and statutory law (WIPO, 2004). Israel established a special IP police force unit through joint efforts of the Ministry of Justice, the Attorney General, the Tax Authority and the Police Units, which highlighted the importance the government placed on protecting IP rights (WIPO, 2004). Israel was amongst the first jurisdictions in the world to adopt a twenty-year patent duration after 1990s, after the United States, EU and Japan, and joined the global TRIPS Agreement (Trade-Related Aspects of Intellectual Property Rights) in 1994 (Pugatch et al., 2010). Israel also became a member of most major international treaties on IP rights, including International Convention for the Protection of New Varieties of Plants (1991 Act) and the Universal Copyright Convention (1952). The legal frameworks in place, coupled with Israel's commitment to international agreements, signalled to the global community that foreign investors and MNEs could confidently establish and develop intellectual property in Tel Aviv.

The dark side of FDI – the effects of FDI in Tel Aviv

FDI provided major contributions towards the growth and development of the Tel Aviv city and the wider Israeli economy (Breznitz, 2007). However, the rapid development and economic expansion, as a result of FDI, also impacted the city in negative ways. Factors such as depleted land capacity, greater income inequality and relinquished control of small firms to raise capital raised concerns and worsened the well-being of the city's inhabitants.

Economic expansion always generated an increased demand for land and with a central economical hub like Tel Aviv, firms and residents have been in an endless battle for more space in the city. MNEs have invested and built new R&D centres and enticed young professional immigrants to live in Tel Aviv, increased which caused a larger consumption of land leading to the city expanding to its outer borders (Felsenstein & Ergas, 2002). However, the poorer inhabitants were asked to flee their homes to allow for the rich population of the city and large real estate development companies that acquired more land on the outskirts of the city. One example was the village of Givat Amal Bet, where Jewish refugees and migrants settled in 1947 fleeing the war, prior to the creation of the Israeli state. They were later denied the right to return to the city or even the right to purchase the land they resided in (McKernan, 2021). As Tel Aviv generated more demand for office space and luxury apartments, the small village on the outer borders was fighting with development companies and the Israeli government. The inhabitants demanded compensation and even the right to access water, electricity and upgrade their homes (McKernan, 2021).

The rise in FDI in Tel Aviv also exacerbated the income inequality. In 2021, Tel Aviv was named the world's most expensive city to live in, which surpassed cities such as Paris or Singapore (O'Hare, 2021). Indeed, the effects of the pandemic contributed to prices soaring, but its reputation as a global tech hub further widened the gap between the working and middle class (McKernan, 2021). This extreme demand caused a surge in house prices which forced lower income households to relocate to cheaper areas away from the city, in zones with fewer economic opportunities (OECD, 2020). The house prices in areas outside the Tel Aviv borders declined, which in turn created an impediment to employment and attracting wider Israeli talent (Eckstein et al., 2012). Therefore, companies based in Tel Aviv experienced a skills shortage, especially in the tech and construction industries. These shortages were pushing firms to look abroad for more skilled workers to attract young talent from high to middle income countries (Tress, 2020). The city attracted foreign professionals to immigrate in Tel Aviv, by creating promotion campaigns based on the famous beaches, nightlife and liberal environment, concentrated in the centre and the metropolitan areas (City Monitor, 2021). However, bringing Western liberal values in the form of wealthy migrants exacerbated the religious segregation of the city. Municipalities in Tel Aviv became divided along ethnic and religious lines, where groups with weak socio-economic status were concentrated in separate neighbourhoods, away from the city's employment opportunities (OECD, 2020).

Another important effect caused by increased FDI was the fact that small firms became dependent on funds from foreign companies, and relinquished control in an attempt to raise capital. During their inception, the start-ups attracted significant FDI, as mentioned above, but since the conflicts which began in 2023 received more attention from the media, foreign investment dropped significantly. At the beginning of 2023, there was a sudden decline in the number of transactions and amounts of foreign investment (Wrobel, 2023a, 2023b). This decline was in part due to a judicial overhaul in 2023, where a controversial law was discussed, where the government could weaken the power and decisions of the Supreme Court, which threatened the democratic values of the country (Berg, 2023).

The decline in foreign investment was exacerbated by the latest conflicts in Palestine, when the Tel Aviv start-ups raised the lowest funding since 2017 (Wrobel, 2024a, 2024b). During the first quarter of 2023, the Finance Ministry reported a drop in FDI by sixty per cent compared to the average figures from 2020 to 2022. The decline was also observed in the number of transactions which also witnessed a reduction of eighty per cent. (Middle East Monitor, 2023). While some companies such as Bain Capital Ventures, GGV Capital and 8VC, publicly expressed solidarity with Israel's actions (Cafiero, 2024), several large MNEs and many other foreign investors were distraught by the conflicts and slowed or ceased activities in the city. One such company was Intel, the American computer manufacturer, who suspended the expansion of its micro processing plant (New Straits Times, 2024). Many citizens were called to support in the conflict, meaning that the start-up employees who were members of the IDF had to leave their jobs to go to war. With an on-going skills shortage, the tech industry was amongst the most affected. This majorly impacted the wider Israeli economy that was relying on taxes from this sector as well as tech exports, amounting for fifty per cent of all exports in 2024 (Wrobel, 2024a, 2024b).

Securing the funds for the war also proved to impact the wider economy, as the government efforts focused on acquiring over fifty five billion USD, which slowed down wider economic growth and dropped by over twenty per cent (Kozul-Wright, 2024). The uncertainty and political instability negatively impacted Tel Aviv, not only because the vibrant atmosphere and nightlife have been silenced by the conflicts, but also because many middle-class migrants chose to leave the city, taking away the knowledge and experience that the Israeli firms were relying upon (Abu Amer, 2023). This illustrated the extent to which the city of Tel Aviv relied on foreign investors, threatening to dismantle the rich innovation culture as soon as liberal values were being threatened.

Conclusions – lessons from Tel Aviv's economic ecosystem

The aim of this chapter was to foster a better understanding of how FDI supported the Tel Aviv's development amidst various tumultuous eras of conflicts. The city's rich history revealed its roots as a small suburb of the Ancient city of Jaffa transforming into a modern liberal hub rising like a European hallmark. In a short time span, Tel Aviv attracted the most amount of FDI in the EMEA region and recorded the highest number of start-ups per capita in the world in tech, manufacturing and telecoms. The United States and Canada became the main benefactors and investment powers, primarily for military aid, causing these start-ups to benefit from the influence of the military., The Israel government required mandatory participation in the army, the start-ups' founders have developed their technology knowledge and an entrepreneurial mindset to further attract foreign investors. The government also played an important role in shaping the FDI environment of Tel Aviv, providing investors with tax breaks, reduced bureaucracy and knowledge of local laws and potential partners. Therefore, the world's tech giants manifested a strong interest in the city, investing in the start-ups, shifting their headquarters to Tel Aviv, creating R&D centres and international collaboration programmes. However, the negative effects of FDI in the city revealed greater inequalities in its society with the city expanding into its outer borders in an attempt to address land resource challenges. The conflicts in 2023 threatened to dismantle the economic growth accumulated since the 1990s. The question remained whether the economic development of Tel Aviv, attributed to FDI, was at risk of being compromised due to investors being discouraged by the ongoing conflicts. Amidst the country's political instability, what strategies could the start-ups adopt to detach from the conflicts and maintain the investors' confidence?

References

Abu Amer, A. (2023). Jews' reverse immigration from Israel is on the rise. *Middle East Monitor*. https://www.middleeastmonitor.com/20231006-jews-reverse-immigration-from-israel-is-on-the-rise/

AlJazeera. (2023). How big is Israel's military and how much funding does it get from the US? *Al Jazeera*. https://www.aljazeera.com/news/2023/10/11/how-big-is-israels-military-and-how-much-funding-does-it-get-from-the-us.

All Israel News. (2023). Tel Aviv is second best tech hub for start-ups, according to new report. https://allisrael.com/tel-aviv-is-second-best-tech-hub-for-startups-according-to-new-report

Bar-El, R. (2019). The economic development of the Mediterranean: The case of Israel. *Athens Journal of Mediterranean Studies*, *5*(3), 189–206. https://www.athensjournals.gr/mediterranean/2019-5-3-1-Bar-El.pdf.

BBC. (2023). Israel Gaza war: History of the conflict explained. *BBC News*. https://www.bbc.co.uk/news/newsbeat-44124396

Berg, R. (2023). Israel judicial reform explained: What is the crisis about? *BBC News*. https://www.bbc.co.uk/news/world-middle-east-65086871

Breznitz, D. (2007). *Innovation and the state: Political choice and strategies for growth in Israel, Taiwan, and Ireland*. Yale University Press.

Cafiero, G., (2024). Has the war on Gaza hurt Israel's economy? *Al Jazeera*. https://www.aljazeera.com/economy/2024/1/27/has-the-war-on-gaza-hurt-israels-economy

City Monitor. (2021). Middle Eastern cities: How Tel Aviv enhanced its tech hotspot reputation throughout the pandemic. *City Monitor*. https://citymonitor.ai/economy/tel-aviv-tech-hotspot-covid-pandemic

Cohan, P. (2013). Four reasons Google bought Waze. *Forbes*. https://www.forbes.com/sites/petercohan/2013/06/11/four-reasons-for-google-to-buy-waze/?sh=43d27953726f

Eckstein, Z., Tolkovsky, E., & Tsur, N. (2012). *Are housing prices in Israel high due to small housing inventory*? Gazit-Globe Real Estate Institute, IDC Herzliya.

FDI Intelligence. (2015). Viva Tel Aviv: How the Israeli city's start-up culture is winning admirers. *Financial Times*. https://www.fdiintelligence.com/content/news/viva-tel-aviv-how-the-israeli-citys-startup-culture-is-winning-admirers-60812

Felsenstein, D., & Ergas, Y. (2002). Investing in an emerging node: Foreign-owned companies in the Tel Aviv economy. In D. Felsenstein, E. Schamp, & A. Shachar (Eds.), *Emerging nodes in the global economy: Frankfurt and Tel Aviv compared* (pp. 57–80). Kluwer Academic Publishers.

Foreign Assistance, US. (2023). https://www.foreignassistance.gov/

Garbi, I., & Garzik, L. (2021). Tel Aviv innovation system. In L. Garzik (Ed.), *Successful innovation systems* (pp. 283–318). Springer. https://doi.org/10.1007/978-3-030-80639-2_16
IDF. (2023). *Startup soldiers: From the IDF to high-tech success*. https://www.idf.il/en/mini-sites/our-soldiers/startup-soldiers-from-the-idf-to-high-tech-success/
Israel21c. (2015). *Israel to offer startup visa for foreign innovators*. https://www.israel21c.org/israel-to-offer-startup-visa-for-foreign-innovators/
Jewish Virtual Library. (2024). *Tel Aviv and Jaffa*. https://www.jewishvirtuallibrary.org/tel-aviv-and-jaffa
Kalman, M. (2013). Tel Aviv stands apart as a hub for tech innovation thanks to one single overriding influence: The Israeli armed forces. *BBC Future*. https://www.bbc.com/future/article/20130911-israel-military-key-to-start-ups
Kozul-Wright, A. (2024). Gaza war extends toll on Israel's economy. *Al Jazeera*. https://www.aljazeera.com/economy/2024/8/23/gaza-war-extends-toll-on-israels-economy
Leichman, A. K. (2020). Tel Aviv counts 107 international R&D centers, aims to entice more. *Israel21c*. https://www.israel21c.org/tel-aviv-counts-107-international-rd-centers-aims-to-entice-more/
Masters, J., & Merrow, W. (2024). *U.S. aid to Israel in four charts*. Council on Foreign Relations. https://www.cfr.org/article/us-aid-israel-four-charts
McKernan, B. (2021). Tel Aviv: Poverty and eviction in the world's most expensive city. *The Guardian*. https://www.theguardian.com/world/2021/dec/12/tel-aviv-poverty-eviction-givat-amal-bet-gentrification-worlds-most-expensive-city
Michaeli, M. (2023). *Tel Aviv—A global startup trailblazer*. DealRoom Tel Aviv. https://dealroom.co/uploaded/2023/03/Tel-Aviv-Report-2023-.pdf?x92057
Middle East Monitor. (2023). Foreign investment in Israel declines 60%. *Middle East Monitor*. https://www.middleeastmonitor.com/20230907-foreign-investment-in-israel-declines-60/
Mitchel, J. (2016). Startup nation: This Israeli company uses military principles to build scalable businesses. *Forbes*. https://www.forbes.com/sites/julianmitchell/2016/07/11/startup-nation-this-israeli-company-uses-military-principles-to-build-scalable-businesses/?sh=28dd838c43cc
New Straits Times. (2024) Foreign investors leaving Israel due to war, says report. *New Straits Times*. https://www.nst.com.my/world/world/2024/06/1066943/foreign-investors-leaving-israel-due-war-says-report
O'Hare, M. (2021). These are the world's most expensive cities in 2021. *CNN*. https://edition.cnn.com/travel/article/world-most-expensive-cities-2021/index.html
OECD. (2002). *OECD investment policy reviews: Israel*. OECD Directorate for Financial, Fiscal and Enterprise Affairs. https://www.oecd.org/daf/inv/investmentstatisticsandanalysis/1956091.pdf
OECD. (2020). *Reducing socio-economic differences between municipalities*. https://www.oecd-ilibrary.org/sites/d6a7d907-en/1/3/2/index.html?itemId=/content/publication/d6a7d907en&_csp_=da64d5c22d31da2590bf0f3aba2f2d6b&itemIGO=oecd&itemContentType=book#:~:textThe%20difference%20in%20disposable%20income,do%20so%20(Panel%20B)
Pugatch, M., Teubal, M., & Zlotnick, O. (2010). *7 Israel's high-tech catch-up process: The role of IPR and other policies*. Intellectual Property Rights, Development, and Catch-Up: An International Comparative Study, Oxford Academic. https://doi.org/10.1093/acprof:oso/9780199574759.003.0007
Razin, E. (2024a). Tel Aviv—Yafo. *Britannica*. https://www.britannica.com/place/Tel-Aviv-Yafo
Razin, E. (2024b). History of Tel Aviv—Yafo. *Britannica*. https://www.britannica.com/place/Tel-Aviv-Yafo/History

Richard, D., & Kane, L. (2019). *15 key questions venture capitalists will ask before investing in your startup*. https://www.forbes.com/sites/allbusiness/2019/04/13/questions-venture-capitalists-will-ask-before-investing-startups/?sh=5d80557c4c44

Rushe, D. (2013). Google buys Waze map app for $1.3bn. *The Guardian*. https://www.theguardian.com/technology/2013/jun/11/google-buys-waze-maps-billion

Sheppard, E. (2018). Sun, sand, sea and ... unicorns? Why Tel Aviv is the world's new startup capital. *The Guardian*. https://www.theguardian.com/business-to-business/2018/aug/02/sun-sand-sea-and-unicorns-why-tel-aviv-is-the-worlds-new-startup-capital

Solomon, S. (2012). Apple said to acquire Israel's Anobit for about $390 million. *Bloomberg*. https://www.bloomberg.com/news/articles/2012-01-11/apple-is-said-to-acquire-israeli-component-maker-anobit-for-390-million?embedded-checkout=true

Solomon, S. (2016). Ben-Gurion University, PayPal to join forces on R&D. *The Times of Israel*. https://www.timesofisrael.com/ben-gurion-university-paypal-to-join-forces-on-rd/

Solomon, S. (2019). Tel Aviv U, Technion among 100 universities with most US patents in 2018. *The Times of Israel*. https://www.timesofisrael.com/tel-aviv-u-technion-among-100-universities-with-most-us-patents-in-2018/

Tress, L. (2020). High tech workforce growing but lacks skilled employees, report says. *The Times of Israel*. https://www.timesofisrael.com/high-tech-workforce-growing-but-lacks-skilled-employees-report-says/

UNHCR. (2013). UNHCR Comments on Law No. 3907/2011 Establishment of Asylum Service and First Reception Service, transposition into Greek legislation of Directive 2008/115/EC 'common standards and procedures for returning illegally staying third-country nationals and other provisions'. https://webarchive.archive.unhcr.org/20230531082427/https:/www.refworld.org/docid/5152beb62.html

US Department of State. (2023). *2023 investment climate statements: Israel*. Bureau of Economic and Business Affairs. https://www.state.gov/reports/2023-investment-climatestatements/israel/#:~:text=There%20are%20no%20limits%20to,and%20residency%20requirements%20are%20transparent

WIPO. (2004). *Enforcement of intellectual property rights: National initiatives, case studies and capacity-building needs*. World Intellectual Property Organization. https://www.wipo.int/edocs/mdocs/enforcement/en/wipo_ace_2/wipo_ace_2_12.pdf

Woods, D. (2016). How Coca-Cola is harvesting innovation energy from startups. *Forbes*. https://www.forbes.com/sites/danwoods/2016/12/06/how-coca-cola-is-harvesting-innovation-energy-from-startups/

Wrobel, S. (2023a). Tel Aviv startup ecosystem ranks 2nd in Europe, Mideast and Africa, behind London. *The Times of Israel*. https://www.timesofisrael.com/tel-aviv-startup-ecosystem-ranks-2nd-in-europe-mideast-and-africa-behind-london/

Wrobel, S. (2023b). Treasury: Foreign investments in Israel plunged 60% in 1st quarter this year. *The Times of Israel*. https://www.timesofisrael.com/foreign-investments-in-israel-plunged-60-in-1st-quarter-this-year/

Wrobel, S. (2024a). Amid war with Hamas, Israeli startup funding drops to six-year low. *The Times of Israel*. https://www.timesofisrael.com/amid-war-with-hamas-israeli-startup-funding-drops-to-six-year-low/

Wrobel, S. (2024b). Tel Aviv moves up to 4th place in annual ranking of global tech ecosystems. *The Times of Israel*. https://www.timesofisrael.com/tel-aviv-moves-up-to-4th-place-in-annual-ranking-of-global-tech-ecosystems/

13

CASE 13: INWARD GREENFIELD R&D FOREIGN DIRECT INVESTMENT AND THE DEVELOPMENT OF SHENZHEN'S INNOVATION ECOSYSTEM

Ludan Wu and Dylan Sutherland

Abstract

We explore the pivotal role of greenfield R&D foreign direct investments (FDIs) in transforming Shenzhen's innovation ecosystem and establishing it as a key R&D cluster in China. Since the 1979 economic reforms, Shenzhen has rapidly developed into an innovative city of world-renown – from simple fishing village to the "Silicon Valley of China". It has built a strong ecosystem in a variety of sectors, including telecommunications, biotechnology, and electronics. Multinational enterprises (MNEs) like Intel, Qualcomm, Apple, and ARM, have set up their R&D centres in Shenzhen. This raises several questions: How has FDI to Shenzhen evolved? How has it used foreign capital and technology, particularly R&D-focused greenfield investments, to transform itself into an innovative centre for China and a key part of the new knowledge-driven economic development model?

Background

As a prominent example of China's reform and opening-up policy, Shenzhen, designated as a Special Economic Zone in 1979, has rapidly developed into an international hub of science and technology innovation through the support of foreign capital construction (Fetscherin et al., 2010). Over 40 years plus of China's economic reforms, it has grown from a small fishing village with an annual output of 0.196 billion yuan to a city with a total economic output of 3,248 billion yuan in 2022 (Bureau, 2023) (see Figure 13.1). Shenzhen has not only reinforced its economic and technological status in the Pearl River Delta, it also holds a central role in the region's future development plans, acting as a key driver in the construction of the

DOI: 10.4324/9781003483410-17

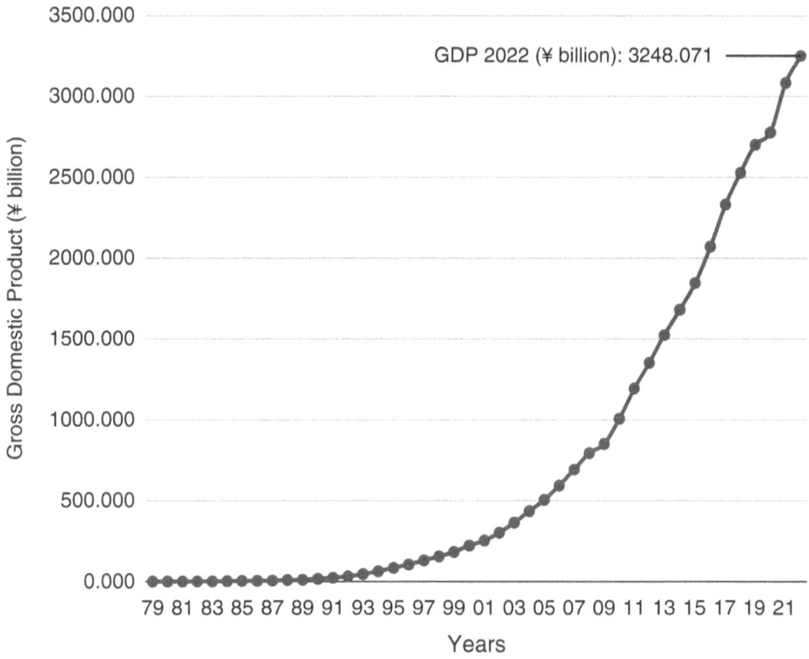

FIGURE 13.1 Gross domestic product of Shenzhen (¥ billion) (1979–2022)

Guangdong-Hong Kong-Macao Greater Bay Area and in the economic and technological advancement of South China (Cheng et al., 2023). Since the reforms began, Shenzhen has pursued several economic goals, including: enhancing exports; attracting foreign investments; and advancing technological innovation, all of which have contributed to its remarkable industrial modernisation (Sheng, 2020). Through its early focus on industrial improvement and active pursuit of foreign investment, Shenzhen has forged an internationalised cluster of technology industries, bolstering regional economic growth and technological innovation.

China's "pioneer members" of reform and opening up (1979–2001)

In the late 1970s, China faced significant social challenges, namely the disparity between the people's growing needs for material and cultural goods and the lagging social production capabilities. To boost economic development, the central government of China decided to open its doors to the world. Shenzhen was chosen as one of the initial four special export zones, a decision influenced by its strategic location and inherent advantages for port development. These zones aimed to increase agricultural exports to

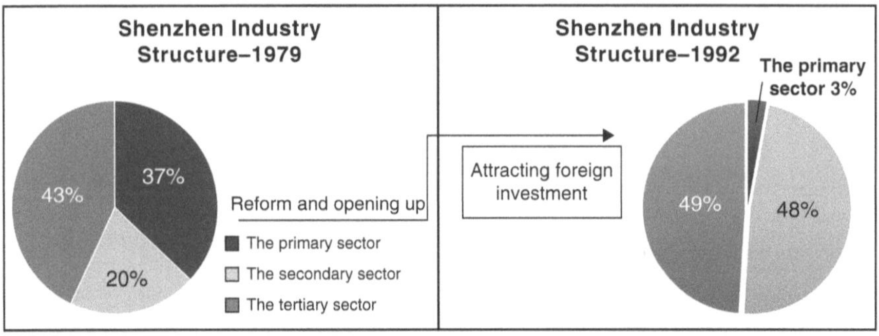

FIGURE 13.2 Shenzhen's economic structure transformation (1979–1992)

generate foreign exchange, fund early industrial infrastructure, and stabilise foreign reserves.

The goal of China's economic reform was to transition from a predominantly agricultural society to an industrialised one. In 1979, Shenzhen's industry structure ratio stood at 37% (primary sector), 20% (secondary) and 43% (tertiary sector). By 1992, with the aid of special economic zone (SEZ) policies, this ratio had shifted to 3% (primary), 48% (secondary), and 49% (tertiary sector) (Bureau, 2010) (see Figure 13.2), signalling Shenzhen's shift from agricultural to industrial development. Greenfield foreign direct investment (FDI) was important in fostering Shenzhen's early growth, which was instrumental in transitioning the city from its agricultural roots to a burgeoning industrial powerhouse. Shenzhen's total actual foreign capital utilisation surged from a modest US$15.37 million to an impressive US$4.902 billion by 2001. This influx was not merely financial; it also facilitated the transfer of technology, management expertise, and global business practices, which were critical in establishing Shenzhen's new industrial sectors, particularly in manufacturing and high technology. The availability of the expansive Chinese market offered substantial potential rewards for foreign investors, making the city a pivotal hub for international business in China.

For the purpose of reform and opening up, the Chinese government implemented a range of policies to attract foreign investment by offering tax incentives, land use rights, and a simplified approval process. Capitalising on these favourable conditions, Shenzhen drew significant investments from Hong Kong, Japan, and Korea. The influx of foreign capital was instrumental in Shenzhen's swift economic growth, markedly enhancing industrial output and contributing to urban infrastructure development and job creation. The city initially predominantly appealed to labour-intensive sectors such as electronics assembly, textiles, and toy manufacturing. During this time, FDI was heavily concentrated in labour intensive manufacturing, in industries with lower technological requirements. While this strategy propelled economic development, it also led to challenges like a homogeneous industrial landscape and environmental concerns.

China's WTO accession (2001–2012): opening the "Window to the World"

With China's accession to the World Trade Organization (WTO) in 2001, Shenzhen earned the title of China's "Window to the World" (Yin et al., 2022). This period was initially marked by significant government-led initiatives aimed at bolstering Shenzhen's role as a global industrial powerhouse. Key policies implemented during this time included the introduction of enhanced tax incentives (2001–2005) for foreign investors, now more specifically targeted at high-tech industries with potential for rapid productivity growth, economies of scale, export market potential and linkages with other sectors. In addition, the establishment of technology transfer frameworks (2003–2007) that encouraged multinational enterprises (MNEs) to set up R&D centres were promoted. Moreover, the central government reformed the nationwide household registration policy (2001–2007), triggering a massive migration of rural labour to urban centres (Du, 2020) in addition to the deep pool of human capital supplied by some of China's leading universities based in and around Shenzhen. Shenzhen therefore experienced a significant influx of labour as well as foreign capital (Du, 2020). These strategic policies were complemented by investments in infrastructure and regulatory reforms aimed at simplifying business operations, making Shenzhen an attractive hub for international trade and manufacturing. The city's SEZ capitalised on these reforms to enhance the competitiveness of key sectors such as electronics, resulting in substantial economic growth.

With WTO membership enhancing international trade conditions and Shenzhen's abundant, cost-effective labour force, the price competitiveness of electronic information products such as electrical machinery, electronics, computer and information components bolstered the SEZ's international competitiveness (Patchell, 2023). The international market's growing demand expanded the Zone's production capacity. Shenzhen's industrial edge extended into the IT manufacturing sector, known for economies of scale and specialised labour division, along with capital-intensive industries, fostering major industrial clusters in communications, new energy, and biomedicine, among others. By 2012, information technology led high-tech industry development; the communication equipment and electronic device manufacturing sector's added value reached 277.214-billion-yuan, accounting for 54.4% of the industry's added value, with high-tech product output at 129.3182 billion yuan, 61% of which were products with independent intellectual property rights (Municipality, 2013).

Initially, local Shenzhen companies, facing competition from foreign companies post-WTO entry, struggled owing to their limited market experience and weaker capabilities vis a vis MNEs. However, they capitalised on the earlier FDI influx, ramping up technological innovation and leveraging global tech resources (PHBS, 2021). Utilising factor upgrading, industrial support, and entrepreneurial innovation, Shenzhen forged expansive domestic and international markets, nurturing advanced production capabilities. This competitive market environment spurred technological advancements. The market and institutional environment of Shenzhen attracted the R&D centres of numerous Fortune 500 MNEs, enhancing the burgeoning high-tech milieu and further harnessing the benefits of large-scale production. Shenzhen thus entered a new phase in attracting foreign investment, optimising investment structures, and enhancing the quality of FDI.

The "Silicon Valley of China" in the new era of the Guangdong-Hong Kong-Macao Greater Bay Area (2020–present)

As the marginal benefits of traditional factors wane and the comparative advantages of the Shenzhen SEZ face challenges, industrial transformation became essential. R&D investment and technological progress became the driving forces of industrialisation. A consistent increase in R&D expenditure in Shenzhen was correlated with a commensurate increase in the number of patents certified over this period (see Figure 13.3). Investment-driven and innovation-driven development strategies are powering the industrial

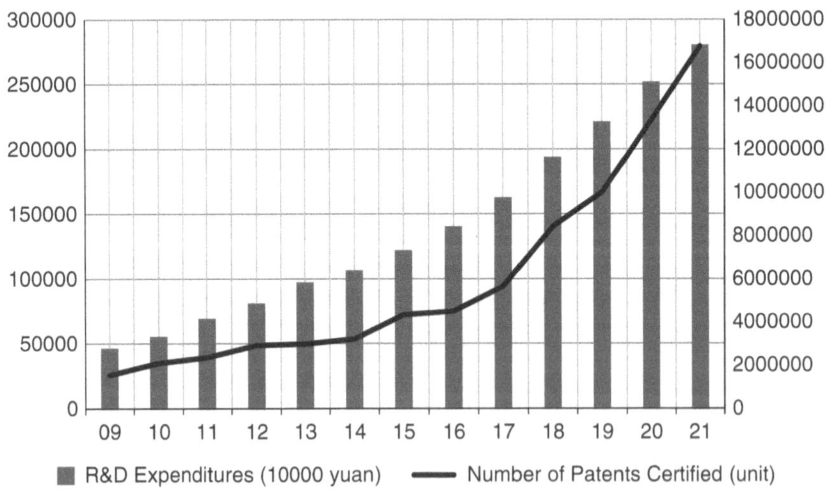

FIGURE 13.3 Shenzhen's R&D expenditure and patent growth (2009–2021)

development, transformation, and upgrading of the Shenzhen SEZ at this stage. After the first decade of the 21st century, Shenzhen built a mature regional innovation system with high-tech industry clusters that benefitted from increasingly visible economies of scale (Dan, 2020).

Recognising the need for high-quality development and using science and technology innovation to generate new momentum, China's central government emphasised during the 14th Five-Year Plan passed on 29 October 2020, by the government's Fifth Plenary Session of the Nineteenth Central Committee, the need to elevate the level of opening up and strongly support the Guangdong-Hong Kong-Macao Greater Bay Area's establishment as an international science and technology innovation hub (Tai et al., 2022). However, the global pandemic and the rise of anti-globalisation trends, along with escalated US-China trade conflicts, introduced uncertainties (Luo & Witt, 2021). The United Nations Conference on Trade and Development's World Investment Report 2020 forecasts a 40% drop in global FDI flows for 2020 and highlights the uncertainty of Shenzhen's foreign investment prospects (UNCTD, 2020).

The impacts of FDI vary across countries and regions. In Shenzhen, FDI has contributed to enhancing the region's innovation capacity both through spill-over effects and via the additional competitive pressures it placed upon local enterprises. At the onset of the 21st century, amid global economic shifts and a deepening commitment to China's open-door policy, Shenzhen began to realign and enhance its approach to FDI (CPRC, 2023b). Addressing the dual challenges of rising labour costs and environmental concerns, the Shenzhen government launched a suite of policy initiatives. These included ramping up financial and tax incentives for high-tech companies, establishing state-of-the-art industrial parks and welcoming international R&D centres of leading MNEs. Such initiatives drew increased FDI into the high tech sector, propelling a rapid evolution and sophistication of Shenzhen's industrial composition. The city notably pivoted its investment focus from labour-centric industries to sectors rich in technology and capital during the 1990s, achieving significant strides in electronics, biotechnology and new materials (Ouyang, 2020). This transformation not only bolstered Shenzhen's status within the global industrial hierarchy but also set the stage for sustained economic growth.

While Shenzhen transformed its foreign investment structure, the city faced new challenges. These include sustaining the competitiveness of its industries, enhancing its capacity for innovation, increasing the application of scientific and technological developments, as well as addressing the environmental and social issues associated with rapid growth. In response, Shenzhen continues to refine its policies, boost investment in science and technology innovation and steer industrial development towards greener and more sustainable practices. The city maintained its focus on strengthening the impact of FDI in the high-tech sector using policy guidance, tax incentives and other measures to encourage high-quality economic growth (Li, 2024). Concurrently, Shenzhen expanded its links with international innovation networks, attracted high-end foreign R&D centres and innovation labs, and promoted the deep integration of local and international markets and technologies.

Despite Shenzhen's significant achievements in attracting R&D investment, the COVID-19 pandemic introduced numerous challenges that negatively impacted this sector. Increased global economic uncertainty led to a decline in investor risk appetite (Luo & Witt, 2021). Disruptions in supply chains resulted in delays and increased costs for Shenzhen's R&D projects. Travel restrictions severely impacted the flow of international talent, thereby hindering Shenzhen's ability to enhance its innovation capacity. Additionally, financial constraints forced many firms to reduce their R&D budgets, which was particularly detrimental to startups and SMEs in Shenzhen. Changes in policies and regulations affected cross-border R&D collaborations and capital flows.

The post-epidemic era

In the post-pandemic era, as the core engine of the Guangdong-Hong Kong-Macao Greater Bay Area, Shenzhen showcased its FDI potential and its pivotal role in economic revitalisation. Specifically, Shenzhen became a key destination for foreign R&D investments in China, with significant FDI from world leading MNEs. As showcased in Figure 13.4, data reflects major contributions from companies like SK Telecom and Siemens Energy AG, investing $82.15 million and $72.66 million respectively, which aligns with

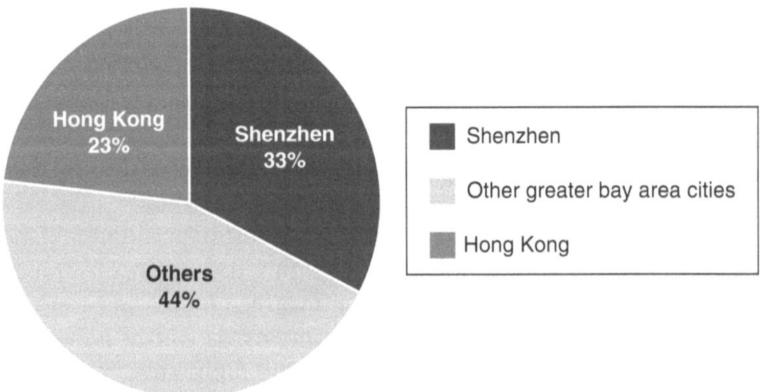

FIGURE 13.4 Inward R&D greenfield investment distribution in the Greater Bay Area from 2014 to 2022 (% of total capital in million USD)

Shenzhen's sophisticated tech infrastructure and supportive business environment. Such substantial investments across various tech sectors, seen in the commitments from POET Optoelectronics, Texas Instruments, and others, underscore Shenzhen's role as a comprehensive hub for high-tech development. These investments enhance Shenzhen's economic dynamism, consolidating its status as an emergent global tech nexus and reaffirming the city's strategic goal in cultivating a setting ripe for technological innovation and sectoral expansion. These investments corroborate the notion that Shenzhen is a more attractive destination for R&D greenfield investment projects. Amidst economic pressures from the US-China trade war, science and technology sanctions from foreign countries, and the impact of pandemics, Shenzhen not only sustained FDI growth but also expedited the enhancement of its industrial and FDI structures. This achieved through policy innovation and the optimisation of industrial strategies, further solidifying its status as a leader in the global high-tech industry.

In 2023, Shenzhen's actual foreign capital utilisation reached 62.62 billion RMB (approximately 8.77 billion USD),[1] the highest in the province. The city witnessed the establishment of 8,002 new foreign-funded companies, a year-on-year increase of 86.6%, indicating that foreign investors' interest in Shenzhen remained strong (ShenzhenDaily, 2024). Additionally, Shenzhen's manufacturing sector experienced a 53.8% year-on-year growth in new foreign-funded companies, and high-tech industries saw a 60.6% increase. This achievement can be attributed to the effective execution of Shenzhen's "20 + 8" industrial cluster strategy and targeted investment promotion in key sectors of the industry chain. Shenzhen's accomplishments stem from its steadfast commitment to marketisation, adherence to the rule of law and continuous improvement of the business environment.

Shenzhen's industrial upgrading and supply chain reshaping, especially in key areas such as chip manufacturing and design, biomedicine, and high-end equipment manufacturing, provided strong support for regional economic recovery and global integration processes. In the post epidemic era, Shenzhen is not only the core engine of economic recovery in the Guangdong-Hong Kong-Macao Greater Bay Area, but also a key force driving the restructuring of the global industrial chain and supply chain. Shenzhen continued to promote the attraction of high-tech foreign investors (XinhuaNews, 2023). This further promoted the technological and industrial upgrading of local companies, accelerating Shenzhen's position in the global supply chain (XinhuaNews, 2023).

In a global economy marked by numerous uncertainties, the approaches taken by Shenzhen potentially illustrate varying impacts of policy innovation, strategic industrial optimisation, and the internationalisation of the business environment on fostering economic growth and attracting foreign investment. Through continuous policy innovation, optimisation of industrial strategies and internationalisation of the business environment, Shenzhen not only drew significant foreign investments but also fostered exemplary economic growth, securing Shenzhen's pivotal position in the worldwide economic rebound. In the future, Shenzhen will continue to play its role as the core engine of the Guangdong-Hong Kong-Macao Greater Bay Area and the global economy, and promote a more open, innovative, and inclusive globalisation process.

Inward greenfield R&D related FDI

In a globalised economy, inward greenfield R&D related FDI has a significant positive impact on the economic growth and technological progress of China (Liu & Zou, 2008). Shenzhen, with its open economic system and advanced industrial policies, became an important destination for global greenfield R&D-related FDI when compared with other Greater Bay Area cities (see Table 13.1). Shenzhen led by a significant margin, boasting $1,217.15 million,

TABLE 13.1 Top 10 GF R&D investors in Shenzhen by capital expenditure (in USD million)

Year	*Investing firms*	*Capital*	*Headline*
2014	SK TELECOM CO., LTD	82.15	SK Telecom opens R&D Centre in Shenzhen, China
2021	SIEMENS ENERGY AG	72.66	Siemens Energy opens innovation, R&D Centre in Shenzhen, China
2021	POET OPTOELECTRONICS SHENZHEN CO., LTD	72.47	POET opens R&D Centre in Shenzhen, China
2017	AIRBUS SE	71.96	Airbus has opened an innovation, R&D Centre in Shenzhen, China
2021	TEXAS INSTRUMENTS INC.	71.25	Growatt and TI open R&D Centre in Shenzhen, China
2021	INTELBRAS	70.64	Intelbras opens R&D Centre in Shenzhen, China
2017	TAOGLAS LTD	70.62	Taoglas opens a IoT R&D Centre in Shenzhen, China
2018	DEUTSCHE LUFTHANSA AG	70.13	Deutsche Lufthansa has opened an innovation, R&D Centre in Shenzhen, China
2018	AIRBUS CHINA LTD	69.95	Airbus China opens an innovation, R&D Centre in Shenzhen, China
2015	INTEL CORPORATION	67.28	Intel opens R&D Centre in Shenzhen, China

Source: Table created based on data provided by Orbis Cross-border Database.

TABLE 13.2 R&D greenfield FDI capital inflows: Shenzhen compared to other top five Greater Bay Area cities from 2014 to 2022 (in USD million)

Shenzhen's R&D capital		*Top five GBA cities' R&D capitals*	
City	*Capital*	*Cities*	*Capitals*
Shenzhen	1,217.15	Guangzhou	875.19
		Hong Kong	863.71
		Foshan	504.01
		Dongguan	204.88
		Huizhou	64.42

Source: Table created based on data provided by Orbis Cross-border Database.

which is higher than any single other Greater Bay Area city reported and exemplifies its dominant position in attracting R&D investments. Guangzhou follows with $875.19 million, then Hong Kong with $863.71 million. In Table 13.2, Shenzhen held the lion's share (33%) of inward R&D greenfield investment across the Greater Bay Area, emphasising its pivotal role in regional tech growth. Hong Kong's significant 23% share also denotes its strong innovation credentials. In high-tech industries, Shenzhen attracted investments from many large MNEs and through these investments it generated significant technological spill-overs that promoted the technological upgrading and industrial development of local companies. This was promoted via the policy support of the Shenzhen government. Shenzhen provides a series of policy concessions for foreign-funded R&D centres, such as tax exemptions and reductions, R&D financial support and intellectual property rights protection. These policies reduce the operating costs of foreign-funded companies and thus improve Shenzhen's competitiveness in attracting FDI, in turn promoting technological spillovers and industrial upgrading.

A major channel for such inward FDI is technology upgrading. As noted by Zhang Yihao, CEO and President of GE Healthcare China this would be impossible without "without Shenzhen's economic vitality, innovative atmosphere, supply chain system, talent pool and international exchange environment" (ShenzhenDaily, 2024). By setting up R&D centres in Shenzhen, international companies not only introduce the world's most advanced technologies but also directly transfer aspects of these technologies and related knowledge to local companies via sub-contracting and cooperation projects with them. Huawei Technologies Co. Ltd. exemplifies this, it having engaged in in-depth co-operation with a number of international technology giants to jointly develop communications technologies. Another important spillover effect of foreign-funded companies is talent training. The R&D centres of international companies in Shenzhen not only provide employment opportunities for local talent but improve their skills and capabilities via training and work experience. Educated to global standards, they contribute significantly within foreign-funded companies and when they transition back to local firms, where they bring with them international insights and advanced expertise. This cross-collaboration enhances the technological prowess and innovative capacity of the entire industry.

Greenfield R&D related FDI encourages technological spill-overs through the collaborative development of the industrial chain (CPRC, 2023a). International companies' investments in Shenzhen are typically part of a larger influx, drawing suppliers and service providers to the city and leading to the formation of industrial clusters. Within these clusters, companies enhance their technological standards and market competitiveness through cooperative synergy (Kerr & Robert-Nicoud, 2020). For instance, the electronic information industry cluster in Shenzhen attracted prominent MNEs like Intel and Qualcomm to establish R&D centres. These centres not only bolster Shenzhen's global standing in the electronics sector but also drive technological advancement and industrial progression among local suppliers and manufacturers (GlobalTimes, 2023). The Shenzhen Bureau of Statistics reported that in 2023, the added value of the high-tech industry accounted for over 40% of the city's GDP, with the electronic information technology and biomedicine industries experiencing the most notable growth. This achievement is attributed to the targeted R&D investment by companies in these high-tech industries.

Increased competition between foreign and domestic firms, lead to the shrinking of the latter's market share or even force them to withdraw from the market, is one challenge FDI has created.

The Shenzhen government, however, takes steps to help local firms, including financial subsidies, tax incentives and technical services, to help local companies improve their technological level and market adaptability (Peter & Arendse, 2022). The optimisation of Shenzhen's foreign investment structure not only attracts high-end R&D-based FDI, but also promotes the upgrading of the local industrial chain. Through the introduction of high-tech industries, Shenzhen promoted the adjustment of industrial structure, enabling local companies to compete in higher industrial chain segments, thus mitigating the effects of intensified direct competition. For example, Shenzhen's new energy automobile industry upgraded the technological level of the whole industry chain through cooperation with foreign-funded companies, and local companies such as BYD gained rapid development through technological innovation in the process (Marcelo et al., 2020).

Shenzhen's embrace of R&D-focused inward FDI is a case of how investment in technology can serve as a catalyst for economic expansion. The city's experience shows the interplay between the beneficial effects of new technologies and the competitive pressure they introduce to existing markets. By effectively harnessing foreign capital, Shenzhen managed to amplify these effects to drive growth. This was made possible through government policies and the recalibration of industrial strategies to foster a conducive environment for innovation. Local companies, too, played a crucial role by adopting new technologies and adjusting to market demands, turning potential obstacles into stepping stones for development. The city transitioned from being a traditional manufacturing hub to a global centre of innovation – a testament to its strategy of leveraging high-tech foreign investment. This transformation solidified Shenzhen's economic infrastructure and increased its participation in the global market, offering a blueprint for other regions seeking to upgrade their economic structure and global market presence. Shenzhen's trajectory illustrates the significant impacts that targeted FDI can have on a region, offering insights into how to attract and integrate foreign capital to enhance industrial sophistication and the competitive edge of domestic Chinese firms on the world stage. Huawei stands out as a case in point.

Note

1 Exchange rate used: 1 RMB = 0.14 USD as of 25 June 2024.

References

Bureau, S. S. (2010). *Shenzhen statistical yearbook*. http://tjj.sz.gov.cn/zwgk/zfxxgkml/tjsj/tjnj/content/post_3086000.html

Bureau, S. S. (2023). Shenzhen Statistical Yearbook [Online]. Available: https://tjj.sz.gov.cn/zwgk/zfxxgkml/tjsj/tjnj/content/post_11182604.html [Accessed 29-03-2024].

Cheng, J., Chen, M., & Tang, S. (2023). Shenzhen—A typical benchmark of Chinese rapid urbanization miracle. *Cities, 140*, 104421.

CPRC. (2023a). *China further supports foreign-funded R&D centers*. https://english.www.gov.cn/policies/latestreleases/202301/18/content_WS63c79b01c6d0a757729e5cf7.html

CPRC. (2023b). *Optimization of Foreign Investment Structure in China*. https://www.gov.cn/yaowen/liebiao/202308/content_6900849.htm

Dan, S. (2020). *Shenzhen miracle to GBA innovation*. https://global.chinadaily.com.cn/a/202008/26/WS5f45a358a310675eafc5579a.html

Du, J. (2020). *The Shenzhen experiment: The story of China's instant city*. Harvard University Press.

Fetscherin, M., Voss, H., & Gugler, P. (2010). 30 years of foreign direct investment to China: An interdisciplinary literature review. *International Business Review, 19*, 235–246.

GlobalTimes. (2023). *Intel builds innovation center in Shenzhen, as US firms expand in China despite 'decoupling'*. https://www.globaltimes.cn/page/202308/1295577.shtml

Kerr, W. R., & Robert-Nicoud, F. (2020). Tech clusters. *Journal of Economic Perspectives, 34*, 50–76.

Li, Y. (2024). *Jan-Oct foreign investment in Shenzhen manufacturing surges nearly twofold*. https://www.ecns.cn/news/2024-03-27/detail-ihcyyfhe2566212.shtml

Liu, X., & Zou, H. (2008). The impact of greenfield FDI and mergers and acquisitions on innovation in Chinese high-tech industries. *Journal of World Business, 43*, 352–364.

Luo, Y., & Witt, M. A. (2022). Springboard MNEs under de-globalization. *Journal of International Business Studies, 53*, 767–780.

Marcelo, D., Dennis, W., Darren, L., & Han, H. (2020). *How Shenzhen became China's Silicon Valley*. https://multimedia.scmp.com/infographics/news/china/article/3100043/shenzhen-special-economic-zone/index.html

Municipality, S. B. O. S. (2013). *Shenzhen statistical yearbook 2012*. https://www.sz.gov.cn/cn/xxgk/zfxxgj/tjsj/tjgb/content/post_1333758.html

Ouyang, S. (2020). *Shenzhen aims to be world hub of innovation*. https://global.chinadaily.com.cn/a/202010/13/WS5f84e256a31024ad0ba7e353.html

Patchell, J. (2023). *China's Greater Bay Area: Agglomeration, external economies, governance and urbanization*. Taylor & Francis.

Peter, U., & Arendse, H. (2022). *Investing in Shenzhen: Industry, economics, and policy*. China Briefing. https://www.china-briefing.com/news/investing-shenzhen-economic-profile-industry-policy-trends/

PHBS. (2021). Economic Report (Shenzhen 2021 Industrial Structure Status and Future Prospects). Peking University HSBC Business School.

Sheng, M. (2020). *Shenzhen reflects the success of reform, opening-up*. https://global.chinadaily.com.cn/a/202008/27/WS5f46f8c9a310675eafc55ba2.html

ShenzhenDaily. (2024). *Shenzhen adds 8,002 foreign firms*. http://qh.sz.gov.cn/en/news/content/post_11149408.html

Tai, M. C., Barry, N., & Eric, H. (2022). *China's roadmap to becoming a science, technology, and innovation great power*. University of California Institute on Global Conflict and Cooperation. https://ucigcc.org/publication/chinas-roadmap-to-becoming-a-science-technology-and-innovation-great-power/

UNCTD. (2020). *World investment report 2020: International production beyond the pandemic*. United Nations Conference on Trade Development.

XinhuaNews. (2023). *Shenzhen, a trailblazer of China's deepened reform, opening-up*. https://english.www.gov.cn/news/202312/20/content_WS65823c61c6d0868f4e8e2601.html

Yin, D., Raffo, J., & Tang, J. (2022). *Global innovation hotspots innovation ecosystems and catching-up in developing countries: Evidence from Shenzhen: WIPO development studies*. WIPO.

14

CASE 14: FOREIGN DIRECT INVESTMENT, INTERNATIONAL COLLABORATION AND KNOWLEDGE COMMUNITY DEVELOPMENT

A case study of Suzhou Industry Park

Juana Du and Charles Krusekopf

Abstract

Suzhou Industry Park (SIP) launched as an international pilot project for innovation zones in Suzhou, a non-hub city south of Yangtze River in China. SIP has played a crucial role in the development of the regional economy and in attracting inward foreign direct investment (FDI). Initial interest and attention didn't guarantee success for the Singapore-Suzhou Industrial Park (SSIP) in terms of realized FDI projects within the zone. The restructuring of SIP in 1999 accelerated its development, and moved its focus from manufacturing to a stronger R&D, service and knowledge economy basis, with a focus on biotech, nanotech and cloud computing. New policies and initiatives were experimented at SIP to encourage FDI, build industrial infrastructure, develop high-technology and industrial clusters and support talent development through international collaborations. Looking forward, new challenges are faced by SIP and registered firms. Those include: will the SIP be able to continue its leading role as an innovation hub and location for research and development in high tech fields in the region? will the SIPs focus shift towards the attraction and development of domestic firms in place of investment and cooperation with foreign firms, given China's increasing focus on domestic technology development, etc.

The year 2024 marks the 30th anniversary of the Singapore-Suzhou Industry Park (SIP), which was launched as an international collaborative project between the Governments of Singapore and China. Given its unique structure representing a public-private partnership spanning two countries, SIP served as a pilot project for innovation zones in Asia. Since its founding, SIP has played a crucial role in the development of the regional economy and in attracting inward foreign direct investment (FDI), making it an ideal model for review and study by both academics and practitioners. This chapter reviews

DOI: 10.4324/9781003483410-18

the development of SIP since its founding, and highlights the changes that occurred over time through restructuring of its operations and shifts in the types of FDI attracted to the zone. The chapter concludes with questions for further exploration and discussion.

Background of Suzhou Industry Park (SIP) and the city of Suzhou

China has utilized the development of innovation zones as a key part of its national strategy to attract foreign firms and investors with a focus in the 1990s to maximize output and exports of manufactured products, and in recent two decades through a focus on attracting investments related to advanced technologies and research and innovation partnerships. The government promoted high-scale knowledge community precincts to attract inward FDI and pilot new policies. In many cases innovation zones have played paramount roles in the regional and local economy, industry and technology development in key sectors, and also helped connect Chinese cities and companies into global city and research networks.

Many early innovation zones were initiated and developed around first-tier cities in China, such as Beijing, Shanghai and Guangzhou (Du & Williams, 2017), due to the unique regional, economic, cultural and policy advantages these major cities were granted by the government after its move towards reform and opening in 1978. After observing the success of the innovation zones in first-tier cities, many non-hub cities and underdeveloped areas and regions began to push for their own innovation zones to boost regional and local development, build specialized industry clusters and promote technological and manufacturing development.

SIP was established in 1994 in Suzhou, a second-tier Chinese city south of Yangtze River with a population of 6.7 million residents, located 100 km to the west of Shanghai and 200 km east of Nanjing, the capital city of Jiangsu Province. The SIP was created as a joint-venture between Singapore and the City of Suzhou, bringing together the strong reputation and management skills developed by Singapore together with the growing interest among foreign firms who wanted to invest in China. The establishment of SIP and the vote of confidence given the area by Singapore helped establish Suzhou as an important location for international companies looking to invest in China. Suzhou offered several advantages for FDI including its geographic proximity to Shanghai and the relatively low operating costs in the area with land and labour costs much lower than within first-tier cities such as Shanghai (Nielsen et al., 2017).

The SIP was intended to attract foreign investors to the Suzhou region, helping to diversify the economy and spread the economic gains from FDI experienced by Shanghai to more cities in the region. Historically, the manufacturing sector, including heavy industries such as iron and steel, played a dominating role in Suzhou's economy along with tourism. Foreign investors played a key role in helping to diversify the city's economy, bringing in a wide range of manufacturing facilities and an increase in investment in research and development and high-tech manufacturing. The GDP of Suzhou in 2023 was 331 billion USD, with a per-capita income of $26,250, which is well above the Chinese national average. The cumulative FDI in Suzhou is $160 billion USD, which ranks it sixth among Chinese cities as a destination for FDI. The SIP played a major role in the attraction of foreign capital and development of international trade within the region, with over $40 billion invested by more than 5,000 foreign firms. Despite having less than 10 per cent of the population and land area within Suzhou, more than one-third of total imports and exports in Suzhou run through the SIP (Suzhou Municipal People's Government, 2024).

Main questions

The SIP offers an interesting case study for the development of innovation zones. First, it was one of the first innovation zones to incorporate an international partnership in its development and management. Second, the zone has undergone an evolution over time as it shifted from a focus more on attracting FDI and basic manufacturing enterprises towards a more advanced innovation zone model that emphasizes education, research and manufacturing in high technology fields through a range of international partnerships, FDI and domestic government and private sector support. The first question to be explored is how has the zone evolved over time in terms of the types of FDI encouraged within the zone, and what supportive mechanisms have the local government and zone managers used to encourage this evolution. Second, what lessons can be learned from the international collaboration aspect of the SIP and its organizational structure as an international partnership? Finally, how has innovation development and FDI within the SIP been affected by changes in Chinese policies under Xi Jinping and shifting attitudes among foreign firms and governments towards cooperation with China, especially in high tech fields?

The establishment of SSIP and local competitions

The establishment of SIP originated in October 1992, when Singapore's Senior Minister Lee Kuan Yew and Deputy Prime Minister Ong Teng Cheong were invited to China by Chinese leader Deng Xiaoping to explore co-operation opportunities. Deng had earlier that year praised Singapore as a model for China in the areas of planned development and economic progress. The two governments decided to collaboratively develop a new township in China that would be based on Singaporean "software" – techniques of municipal and industrial zone planning and management that had been successful in the development of new townships in Singapore, such as Jurong. This newly planned town was meant as a demonstration zone and specially designated location to experiment new policies and attract foreign investors, who were expected to feel more comfortable and confident about investing in an area planned and managed by Singapore with more advanced management philosophy, practices and infrastructure.

An initial agreement was reached in 1994 to create the Singapore-Suzhou Industrial Park (SSIP) with the Chinese side providing the land and approvals necessary for the project, and the Singaporean side providing the development capital and management expertise. The Singaporean side held 65 per cent of the shares in the project, and the Chinese side, led by the Suzhou municipal government, held 35 per cent (Zhao & Farole, 2011). Management and cooperation between the two governments were demonstrated at three levels: a direct central-government-to-government agreement and commitment at the highest levels of both national governments; a second operational management committee made up of the Suzhou municipal government and a representative of the Singapore government; and a third level focused on the establishment of a joint-venture corporation owned by the two governments responsible for town planning, property development, marketing and estate management (Han, 2008).

High-level government involvement in the project ensured that it received special attention within China, and Singapore's involvement ensured widespread notice in the international community. This was key, as, at the time, the international community retained some scepticism of China's commitment to reform in the wake of the crackdown on government protestors that occurred in June 1989 in Beijing's Tiananmen Square and other areas of China and the subsequent chill in international relations. Politically, the project fulfilled Singapore's desire to develop a special link to China, and allowed China to trumpet an international cooperation agreement at a time when it was still under sanction from most western governments.

The project experienced some early success through information sharing and exchanges of government officials. For instance, government officials from the Suzhou government were sent to Singapore to study how Singapore managed town planning and residential and industrial development. The high-profile project raised awareness of Suzhou, which was a small non-hub city located between the much larger cities of Shanghai and Nanjing along the Yangtze River, and numerous delegations of international companies visited the site when looking for locations to open manufacturing operations in China.

Initial interest and attention however didn't guarantee success for the SSIP in terms of realized FDI projects within the zone. The biggest challenge the SSIP faced was competition for foreign investors from other development zones in the city of Suzhou – in particular the much larger Suzhou New District (SND), an area of land controlled by the Suzhou municipal government that surrounded the original SSIP land area. The SND comprised 208 km^2 of land, an area much larger than the 80 km^2 in the SSIP. Foreign companies looking for an investment location were steered towards the SND by the Suzhou municipal government because it had 100 per cent control over this area and only a minority (35 per cent) stake in the SSIP (Han, 2008). It became evident that a key weakness of the arrangement was that the initial agreements and development plans for the SSIP were negotiated between the central Chinese government and the Singaporean government, but while the initial concept fulfilled national development goals, it did little to support the interests of the local Suzhou government.

In 1999, facing rising costs and slow development prospects, the SSIP ownership structure was changed, with the Singaporean government relinquishing its majority stake while the Suzhou government took over 65 per cent of the shares and the overall management of the project. The Suzhou government quickly unified the management of the SSIP and SND, creating the 288-km^2 Suzhou Industrial Park (SIP) that merged the original land of SSIP and the land of SND. The restructured SIP retained government-to-government status, with Singapore still holding a 35 per cent share but ceding control over the management and development of the zone to the Suzhou government. Singaporean companies remained deeply engaged as developers and tenants in the zone, but the management of the zone and the surrounding area was under the control of the Suzhou city government allowing for improved regional planning and more efficient local oversight of the zone and the connecting infrastructure.

New development brought by the restructuring of SIP

This restructuring accelerated the development of SIP. The zone averaged output growth of 30 per cent per year from the late 1990s until 2013. The SIP has attracted investments from more than 4,900 foreign invested enterprises (including 88 Fortune 500 companies) that have invested more than US$45 billion in the zone. More than 18,000 domestic companies have invested in the zone, and it ranks second among national development zones in the National Comprehensive Development Index (The World Bank, 2011). The SIP is well connected to the national transportation system, and has its own high-speed rail station that allows access to Shanghai in only 23 minutes. It houses more than 1.2 million residents, and its high-quality residential and retail offerings make it the most desirable residential location in the area for both international and domestic residents (Ma et al., 2013).

In recent years, the SIP has worked to move its focus from manufacturing to a stronger R&D, service and knowledge economy basis, with a focus on biotech, nanotech and cloud computing. Advanced manufacturing and technology firms are well represented in the SIP. Global firms including Microsoft, IBM, Siemens, Philips, Samsung, Nokia, Honeywell and Fujitsu have operations in the SIP. This shift has been characterized as the move from "Industrial Park 1.0" to "Industrial Park 2.0." To achieve this goal, the SIP has worked to improve living amenities to provide an attractive environment for knowledge and service workers; developed the Dushu Lake Science and Educational Innovation District within the boundaries of the zone; encouraged lower-end manufacturing facilities to move out of the park to make room for higher-tech firms and developed specialized areas within the park, including a nanotech zone known as "Nanopolis," a biotech zone, and an international science and technology zone.

Experimental policies and initiatives to encourage FDI

The SIP served as a pioneer for a variety of new policies and a demonstration zone of industrial parks in China. It was among the first national eco-industrial and intellectual property rights demonstration zones, and became China's first experimental area on preferential policies for technologically advanced service industries, China's first outsourcing demonstration base, and China's only base for service trade innovation and business tourism. SIP is recognized as an important window of China's reform and opening-up and a successful model of international cooperation and served as the first open innovation experimental area of China (Min & Ding, 2018).

- Experimental policies of innovation zone to encourage FDI.

SIP has served as a pioneer for a variety of new policies of innovation zones as international joint ventures. Consequently, those policy initiatives have been implemented in other innovation zones in China. The inward FDI in Suzhou has tremendously increased in the last decade. For instance, the inward FDI in Suzhou in 2023 reached $6.9 billion USD (Suzhou Municipal People's Government, 2024).

The SIP utilized its unique connections to Singapore to develop its status as a financial centre, hosting branch offices of 30 domestic and international banks. It was the first development zone in China where firms were allowed to source renminbi (RMB) loans from Singaporean banks, a move that significantly cut borrowing costs. The area has also been a leading experimental area for RMB convertibility, again utilizing the financial expertise of Singapore-based banks and financial institutions to support international trade and operations by firms registered in the SIP. Those policy initiatives largely help the MNEs registered in the zone to make investment choices, and encourage inward FDI in the innovation zone. The benefits of those new financial policies have also been a major motive for several MNEs to set up their subsidiaries and operations in SIP when they were considering the choices of locations in China and Asia Pacific market (Cai et al., 2005).

New technology development and collaborations fostered through FDI in research and development projects have been supported by a series of new policies pioneered in the SIP. The SIP has encouraged companies to establish R&D operations, and it now houses over 2,000 R&D centres (Suzhou Industry Park, 2024). Many well-recognized and advanced manufacturing and technology MNEs have operations in the SIP. Biomedicine, nanotechnology and artificial intelligence are three pillar industries in SIP, which have realized an average 20 per cent growth rate in recent years. Oxford University's first overseas centre for research in physical and engineering science, the Oxford Suzhou Centre of Advanced Research (OSCAR) was opened in SIP, and the first patent application from the OSCAR collaboration was filed for a novel testing system for COVID-19 (Suzhou Industry Park, 2024). This development was recognized with an award for Pandemic Service by the Royal Academy of Engineering.

- Policies of innovation zones to build industrial infrastructures

The innovation zones and its management committee developed the blueprint and strategies that guided the industrial and economic development of the innovation park. The overall development strategy and policies put the innovation zone in a unique position to attract inward FDI. For instance, the zone hosts the National Animation Park and the National 3D Movie Park, and several facilities to support animation and 3D movie production. In addition, an Eco Science Park, an Eco Industrial Park, an Information Park and a Sino-China friendship library were developed in the innovation zone, to encourage firms engaging in environmental technology design, green finance, IT and green building research and design.

The government invested to build infrastructure for SIP which became shared resources and unique advantages of the industrial park. Those infrastructures served as the precincts to develop a knowledge community of international firms and investors. Being physically located in the SIP, connecting those firms as knowledge actors which actively engage in knowledge sharing and transfer practices. Those shared working spaces in SIP have been venues to encourage conversations, inspire initiatives and ideas and facilitate collaborations among firms, management committees and government offices.

In addition, MNEs in the zones are provided with government subsidies and financial aid to set up new research and development facilities. Those policies have been proved successful in boasting a large number of registered MNEs to invest and operate in the innovation zone. It is noted that the SIP started one-stop service model to provide a 360-degree services to registered firms and professionals in the innovation zones. This covers the area of policy services, legal consultations, financial services and technology support. This community service model originated and developed from the Singaporean management philosophy at its early stage, and was widely adopted in the SIP in the following years. The SIP also provided social services to attract high skill workers including hospitals, high end retail shopping and high-quality schools. This community building and management practice created a high-quality living environment that has been copied by other innovation parks in China. This service model helped registered firms and investors to quickly learn and adapt to the local investment environment and fully utilize the SIP policies.

- Policy to encourage the advancement of high-technology and industrial clusters.

Nanotechnology, which focuses on the development of new materials, micro-manufacturing techniques and biotechnologies, has been a special area of focus within the SIP. In 2010, the SIP launched "Nanopolis," the world's largest district focused on nanotech research and commercialization. The first phase of the project was completed in 2013, and houses over 100 nanotech companies and more than 20 university and research institutes, including the China-Finland Nano Innovation Center and the Holland High Tech Center (China). Altogether, US$1B is being invested in the development of Nanopolis, with more than 1.5 million km^2 (16 million square feet) of research, training, and production centres employing more than 10,000 nanotechnology experts. In addition to nanotechnology, the SIP has encouraged companies to establish research and development operations, and it now houses over 300 research and development centres employing more than 15,000 researchers (China-Finland Nano Innovation Center, 2015). The research centres are generally associated with international companies operating in the zone, including Emerson, Bosch, Samsung and Panasonic (Suzhou Industrial Park Administrative Committee, 2015).

This development demonstrates the success of the high-tech industrial strategy of the SIP. Instead of the traditional model of building an industry park to attract high-tech firms moving in, the SIP strategically identified nanotechnology industry as a leading sector in SIP, and actively developed industrial clusters. Nanopolis in SIP started to build since 2011 and then became the leader of nanotechnology in the region, and a knowledge community around nanotechnology has developed involving partnerships with nanotech-related organizations from over 20 countries and regions, including Singapore, Canada, the United States, Germany, the United Kingdom and Finland. Those partnerships have expanded from purely nanotechnology to related areas including nanomaterials and pharmaceuticals.

- Policy to support talent development.

Since its establishment, talent and professional development have been one of the foci in the SIP. The financial strength of the SIP government, which has a large tax base because of the increasing number of international and domestic companies operating in the zone, allows it to support a number of initiatives such as talent attraction subsidies that attract high-quality professionals and skilled workers to the area. SIP has focused on the development of high-quality higher education through the development of branch campuses of famous Chinese universities such as Renmin, Soochow and Nanjing Universities, and international partnership schools and research institutes with UCLA, Oxford and Liverpool. In this regard, Suzhou was following the lead of Shenzhen, a special economic zone that focused on technological upgrading through the strategic development of a series of campuses for local, national and international universities starting in the 1990s.

In 2002, the SIP created the Suzhou Dushu Lake Science and Education Innovation District (SEID), a 25-km^2 area within the SIP that now houses campuses or research facilities for 27 universities. The SEID is one component of an overall talent development programme sponsored by the SIP. In 2007, the SIP initiated the Technological Talents Program to ensure that local technology firms had the personnel they needed to support both research and manufacturing operations. In 2010, the SIP initiated the Jingji Lake Double Hundred Talent Program to attract new talented employees with advanced degrees and to offer existing employees opportunities to improve their professional training and explore opportunities to start new companies. Starting in 2011, the SIP committed RMB200M per year (US$30M) to attract highly talented people to relocate to the SIP (Suzhou Municipal People's Government, 2024).

To further boost the recruitment of foreign talents, the Suzhou Free Trade Area which is mainly located in the SIP, released *Several Measures to Achieve Better Work and Life Services for Foreign Talents (Trial)* on February 2021. It included 19 measures to facilitate foreign talents' entry, work and exit in Suzhou, and improved the incentive mechanism for foreign talents and optimized social service systems for Foreign talents (China Briefing, 2021).

It is worth noticing that most of those policy experiments go beyond the municipal level and connect SIP with knowledge actors both locally and internationally, such as MNEs, global investors, financial institutions and other service agents, etc. Those business activities initiated and hosted by SIP led to the increase in cross-city connectivity in Suzhou, and upgraded the role of Suzhou city in regional city networks. The city of Suzhou has been well-known because of SIP, and the local GDP continually ranked fourth in China in the last decade. SIP attracts young talents, professionals and graduates to move to the region for employment. Fresh graduates not only come from hub cities nearby, such as Shanghai and Nanjing, but also cities from other regions, including northern China.

The upgraded role of Suzhou City has also been demonstrated through international collaborations of higher education programs and institutions. For instance, the SIP focused on foreign educational partnerships when developing the SEID, an idea fostered by the collaboration between Singapore and the SIP. In 2012, the SEID was granted the title Pilot Area for Higher Education Internationalization by the Chinese Ministry of Education, paving the way for local institutions such as Soochow University to offer programs in English. This designation assisted in the development of innovative partnerships between foreign and local universities. As noted, "The Suzhou area is at the vanguard of new ways of thinking about higher education. We are among the first industrial parks going abroad to attract international education institutions. There has been lots of investment recently into world-leading universities here" (Hu & Zhou, 2015). As the first pilot area for Higher Education Internationalization, the SEID hosts around 400,000 people with around 100,000 students.

The next chapter for SIP

The year 2024 is the 30th anniversary of SIP. So far, it has attracted more than 5,000 foreign investment projects, and has received more than $40 billion US dollars of FDI. Looking forward, SIP and registered firms are facing new challenges in the innovation zones. For instance, for businesses registered in SIP, how can sustainable business practices face increasing operational costs and local competition in the Yangtze Delta River region? For SIP, how to continue to develop its competitive advantage as a leading innovation park in China attracting high quality investment from top international and domestic firms? How to improve public community services and the efficiency of management committees for sustainable growth?

It will be interesting to follow the development of the SIP as of 2024 during its next 30 years to better understand China's ability to continue to innovate and advance to become a leading global economy, not only in the manufacturing of basic products, but in high-tech fields and research economies equal to those in the West. Facing recent international security concerns and new regulations, what changes have impacted the collaboration among those foreign firms and local businesses? Given tensions between China and foreign governments and companies, especially in areas of high-tech development, will the SIP be able to continue its leading role as an innovation hub and location for research and development in high tech fields such as nanotechnology? Given China's increasing focus on domestic technology development, will the SIPs focus shift towards the attraction and development of domestic firms in place of investment and cooperation with foreign firms? SIP will be an interesting test case to understand if China can maintain its goal to become an innovation economy, while also increasing tight political, economic and security controls over its people, companies and investors.

References

Cai, X., Gao, L., & Yeoh, C. (2005). *Regionalization and Singapore's transborder industrialization: A new perspective on Suzhou Industrial Park (2005)*. Pacific Rim Conference, Hong Kong, 15–17 January 2005. Research Collection Lee Kong China School of Business.

China Briefing. (March 16, 2021). *Incentives and favorable policies available in Suzhou Industrial Park*. http://www.china99.org/index-1185.html

China-Finland Nano Innovation Center. (2015). *Suzhou Industrial Park—Your partner to success*. http://www.nanoinnovationcenter.com/?page_id=277

Du, J., & Williams, C. (2017). Innovative projects between MNE subsidiaries and local partners in China: Exploring locations and inter-organizational trust. *Journal of International Management, 23*(1), 16–31.

Han, M. (2008). *The China-Singapore Suzhou Industrial Park: Can the Singapore model of development be exported?* National University of Singapore.

Hu, H., & Zhou, F. (March 27, 2015). *A frontier of innovative education. China Daily Europe*. Invest Ottawa. April 16, 2014. ZDG International Incubation Centre takes four Ottawa knowledge-based companies to next level of innovation. http://investottawa.ca/zdg-international-incubation-centre-takes-four-ottawa-knowledge-based-companies-next-level-innovation/

Ma, X., Delios, A., & Lau, C. M. (2013). Beijing or Shanghai? The strategic location choice of large MNEs' host-country headquarters in China. *Journal of International Business Studies, 44*(9), 953–961.

Min, Z., & Ding, Y. (2018). Forty years of China's reform and opening policy: Innovative transformation of Suzhou Industrial Park and its connection with the one belt and one road initiative. *Global Economic Observer, 26*(2), 212–225.

Nielsen, B. B., Asmussen, C. G., & Weatherall, C. D. (2017). The location choice of foreign direct investments: Empirical evidence and methodological challenges. *Journal of World Business, 52*(1), 62–82.

Suzhou Industrial Park Administrative Committee. (2015). *China-Singapore Suzhou Industrial Park*. http://www.sipac.gov.cn

Suzhou Municipal People's Government. (2024). *The economic and social development in Suzhou Industry Park*. https://www.suzhou.gov.cn/szsenglish/gyyq/202108/7fdbdb71544b401e8713bd03cf5f97ef.shtml

The World Bank (2011). *The world development report 2011: Conflict, security and development*. https://en.wikipedia.org/wiki/The_World_Development_Report_2011

Zhao, M., & Farole, T. (2011). Partnership arrangements in the China-Singapore (Suzhou) Industrial Park: Lessons for joint economic zone development. In T. Farole & G. Akinci (Eds.), *Special Economic Zones: Progress, emerging challenges, and future directions*.

PART IV

Sustainable Development and Resilience in Cities through FDI

Abstract

As Foreign Direct Investment (FDI) flows into cities around the world in search of returns for investors and economic benefits for local city communities, the issue of responsibility has come increasingly under the spotlight. Responsibility can be seen in terms of how FDI flows align with United Nations Sustainable Development Goals (UN SDGs). And, it can be assessed in terms of indicators for Environmental Social and Governance (ESG)-based investing and accountability. At a corporate level, Multinational Enterprises (MNEs) can report on their global strategies, stances, and intentions in terms of responsible investing. But it is in the host countries and cities into which FDI flows where we see the imperatives for operational and managerial responsibility. The success or failure of an MNE's corporate strategy for responsible investing will ultimately be determined by the lower-level activities pursued in cities around the world where the issues to be addressed by FDI are most acutely felt. Part IV now explores responsibility through FDI in cities with a focus on cases relating to sustainable development and resilience in cities. This is not just a third-world issue, or one related to cities in politically unstable countries, or conflict and warzones. It is also an issue that affects FDI flows into richer, more stable, developed countries. Here, we also find cities struggling with how to adapt to broader global trends in terms of sustainability and social and environmental good. Cities themselves can play an important part in how inward FDI is used to address global challenges at a local level, and how this FDI can be influential in establishing outcomes in cities that benefit a wide range of stakeholders.

Sustainable development in cities through FDI

We can consider two lines of thinking about the role of Foreign Direct Investment (FDI) in sustainable development in cities. Firstly, there is a narrow view relating to the specific issue of energy use and carbon emissions through

DOI: 10.4324/9781003483410-19

FDI. The argument here is that an increase in demand for energy is brought about through FDI, both in the investments made by Multinational Enterprises (MNEs) and in the partner and supplier organizations within the ecosystem of investment. This is due to increased production and consumption in the city because of FDI. The question of a direct effect on emissions is understandably valid given many examples of MNE activity in the world (such as in the oil and gas sector), which have led to environmental damage and erosion of natural capital. In many cities, the quest for securing FDI to boost economic development and spillovers could mean that policymakers and regulators have downplayed the issue of environmental impact. Indeed, this may have been the case in the past, especially in BRIC countries (Pao & Tsai, 2011). However, we noted earlier in this book how meta-analysis shows FDI has a zero or negative impact on environmental emissions when considering the totality of studies on this (Demena & Afesorgbor, 2020). Demena and Afesorgbor (2020) conducted an authoritative meta-analysis of studies on this topic, showing this negative effect after accounting for publication bias (the pressures that researchers are under for a preference in finding either a positive or negative effect). They first show that, in 83 studies conducted between 2001 and 2018, there were both negative and positive impacts of FDI on environmental emissions identified. And the results were very split: 54% of these studies showed a negative impact on emissions (significant and non-significant), while 46% showed a positive effect (significant and non-significant) (see Demena and Afesorgbor, 2020, Figure 1, p. 3). They then use meta-analysis techniques to show that the effect is close to zero overall, and when publication bias and heterogeneity are accounted for, the effect becomes negative. Clearly, there has been much debate on this effect, with many examples of both positive and negative findings.

Secondly, we can think about sustainable development through FDI in more broader terms: it is not just about carbon emissions. It is instructive to refer to the United Nations Sustainable Development Goals (UN SDGs) in this respect. It has been noted that MNEs have been slow to respond to the SDG agenda, despite all UN countries adopting them (Van Tulder et al., 2021). Nevertheless, empirical results show that the more internationalized a firm is, the more likely it is to engage with SDGs (DasGupta et al., 2022). The UN SDGs include (1) eradicating poverty, (2) reducing hunger, (3) supporting health and well-being, (4) quality education, (5) gender equality, (6) clean water and sanitation (see Amiraly, in this book), (7) providing affordable and clean energy, (8) providing decent work and economic growth, (9) supporting industry, innovation, and infrastructure (see Saittakari and van den Berghe, in this book), (10) reducing inequalities, (11) helping build sustainable cities and communities, (12) supporting responsible consumption and production, (13) climate action, (14) preserving life below water and (15) on land, and (16) reinforcing peace, justice, and strong institutions comprise these goals.

The 17th goal relates to creating partnerships for the goals[1]. The issue of carbon emissions through FDI is directly linked to goals 6, 7, 11, 13, and potentially indirectly linked to others. The point here is that FDI can have a role to play beyond carbon emissions in all the goals. Aust et al. (2020) show that FDI has positive effects on some of the goals – but not others – in a study of 44 African countries. Their study shows that FDI had a more important role to play (positive and significant) in achieving overall SDG goals (measured through an overall SDG score) compared to domestic public financing which was not significant. They show FDI to support goals 1 (no poverty), 7 (clean energy), 9 (industry, innovation, and infrastructure), and 14 (life below water), and 16 (peace, justice, and strong institutions). However, they find a negative relationship between FDI and goal 13 (climate), supporting the 'pollution haven' hypothesis and providing a counterpoint to Demena and Afesorgbor (2020), noted above. The important point to note is how FDI can have a positive impact on a broad range of UN SDGs, over and above domestic public finance, and how these goals are often inter-linked (see also Williams et al., 2022).

Resilience of cities through FDI

We described in Part I how cities in advanced countries can be sensitive to disruptive events and shocks, including both natural and manmade disasters. This vulnerability matters for the global population in cities in all types of countries – not just advanced ones – as more and more people are drawn to live and work in cities globally (Hernantes et al., 2019). Cities' ability to be resilient and maintain infrastructure, economic stability and social cohesion in times of crisis can be important to MNEs that have invested – or are considering investing – in the city. Furthermore, FDI can help build and support the resilience of cities, i.e., their ability to cope in the short term as disruptions arise and recover more fully over the longer term. Resilience – the ability to cope with disruptions and return to a normal or new functioning state – is not just a characteristic of cities that may entice investors, it can also be an outcome of FDI.

Various empirical studies point to the role of FDI in supporting the capacity of cities to respond effectively to disruptions and shocks. FDI that helps host locations develop as smart cities is an example of this. Smart cities have been shown to reduce the negative impact of climate risks on FDI at the city level (An et al., 2022). Smart cities are seen to be more resilient to disruptions and shocks compared to 'non-smart' cities because of their digital abilities in collecting and processing information that guides decision-making during times of crisis (Jayathilaka & Park, 2022). FDI can help cities develop their digital capabilities for the long term, for instance, through digital enabling projects (Stephenson et al., 2022). In addition, models for developing resilience in cities have emerged, such as the Resilience Maturity Model

(Hernantes et al., 2019). This emphasizes roles for a wide range of stakeholders in all aspects of anticipating and coping with disruption in cities. This includes international organizations that can act as conduits to reinforce linkages with other cities, help with expertise, standards, and training, and that can also offer capabilities in analysing big data to enable response and recovery capabilities.

The role of FDI in supporting peaceful outcomes in countries that are affected by violent conflict and war has been debated in the literature. These contexts are rife with disruptions in their cities, including street-level violence. The Business for Peace (B4P) field has analysed and debated this issue, not just from the perspective of local businesses, but also through the actions of MNEs (Katsos & AlKafaji, 2019; Oetzel & Miklian, 2017; Williams, 2024). A key issue is whether the actions of MNEs in cities in conflict zones will act to stabilize and contribute to peace, or whether they can make matters worse, for instance by supporting or siding with one faction over another. How MNE managers deal with issues in cities beset by violence lies at the crux of solving this issue. Scholars have identified specific leadership abilities in violent contexts for business leaders, including the ability to bring conflict actors together, to work in the interests of the local community, and to take a long-term perspective (Katsos and Fort, 2016). Through such leadership MNEs can help to create a 'peace dividend' in a conflict-afflicted city (Miklian et al., 2016).

Knowledge transfer and knowledge management

In FDI's role in sustainable development and building resilience in cities, the MNE is seen as a disseminator of knowledge and skills. Their subsidiaries act as conduits for know-how and best practices to be disseminated into local city communities and stakeholders, for the benefit of those communities. In much of the literature on the knowledge-based view of the MNE, subsidiaries are seen as learning agents, important nodes in a network of global operations that allow the MNE to gather and harness knowledge globally through interactions between external communities and internal ones (Tallman & Chacar, 2011). When operating in locations in which sustainable development and resilience in the locale are a high priority, the MNE will still need to be able to operate in this mode, i.e., to learn. Problems and solutions in the realm of sustainable development will have some similarities from one context to another, and so this learning will be important. It will enable the MNE to understand what practical solutions have worked well, and what has worked less well, and transfer this learning internally from one location to another. Nevertheless, for the MNE to make an impact in terms of sustainable development and resilience in a city, its investment will need to involve managers on the ground who can direct knowledge and skills outward into local projects aimed at public good (Katsos & AlKafaji, 2019; Oetzel & Miklian, 2017; Williams, 2024).

Knowledge transfer involving MNE subsidiaries has been extensively studied. The received wisdom asserts that managers and employees within subsidiaries will need to be willing and able to share knowledge for it to have an impact. Willingness is connected to motivation; individuals must feel there is a purpose and a reason for disseminating knowledge. Ability is linked to skills and having the capacity to communicate the right way at the right time. Collectively, this willingness and ability has been referred to as disseminative capacity (Minbaeva & Michailova, 2004). This contrasts with the concept of absorptive capacity of MNE subsidiaries which relates to their willingness and ability to recognize new knowledge, assimilate it, and use it (Minbaeva et al., 2014).

Much of the early research into knowledge transfer and knowledge sharing took a purely internal perspective. More work has been done in recent years on interactions between internal and external communities, although this has not always been focused on sustainable development and resilience explicitly (Lee & Williams, 2007; Tallman & Chacar, 2011). Scholars have woken up to the importance of local employees and managers in MNE subsidiaries in terms of them having an impact in local communities through the transfer of knowledge and skills of the corporation. This is reflected in work on peacebuilding in MNE subsidiaries (Williams, 2024), subsidiary identity and impact on SDGs in the local context (Liou & Rao-Nicholson, 2021), and subsidiary size and experience being positively related to societal impact by the subsidiary (Reimann et al., 2015).

The cases in Part IV

There are four cases in Part IV, which explore FDI and cities through the lenses of sustainable development and resilience. The cases are set in Chennai, Lviv, Redcar, and a case set in the Nordics that covers two different cities: Skellefteå and Lappeenranta. Collectively, these cases show how the themes of sustainable development and resilience resonate in both developed country contexts (Redcar – United Kingdom, and Skellefteå – Sweden and Lappeenranta – Finland) as well as transition and emerging countries (Lviv – Ukraine, and Chennai – India). The need for revitalization and rebuilding of city economies is seen in countries of all levels of economic development. What differs are the reasons for economic demise or hardship in the city in the first place. Sometimes these reasons are deeply rooted in history and geopolitics. Sometimes they are sudden, such as the case with the onset of war and violence. Sometimes they are related to gradual economic change. The cases show

how FDI can aim to have a range of effects when sustainable development is included in its motive, or to assist a recipient city in its resilience in a broader disruptive environment.

- Chennai: Diffusing Water Management Practices through FDI

Chennai, the capital of Tamil Nadu, and India's fifth largest city[2] was beset with water-related issues for decades. It had been reported that rapid urbanization and land redevelopment had led to the abundant lakes and water resources of the city area being under-utilized to the point that the city had effectively 'run out of water'[3]. The case shows how the transfer of management and technical knowledge from an international company with a presence in the city is a feature of FDI that can have potential benefit for the city. The company had advanced capabilities in water systems and management. The case takes a micro-level perspective to show how the transfer of this knowledge is not as straightforward as it may sound, and that it is necessary to identify and overcome impediments to knowledge transfer if FDI is going to be effective in helping cities with sustainable development through practice transfer.

- Lviv: Prompting FDI in a Context of War and Violent Uncertainty

Lviv is the sixth largest city in Ukraine and the largest in the west of the country. It has the motto: 'Lviv is open to the world'. The military conflict in Ukraine had cost over one million lives and caused immense destruction of physical assets and infrastructure in its first two years. Considering investing in this type of context so soon after the onset of a major war will not seem obvious to many. The case shows how the investment promotion agency – UkraineInvest, based in Kyiv – continued to be active after the onset of war, and how it helped bring about regulation change that would entice an Irish construction company to start planning for a new investment in Lviv. The goal was not only to help Ukraine re-construct in the longer term but also to offer new opportunities for the investor across Eastern Europe, from the Lviv location.

- Redcar: Long-Term Recovery through Industrial Transition

The Teesside Steelworks in Redcar, northeast of England, had been running for over a century. Multiple crises and shocks led to its eventual closure and demolition in 2021. Shocks came from global competitors and the forces of environmental transition. Without an economic transformation at Redcar, the local cities of Middlesbrough, Stockton-on-Tees, and Hartlepool (all part of a wider metropolitan area of Tees Valley with 700,000 inhabitants) would continue to be economically depressed. Steelmaking had been part of the social and cultural fabric of the region for decades. The case shows how a special economic zone was created: Tees Valley Freeport, and how this began to attract FDI in newer green industries. This led to plans to build a renewable energy plant and a factory for manufacturing wind turbines.

- Skellefteå and Lappeenranta: Attracting and Embedding FDI for Green Projects

Skellefteå in northern Sweden is a city of almost 80,000 inhabitants and Lappeenranta in eastern Finland one with 73,000 inhabitants. The case provides insight into how both cities attracted FDI for Greentech projects and the conditions that facilitated the need for this type of FDI in these different locations. Skellefteå had experienced a construction boom and MNEs were drawn in to help execute this physical expansion. It also hosted a new lithium-ion battery gigavolt factory built by a company initially set up by Tesla executives and it received funding from various international sources. There was a strong international orientation in Skellefteå's experience, despite its geographic location in the north-east of Sweden. In Lappeenranta, foreign MNEs invested in thermal energy storage and power reserves. While at different stages of development, the two cities show the importance of having a stable industrial environment at the city level that can capture the benefits of new technological capacity for the sustainable development of cities through FDI.

Notes

1 https://sdgs.un.org/goals
2 https://worldpopulationreview.com/cities/india
3 https://economictimes.indiatimes.com/news/politics-and-nation/how-chennai-one-of-the-worlds-wettest-major-cities-ran-out-of-water/articleshow/80680182.cms?from=mdr

15

CASE 15: DIFFUSING WATER MANAGEMENT KNOW-HOW BETWEEN A FRENCH MNE AND AN INDIAN UTILITIES COMPANY IN CHENNAI, INDIA

La mayonnaise n'a pas pris

Akil Amiraly

Abstract

To improve the management of the public water supply service in the city of Chennai, the French utility company Veolia provided to Chennai Metro Water technical assistance from 2002 to 2006, under the institutional support of an international donor, the World Bank. The project allowed for the contractor Veolia to support Metro Water in developing the following functions: management, forecasting, operational management and maintenance of the water distribution network at a pilot-zone level. This case illustrates how instilling managerial and technical changes in public water utilities through foreign direct investment is a challenging task. The conflict of corporate cultures (demand driven versus offer driven), differences in appreciating the necessity to supply 24/7 water service in a context where public utilities were not able to supply enough water, and the issue around water tariffs made the challenge even more difficult.

Technical assistance as part of FDI into Chennai in the early 2000s

Veolia, a worldwide leader in the sector of water supply and sanitation, had a century-long tradition of providing its water supply service to municipalities in Europe and beyond. It started its first operation in France in Lyon (1853), soon after the creation of the Compagnie Générale des Eaux by Napoléon III. Industrialisation along with demographic and urban growth led cities to adopt emerging models of supplying water with the technical concourse of private utilities. The company initiated its foreign operations by the end of the 19th century with Venice (1880), followed by Constantinople (1882) and

DOI: 10.4324/9781003483410-20

Porto (1883). Beyond water, it had developed additional expertise in essential services[1] such as waste management and energy.

Providing technical assistance in Chennai

The development of Veolia's activity on Indian soil was nothing but a sinuous pathway. In the early 2000s, a series of projects intended to improve the public supply of water in Indian cities and involving the participation of foreign water utilities with Indian municipalities were initiated. These projects materialised in pilot projects first, and in some cases were translated into a service covering a significant share, if not the full scale of a city. The French water company Veolia stood out for multiple reasons: the number of projects it initiated, the managerial and technical innovations it developed with its Indian public counterparts, and for facilitating the entry of local private water utilities into the sector and helping them acquire new knowhow.

The perseverance of the company into getting into partnerships through a series of pilot projects with well-established public water utilities paid off. In 2005, a twinning consultancy arrangement was signed with the State of Karnataka involving four cities, at pilot zone levels. The company was assigned the management of the water supply service of the entire city of Nagpur, for a 25-year duration in 2012, and in 2013, part of the management of the water supply of Delhi for 15 years.

However, these milestones should not hide the fact that the initial stages of the development of the company in the Indian context were bumpy. One of the foundational grounds for its development in India was the technical assistance it provided to the Chennai Metropolitan Water Supply and Sewerage Board (CMWSSB) between 2002 and 2006. That project was among the first launched in India by the company following consultancy projects with the city of Jamshedpur in the late 1990s. The exploration of the Indian subcontinent by the company came more than a century after its first development in Europe.[2]

The technical assistance of Veolia in Chennai was aligned with the core policy of the World Bank in developing countries from the 1990s to the early 2000s. During that decade, the principles of the "Washington Consensus" constituted the founding element of the policy of international institutions. This policy, which advocated market liberalisation and the privatisation of certain state production tools, was to attract growth and investment. Foreign direct investment (FDI) played a significant role: foreign companies brought technical expertise, and access to financial resources that local institutions were often missing in emerging countries. However, if FDI could be instrumental in the success of infrastructure projects, their outcome depended on external factors as well. And at times the rules of the game were set to benefit to the international players over the local ones: a situation extensively narrated by Joseph Stiglitz.[3]

Through interviews with representatives of Veolia in France and in India in 2005–2006, and evidence taken from documentation, we describe the way the technical assistance evolved and the rationale of actions as seen from both sides (Veolia and CMWSSB).

The agreement: Transfer of knowledge between Veolia and Chennai Water Board

Objective of the technical assistance

The technical assistance general objective specified the functions to be supported:

> The general objective of the technical assistance is for the contractor to support Metro Water in developing the following functions: management, forecasting, operational management and maintenance of the water distribution network. The contractor will ensure the efficient management of the structure, particularly from a cost point of view.
>
> *(CMWSSB, 2000, p. 42)*

The agreement expressly mentioned the need to create optimum conditions for technology transfer. The service provider was expected to make available its experience and know-how in a wide range of activities, using the latest management techniques.

Metro Water's expectations covered the main managerial and technical functions involved in managing a water distribution service:

> Within the framework of this technical assistance, the partner's contribution should focus on the technical and managerial aspects of the following functions: (a) management and finance, (b) operational management and maintenance, (c) engineering and (d) human resources management.
>
> *(CMWSSB, 2000, p. 43)*

The transfer of know-how was expected to be part of the technical assistance.

Management of the technical assistance

The agreement stipulated the need for teamwork on both sides:

> The proposed partnership will be characterized by teamwork between the two parties, unlike traditional customer-consultant relationships. Its

> purpose is a direct transfer of managerial and technical skills and tools relating to Metro Water's various functions.
>
> *(CMWSSB, 2000, p. 43)*

While the chosen company had some leeway in the way it conducted the assistance, the managerial structure was clearly defined by the contract:

> The organization of activities to meet the customer's needs will be the responsibility of the partner. As far as possible, assistance should be provided by a permanent, experienced team from the company (and not by external consultants hired for the occasion) seconded to Metro Water to assist their counterparts. Metro Water undertakes to make available the necessary and competent personnel for training, and to provide a working environment and adequate material conditions to facilitate the partner's mission.
>
> *(CMWSSB, 2000, p. 43)*

The functions of each party were well specified:

> Four advisors (operational management and maintenance, technical and engineering, finance and administration, personnel and human resources) will be appointed to reinforce the skills of the Metro Water Board. They will be assisted by ad hoc experts in these fields. A general manager will also be appointed. The team leader will be drawn from the team of consultants. The role of the advisors and experts will be to advise Metro Water's senior management on the implementation and operational management of procedures, practices and systems. The partner will also advise Metro Water in its relations with third parties.
>
> *(CMWSSB, 2000, pp. 43–44)*

Perspectives from the two sides

Veolia: Sharing know-how without transferring it

The mindset behind the project

According to one of the project managers for India at Veolia in Paris, technical assistance was a transfer centred on an abbreviated dissemination of a knowledge model. For the company, it was a matter of making its know-how known to the Indian customer, rather than delivering it outright:

> There is a transfer of tools, methods and procedures. In this way, the meter is a concept that is transferred. The tool is bought by the Indians. We advise

> them on the purchase: it's not our job to sell equipment, and that's not what we margin on.

Technical assistance was a kind of preliminary action, leading the customer towards a more comprehensive offer. The latter would take the form of a management contract along the lines of a service delegation contract, Veolia's longer-term objective in India.

The project manager stressed that the elements transferred to Metro Water were marginal compared to the real know-how of Compagnie Générale des Eaux (CGE), the subsidiary of Veolia in India, in terms of management, network maintenance and customer relations. The technical assistance was viewed less as a technology transfer, and more of a marketing operation.

According to the respondent, CGE staff were not in the process of transferring knowledge:

> The prevailing mindset is *I show it because I'm asked* to. Culturally, transfer is not so easily disclosed.

For the Veolia India zone manager, transfer was more in the nature of the people at Seureca, Veolia's design office:

> At Générale des Eaux, we want to keep control of our knowledge. We don't transfer to structures, but to our managers. It's a business model that integrates and absorbs (…) The managers integrated into Veolia are based on the Veolia Water model.

Training at the heart of the transfer

A series of questions raised by the Head of the Veolia India zone during a steering committee meeting suggest that the elements transferred were not spreading or were operating very slowly on the Indian side. Veolia's involvement was anecdotal, being limited to the management of Metro Water's Board of Directors. It seemed that the work was not continued beyond the end of the project, and the technologies and management methods were not taken over by the recipients.

An exchange of views emerged during this committee meeting, stressing the limits of the transfer from Veolia. One of the project managers pointed out that the management approach was being appropriated through training (more and more Indians in the projects were being recruited directly by the company). The head of the India zone noted that in the field, the people in charge did not necessarily have an inclination for training: the dissemination of knowledge was not that easy, the transfer did not go through the structure, it was limited to the managers.

In the field, the last Veolia project engineer still working in Chennai indicated that the technical assistance only achieved 50% of its objectives. The lack of involvement by mid-level employees on the Indian side, coupled with their lack of interest in the knowledge and technology transfers achieved, largely explained the project's outcome.

Some people within the utility had learned a great deal, particularly on the pilot metre installation project, but such involvement was confined to a minority. Metro Water's senior managers were aware of the value of the project and the training opportunities it offered. However, this interest failed to spread to the lower hierarchical levels.

For the project manager in Paris, the nature of the contract did not allow for a transfer of knowledge:

> Technical assistance is a way for Veolia to demonstrate its knowledge, without actually transferring it. To communicate this knowledge, the management contract is the solution.

In his opinion, the transfer did not happen:

> The service business involves operating a service on behalf of an entity. What is sold is the quality of management and human resources. So, there is no transfer and no willingness to transfer.

A former accountant at Veolia in Chennai had a critical view of the company's management of the project and the positioning of Metro Water employees in the transfer:

> The aim of CGE was to train them, which was not achieved in most areas, with a few exceptions.

He added that there was no specific training for metre installations:

> We should have trained them as part of the water meter rollout.

Similarly, the project engineer in Chennai noted that there was no training designed independently of the operational side of the project. The trainees were put into real-life situations, without books or manuals, with the support of expatriates and local CGE engineers. The latter, who communicated in Tamil and English, experienced no major difficulties in communicating data.

The view from Veolia executives

From 1998, the year Veolia set up in India, to 2004, the Indian business was supervised by Veolia UK and the management of the subsidiary in Delhi was entrusted to expatriates. From 2004, the Indian subsidiary was attached to the CGE head office in Paris. During the first phase, the management of the Chennai project, the company's first activity in India, was entrusted to a team of expatriates from the United Kingdom (including consultants) and locals.

Several people we spoke to who had worked with the team emphasised the ethnocentric nature of expatriates' management. According to the project engineer in Chennai, the expatriates had a presumptuous attitude towards their Indian counterparts: they had not broken with their self-centred practices. Their personal involvement in the project was rather limited, and individual interests took precedence over collective ones.

The only French consultant who provided technical assistance to Veolia UK in 2001 on the financial aspects of the Chennai project shared his analysis:

> The English involved have no awareness of the problems. They don't give a damn, they have absolutely no interest in the country. The head of mission at the time was an old-fashioned Englishman, who transposed his model without any regard for the Indian world.

His colleague, a former accountant of Veolia in Chennai, pointed out that this tendency of expatriates to transpose their way of doing things from their home environment to the Indian city context was compounded by their inability to respond to requests for information from Metro Water executives. This situation created frustration among the latter and raised questions: employees started to wonder whether the expatriates were experts in their respective fields.

In the initial phase of the project, Veolia's UK representatives adopted an attitude exclusively focused on achieving their objectives, regardless of the situation of water distribution and the water company in Chennai.

There was a perception that those expatriates in charge of the Indian business were not focused on solving problems for the Indian water company, but exclusively on Veolia's short-term interests:

> Their aim is to place a contract, to take action quickly, with an immediate result, of a technical nature, with very short-term improvements, cosmetic measures. (...) They try to sell things with a sales pitch and apparent results. (...) It's a question of placing 2-3 experts who are trying to sell [their] software and old-fashioned hardware.

In the end, the contribution made by Veolia's French and UK teams in terms of transferring technical and managerial know-how was perceived as being marginal. The former adopted a posture of retention that inhibited effective transfer; the latter followed a purely mercantile and post-colonialist logic, transferring almost obsolete equipment to the Indian side.

Metro Water: Showing an interest in know-how without getting too involved

Seen from afar, technical assistance sets an example

The technical assistance contract financed by the World Bank from 2002 to 2004 was extended for a further year at Metro Water's request, using its own funds. For the Director of Veolia India in Delhi, this extension by the Indian side indicated their complete satisfaction with the work carried out by the company.

The project engineer in Chennai pointed out that the installation of water metres had gained the attention of Metro Water's Board of Directors and the Municipality. In addition to Chennai, representatives from other Indian cities, including Bangalore, Hyderabad and Vijayawada, expressed their interest in installing the metres after visiting the pilot project site. In January 2006, the city of Delhi asked for precise data on the installation of the metres. The project was also cited as a reference by Veolia Water's competitors in India. This pilot project opened an avenue for forthcoming projects for the company, starting with technical assistance in four cities in Karnataka, namely Belgaum, Hubli-Dharwar, Gulbarga, between 2005 and 2012, followed by a management contract with the city of Nagpur in 2012.

The opinion of the head of the Veolia India zone in Paris was much more nuanced. According to him, the success of the transfer needed to be put into perspective: it was carried out within the institutional framework of the World Bank, in a pilot zone of 1,500 connections, which concentrates a tiny proportion of the population, in a context of strong resistance to the transfer.

He wondered about the reasons behind the strong resistance to foreign techniques in Chennai:

> We have to see whether at the outset both parties had the transfer as an objective. In the case of the project, this was the case because the World Bank was behind it.

Seen closely, a possible lack of commitment to the project

The India manager's concerns were echoed throughout the organisation. There were indications that the Indian side had demonstrated little interest in the project, at various levels of Metro Water's hierarchy, both at employee and director levels.

According to Veolia's accountant in Chennai, the company's teams were not exempt from criticism. He questioned the way the project was being managed and described the failure of each party to meet deadlines as an indicator of poor management. On the one hand, there was Veolia's willingness to negotiate additional deadlines for the delivery of the evaluation report, with the aim of increasing its revenues and prolonging its presence within Metro Water. On the other hand, the water company was successively postponing deadlines in the work completion phase:

> The public operator is taking it lightly, without showing any signs of aggression or annoyance. Metro Water should have been behind us to push us to complete the project on time.

The Veolia employee noted that neither party wanted to invest heavily in the project:

> On their side, they had no desire to learn, to adapt the transferred technology. (...) Each CGE expert had an alter-ego on the Indian side for each of the activities. We should have passed on our knowledge and trained them. We did not. Nor did they ask us to: Public structures operate as they see fit. The administrators only act according to the directives of the ruling powers. (...) Their objective was to obtain nothing else than the World Bank loan.

The fact that managers were not naturally demanding was a natural attitude for Veolia Water's consultant and financial advisor in the context of technical assistance. What was less natural, in his opinion, was the short-term vision shared by both parties:

> There's no one to buy out the other. (...) It's difficult to move forward: External help is a joke, and the Indians won't accept any criticism, however justified .... the blame is shared. In the case of Chennai, two positions are diametrically opposed: on the Veolia side: *We sell you this system, buy it, we help you use it*; on the Indian side: *But what? Everything works perfectly.*

The chief sanitation engineer at the World Bank in New Delhi was equally sceptical. He pointed out the lack of involvement of the Indian side in the project:

> The willingness to learn is virtually nil. I'm not blaming the individual, but the system. It doesn't encourage people to learn in the sense that it doesn't give them the time.

Employees' partial support for the project

Resistance to the project was also perceptible at Metro Water's employee level, according to the accountant:

> Nothing is possible without the employees' assent. (...) From the outset, there was strong employee opposition to the project. They thought we were recommending downsizing. They were expressing their opinion independently. If you asked them about the content taught by CGE, they couldn't answer (...) Also, the high mobility of employees makes it difficult to pass on knowledge.

His colleague, a project engineer, confirmed this:

> Half the employees have a proven interest in technical aspects, while the other half show no interest in learning.

He did, however, recognise one advantage of the high mobility of Metro Water's technical assistance staff: the ability to train many employees at different hierarchical levels over a three-year period.

The French consultant noted, however, that the situation was not totally blocked on the Indian side:

> There are people who think, who are conscientious. Situated in subordinate, intermediate positions, they are aware of the problems. Conversely, for well-established leaders, everything's fine, we don't need anyone.[4]

He then evoked Peter's Principle:

> "In a hierarchy, every employee tends to rise to his/her level of incompetence". This principle leads to Peter's corollary: "In time, every post tends to be occupied by an employee who is incompetent to carry out its duties."

This consultant's experience in achieving his objective – the implementation of a financial management tool – revealed both the existence of real skills which were not valued by senior management:

> I managed to find a guy in his corner with his software. I struggled to get his thing, an Excel modelling tool. I've improved a lot of data. It gave me a quantified view of the accounts ... for different groups: Operations, accounts, financing, etc. It's a management tool with a real asset. (...)

He was in his corner, the only one interested, and he had to do it because of the World Bank's request. Disillusioned and old, he didn't believe in it anymore.

Conclusion

The case reveals that the transfer of know-how was not fully achieved. None of the parties showed a strong desire to carry out the transfer in practice. Veolia was not ready to fully transfer know-how, and commitment by Metro Water employees was highly uneven. Several factors seemed to have coalesced in this situation, starting with the very format of the project. It took place in a limited timeframe, in a confined organisational environment (a project team, a project office), in a circumscribed space (the pilot zone for the metre installation operation) with substantial human and technical resources (permanent staff and consultants, management tools, organisational methods). While this level of resources should have been an asset, in reality "the mayonnaise didn't take" (to coin the French expression, "la mayonnaise n'a pas pris"). External company representatives tried to promote their own tools, methods and models without showing sufficient interest in those of their partners. Conversely, the latter knew that this project was only for a short time, and this fed through to their level of commitment to transferring know-how. The learning process followed a top-down approach, from the giver to the receiver. This corresponded to the transposition of imported objects and knowledge without adaptation. A bottom-up approach would have enabled an integration of the latter's logics and modes of action, creating a breeding ground for innovation and the creation of hybrid management tools and models.

Notes

1 The sector of water supply and sanitation constitutes Veolia's principal business interest (40.6% of its turnover), followed by waste management (32.4%) and energy (27%), where it stands as the European leader. It employed nearly 218,000 employees in 2023 across all five continents. Its shareholders were diverse, and employees were the largest group of owners of shares (7.5%), followed by multiple pension funds from France and elsewhere. Veolia is listed on the Paris Stock Exchange.

2 The company started its operation more than 170 years ago in Lyon (1853), soon after the creation of the Compagnie Générale des Eaux by Napoléon III. Veolia has a century-long tradition of providing its water supply service to municipalities which started with Venice (1880), followed by Constantinople (1882) and Porto (1883). It is a worldwide leader in the sector of water supply and sanitation (40.6% of its turnover), followed by waste management (32.4%) and energy (27%) where it stands as the European leader. It employed nearly 218,000 employees in 2023 across the five continents. Its shareholders are diverse, and employees are the first owners of shares (7.5%), followed by multiple pension funds from France and elsewhere. It is listed in the Paris Stock Exchange.

3 Stiglitz J. (2002). *Globalization and its discontent*. W.W. Norton.
4 Laurence, P., & Hull R. (1970). *The Peter Principle*. Pan Books.

Bibliography

Chennai Metropolitan Water Supply and Sewerage Board (2000). Second Chennai water supply project: Agreement for twinning arrangement consultancy. *CMWSSB*.

Interview with the Chief Sanitation Engineer, World Bank, Delhi, February–March 2006.

Interview with the Director of Veolia Water India, Delhi, February–March 2006.

Interview with the Financial Advisor, Technical Assistance, Veolia UK, Aix-en Provence, June 2005.

Interview with the former Accountant, Technical Assistance, Veolia India, Chennai, June 19, 2006.

Interview with the Project Engineer, Technical Assistance, Veolia India, Chennai, April–June 2006.

Interview with the Project Manager, Veolia, India zone, Paris, June 2005.

Minutes, Steering Committee n°2, Institut Veolia, Paris, September 27, 2005.

16

CASE 16: FDI ON THE FRONTLINES

Kingspan's wartime investment in Lviv

Courtney Fingar

Abstract

After the full-scale Russian invasion of Ukraine in February 2022, national investment promotion agency UkraineInvest faced a crisis on many fronts, with an urgent need to reassure existing investors in Ukraine but also to attract new investment in the face of a plummeting GDP and falling investment flows. Led by then-CEO Sergiy Tsivkach, the agency put out an urgent call to the international business community to not hold back on investing in Ukraine. This was alongside work to improve the country's investment environment, with a new investment law put into place a year and a half after the invasion. Irish multinational Kingspan heeded the call and announced that it would invest more than €200m in a new Building Technology Campus in Ukraine. It selected a site near the western Ukrainian city of Lviv. The announcement gave a major morale boost to UkraineInvest and the country in general, and helped spark interest and investments from other international companies. This case examines the decision-making process Kingspan went through and the significance of planned investment in the context of wartime Ukraine.

When Russia launched a full-scale invasion of neighbouring Ukraine on 24 February 2022, with chilling images broadcast around the world of a column of tanks rolling towards capital city Kyiv, foreign direct investment was the last thing on anyone's mind – except for Sergiy Tsivkach, then CEO of Ukraine's national investment promotion agency.

Tsivkach was suddenly faced with the task of not only keeping his agency, UkraineInvest, and its staff functioning amidst the disruptions and traumas of war, but also reassuring and supporting both domestic and foreign companies operating in Ukraine.

DOI: 10.4324/9781003483410-21

Tsivkach recounted: "Everyone was shocked, even though we knew from watching the news it might happen."

Tsivkach (2024) said:

> Some of our staff had to relocate from the most affected areas, but it didn't stop us being connected. Our main responsibility was to support businesses. We were completely focused on our investors. We had to help avoid panic and also show our support for the Government of Ukraine.

The proverbial phone was ringing off the hook with investors seeking information, reassurance or practical help. "We jumped on that line of support for them. We had Teams meetings with them daily to coordinate what to do," he said.

UkraineInvest was established in 2016. As a full-fledged government institution and consultative body, its remit was supporting investors with advice and credible information on investment and business expansion in Ukraine. At the time of the 2022 invasion, the agency had approximately 30 employees.

The invasion began with a series of airstrikes targeting military installations, communication centres and strategic locations across Ukraine. Simultaneously, Russian ground forces, including tanks, artillery and infantry advanced into Ukrainian territory from multiple directions. A humanitarian crisis quickly erupted, with thousands of civilians fleeing their homes to escape the violence.

Ukraine's military, though significantly outnumbered and outgunned, put up a determined resistance, engaging in fierce battles to defend its territories. The initial phase of the invasion saw rapid territorial gains by Russian forces, including the capture of several Ukrainian cities and towns. There was also widespread destruction of Ukraine's infrastructure. However, Ukrainian forces managed to mount effective defences in some areas, slowing down the Russian advance and inflicting casualties on their troops.

The Battle of Kyiv was a pivotal and highly significant event during the early stages of the invasion. Kyiv, as capital, held immense symbolic and strategic importance, making it a primary target for both Ukrainian defenders and advancing Russian forces.

The battle began with intense fighting in the outskirts of Kyiv as Russian troops attempted to encircle the city and seize control of key transportation routes, including highways and railways. Ukrainian forces, bolstered by civilian volunteers and militias, defended the city strongly, employing a combination of conventional military tactics and guerrilla warfare.

Street-to-street fighting ensued as Ukrainian troops and volunteers fiercely resisted the Russian advance, often engaging in close-quarters combat.

The battle for Kyiv quickly turned into a gruelling urban warfare scenario, with both sides suffering significant casualties.

Despite facing overwhelming odds, Ukrainian defenders managed to hold strategic positions within the city, preventing the Russian forces from achieving a swift victory.

The battle lasted for several weeks, with both sides sustaining heavy losses. The city remained under Ukrainian control, dealing a significant blow to Russia's objectives in the region and bolstering international support for Ukraine's resistance efforts.

Throughout this fraught period, UkraineInvest, which is headquartered in Kyiv, managed to continue its operations without major interruption. The defence of the capital bolstered the morale of the agency, as it did for Ukraine itself, and thoughts turned already to reconstruction. There was an awareness that Ukraine's investment environment needed to be reinforced just like its military defences.

Tsivkach (2024) recalled:

> After the first few weeks of the invasion, when Kyiv didn't fall and we saw that we could protect ourselves, we looked at the damage that had been done and thought about the legislation to support investors and our investment incentives.
>
> Part of our team was focused from mid-March 2022 on the development of proposals to improve legislation that would enable more investors to come and rebuild Ukraine. We were already thinking about that.

The proposals were submitted to the Minister of Economy in 2022 and approved by the Prime Minister. The new investment legislation was passed by the Parliament in 2023.

The "Law On Amendments to Certain Legislative Acts of Ukraine on Implementation of Investment Projects with Significant Investments" went into force on 17 September 2023. The law brought in the following key changes:

- Lowered the investment threshold for accessing incentives from €20 million to €12 million;
- Expanded the list of eligible projects to include electronic communications, energy-efficient construction materials, bioethanol production for fuels and others;
- Provided state support for up to 30% of qualifying investments;
- And introduced new forms of state support, such as compensation for the cost of infrastructure objects and expenses for connecting to engineering and transport networks (CMS Law-Now, 2023).

The law also brought in new tax incentives, simplified the provision of land necessary for investment projects and consolidated investor guarantees through direct agreement with the Ukrainian government for 15 years (IEA Law No. 1116, 2023). Although it was an initiative offered by the UkraineInvest, its final version was a group effort of both the Ministry of Economy and the government of Ukraine more generally.

"March of 2022 was difficult since there was not much investment and to improve the situation UkraineInvest drafted a proposal to decrease the threshold which would help attract investors," Tsivkach said.

> After the initiative was implemented the new system became more flexible and investor-friendly. Rules on investor company size were rearranged and while in the past UkraineInvest would work only with big companies, after the new legislation the agency's services were available to any ambitious company with even a minimum of 10 employees.
>
> *(Tsivkach, 2024)*

The reforms were well timed. It was clear that inward investment was urgently needed to help keep Ukraine's economy afloat and to assist with reconstruction. The economic impact of the war was immediate, and severe. Before the invasion, it was estimated that Ukraine's GDP growth rate for 2022 would be 3.4%. However, due to the destruction of infrastructure and economic slowdown caused by the invasion, in 2022 Ukraine saw its GDP plummet –29% (Ukrainian Government, 2024).

UkraineInvest, though it had its hands full looking after existing international investors and domestic companies, felt strongly that the promotion of new investments was not to be shelved for some future post-war date.

Tsivkach said:

> We are practical people and at UkraineInvest our aim was to explain the potential to businesses that may invest in the country. And unfortunately we had a lot of potential for business due to damage to houses, bridges, facilities, buildings and manufacturing sites.
>
> We had to transfer this damage into an opportunity and present it to the world.

Armed with the new incentives and improved framework for investment, UkraineInvest put out a call to the international business community through newspapers, webinars, news outlets and social media platforms. "There is no need to wait until the end of the war. Our message to the international business community is clear: Ukraine is not only strong and free, but open for business," Tsivkach declared in a statement on UkraineInvest's website in 2023 (UkraineInvest, 2023).

Kingspan heeds the call

Less than four months after the start of the invasion came news of a major inbound investment: Kingspan, a global leader in advanced insulation and energy-efficient building solutions, said it would invest more than €200m in a new Building Technology Campus in Ukraine (Kingspan Group, 2022). Ireland-based Kingspan had more than 220 manufacturing facilities and more than 22,500 employees across more than 70 countries around the world.

It would be one of the first foreign companies benefitting from Ukraine's new incentives scheme.

Billed as a state-of-the-art facility geared towards meeting rapidly growing demand for energy-efficient buildings, the group's Ukraine campus would manufacture advanced insulation and district heating products and eventually create more than 600 jobs. The low-carbon facility will be powered by solar and wind energy.

Kingspan had previously announced its total exit from the Russian market. In April of 2022, the company divested its Russian operations – which consisted of two factories and a commercial structure – to local management and sold the assets to local partners (Kingspan group/Stenson, 2024).

Welcoming both announcements, Ukraine's Foreign Minister Dmytro Kuleba said: "Our goal is not solely renewal and rebuilding of the destruction caused by Russian aggression but also the creation of a completely new, modern and innovative economy leveraging leading urban development expertise and green technologies."

He added:

> For this reason, based on President Volodymyr Zelenskyy's vision, we created the Recovery Plan for Ukraine, and Kingspan's project meets both the spirit and the goal of our plan. We invite the international business community to follow this example by withdrawing completely from Russia and relocating their businesses in Ukraine. This will benefit both: a company's standing and its long-term strategy.

Commenting during a visit to Kyiv to kickstart the project, Gene Murtagh, CEO of Kingspan Group, said:

> This investment sits at the crossroads of three crises: the climate crisis, the energy security crisis, and the crisis caused by the Russian war against Ukraine. The new Building Technology Campus we are planning will make positive contributions on all three fronts, supporting Ukraine as it rebuilds its economy, meeting demand across central and Eastern Europe for energy efficient buildings, and helping Europe to reduce reliance on oil and gas imports. (Kingspan Group, 2022)

Although the investment was important both practically and symbolically for Ukraine, supporting Ukraine and its reconstruction was not the main motivation for Kingspan, according to Mike Stenson (2024), project director for the Ukraine facility.

Stenson said:

> It was exclusively a business decision at that time. However, as we began to engage at every level in Ukraine, inevitably you get somewhat emotionally caught up in what [the Ukrainians] are going through, even if our primary driver was business.

A number of the company's divisions that operate in eastern Europe were looking for incremental manufacturing-related capacity in eastern Europe. "We have a significant presence in Slovakia, Hungary, Poland and Czech Republic. All these were considered as part of the process," Stenson said.

> Our view was if we want to put something together in one location covering everything, it might be better to look at a super-site somewhere in Eastern Europe and Ukraine entered the equation. We realised we could manufacture there and export back into the EU.

He stressed the investment would be incremental and not a replacement of any existing investment elsewhere.

Tapping into the reconstruction opportunities were not irrelevant, however. "A lot of damage was done to infrastructure in Ukraine, so there is an opportunity to avail of competitively selling products which are needed in the rebuild," Stenson (2024) said.

Not alone on the FDI front

Kingspan was not the only foreign company investing in Ukraine in the wake of the invasion.

There was an understandable drop off in investment into the country, exacerbated by a global downturn in FDI volumes. According to UNCTAD's World Investment Report (2024), FDI flows to Ukraine fell to $848 million in 2022, down from $7.3 billion one year earlier. But several investors showed fortitude in the face of the Russian onslaught. UkraineInvest said it attracted $500 million in inward investment in the year following the invasion (Mathews & Sraders, 2023).

Since the full-scale war broke out, German multinational chemical and consumer goods company Henkel invested about €1.5M in its Ukrainian factories in order to modernise production, despite damage to some of its facilities from the fighting (Ukrainian Business News, 2023). Like Kingspan, Henkel exited the Russian market in April 2022.

US cybersecurity firm Hold Security chose Kyiv for its second European office in late 2021 and launched its Ukrainian operations just 18 days after Russia's invasion. Online games developer SciPlay, which had been active in Ukraine since 2020, said it expanded its headcount in the country by more than 60% since the war began (Myles, 2023).

Meanwhile, Swedish truck manufacturer Scania went ahead with plans to open a new workshop in Brovary, a city in Kyiv Oblast, despite its factory in Bucha having been seized by Russian troops when they invaded the city in March 2022 (it regained control a month later when the city was liberated).

Scania's exit from the Russian market was announced on the company's official website in March 2023.

Other announcements followed throughout 2023.

Carlsberg Group, the Danish beermaker, confirmed investments of €40 million in Ukraine, adding a new production line at its Kyiv brewery and increasing the production capacity of canned products by 80%. The group started its operations in Ukraine in 1996 and was one of the largest international investors in the FMCG sector ever since, investing more than €1 billion in the country (Carlsberg Group, 2023). In 2022, Carlsberg Group also announced its plans to leave Russia and in 2023 signed a final agreement on selling its business there.

Pharmaceutical giant Bayer announced an investment of €60 million from 2023 onwards in its corn seed production facility in Pochuiky (Bayer, 2024), while steel and mining company ArcelorMittal announced plans in April 2023 to build a new tailings storage facility in Kryvyi Rih, a city in central Kyiv that is the hometown of President Zelensky (EcoPolitic, 2023).

Bayer said it was reconsidering investment levels and production procedures in Russia after the invasion but continued operating in the country (Reuters, 2022).

American tobacco company Philip Morris International said it planned to invest more than $30 million in the launch of a new production facility in the Lviv region (Philip Morris International, 2023). Philip Morris also continued doing business in Russia despite announcing plans to exit the market in 2022.

Such expansions by existing investors – and the fact they didn't cut and run – gave a boost to Ukraine's FDI efforts and provided sorely needed reassurance. "These examples were pivotal for the promotion of Ukraine," Tsivkach (2024) said. "For investors it is important to not only see an opportunity but also to see that others are already succeeding in the country."

But Kingspan's investment was especially meaningful. It wasn't Kingspan's first foray into Ukraine: the company had a sales presence in the country since 2005. But this was its first major investment and first production facility there. In the past an investment in the East of Ukraine was considered but not advanced back in 2008 to 2010.

"Kingspan was a very important case for Ukraine. Attracting such a significant greenfield investment during this difficult time was massive for us. This became a flagship project for UkraineInvest to present to the world," Tsivkach said.

"Afterwards a few companies from the construction materials industry approached us from European countries and the United States. Now several projects are being developed in Ukraine to penetrate this market. They wanted to follow Kingspan's example."

A notable ripple effect came in April 2024 when ArcelorMittal, a world leader in construction solutions, announced it would build a €40 million modern production facility in Kyiv to support reconstruction (Ukrainian Business News, 2024).

"The promotion of the Kingspan case helped attract ArcelorMittal," Tsivkach said. "This is how they initially contacted UkraineInvest."

The perils and mundanities of conflict investment

Investing in active conflict zones poses a myriad of challenges for companies, ranging from security risks to operational hurdles. However, Kingspan's project director Stenson (2024) said, barring a few notable examples, the company mainly faced more typical FDI hurdles with its Ukraine project.

He explained:

> There was nothing in the early stages that jumped out, other than the complications related to getting a project team in place in the middle of a war zone and the risk of conscription. There is more difficulty in going in and out of the country, and getting through border crossings.

More significant were what he called "peculiarities in the way Ukraine is set up to do investment" that Kingspan was not aware of at the outset. Availability of land and access to utilities was a primary issue.

"We were looking for a 50-hectare site, which is enormous. The likelihood was small of finding that," he said. "In terms of Industrial policy, Ukraine needs to do more to attract inward investors and have zoned land which is available with utilities nearby. We don't have any of that."

The newly unveiled investment incentives proved attractive also to Kingspan. He explained:

> The resolution allows for up to 30% of capital investment to be given back in the form of tax write offs, which is helpful. Also, where there is no power, road or rail, the state will compensate or partly compensate what an investor would spend in that space, within the constraints of the 30% limit.

> If we spend x millions on power or roads, we can work with the state and we get less in terms of tax relief but get this capital up-front as compensation.

These were deemed as highly beneficial incentives, but meant there were quite a few legalities to work out about them. Though guidance and support from the state was needed, and appreciated, Kingspan was at pains to avoid any special treatment.

"We were very aware of the historical issue with corruption in Ukraine. It is getting better but is still there," Stenson said.

> In every meeting we have with officials we say we're not looking for anything special for Kingspan. We can't afford to have doubts about that. We want help on what the law allows for in terms of compensation or investment support, we want to figure out how to get it, but we will never look for anything unusual or special.

The site-selection search led Kingspan to the outskirts of Lviv, where the company has had an office since 2009.

"We wanted something close to the border that could serve as a beachhead for further expansion into the rest of Ukraine. The opportunity to go east from there remains," Stenson said (2024).

Lviv was the largest city in western Ukraine, with a population of just over 700,000. The Lviv region shared a 278-km border with Poland and therefore the European Union. Although only the sixth-largest city in Ukraine, Lviv was one of the main cultural centres for the country and was second only to capital Kyiv in cultural, political and religious importance.

Lviv boasted a well-educated and skilled workforce, with a strong emphasis on technology, engineering and IT-related fields. The city was home to several prestigious universities and technical colleges, producing a steady stream of talent in areas such as software development, cybersecurity and digital marketing. This pool of skilled professionals had attracted numerous multinational companies to establish outsourcing and R&D centres in Lviv.

In the years ahead of the invasion, Lviv had seen significant investment in infrastructure projects aimed at enhancing connectivity and supporting economic growth. This included the expansion and modernisation of transportation networks, such as roads, railways and airports, as well as the development of industrial parks and special economic zones to attract investment in manufacturing and logistics.

Its relative safety compared to other parts of Ukraine and proximity to the rest of Europe made Lviv a hub for war-time humanitarian efforts, providing support to internally displaced persons fleeing from conflict-affected areas in eastern Ukraine. The city saw a large influx of refugees seeking shelter, food and medical assistance, putting a strain on local resources. The conflict also had repercussions on Lviv's economy, particularly in sectors like tourism and trade.

Lviv, although not directly on the frontlines of the conflict, nonetheless experienced heightened security concerns. Kyiv and major eastern cities such as Kharkiv have borne the brunt of Russian bombardment, but Lviv was not immune from shelling. The city suffered deadly missile attacks in March and April 2022, ahead of Kingspan's investment announcement (Aljazeera, 2022; BBC News, 2022).

Kingspan remained undeterred. The company took possession of the land in late March 2024. Kingspan expected construction on the facility to begin in late 2024 or early 2025, with production launching between Feb and May 2026. The company intended to make a go-or-no-go decision in November 2024.

"The project is a year and a bit behind schedule, but that's okay, war is still going on. Even if we were ready, we're not sure we would proceed with the build right now," Stenson said.

A local project team – all Ukrainian – was assembled, and after initial training, the facility was planned to be staffed and managed solely by local hires. Half or more of the products manufactured at the facility would be for export. "We're excited and enthusiastic about the team we've put in place to make this happen," Stenson (2024) said.

As to whether the outcome of the war might impact the eventual plans and whether a loss by Ukraine would halt the project, Stensen said, "It depends what it means by Ukraine losing."

"Would Russia occupying more than 20% of Eastern Ukraine impact us? Probably not. We might end up delaying if Russia pushed to the Dnipro River," he said, of the river which flows through the heart of Ukraine and broadly separates its east from west. "Whatever the [post-war] agreement is will be much more important."

Meanwhile, Stenson remained broadly optimistic about Ukraine's longer term prospects as an investment destination.

"State support in Ukraine is reasonable and developing. They need to do more in relation to business parks and provision of utilities, and keep working on the anti-corruption drive," he said. "But with a bit of help from outsiders they will make it an attractive place to do business."

References

Aljazeera (2022). *7 killed in Lviv as Russia steps up attacks before Donbas push*. https://www.aljazeera.com/news/2022/4/18/six-killed-lviv-russia-steps-up-attacks-before-donbas-push?traffic_source=KeepReading

Bayer (2024). *Bayer's effort in Ukraine*. https://www.bayer.com/en/ukraine

BBC News (2022). *Ukraine war: 'Sky turned red' as missiles hit Lviv military base*. https://www.bbc.com/news/world-europe-60728208

Carlsberg Group (2023). *Carlsberg Ukraine presents one of the largest investment projects of 2023*. https://www.carlsberggroup.com/newsroom/carlsberg-ukraine-presents-one-of-the-largest-investment-projects-of-2023/
CMS Law-Now (2023). *Ukraine advances legislation for state support of projects with significant investments*. https://cms-lawnow.com/en/ealerts/2023/09/ukraine-advances-legislation-for-state-support-of-projects-with-significant-investments
EcoPolitic (2023). *ArcelorMittal is building a toxic waste tailings facility in Kryvyi Rih*. Available at: https://ecopolitic.com.ua/en/news/u-krivomu-rozi-arselormittal-buduie-hvostoshovishhe-z-toksichnimi-vidhodami-2/
IEA (2023). *State support for investment projects with significant investments in Ukraine (law no. 1116) – policies*. https://www.iea.org/policies/18076-state-support-for-investment-projects-with-significant-investments-in-ukraine-law-no-1116
Kingspan Group (2022). *Kingspan to invest €200m in new state-of-the-art Ukraine facility*. https://www.kingspangroup.com/en/news-insights/kingspan-to-invest-200m-In-new-ntate-of-the-art-ukraine-facility/
Mathews, J., & Sraders, A. (2023). The man responsible for promoting investment in Ukraine says the country has attracted $500 million since the start of the war. *Fortune*. https://fortune.com/2023/09/29/500-million-invesments-in-ukraine-since-war-started-ukraineinvest/
Myles, D. (2023). *Staying put: The bumpy ride of investing in Ukraine through war*. FDI Intelligence. https://www.fdiintelligence.com/content/news/staying-put-the-bumpy-ride-of-investing-in-ukraine-through-war-82119
Philip Morris International (2023). *Philip Morris invests 30 million dollars in new production in Ukraine*. https://www.pmi.com/markets/ukraine/uk/media-center/details-news/article-philip-morris-investment-in-Ukraine-2023
Reuters (2022). *Bayer says it will continue supplying Russia with agricultural inputs*. Reuters. https://www.reuters.com/business/healthcare-pharmaceuticals/bayer-says-it-will-continue-supplying-russia-with-agricultural-inputs-2022-08-15/
Stenson, M. (2024). *Interviewed by Courtney Fingar*. 21 March, Online Zoom interview.
Tsivkach, S. (2024). *Interviewed by Courtney Fingar*. 22 March, Online Zoom interview.
UkraineInvest (2023). *Guide: Rebuilding Ukraine with the private sector*. https://drive.google.com/file/d/15aM5yqKtocog9DvViLkATAFHzZdcmtZv/view
Ukrainian Business News (2023). *Since the war, Henkel has invested about €1.5M in its Ukrainian factories*. https://ubn.news/since-the-war-henkel-has-invested-about-e1-5m-in-its-ukrainian-factories/(Accessed 14 April 2024).
Ukrainian Business News (2024). *ArcelorMittal Construction is investing €40M in the production of construction materials to rebuild Ukraine*. https://ubn.news/arcelor-mittal-construction-is-investing-e40m-in-the-production-of-construction-materials-to-rebuild-ukraine/
Ukrainian Government (2024). *Sustainable economy*. https://www.kmu.gov.ua/en/the-government-priorities/sustainable-economy
UNCTAD (2024). 'World Investment Report 2024' https://unctad.org/publication/world-investment-report-2024

17

CASE 17: REVITALISING TEESSIDE, UK

The remarkable journey from loss-making steelworks to a renewable energy hub through FDI and local government support

Maurice Wokke

Abstract

Once a major player in the UK steel industry, Teesside Steelworks planned a transformation into a renewable energy hub. In North East England, steel production on the banks of the river Tees had shaped the region's economy for over a century. However, global competition, stricter environmental regulations and economic downturn led to its eventual closure. Attempts to continue operations through foreign acquisitions failed, leaving the site abandoned and the local economy declining. In response, recent efforts repurposed the steel site, taking advantage of its strategic coastal location, industrial infrastructure and Freeport status. Creating the Tees Valley Freeport attracted significant foreign direct investment (FDI) in green industries, including planning a greenfield renewable energy plant and a wind turbine monopile manufacturing plant. Other key projects, such as a carbon capture initiative, aimed to create a low-carbon industrial hub. With strong government support and strategic planning, the Tees area was prepared to become a leading player in the UK's energy transition, showcasing the potential for regeneration and sustainable development in post-industrial regions.

Introduction

In North East England, Teesside Steelworks, also known as Redcar or Teesside Cast Products (TCP), had been a crucial part of the British steel industry since the 19th century. It was once one of Europe's largest steel production sites, with the continent's second-largest blast furnace in operation. Over the years, the steel site faced significant challenges, including global competition, economic decline and stricter environmental regulations, which led to

DOI: 10.4324/9781003483410-22

instability, ownership changes and eventually the bankruptcy of the steelworks. Recent developments in 2022–2023 aimed to repurpose the formal steel site for new industrial uses and promote innovation and sustainable development. The River Tees area where the steelworks was located was a major supplier of high-quality steel to key sectors such as construction, automotive, shipbuilding and railways, supporting UK infrastructure and economic development. The steel site's strategic location, with a deep-sea port and access to crucial transportation routes, enabled efficient production and distribution. This case study aimed to highlight Teesside Steelworks, examining its historical significance, economic impact, challenges and ongoing development efforts. By exploring these facets, the case study aimed to highlight the role of the steelworks in the UK steel industry and its impact on the local community and economy. It sought to understand the factors that had shaped its journey and provide insight into the European steel industry's broader trends and issues.

Historical background

Britain achieved a leading position in the global steel industry in the mid-19th century thanks to its favourable access to cheap raw materials and advanced technical skills. The areas around the banks of the River Tees from Middlesbrough to Redcar played a crucial role in developing steelmaking technology in this era. This strategic location was close to the iron ore deposits in Cleveland Hills and the coal mines in Durham. At the height of industrial activity, nearly a hundred blast furnaces were operating in that area. Although new technologies were not necessarily invented in the River Tees area, Teesside played a crucial role in adopting, refining and advancing steelmaking processes, contributing to the region's reputation as an industrial innovation centre. In the 19th century and early 20th centuries, Britain was characterized as an 'export-oriented economy.' It was often argued that the expansion of industrial production depended significantly on the performance of key export sectors, as roughly 30% of industrial production was destined for overseas markets. To illustrate as Hatton (1990, p. 576) puts it, in 1907 exports accounted for 84% of cotton textiles, 57% of woollen goods and 40% of iron and steel, mechanical engineering, and shipbuilding production. However, as the 20th century dawned, this lead gradually diminished, with the United States and Germany taking over the position. Taking advantage of vertical integration, new access to cheaper raw materials, larger average plant size, improved operational efficiency and more concentrated industry, these countries took over Britain's former dominance in the international steel trade.

The 1960s and 1970s marked the era of establishing new European coastal steel sites. Examples of these coastal sites were Sidmar (Belgium),

Dunkerque (France), Fos-sur-Mer (France), Italsider Taranto (Italy), Hamburger Stahlwerke (Germany) and the Teesside Steelworks in Redcar United Kingdom. Most of these coastal sites had an efficient layout with modern technology compared to the more vintage inland steel sites. Coastal steel sites with a deep-sea port have access to bulk carriers and the global raw material market (e.g., coal and iron ore), a competitive advantage vis-à-vis inland located competitors (as noted by) Fleming (1967). They were not dependent on local resources and could benefit from the dynamics of the international trade markets. The Teesside Steelworks was strategically located on the banks of the river Tees between the city of Middlesbrough and the towns of Redcar, and Hartlepool in North East England, significantly impacted the socio-economic landscape of these surrounding areas. With populations of approximately 140,000, 30,000 and 92,000 (year 2022), these towns heavily depended on the steelworks.

Changes in the industrial context

The 1980s to the 1990s saw significant transformations in the European steel industry, characterised by overcapacity and the privatisation and restructuring of several leading companies. A notable example was the British Steel Corporation (BSC) privatisation in the United Kingdom (UK), initiated under Prime Minister Margaret Thatcher's government. After privatisation, the BSC merged with the Dutch steel maker Hoogovens to form one of Europe's leading steel firms in 1999. The Teesside Steelworks was one of the five crude steel-producing facilities with blast furnaces in this new firm, named Corus. Due to a steel crisis in the early 2000s, Corus faced losses and was forced to implement a large restructuring programme to become profitable. This included divestment in downstream activities and the closure of Llanwern's heavy-end steel site in South Wales. As a result of its financial struggles, Corus became a target for foreign investors, leading to its acquisition by Tata Steel from India after a bidding contest with the Brazilian steel firm CSN in 2007. This acquisition made Tata Steel one of the ten largest steel producers in the world in terms of production capacity. At the time of Tata Steel's acquisition of Corus, the steel industry was booming, driven mainly by the expansion of China's economy and its high demand for steel products. This hunger for steel led to historically high prices for steel, and resulted in a profitable period for Corus.

Economic challenges

However, this economic boom was short-lived and ended shortly after the start of the Global Financial Crisis (GFC) in 2008. The GFC hit the steel industry unexpectedly hard. While the profit of European steel mills in Q3 2008 was at an all-time high, 30% of steel production was idled by the end of the year, leading to loss-making operations throughout Europe in the following years. The United Kingdom's steel industry suffered significantly and ultimately did not recover. After stable production levels of around 15 million metric tonnes of crude steel per annum in the years before the GFC, the total crude steel production in the United Kingdom declined with a –7% Compound Average Growth Rate (CAGR) to production levels of 6 million tonnes in 2022 (WSA, 2009; 2024). Before the GFC, the United Kingdom was a steel-exporting country with a net trade balance of approximately 2 million metric tonnes annually. This position gradually changed to net zero, where steel exports and imports were balanced at approximately 7 million metric tonnes in 2015. The outdated infrastructure of the steel sites led to high production costs, and this, combined with a strong British Pound compared to currencies like the Euro, resulted in increased imports.

Eventually exports had declined to 3.3 million metric tonnes, while imports fell to 5.4 million metric tonnes (with a value of $8.7 billion), resulting in a net import of 2.1 million metric tonnes in 2015. The largest crude steel producers in the United Kingdom were Tata Steel UK Limited, Hebei Jinge Group Co. Ltd. and Celsa (UK) Holdings Ltd. The top three countries exporting to the United Kingdom were Turkey, Germany and Spain (International Trade Administration, 2024). An example of an outdated infrastructure of the steel sites was Scunthorpe; this site produced Long products with virgin steel made from coal and iron ore. Examples of Long products are products like wire rod, sections and rail. These products were often used in construction while the so called flat products are products used in automotive, white and yellow goods and canning industry. Producing Long products with blast furnaces was not cost-competitive compared to the industry standard of using recycled steel with Electric Arc Furnaces (EAF) as explained by Medarac et al. (2020). The steel site in South Wales struggled with producing high-quality Flat products due to a lack of capabilities and an inefficient steel site. Finally, the apparent steel use in the United Kingdom declined from 11.7 million metric tonnes in 2008 to 9.4 million tonnes in 2022 (WSA, 2009; 2024).

The end of an era

During the GFC, Teesside Steelworks suffered more than other European mills, and the site was mothballed in 2009. In 2011, the Thai-based Sahaviriya Steel Industries (SSI) acquired Teesside Steelworks for £291 million and restarted the production of crude steel and cast products in 2012 (BBC, 2012). The business model implemented by SSI at Teesside Steelworks contrasted with the efficient Integrated mill concept. An Integrated mill produces hot-rolled products from iron ore and coal by combining raw material agglomeration, coke production, blast furnaces, a basic oxygen steel plant and a hot mill at the same location. This setup optimises efficiencies, site logistics and the utilisation of works-arising gases, making it competitive against other mills. In contrast, the semis produced at Teesside Steelworks were exported and milled overseas, resulting in inefficient energy use and a high-cost price. Semis are the first solid steel product upon solidification of liquid steel and are products like billets, or slabs. The one-blast furnace site configuration at Teesside Steelworks was once a competitive advantage in Europe, featuring one of the continent's largest blast furnaces. However, with a declining market for steel, this asset footprint became a liability due to the high minimum operating speed of the furnace. This rigidity made it difficult to reduce production volume when needed. Stricter environmental rules and regulations required additional investments in the steel site to comply with the new emissions levels. In 2015, the strong British Pound and high energy prices caused a new steel crisis in United Kingdom, severely impacted steel-producing firms and their customers, including Caparo, Crown, Tata Steel UK and SSI Teesside Steelworks (House of Commons Library, 2016). SSI Teesside Steelworks entered liquidation, leaving the Redcar community with an abandoned steel site on the polluted ground, thousands of redundant steelworkers, and additional thousands of redundant jobs in the local area. The Redcar MP, quoted in the BBC News on October 15, 2015, accused the government of 'industrial vandalism' by not keeping the site operational (BBC, 2015). A stand-alone scenario for the steelworks' coke ovens was not considered as a feasible solution because the coke ovens made a loss of £2 million per month due to overcapacity in the steel industry across the world. The closure of the steelworks had a significant impact on the local economy, further endangering the already vulnerable population. The city of Middlesbrough and the towns of Redcar and Hartlepool not only experienced higher unemployment rates but also exhibited lower education levels compared to national averages. Compared to the national average unemployment rate for the United Kingdom which was approximately 4.8% as of 2021. By comparison, unemployment rates in Middlesbrough (7.7%), Redcar (6.1%) and Hartlepool (7.2%) are significantly higher, highlighting significant regional economic challenges. The UK average for residents without qualifications was around 22%, while Middlesbrough, Redcar and Hartlepool had higher rates of 27%, 25% and 29% respectively. Similarly, higher education levels in these cities (14–15%) were lower than the national average of around 40%.

Comparable cases in the European steel industry

The steelworks at Teesside was not the only coastal site closed in the last decades; out of the thirteen coastal steel sites operating in the European Union in 1980, Llanwern (United Kingdom), Cornigliano (Italy) and Lucchini

(Italy) closed their heavy end while the downstream operations remained in operation. Furthermore, Bagnoli in Italy, for example, was closed entirely in the 1990s. These were examples of coastal steel sites with initial competitive location advantages vis-a-vis inland competitors that did not survive at the end. Because of the location advantage, closing a coastal steel site or its heavy-end could open the door for new opportunities. In 2005, the heavy-end of the Cornigliano coastal steel plant in Italy was closed while downstream operations continued. Similarly, the former Llanwern heavy-end in South Wales was cleaned and redeveloped into residential and recreational spaces, while downstream operations remained in operation. However, the Bagnoli site in Italy remained undeveloped and polluted, highlighting the challenges of industrial decay.

Transformation into a renewable energy hub

To create an attractive business environment, the Tees Valley was granted Freeport status to create high-quality jobs for local people (UK Parliament, 2023). Freeports are special areas established by the government to encourage investment in regions that had 'historically missed out.' The South Tees Development Corporation expected 20,000 jobs would be created over the next 25 years, mainly in green industries (Tees Valley, 2023a). Next to the former steelworks, the Tees Valley Freeport covered the region including Teesport, the Port of Middlesbrough, the Port of Hartlepool, Redcar Bulk Terminal, LV Logistics, Wilton International and Teesside International Airport. In 2016, the South Tees Site Company Limited was established as a joint venture between the Department of Business, Energy and Industrial Strategy, and the South Tees Development Corporation. This entity initially focused on ensuring the safety of the former steelworks and mitigating any safety risks. The company became a wholly-owned subsidiary of the South Tees Development Corporation in 2020. After the decommissioning of the steel site, the stranded assets had to be demolished and extensive remediation of the site was necessary. The estimated costs for these demolition, construction and site remediation efforts ranged around £482.6m with the government contributing £246 million (MRW, 2023). This total investment included the demolition of key steel making assets, such as the blast furnace, sinter plant and coking plant, among others. The demolition included all former TCP assets while downstream assets, like for example, the British Steel Beam plant remained in operation.

The redevelopment of the premises was crucial for the establishment of new industries. The site still had strategic advantages including a deep-sea port, access to the high-voltage grid and extensive infrastructure links, all of which were remnants of the former Teesside steelworks. The steelworks was a hub of industrial symbiosis, housing not only the steel mill operations but also companies such as Anglo American (a mining company), Linde Group (an industrial gases company), Heidelberg Cement Group, Redcar Bulk Terminal and several energy companies, many of which remained active in the area after the steel sited ended operations. Among the new key projects to be developed, MGT Teesside planned to build a £650 million renewable energy plant. In addition, Net Zero Teesside Power (NZT Power) was preparing to build a gas-fired power station equipped with carbon capture technology. This initiative also included the development of a CO_2 transport, utilisation and storage infrastructure (CCUS) for the Tees Valley, collectively valued at approximately £4 billion domestically funded. In addition, Circular Fuels Ltd, a British company, planned to set up a £150 million plant in Teesside that could produce 50 kilotons of clean fuel annually from 220,000 tons of non-recyclable household and industrial waste. NWG Living Water has announced two projects with a combined investment of £27 million domestically funded, aimed at improving the sewerage network and environmental protection in Teesside (Tees Valley, 2023b).

South Korean company, SeAH, was preparing £450 million foreign direct investment (FDI) in SeAH greenfield Wind's monopile production facility at Teesworks. This facility was known for its significant advancements, including manufacturing steel monopiles for wind turbines (GOV.UK, 2023). Once completed, the 800-meter building would be the largest monopile facility in the world and the first of its kind in Britain. In 2023, Blastr Green Steel from the Nordics signed a Memorandum of Understanding (MoU) with Redcar Bulk Terminal to explore the potential for a FDI in a greenfield future pellet plant at the former steelworks premises (Blastr, 2023). These pellets would serve as feedstock for new low-CO_2 direct reduction iron plants, which were expected to be built in Europe and worldwide for the manufacturing of green steel. British Steel (Jingye Group) received planning permission to build an EAF on the former steelworks site in 2023 (BBC, 2023). With this project Jingye Group (China) was preparing a greenfield FDI in a new steel site including an EAF, a ladle furnace, a vacuum degasser and two continuous casters. The new steelworks would supply both the British Steel Beam plant in Teesside and the Skinningrove Works in North Yorkshire. In addition, British Steel had been contracted to supply more than 30,000 tonnes of steel, using recycled steel from the former steelworks to produce semis for SeAH's Wind monopiles. All these planned greenfield investments had the potential to establish a new industrial symbiosis and to utilise the current exported steel scrap from the United Kingdom, creating a low-carbon energy hub and green steel facility. This transformation would be the result of 10 years of strategic planning and changes in a former loss-making polluting site into a renewable energy hub through FDI and local government support with thousands of jobs secured.

Conclusion

The history of Teesside Steelworks reflected the wider story of the British steel industry, once a world leader, now facing industrial change and economic challenges. The transition from traditional integrated steel production to a more diversified industrial base was marked by the closure of the heavy end and the demolition of these plants. While difficult for the industry and the local community, this shift has paved the way for new opportunities. Teesside was a good example of a steelworks in transformation. With significant government support, the site was cleared, retaining coastal benefits such as a deep-sea port, high-voltage grid connections and existing industrial infrastructure. The presence of symbiotic industries, such as energy companies and the cement industry, further increased the potential for redevelopment. The establishment of a Freeport in the Tees area was a crucial step in attracting new businesses and FDIs. This initiative appealed not only to domestic companies but also to foreign investors in the steel and energy-related sectors. The Tees Valley region, once burdened by a loss-making steelworks in Redcar, now held the promise of becoming a new industrial cluster. This transformation had the potential to generate thousands of new jobs and position Tees Valley as a leading hub in the energy transition, driving innovation and economic resilience. In conclusion, the evolution of Teesside Steelworks from a liability to a rapidly growing centre of industrial activity was an example of the potential for successful regeneration of former industrial sites. With strategic investment and government support, Teesside played a crucial role in the future of the UK industrial and energy landscape.

References

BBC. (2012). Teesside steel plant's £291m sale secures 700 jobs. https://www.bbc.com/news/uk-england-tees-12503390.

BBC. (2015). SSI Steelworks: MPs clash over closure of Redcar. https://www.bbc.co.uk/news/uk-england-tees-34518649

BBC. (2023). Design of new Electric Arc Furnace revealed. *BBC News*. https://www.bbc.com/news/articles/cgxj0ewnxv2o

Blastr. (2023). *Blastr Green Steel signs a Letter of Intent with Redcar Bulk Terminal to explore the development of a pellet plant in Teesside, UK*. Green Steel Press Release. https://www.blastr.no/resources/230710-Blastr-signs-a-Letter-of-Intent-with-Redcar-Bulk-Terminal_v3.pdf

Fleming, D. (1967). Coastal steelworks in the common market countries. *Geographical Review, 57*(1), 48–72.

GOV.UK. (2023). *Ground-breaking UK Export Finance deal secures huge investment in North-East England*. https://www.gov.uk/government/news/ground-breaking-uk-export-finance-deal-secures-huge-investment-in-north-east-england

Hatton, T. (1990). The demand for British exports, 1870–1913. *The Economic History Review, 43*(4), 576–594.

House of Commons Library. (2016). *Steel in crisis: Timeline and events in Parliament*. https://commonslibrary.parliament.uk/steel-in-crisis-timeline-and-events-in-parliament/

International Trade Administration. (2024). *U.K. trade*. https://www.trade.gov/media/9063#:~:text=The%20U.K.'s%20deficit%20in,million%20metric%20tons%20in%202021

Medarac, H., Moya, J., & Somers, J. (2020). *Production costs from iron and steel industry*. Publications Office of the European Union.

MRW. (2023). *Government to probe sale of scrap from Redcar steelworks*. https://www.mrw.co.uk/news/government-to-probe-sale-of-scrap-from-redcar-steelworks-09-06-2023/

Tees valley. (2023a). *South Tees Development Corporation & Group Statement of Accounts 2022/23*. https://teesvalley-ca.gov.uk/about/leadership/mayor/the-mayors-priorities/teesworks/

Tees valley. (2023b). *The roadmap to net zero 2040 for the Tees Valley Industrial Cluster*. https://teesvalley-ca.gov.uk/business/energy-low-carbon/

UK Parliament. (2023). *Performance of investment zones and freeports in England*. https://publications.parliament.uk/pa

WSA. (2009). *Worldsteel in figures 2009*. https://worldsteel.org/wp-content/uploads/2009-World-Steel-in-Figures.pdf

WSA. (2024). *Worldsteel in figures 2024*. https://worldsteel.org/data/world-steel-in-figures-2024/

18

CASE 18: GOING FOR GREEN

Competing for Green FDI projects in the Nordics

Iiris Saittakari and Douglas van den Berghe

Abstract

This chapter focuses on Green foreign direct investment (Green FDI) in the Nordics – a region with ambitious climate plans. While FDI has typically gone to capital cities and their surroundings, Green FDI is changing the name of the game as it is often planned in non-capital cities. This creates both challenges and opportunities for these cities. It is built on the notion of absorptive capacity and identified the fundamentals which must be in place for a city to first attract FDI projects, and then capture the full potential benefits from them. The analysis suggests that domestic-owned firms – both private and publicly owned – are important in creating the necessary local expertise and absorptive capacity for attracting FDI. Creating the needed absorptive capacity to reap long-term benefits of Green FDI requires close collaboration and cost and resource sharing between the local municipalities and the national government, stable and predictable policy environment, and ensuring that local companies are included in the new local ecosystems.

Introduction

Multinational companies' (MNCs') Green foreign direct investments (Green FDI) contribute to environmental objectives and especially the reduction of greenhouse gas emissions (Sauvant et al., 2021). Prime examples of necessary Green FDI include renewable energy projects like wind and solar farms, along with large-scale industrial production facilities for batteries and green steel.

In this chapter, we focus on Green FDI in the Nordics – a region with ambitious climate plans. Finland aims to achieve carbon neutrality by 2035 (Finland's Ministry of the Environment, 2023), while Sweden has set a target

DOI: 10.4324/9781003483410-23

to reach net zero by 2045 (Government Offices of Sweden, 2021). Norway, on the other hand, aims to reduce greenhouse gas emissions by 90–95% by 2050, compared to 1990 levels (Norwegian Ministry of Climate and Environment, 2021). With a long and windy coastline and sparce population, Northern parts of Finland, Sweden and Norway are ideal for providing wind energy required, e.g., in the production of green steel. Green FDI requires vast amounts of land, which is why 80% of them go to non-capital areas (Perpiña Castillo et al., 2024). Therefore, while FDI has typically gone to capital cities and their surroundings (Goerzen, 2024), Green FDI is changing the name of the game. This has a profound impact for non-capital cities.

Next, we discuss the trends and drivers of Green FDI, using Finland as an example. We then zoom into the opportunities and challenges that Green FDI poses for non-capital cities with an example of Skellefteå, Sweden, which is hosting one of the largest green investments thus far in the Nordics. Based on these case examples, we discuss the concept of absorptive capacity in the context of cities. We conclude with key takeaways for countries and cities in attracting and benefitting from Green FDI.

Green investments in Finland

An open Green Investment Database[1] provided by the Confederation of Finnish Industries (EK, 2023) illustrates that the investment plan boom for green investments in Finland started picking up in 2021. By 2024, planned green investments had exceeded 260 billion euros in Finland alone, with over 100 billion euros from foreign investors. Despite this impressive magnitude, less than 20 billion euros had reached the investment decision by 2024, suggesting that even Finland is in the early stages of green transition. If these green investment plans do not convert into actual investments, the ambitious climate goals may not be achieved.

We manually divided the number of all investment plans based on their ownership into (1) foreign-owned investor (27% of the number of investments), (2) domestic private investor (48%), and (3) state or city-owned investor (26%). The examination of investments by cities showed that all three types of investors were typically present, suggesting the importance of various types of players in advancing the green transition. When examining the investment phases, it becomes clear that investments which had reached either the 'decision' stage or the 'start of operations' were largely populated by domestic private firms and state- or city-owned firms, as illustrated in Table 18.1. Furthermore, 'planning' and 'feasibility study' phases had relatively more FDI in addition to domestic private firms. This suggests that while domestic private firms had a significant role in having projects in all phases, state- or city-owned companies have been making green investments slightly ahead of foreign investors in Finland. The data further reveals

TABLE 18.1 Investment phases by different types of investors in Finland (number of green investment projects)

	FDI		*Domestic private firm*		*State or city-owned firm*		
City	*#*	*%*	*#*	*%*	*#*	*%*	*Grand total*
Start of operations	19	19%	46	46%	34	34%	99
Investment decision	22	20%	46	43%	40	37%	108
Planning	77	31%	129	51%	46	18%	252
Feasibility study	13	36%	16	44%	7	19%	36
Discontinued	3	50%	2	33%	1	17%	6
Grand Total	**134**	**27%**	**239**	**48%**	**128**	**26%**	**501**

that especially city- or state-owned electricity companies have an important role in paving the way for local carbon-neutral ecosystems and making cities attractive for Green FDI. This requires long-term engagement and vision from the policymakers and is done in cities by investing in solar power, (district) heating, biogas, energy storage, waste heat and heat pumps, as illustrated in Table 18.2. In the level of the country, the transmission grid is the most significant investment and plays a major role in facilitating green transition

TABLE 18.2 Green investments planned by state- and city-owned firms in Finland, 2021–2024

Type of green investment	*Investment (M€)*
Transmission grid	8,000
Offshore wind	3,276
Batteries	2,700
Energy storage	2,612
Hydrogen	1,730
Nuclear Power	1,000
Solar Power	392
Heating	286
Heat pumps	252
Bioenergy	252
Waste heat	141
Biogas	140
Carbon capture	138
Circular economy	80
Hydropower	20
Other	2
Grand Total	**21,019**

by ensuring there is enough capacity to transfer renewable energy. To reach the carbon neutrality goals, investments are needed both in green energy supply (e.g., wind and solar power) and demand (e.g., green steel). Storage (e.g., hydrogen, energy storage batteries) is also important to balance the fluctuating energy demand and supply.

To further illustrate the interplay of green investments by the state- or city-owned firms, domestic private companies and FDI, we briefly turn to a city of Lappeenranta, the European Green Leaf Award winner in 2021. The city in Eastern Finland has a population of 73,000 people and is a leader in Finland regarding the number of green investments that have reached the investment decision stage. Like in most cities in Finland, domestic-owned MNCs have had an important role in leading green transition and creating relevant expertise in Lappeenranta. For example, in 2012, the Finnish forestry company UPM invested 179 million euros in the world's first biorefinery that produces wood-based renewable fuels (UPM, n.d.). Furthermore, the city-owned electricity and heating companies have invested in heating, energy storage and bioenergy, showcasing their crucial role in creating carbon neutral ecosystems locally. Relatedly, green investments made by foreign MNCs in Lappeenranta are linked to thermal energy storage based on technology provided by a local university spinoff. In a larger scale, a French MNC Neoen is building the largest power reserve in the Nordics in Lappeenranta by 2025 (Morvant, 2023). It will provide significant support to the Finnish electricity grid, enhancing its stability and reliability. It is thus an example of a non-equity public-private collaboration that is increasingly prominent in green investments.

Vaasa, on the other hand, is a city of 69,000 people on the West coast of Finland. The city won the European Green Leaf 2026 award and has formed its strategy around becoming the 'Energy capital' of the Nordics. According to its strategy, children start studying energy-related topics already in kindergarten (EnergyVaasa, 2024). Vaasa region is the home of EnergyVaasa, the largest energy technology ecosystem in the Nordic countries. EnergyVaasa has been taking shape since 1990s, with lead firms of Wärtsilä, a Finnish MNC focused on ship engines, and ABB, a Swiss-Swedish energy technology company that had acquired a Finnish company called Strömberg. The engineering and electrotechnical industries, in collaboration with local universities and the municipality, have established a solid foundation for the future battery chemistry sector (Rosenblad, 2023). In 2024, EnergyVaasa consisted of over 180 companies, employed 13,000 people and had invested 250 million euros on R&D (EnergyVaasa, 2024). Furthermore, 80% of the turnover came from exports, emphasizing the importance of outward FDI activities in making the region attractive for inward FDI.

Lappeenranta and Vaasa are typical examples of the importance of domestic-owned firms – both private and publicly owned – in creating necessary local expertise for attracting FDI. Additionally, local universities have had a crucial role in building the expertise.

Opportunities and challenges brought with green investments – city of Skellefteå, Sweden

Green investments such as green steel or green battery production facilities are large employers, so they have a profound impact on the city hosting it. Next, we will discuss the city of Skellefteå in Sweden, which is home to Northvolt, the first green gigafactory in operation in the Nordics. Skellefteå is a city in Northern Sweden with a population of 75,000 (Skellefteå, 2024). With estimated 15,000 new residents by 2030 (Skellefteå, n.d.), Skellefteå was faced with unique opportunities as well as challenges due to Northvolt's mega-size green investment. After introducing the company, we will explore this from the perspectives of employees, infrastructure, and local ecosystems.

Company

Northvolt, a Swedish startup founded in 2015 by former Tesla executives, has been the forerunner of green investments in the Nordics. The company's significant breakthrough was in 2017 when it secured its first industrial partner, a Swedish-Swiss technology company ABB (Northvolt; https://northvolt.com/), signifying the important role of existing local companies in the development of startups. Furthermore, despite being founded in its home country Sweden, Northvolt has significant foreign ownership. By 2024, Northvolt had secured over $13 billion in equity and debt from commercial banks worldwide, including European Union's European Investment Bank (EIB), the Nordic Investment Bank (NIB),[2] asset management companies, institutional investors, and European car manufacturers.

Northvolt chose the initial location for its lithium-ion battery gigafactory in Skellefteå, located in Northern Sweden. The company had considered eight cities in Sweden and two in Finland (Vaasa and Kotka-Hamina). However, according to the CEO Peter Carlsson, Skellefteå was chosen due to its easy access to a harbor, train connections, energy benefits and the fact that the region "really, really wanted us to come" (Carlsson, as cited in Ekblom & Paulsson, 2023).

Employees

Skellefteå was chosen as the location for Northvolt's gigafactory even though the CEO acknowledged it would be "a certain challenge" to get people to move so far north (Ekblom & Paulsson, 2023). This has proven to be a challenging task indeed, as Skellefteå is located 9-hour drive North from

Stockholm, the capital of Sweden, and only a few hundred kilometers south from the Arctic Circle.

Northvolt and its suppliers have been constantly recruiting new employees. The demand for Northvolt in 2024 was over 2,500 employees in addition to 1,500 employees that had been recruited already (Siirilä, 2023). Another 1,000 employees were needed for suppliers, as well as public and private services that come with the population growth. To solve the issue, the Region Västerbotten, Skellefteå municipality, the Swedish Public Employment Agency and Northvolt had a joint "Relocate Skellefteå" project in which they targeted unemployed people in Stockholm, Gothenburg and Malmö to move to Skellefteå to live and work (Skellefteå, 2020). They invested 70 million Swedish kronor (EUR 6.2 Million) to recruit unemployed from Southern Sweden to Skellefteå with poor results (Folkbladet, 2023).

In 2023, Northvolt had a road show to recruit employees also in Finland. It organized recruiting events on the west coast, including Oulu, Kokkola, Vaasa, Pori and Turku. These cities are known for their expertise in green technologies and have a large population of Swedish speaking Finns. Finns are also used to the long, dark, and cold winters, and thus accustomed to the climate in Northern Sweden. In Finland, however, there were concerns that there will not be enough workers for the green investments taking place in Finland, and the intense recruitments by Northvolt was not making the situation easier (Mainio, 2022).

Infrastructure and housing

The radically increasing population also required housing and other infrastructure that needed to be built quickly. Skellefteå was preparing to have 15,000 new residents by 2030 (Skellefteå, n.d.), a 20% increase in population in less than a decade. There were also additional 5,000 workers living in the area during construction (Palmén, 2023). Housing had become a bottleneck as inflation and increasing interest rates had stalled construction in Sweden. The chairman of Skellefteå's city council stated that they were "working around the clock to get hesitant builders insured and new operators to replace those who gave up" (Palmén, 2023). On the other hand, the demand had led to increasing prices. The prices of detached houses had risen the most across Sweden (Kurki-Suonio, 2021), making them out of reach for first-time homebuyers.

The city also had to invest heavily in other infrastructure to accommodate the growing population. This included expanding health centers and developing new neighborhoods with water and waste management systems. New international schools and daycares as well as other leisure activities were needed to make the city attractive for families. A large share of these investments had to be paid by the city. As stated by the chairman of the city council:

"We didn't realize that the municipality would be so alone in the middle of all that" (Palmén, 2023). The state of Sweden had promised to help with the broader infrastructure, such as roads, railways, ports and airports but other investments needed to be paid by the city. Therefore, the city of Skellefteå's debt had increased from 170 million to 1.9 billion kronor during Northvolt's investment (Palmén, 2023). While investments in infrastructure were necessary to accommodate the growing population and future tax revenues, they pose a risk for a small city like Skellefteå.

Cities generally benefit most when workers move to the area with their families. Therefore, the city also needed to invest in cultural services to enhance life beyond work. To avoid a "fly-in fly-out" culture, where workers periodically come to Skellefteå for work and pay their income taxes elsewhere, it's crucial to make workers feel welcome in the city. After all, the city benefits from the increased population mainly through income tax revenues.

Local ecosystems

When a gigafactory, such as the one in Skellefteå, was built, it was not self-evident that local companies were able to tap into the Northvolt's local ecosystems by, e.g., becoming sub-contractors. Local companies had to first collaborate among themselves to form larger entities to fulfill the requirements of such large-scale operation. A key takeaway that other cities have learned from Skellefteå is that large investments require large scale contractors. Large MNCs are often brought in as suppliers and contractors rather than employing multiple small local firms. Therefore, the cities need to prepare their local businesses to collaborate and create supplier databases before the construction starts (source: authors' interview). In other words, the extent to which the local community will benefit from the new green investment largely depends on their absorptive capacity, which we elaborate next.

How to attract Green FDI to a city and benefit from it: the role of absorptive capacity

Attracting FDI to countries and cities is a well-researched topic and is the core task of Investment Promotion Agencies (IPAs). Apart from all the different promotion techniques and efforts, to successfully attract and benefit from FDI, cities must have enough absorptive capacity. The concept of absorptive capacity (AC) has its origins in the strategic management literature in the context of firms (Zahra & George, 2002). However, it has also been adopted by researchers in the field of economic development and FDI. AC is defined as a host-country's ability to capture potential benefits from FDI, and such ability is proxied by government FDI policy (Tang & Zhang, 2016).

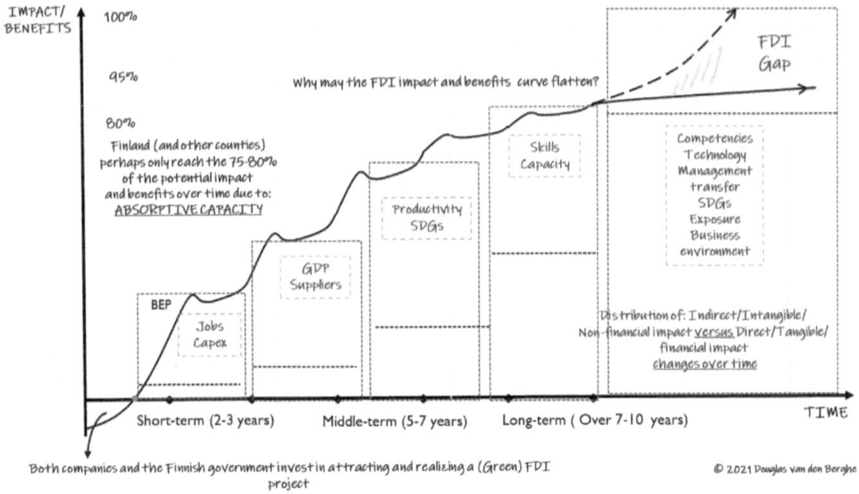

FIGURE 18.1 Host locations' absorptive capacity for FDI

Source: AMCHAM Finland report and van den Berghe (2021).

The economic development literature refers to AC as a prerequisite to have positive spillovers or externalities of FDI to the host economy (e.g., Criscuolo & Narula, 2008; Filippetti et al., 2017). We extend the concept of AC and argue that it is also necessary to *attract* FDI in the first place. This broader concept of AC identifies the *fundamentals* which must be in place for a country or city to first attract FDI projects, and then capture the full potential benefits from them, as illustrated in Figure 18.1 and described next.

Attracting FDI

Building necessary AC to attract Green FDI requires both local specialization as well as national collaboration and support. Expertise created by domestic (both private and city- or state-owned) firms is an important part of AC, as showcased by the cities of Lappeenranta and Vaasa. Thriving domestic firms provide local ecosystems that are attractive for FDI and ideally also form a local supplier and contractor base for the foreign firm.

The preparations for each FDI may take multiple years prior to the investment decision. Countries and cities thus invest a significant amount of resources in attracting FDI by allocating their officials' working time and investing in needed infrastructure. Even though not all investments (e.g., railroads, electricity infra) belong for the city, non-capital cities take a major risk in investing in local infrastructure as illustrated by the case of Skellefteå. The questions that these cities need to address include: *How much to invest prior to investment decision? How much does schools, daycares and hospital capacities need to be increased to accommodate increasing workforce?* These non-capital cities, however, cannot do it alone. National governments typically have regional assistance if a significant factory is being closed. Such instruments ex-ante before a major investment would help the city to build their AC without having to take on massive debt as in the case of Skellefteå. The instruments could also give support to the city if the company goes out of business.

Reaping the long-term benefits of FDI

FDI is a long-term commitment for a company and a city. Without the fundamentals - absorptive capacity for FDI "- it will be difficult to not only attract FDI *but also* generate and reap the long-term benefits of FDI". This is illustrated in Figure 18.1. There are several observations which can be derived from the figure, which are specifically applicable for Green FDI – due to its large magnitude and long-term characteristics.

- The relationship between the benefits of FDI for a host location, as well as the investing company, are initially negative and the break-even point (BEP) is after approximately 2–3 years when the company has created jobs and invested the funds and are starting to make profits – hence starting to pay taxes (employers and income tax). Over time, the benefits and impact develop progressively, but may occasionally fall back due to setbacks in the FDI operations of a company.
- After the break-even point, the local benefits of FDI are more direct and tangible (measurable) for the cities and country, such as new jobs created, capital expenditures, GDP growth, and involvement of first and second tier suppliers. All these initial short- and mid-term benefits are quantifiable and can be clearly measured.
- After the mid-term (5–7 years), the impact or benefits of FDI are more indirect or intangible and thus difficult to measure. These include skills and capacity enhancement, building competencies, knowledge management and technology transfer, exposure of business environment to global MNCs, visibility of the country on the global FDI scene, and a gradual change in mindset to FDI and perhaps globalization due to the economy's exposure to FDI.
- Over time the benefits curve tends to flatten. For Finland this is relatively late, as a developed economy can more easily absorb FDI and also has the institutions in place for FDI to flourish. Let's assume for Finland – and many other developed countries in the EU – that the FDI benefits curve flattens in the long term, and at a stage when more or less 80% of the benefits and impact have been realized. The curve may flatten due to a lack of political

commitment toward FDI by the government (e.g., by not solving the challenges and barriers for foreign companies now operating in the country), implementation of new policies that may be detrimental or challenging to further FDI or a lack of appropriate facilitation and aftercare policies and activities by the IPAs. The curve may flatten less when new commercial opportunities arise through increased exports beyond the immediate region, as in the case of Energy Vaasa.

(Source: AMCHAM Finland report & van den Berghe, 2021)

Figure 18.1 is an example of how AC is instrumental in both attracting (Green) FDI, but also in the further growth of a FDI project over time through the right policies, support activities and solving barriers and challenges to FDI. This way governments can reap the full benefits of a FDI project and avoid what we have called a "FDI Gap". The case of Finland is taken here as an example, but Figure 18.1 may also be applicable to many other developed and developing countries.

Creating AC requires specific national and city policies that directly (e.g., incentives) or indirectly (e.g., labor, immigration and tax policies) affect relevant domestic and foreign investments. These policies must be transparent, understandable for investors, predictable and stabile. They must be constant for the next 5–10 years. If policies change with each new election, the regulatory environment is unpredictable and challenging for (foreign) companies to operate. Regulatory and policy decision-making also need to be consistent across different departments. Collaboration between different levels of government and policy is required (national – regional – city) to ensure the needed absorptive capacity for both attracting and maximizing the benefits of the FDI. Vaasa is a prime example of a city that has had consistent policies around the formation of EnergyVaasa.

Lessons learned for cities attracting and benefiting from Green FDI

In this chapter, we have focused on Green FDI in the Nordics – the first industrialized region to reach net zero. We used the Confederation of Finnish Industries' Green Investment Database and cities of Lappeenranta and Vaasa to show the important role of domestic companies (private owned and state- and city-owned) in paving the way for inward FDI in green transition. We also discussed the opportunities and challenges with large Green investments with an example of Skellefteå in Sweden. The chapter also elaborated on the necessary absorptive capacity for Green FDI to both attract and have a greater impact on the host local economy.

The case studies give valuable insight for policy makers and practitioners in the field of Green FDI. First, while Green FDI – often changing the nature and character of a local economy and community – can certainly contribute to the local ecosystems, domestic investments should also precede FDI to create the necessary absorptive capacity for Green FDI to grow, nurture and generate a long-term impact on the local and national economy. This is the case for any type of FDI but especially for Green FDI – where infrastructural investments are high. However, local cities cannot absorb these high infrastructural costs without receiving national-level support. To create the needed absorptive capacity, the Green FDI often requires a close *collaboration and cost sharing* between the local municipalities and the national government and policy makers.

Second, FDI in general requires a *stable and predictable policy environment*. Given the massive investments associated with Green FDI, policies should be predictable and stable. Changes in national regulations, taxation or investment policies can significantly affect not only inward FDI but also the strategies of local cities and municipalities. These entities are working to build absorptive capacity—especially through substantial infrastructure investments—to support Green FDI. National policy makers, if committed to the net zero agendas, should be aware of this and avoid electoral changes in their policies that can jeopardize earlier domestic investments made.

Third, Green FDI often brings its own suppliers, who have specialized capabilities and expertise in green industries, resulting in limited involvement of local suppliers. This brings in the unique challenge for local and national FDI policy makers to create specific linkage programs and specific behavioral incentives that can enhance the expertise and capabilities of the local firms so that the MNCs can involve them in their projects rather than bringing suppliers from abroad. This would increase the spillover effects associated with the entry of the Green FDI.

Finally, the green investment data shows that only a small number of green investment plans have reached the investment decision phase. Cities are thus in very different phases of attracting Green FDI in the Nordics. While Skellefteå has been the forerunner, many other cities have been learning from it while working on securing the investment decisions in their cities. This requires a unique and tailored set of investment attraction activities that consider the legacy of the city. At the end, each Green FDI decision contributes toward the needed five trillion USD in annual investments that are required to fund the global green transition (IMF, 2023).

Notes

1 The database contains investments collected from open sources and it may not cover all investments. Onshore wind not included in the figures.
2 International financial institution of the Nordic and Baltic countries, headquartered in Helsinki, Finland.

References

AMCHAM Finland report and van den Berghe. (2021). *Finland FDI vision: The building blocks for Finland's economic growth and future resilience.* https://amcham.fi/fdi-vision-for-finland/

Criscuolo, P., & Narula, R. (2008). A novel approach to national technological accumulation and absorptive capacity: Aggregating Cohen and Levinthal. *The European Journal of Development Research, 20,* 56–73.

EK. (2023). *Confederation of Finnish industries.* Green investments in Finland database. https://ek.fi/en/current/news/the-data-dashboard-tracks-finlands-green-investments/

Ekblom, J., & Paulsson, L. (2023, February 21). *This icy Swedish town is at the forefront of a $100b green tech boom.* Australian Financial Review. https://www.afr.com/property/commercial/this-icy-swedish-town-is-at-the-forefront-of-a-100b-green-tech-boom-20230220-p5cm1x

EnergyVaasa (2024) EnergyVaasa in short. https://www.vaasa.fi/energyvaasa-in-short/

Filippetti, A., Frenz, M., & Ietto-Gillies, G. (2017). The impact of internationalization on innovation at countries' level: The role of absorptive capacity. *Cambridge Journal of Economics, 41*(2), 413–439.

Finland's Ministry of the Environment. (2023). *Finland's report on the implementation of the new urban agenda.* https://ym.fi/documents/1410903/40549091/NUA+Report_FINLAND.pdf/faebd276-1078-698e-8a0b-b2e779644ce8/NUA+Report_FINLAND.pdf?t=1646145920610

Folkbladet. (2023, March 2). *Skellefteå har drivit Sveriges sämsta bemanningsprojekt.* https://www.folkbladet.nu/2023-03-02/skelleftea-har-drivit-sveriges-samsta-bemanningsprojekt

Goerzen, A. (2024). Global cities. In C. G. Asmussen, N. Hashai, & D. Minbaeva (Eds.), *Encyclopedia of international strategic management* (pp. 118–120). Edward Elgar Publishing.

Government Offices of Sweden. (2021). *Sweden's climate policy framework.* https://www.government.se/articles/2021/03/swedens-climate-policy-framework/

International Monetary Fund (IMF). (2023). *Global financial stability report.* https://www.imf.org/en/Publications/GFSR/Issues/2023/10/10/global-financial-stability-report-october-2023

Kurki-Suonio, O. (2021, December 2). *Euroopan suurin akkutehdas valmistuu kohta Pohjois-Ruotsiin, jossa on käynnissä uusi kultakuume - Miksi kymmenien miljardien eurojen vihreät investoinnit menevät juuri Ruotsiin?.* Talouselämä. Euroopan suurin akkutehdas valmistuu kohta Pohjois-Ruotsiin, jossa on käynnissä uusi kultakuume – Miksi kymmenien miljardien eurojen vihreät investoinnit menevät juuri Ruotsiin? | Talouselämä (talouselama.fi).

Mainio, T. (2022, December 20). *Ruotsalainen Northvolt etsii Suomesta työntekijöitä kissojen ja koirien kanssa – Moni muukin rekrytoi Pohjois-Suomessa.* Talouselämä. Ruotsalainen Northvolt etsii Suomesta työntekijöitä kissojen ja koirien kanssa – Moni muukin rekrytoi Pohjois-Suomessa | Talouselämä (talouselama.fi).

Morvant, C. (2023, December 27). *Neoen launches construction of Yllikkälä Power Reserve Two in Finland, the largest battery in the Nordics.* Neoen. https://neoen.com/en/news/2023/neoen-launches-construction-of-yllikkala-power-reserve-two-in-finland-the-largest-battery-in-the-nordics/

Norwegian Ministry of Climate and Environment. (2021). *Norway's climate action plan for 2021–2030* (Meld. St. 13 (2020–2021) Report to the Storting (white paper)). https://www.regjeringen.no/contentassets/a78ecf5ad2344fa5ae4a394412ef8975/en-gb/pdfs/stm202020210013000engpdfs.pdf

Palmén, J. (2023, July 9). *Pienet kunnat jäivät yksin vastuuseen jätti-investoinneista Ruotsissa – "Emme tienneet, mihin ryhdyimme".* Talouselämä. Pienet kunnat jäivät yksin vastuuseen jätti-investoinneista Ruotsissa – "Emme tienneet, mihin ryhdyimme" | Talouselämä (talouselama.fi).

Perpiña Castillo, C., Hormigos Feliu, C., Dorati, C., Kakoulaki, G., Peeters, L., Quaranta, E., Taylor, N., Uihlein, A., Auteri, D., & Dijkstra, L. (2024). *Renewable energy production and potential in EU rural areas*. Publications Office of the European Union.

Rosenblad, L. (2023). *Kehittyvä Vaasan seutu: VASEK 2003–2023.* https://www.vasek.fi/assets/Quicklinks/2024/05/Vasek_20_kirja_FI.pdf

Sauvant, K. P., Stephenson, M., & Kagan, Y. (2021). *Green FDI: Encouraging carbon-neutral investment*. Columbia FDI Perspectives (316).

Siirilä, M. (2023, January 18). *Akkuvalmistajan kiertue vieraili Vaasassa ja Kokkolassa – opiskelijat ja kokeneet teollisuustyöntekijät kiinnostuneita työstä Ruotsissa*. Yle Uutiset. https://yle.fi/a/74-20013388

Skellefteå. (n.d.). *Välkommen till Skellefteå!* https://skelleftea.se/

Skellefteå. (2020, October). *Reflections on competence, education and skills supply* [PowerPoint slides]. Microsoft PowerPoint – Espon.

Skellefteå. (2024). *Skellefteå residents are now more numerous than ever*. https://skelleftea.se/platsen/eng/move-here/moving-to-skelleftea/arkiv/news/news/2023-10-16-skelleftea-residents-are-now-more-numerous-than-ever

Tang, Y., & Zhang, K. H. (2016). Absorptive capacity and benefits from FDI: Evidence from Chinese manufactured exports. *International Review of Economics & Finance, 42*, 423–429.

UPM. (n.d.). *UPM Biofuels*. https://www.upm.com/businesses/upm-biofuels/

Zahra, S. A., & George, G. (2002). Absorptive capacity: A review, reconceptualization, and extension. Academy of Management Review, 27(2), 185–203.

CONCLUDING COMMENTS

Diversity, but a lot in common

The cases presented in this book provide a rich and diverse insight into the phenomenon of Foreign Direct Investment (FDI) and cities. This diversity is seen in many ways, too many to mention all here. We highlight three sources of diversity that we think are important.

Firstly, we see cases (such as London (Dettoni), New York (Smith), cities in Flanders (Zhang and Zhu), Bagamoyo (Hoelscher) and Chennai (Amiraly)), where the outcomes were less than ideal, where things did not turn out as intended or hoped. At least one of the parties in the case may have suffered financially or been disappointed with the outcome in another way. On the other hand, we see more successful cases, where positive outcomes from FDI at city level are discernible (such as the stories of Johannesburg (Castellani et al.), Paris (Colovic), Shenzhen (Wu and Sutherland) and Suzhou (Du and Krusekopf)). And we see other cases where positive effects are desired, but at the time of writing the case, the outcomes were not yet clear (such as Lviv (Fingar) and Redcar (Wokke)). The first reflective point is on the nature of outcomes and how success can be clear, less clear, or not present at all. This diversity of outcomes speaks squarely to the broad array of risks that accompanies FDI in cities, and how, despite best intentions, risk is not always well-understood, appreciated or effectively dealt with. It speaks to the fundamentally entrepreneurial nature of FDI at city level, how opportunities may be seen as such by some actors, but not by others. Some actors make proactive decisions to bear risk by proceeding with investment into cities, whereas others may be more cautious and deterred, despite the efforts of investment promotion agencies and other bodies offering incentives and inducements that can dampen perceived risk.

DOI: 10.4324/9781003483410-24

A second source of diversity in the case material presented in this book concerns the level of analysis. Some cases are clearly at a macro level (such as Johannesburg (Castellani et al.), Paris (Colovic), Tel Aviv (Steriu) and Ho Chi Minh City (Becker)) while others are at meso- and micro-levels, revealing the dynamics of projects (Cambridge (Fear et al.), Hamburg (Arnold) and Chennai (Amiraly)). FDI and Cities is not a topic that should be appreciated at only one level of analysis. It is important to be able to understand the macro when dealing with the micro. And it is important to understand how the micro and the meso will inform the longer-term trends and trajectories at a macro level. The multi-level nature of the phenomenon has implications for all kinds of actors with an interest in the phenomenon, on the academic and research side of the coin, as well as on the policy and business side.

A third source of diversity lies in whether the case writer has chosen to emphasize the experiences of a particular investor or investors (such as the cases on Gorillas (Smith), Kingspan (Fingar), China State Grid and Eandis (Zhang and Zhu), Intel Extreme Masters (Irwin-Hunt) or Veolia (Amiraly)), or whether the analysis does not have any one central investing MNE in the storyline, but is centred more around the changes taking place in cities (Cambridge (Fear et al.) and Redcar (Wokke)). Here, we see differences in the preference of the case writer(s) in terms of emphasis on a particular investor, or more city-centric picture. This is important to acknowledge because the idiosyncratic features of investor-city interaction and performance can be visible when a specific investor is known and included in a narrative of a specific city. But it also shows how we can still learn about FDI and cities when the storyline is more city-centric. Indeed, the learning points we can take away from each case will differ depending on whether the story is told through the eyes of one or a few investors, as well as through the eyes of the city, or only through the eyes of the city.

Despite these sources of diversity (and there are likely to be many more that we encourage the reader to reflect upon), there are also some common themes. Again, there may be more areas of common thematic interpretation that we do not consider, but we highlight three important ones here.

One common theme relates to the telling of stories of FDI at city level. We found as we conducted this project how willing the authors were to tell a story about FDI in a given city or city region. All found an angle, and a context that they were expert and interested in – even passionate about – and which they could use to research and describe key events over time. This story-telling approach is a powerful tool in our efforts to create and disseminate knowledge about FDI and cities. The phenomenon is not static, and there are severe limitations with analysing it in a cross-sectional manner, at one point in time. Investors are constantly learning from their successes and mistakes, and they try and improve how they approach investment challenges based on their learnings. Cities are complex and highly dynamic, with many interlocking and evolving agencies and bodies with an interest in harnessing and managing FDI. They, too, learn over time through the outcomes of previous investment activities and efforts. These dynamics include the ongoing feedback and signals these agencies receive from market participants. All our cases reflect this dynamism in one way or another; they all have a story-telling ethos.

This leads to a second area of commonality across the cases in this book, which concerns the extent to which the cases can help to refine theory or develop new theory. We need to be muted in our claims here because the book was not developed with any one theory in mind, or with a purpose of testing any given theoretical framework. As noted earlier, many theories are potentially applicable, including institutional theory, theories from economic geography, a range of theories from the academic field of international business, and many firm- and investor-centric theories. It would have been a monumental – and potentially confusing – task to tackle all of these in one volume. That said, what the case data on FDI and cities in this book allows is a critical reflection on theory. Sometimes, theory is reductionist, simplifying phenomena for the purposes of clarity and argumentation. In most cases, theories have known defects and limitations, acknowledgements about where they may work better and in what situations they are relevant. We do not have one single theory on FDI and cities. But our case data does allow theory to be discussed and debated. It does so because it contains information about context, about actors, about decisions that are made, about events occurring over time, and about outcomes. While we leave it to the reader to scrutinize theory considering the case data presented here, it might also be possible to use one or a selection of cases in this book to put together the tenets of new theory, new models and frameworks, which can be used to guide logic and thinking about how the international investment environment works and why it works in the way it does. We build on this point below.

A third common theme is that all the cases presented can contribute to policy debate and development, including in contexts different from the focal city in each case. It is because we have insights into how decisions and actions involving organizations and institutions in different contexts lead to outcomes, that we can pose some basic but powerful policy-oriented questions: Would that work here? Why don't we try that? Could that happen here? Do we need to exercise caution given what we see in this case? While the exact nature of policy debate and development differ across the cases in this book, they do all allow a reflection on policy for FDI in any given city. Much of the nomenclature, concepts and semantics used in the cases documented can be the basis for critical reflection in policy. The concepts revealed include the city as a landing pad (Hamburg (Arnold)), how to build a unified shop window (Cambridge (Fear et al.)), leveraging city-city collaboration over a long-time frame (Suzhou (Du and Krusekopf)), facilitating FDI on the back of a high-profile domestic downfall (Helskinki (Lemagnen)), and investing into conflict zones while others are de-investing (Lviv (Fingar)). These are just some examples of central concepts and themes within the case data that could be used when developing policy around FDI and cities in other locations. We would argue that all cases in this book could be used – where appropriate – as a reference point for policy in other contexts.

Benefits for learners

Learning about FDI and cities through cases is not confined to solo reading. We encourage the use of group case discussions on the storylines and phenomena revealed in this book. Developing skills in listening to others' opinions on FDI and cities, including others' interpretation of the events and outcomes, can help learners expand their understanding and knowledge. This is particularly important in groups where others may have personal experience in some of the cities described, or of the agencies, the investors and their industries. This personal experience can be used to complement knowledge encapsulated in any articulated case. As noted above, the case data has implications for policy reflection, as well as theoretical reflection, and we encourage readers to consider both types of implications in their appraisal of case data on FDI and cities.

Learning from case data on FDI and cities can also help learners plan and develop their careers. It may open career opportunities and paths that they had not previously considered, such as becoming involved in investment promotion agencies, city planning or the sustainable development policy units of MNEs. Many of these organizations and organizational units are mentioned in the cases in this book. Important to note is that they are all employers. They all rely on human resources and human capital to function, and the cases offer a glimpse into the skillsets and abilities that are needed for a career in investment promotion, implementing FDI projects and harnessing positive outcomes in city locations around the world.

Making an impact in the field of FDI and cities through effective leadership builds on this. Through an expanded case knowledge of what has worked, why it has worked and how it has worked, learners will be able to assume positions of authority and responsibility in which they are able to exert impact in a positive way. Leadership themes are highlighted in many of the cases, including Cambridge (Fear et al.), Katowice (Irwin-Hunt) and green FDI projects in the Nordics (van den Berghe and Saittakari). Questionable leadership practices in the context of FDI and cities are also exposed in some of the other cases, and we will allow the reader to reflect on these. Relatedly, the issues surrounding political forces and the importance for leaders to understand and negotiate the challenges put up by political forces are highlighted in some of the cases (e.g., Bagamoyo (Hoelscher)). In this sense, learners can use the case material presented here to explore leadership capabilities in relation to political influence.

Implications for academic researchers

Academic researchers can use case material to expand their ideas for research and impact work, as well as in class for teaching and case learning. But they can also become actively involved in researching and writing case material on the topic of FDI and cities. Some of the benefits of doing this include gaining close personal familiarity with the phenomenon, with the actors involved, the decision-making processes they go through, and the challenges they strive to overcome. This is particularly evident when developing cases based on primary data and close connection with the phenomenon at a micro level (Chennai (Amiraly) and Gorillas (Smith) in this book). Working alongside representatives from industry and the investment world on case development (such as with the Cambridge case (Fear et al.) and the Paris case (Colovic)) can also help academics to nurture their understanding of the nuances and details of the phenomenon. This inevitably has a spillover into academics' theoretical work and academic article publishing. It can inspire and help guide the choice of topics for academics to work on in the future.

As an example, one such area that is consistently raised in the cases is the role of investment promotion agencies, and investment promotion actors collaborating in ecosystems for investment at city level. This is a topic that has not received sufficient academic attention in our view. Case writing projects can yield first-hand insights and ideas about how to approach topics such as these and can provide academics with bountiful evidence for introducing new concepts into the academic literature.

Returning to the issue of theory development, we made the point above that it could be possible to use a selection of the cases presented in this book – perhaps alongside other case material – to develop entirely new theoretical propositions and frameworks in an inductive way. One way to approach this could be to use systems thinking and systems approaches, scrutinizing the case storylines and developing systems diagrams showing outcomes alongside various factors and activities that lead to those outcomes. Incorporating a diverse range of FDI and city case data as an 'input' to this process will increase the chances of yielding a fully developed systems view. The stance taken would be a holistic one, countering the norm of reductionist thinking that sometimes accompanies deductive theoretical development. We encourage scholars to consider engaging with case stories on FDI and cities on a holistic basis to avoid the risk that important variables or logic are omitted.

Implications for policymakers and consultants

As noted above, while all the cases concern the topic of FDI and cities in one way or another, there is great diversity in the case data in terms of outcomes. Some stories show a more successful outcome, others less so. For those reviewing and developing policy for cities or for investors, understanding the root causes of success and failure in other city settings is vitally important. One needs to be careful about interpreting and transferring learning from one specific case into an entirely different context. Differences due to level of economic development, political regime, time frame and investor sentiment will all conspire to influence this problem of generalizing or transference of learning. Nevertheless, taking the cases collectively as a body of knowledge on FDI and cities, heuristics can be developed in policy agents and those who consult for them. Such heuristics can recognize that knowledge is not perfect, and that due diligence and risks associated with transferability of learning need to be managed. The process by which investment policymakers and consultants learn should involve the study and reflection of case data, including discussion in groups. This will allow opinions to be formed not so much on 'if,' but on 'how' case knowledge can be applied from settings that are different to those in which the focal policy environment is situated. Such case knowledge can be internalized and combined with own experiences to allow an individual to contribute to policy development in a group in an informed way. So, one main implication for policy development is for policymakers to view case collections of FDI and cities as bodies of knowledge that can guide heuristics in any given setting. This should allow them to foresee risks and provide unbiased and well-grounded advice. It may also allow them to innovate in policy development, building on the concepts and ideas that are in use in investment promotion in one location, into a focal city.

The cost of this for the individual policymaker or consultant is twofold: (1) gaining access to case knowledge on FDI and cities and (2) spending the time to read (and re-read) case stories, in order to elicit key learnings applicable to the individual and their project demands. These barriers are not insurmountable. In the same way that many consultants subscribe to sources for quantitative data on FDI at the city or regional level, it may be necessary to subscribe to case libraries and books containing bodies of knowledge about FDI and cities based on cases, and that have a qualitative or hybrid narrative. Also, in the same way, that academics can benefit from taking part in case research and writing on FDI and cities, so can (should) policymakers and consultants. Indeed, they are likely to hold a privileged position, deeply embedded in the phenomenon, and with access to many contacts and strands of evidence that can be used to formulate and articulate new and revealing cases on FDI and cities. Taking part in case writing – perhaps alongside academic writers – will allow knowledge to be surfaced, reflected upon and annotated in the interests of improving the abilities of policymakers and consultants.

Implications for investors

Finally, we believe that the cases contained in this book have implications for investors – for MNEs seeking to expand internationally, either for the first time or as a subsequent investment building on previous investments. Case data on FDI and cities can help the bearers of risk. Firstly, the cases suggest that investors need to think very carefully about the dynamic characteristics of cities, not just of countries they are being drawn to. Sure, they need to understand how the city works for the country, and how the country context influences the investment environment in the city. But they also need to know how the city will work for the MNE, and how the MNE will contribute to the city. We know that the majority of the world's FDI goes into cities and that this is likely to intensify in the future. How cities change, how they develop and how their demand and supply-side conditions evolve over time are important to understand. Cases allow this dynamism to be appreciated, and for the temporal dimension to be as relevant to the decision-makers in MNEs as other factors and inducements. What happens following the investment? Is there an aftercare component? What will it involve? Thinking carefully about the potential evolutionary paths can be reinforced by using case stories as part of the body of evidence when conducting analysis and due diligence.

Secondly, the cases in the book suggest that investors should also see investment from the city's point of view. What will the city gain from the investment? How can the investment complement existing initiatives and the direction of travel for the city? How can concerns and criticisms relating to FDI into cities be assuaged? Case evidence and case knowledge can help in answering these and similar types of questions. Working authentically and meaningfully with city representatives, understanding their pain points and how the investment will contribute towards alleviating and resolving those pain points – as opposed to exacerbating them – is essential. The cases suggest that this can be achieved by taking a long-term view of engagement with the city not as just a temporary host organism that the MNE latches on to, but as an environment in which the MNE can settle into and become an intricate part as the city continues its journey through history.

Final note

In sum, engaging with cases on FDI and cities allows us to create and share knowledge about the phenomenon. The cases presented in this book show how this knowledge is shared amongst a broad range of people, including investors, investment promoters, consultants and academics. While it is not possible to capture the universe of case knowledge in one volume, the implications for learners, academics, practitioners in the investment promotion community, and investors, show how important it is for all parties with an interest in FDI and cities to become immersed in case data. This can be brought about not only by reading and discussing cases but by researching and writing them too. This immersion will allow interested parties to learn from the experiences of others and contribute to the learning of others. It is especially relevant when those experiences are based on personal journeys, participation in events and projects undertaken or based on new and original case research. Being part of this immersion into case data on FDI and cities will allow knowledge to be shared by a wide range of participants in a way that we hope will be useful and impactful for investors and the cities they invest in.

REFERENCES

Agnew, K., & Lyons, R. C. (2018). The impact of employment on housing prices: Detailed evidence from FDI in Ireland. *Regional Science and Urban Economics, 70*, 174–189.

Allard, G., Martinez, C. A., & Williams, C. (2012). Political instability, pro-business market reforms and their impacts on national systems of innovation. *Research Policy, 41*(3), 638–651.

Allard, G., & Williams, C. (2020). National-level innovation in Africa. *Research Policy, 49*(7), 104074.

ALshubiri, F. (2024). Do foreign direct investment inflows affect tax revenue in developed and developing countries? *Asian Review of Accounting, 32*(5), 781–810.

An, Y., Liu, N., Zhang, L., & Zheng, H. (2022). Adapting to climate risks through cross-border investments: Industrial vulnerability and smart city resilience. *Climatic Change, 174*(1), 10.

Anttiroiko, A. V. (2015). City branding as a response to global intercity competition. *Growth and Change, 46*(2), 233–252.

Audretsch, D. B., & Belitski, M. (2017). Entrepreneurial ecosystems in cities: Establishing the framework conditions. *The Journal of Technology Transfer, 42*, 1030–1051.

Aust, V., Morais, A. I., & Pinto, I. (2020). How does foreign direct investment contribute to Sustainable Development Goals? Evidence from African countries. *Journal of Cleaner Production, 245*, 118823.

Awokuse, T. O., & Yin, H. (2010). Intellectual property rights protection and the surge in FDI in China. *Journal of Comparative Economics, 38*(2), 217–224.

Basu, P., & Guariglia, A. (2007). Foreign direct investment, inequality, and growth. *Journal of Macroeconomics, 29*(4), 824–839.

Beaverstock, J. V., Smith, R. G., & Taylor, P. J. (1999). A roster of world cities. *Cities, 16*(6), 445–458.

Belderbos, R., Du, H. S., & Slangen, A. (2020). When do firms choose global cities as foreign investment locations within countries? The roles of contextual distance, knowledge intensity, and target-country experience. *Journal of World Business, 55*(1), 101022.

Belderbos, R., Du, S., & Somers, D. (2014). *Global cities as innovation hubs: The location of R&D investments by multinational firms*. DRUID Academy.

Bhawe, N., & Zahra, S. A. (2019). Inducing heterogeneity in local entrepreneurial ecosystems: The role of MNEs. *Small Business Economics, 52*(2), 437–454.
Blevins, D. P., Moschieri, C., Pinkham, B. C., & Ragozzino, R. (2016). Institutional changes within the European Union: How global cities and regional integration affect MNE entry decisions. *Journal of World Business, 51*(2), 319–330.
Bono, P. H., David, Q., & Desbordes, R. (2024). International attractiveness of cities: The drivers of urban FDI. *Review of International Economics, 32*(5), 2319–2343.
Buckley, P. J., & Meng, C. (2005). The strategy of foreign-invested manufacturing enterprises in China: Export-orientated and market-orientated FDI revisited. *Journal of Chinese Economic and Business Studies, 3*(2), 111–131.
Campos, N. F., & Giovannoni, F. (2007). Lobbying, corruption and political influence. *Public Choice, 131*, 1–21.
Castellani, D., & Lavoratori, K. (2019). Location of R&D abroad—An analysis on global cities. *Relocation of Economic Activity: Contemporary Theory and Practice in Local, Regional and Global Perspectives*, 145–162.
Castellani, D., Lavoratori, K., Perri, A., & Scalera, V. G. (2022). International connectivity and the location of multinational enterprises' knowledge-intensive activities: Evidence from US metropolitan areas. *Global Strategy Journal, 12*(1), 82–107.
Chakravarty, D., Goerzen, A., Musteen, M., & Ahsan, M. (2021). Global cities: A multidisciplinary review and research agenda. *Journal of World Business, 56*(3), 101182.
Chintrakarn, P., Herzer, D., & Nunnenkamp, P. (2012). FDI and income inequality: Evidence from a panel of US states. *Economic Inquiry, 50*(3), 788–801.
Choi, S. B., Lee, S. H., & Williams, C. (2011). Ownership and firm innovation in a transition economy: Evidence from China. *Research Policy, 40*(3), 441–452.
Daniele, V., & Marani, U. (2011). Organized crime, the quality of local institutions and FDI in Italy: A panel data analysis. *European Journal of Political Economy, 27*(1), 132–142.
DasGupta, R., Kumar, S., & Pathak, R. (2022). Multinational enterprises' internationalization and adoption of sustainable development goals. *International Journal of Managerial Finance, 18*(4), 617–638.
De Beule, F., & Zhang, H. (2022). The impact of government policy on Chinese investment locations: An analysis of the Belt and Road policy announcement, host-country agreement, and sentiment. *Journal of International Business Policy, 5*(2), 194–217.
De Jong, M., Joss, S., & Taeihagh, A. (2024). Smart city development as spatial manifestations of 21st century capitalism. *Technological Forecasting and Social Change, 202*, 123299.
Demena, B. A., & Afesorgbor, S. K. (2020). The effect of FDI on environmental emissions: Evidence from a meta-analysis. *Energy Policy, 138*, 111192.
De Villiers, J. C. (2009). Success factors and the city-to-city partnership management process—From strategy to alliance capability. *Habitat International, 33*(2), 149–156.
Du, H. S., Belderbos, R., & Somers, D. (2022). Research versus development: Global cities and the location of MNCs' cross-border R&D investments. *Regional Studies, 56*(12), 2001–2018.
Du, H. S., & Colovic, A. (2024). The impact of global city location intensity on MNE performance: Leveraging learning and connectivity. *Long Range Planning, 57*(1), 102409.
Dussaux, D., Dechezleprêtre, A., & Glachant, M. (2022). The impact of intellectual property rights protection on low-carbon trade and foreign direct investments. *Energy Policy, 171*, 113269.
Ecker, B., van Triest, S., & Williams, C. (2013). Management control and the decentralization of R&D. *Journal of Management, 39*(4), 906–927.
Edey, M. (2009). The global financial crisis and its effects. *Economic Papers: A Journal of Applied Economics and Policy, 28*(3), 186–195.

Eva, M., Cehan, A., & Lazăr, A. (2021). Patterns of urban shrinkage: A systematic analysis of Romanian cities (1992–2020). *Sustainability, 13*(13), 7514.
Gil, C. (2020). The sister cities program and tourism. *Journal of Hospitality and Tourism Management, 45*, 182–191.
Glaeser, E. L., & Resseger, M. G. (2010). The complementarity between cities and skills. *Journal of Regional Science, 50*(1), 221–244.
Hensher, D. A., Wei, E., & Beck, M. J. (2023). The impact of COVID-19 and working from home on the workspace retained at the main location office space and the future use of satellite offices. *Transport Policy, 130*, 184–195.
Hernantes, J., Maraña, P., Gimenez, R., Sarriegi, J. M., & Labaka, L. (2019). Towards resilient cities: A maturity model for operationalizing resilience. *Cities, 84*, 96–103.
Hoskisson, R. E., Eden, L., Lau, C. M., & Wright, M. (2000). Strategy in emerging economies. *Academy of Management Journal, 43*(3), 249–267.
Iammarino, S., McCann, P., & Ortega-Argilés, R. (2018). International business, cities and competitiveness: Recent trends and future challenges. *Competitiveness Review: An International Business Journal, 28*(3), 236–251.
Inkpen, A. C., & Pien, W. (2006). An examination of collaboration and knowledge transfer: China–Singapore Suzhou Industrial Park. *Journal of Management Studies, 43*(4), 779–811.
Jayathilaka, U. R., & Park, G. C. (2022). Smart cities and FDI. *Applied Research in Artificial Intelligence and Cloud Computing, 5*(1), 19–28.
Katsos, J. E., & AlKafaji, Y. (2019). Business in war zones: How companies promote peace in Iraq. *Journal of Business Ethics, 155*, 41–56.
Katsos, J. E., & Fort, T. L. (2016). Leadership in the promotion of peace: Interviews with the 2015 Business for Peace honorees. *Business Horizons, 59*(5), 463–470.
Kaufmann, D., Kraay, A., & Mastruzzi, M. (2009). Governance matters VIII: aggregate and individual governance indicators, 1996–2008 (World Bank Policy Research Working Paper No. 4978).
Kim, H. M. (2024). Foreign direct investment and urban growth in Vietnam: Spatial, economic, and demographic perspectives. *Asian Geographer, 41*(2), 167–184.
Kola-Bezka, M., & Kuzel, M. (2023). Global cities and multinational enterprises: Integrating the existing concepts for future research studies. *Bulletin of Geography*. Socio-economic Series, *60*, 101–125.
Lee, S. H., & Williams, C. (2007). Dispersed entrepreneurship within multinational corporations: A community perspective. *Journal of World Business, 42*(4), 505–519.
Liou, R. S., & Rao-Nicholson, R. (2021). Multinational enterprises and Sustainable Development Goals: A foreign subsidiary perspective on tackling wicked problems. *Journal of International Business Policy, 4*(1), 136–151.
Liu, X. (2021). Chinese Multinational enterprises operating in western economies: Huawei in the US and the UK. *China's big power ambition under Xi Jinping* (pp. 219–236). Routledge.
Lorenzen, M., Mudambi, R., & Schotter, A. (2020). International connectedness and local disconnectedness: MNE strategy, city-regions and disruption. *Journal of International Business Studies, 51*(8), 1199.
Luo, Y., & Peng, M. W. (1998). First mover advantages in investing in transitional economies. *Thunderbird International Business Review, 40*(2), 141–163.
Majocchi, A., & Presutti, M. (2009). Industrial clusters, entrepreneurial culture and the social environment: The effects on FDI distribution. *International Business Review, 18*(1), 76–88.
Mazzoleni, R., & Nelson, R. R. (2007). Public research institutions and economic catch-up. *Research Policy, 36*(10), 1512–1528.
McDonald, C., Buckley, P. J., Voss, H., Cross, A. R., & Chen, L. (2018). Place, space, and foreign direct investment into peripheral cities. *International Business Review, 27*(4), 803–813.

Metaxas, T. (2010). Cities competition, place marketing and economic development in South Europe: The Barcelona case as FDI destination. *Theoretical and Empirical Researches in Urban Management, 5*(14), 5–19.
Meyer, K. E., & Tran, Y. T. T. (2006). Market penetration and acquisition strategies for emerging economies. *Long Range Planning, 39*(2), 177–197.
Miklian, J., Schouten, P., & Ganson, B. (2016). From boardrooms to battlefields: 5 new ways that businesses claim to build peace. *Harvard International Review, 37*(2), 1–4.
Minbaeva, D., Pedersen, T., Björkman, I., Fey, C. F., & Park, H. J. (2014). MNC knowledge transfer, subsidiary absorptive capacity and HRM. *Journal of International Business Studies, 45*, 38–51.
Minbaeva, D. B., & Michailova, S. (2004). Knowledge transfer and expatriation in multinational corporations: The role of disseminative capacity. *Employee Relations, 26*(6), 663–679.
Mykhnenko, V., & Turok, I. (2008). East European cities—Patterns of growth and decline, 1960–2005. *International Planning Studies, 13*(4), 311–342.
Ning, L., Wang, F., & Li, J. (2016). Urban innovation, regional externalities of foreign direct investment and industrial agglomeration: Evidence from Chinese cities. *Research Policy, 45*(4), 830–843.
OECD (2006). *Competitive cities in the global economy*. Organisation for Economic Co-operation and Development.
Oetzel, J., & Miklian, J. (2017). Multinational enterprises, risk management, and the business and economics of peace. *Multinational Business Review, 25*(4), 270–286.
Pao, H. T., & Tsai, C. M. (2011). Multivariate granger causality between CO_2 emissions, energy consumption, FDI (foreign direct investment) and GDP (gross domestic product): Evidence from a panel of BRIC (Brazil, Russian Federation, India, and China) countries. *Energy, 36*(1), 685–693.
Poelhekke, S., & Van Der Ploeg, F. (2009). Foreign direct investment and urban concentrations: Unbundling spatial lags. *Journal of Regional Science, 49*(4), 749–775.
Porter, M. E. (1990). *The competitive advantage of nations*. Free Press, MacMillan.
Prime, P. B. (2012). Utilizing FDI to stay ahead: The case of Singapore. *Studies in Comparative International Development, 47*, 139–160.
Reckien, D., & Martinez-Fernandez, C. (2011). Why do cities shrink? *European Planning Studies, 19*(8), 1375–1397.
Reimann, F., Rauer, J., & Kaufmann, L. (2015). MNE subsidiaries' strategic commitment to CSR in emerging economies: The role of administrative distance, subsidiary size, and experience in the host country. *Journal of Business Ethics, 132*, 845–857.
Rogoff, K. S., & Yang, Y. (2024). A tale of tier 3 cities. *Journal of International Economics, 152*, 103989.
Sassen, S. (1993). Rebuilding the global city: Economy, ethnicity and space. *Social Justice, 20*(3/4, (53–54), Global Crises, Local Struggles, Fall–Winter 1993), 32–50.
Scholvin, S., Breul, M., & Diez, J. R. (2019). Revisiting gateway cities: Connecting hubs in global networks to their hinterlands. *Urban Geography, 40*(9), 1291–1309.
Serikzhanova, S. S., & Aldangarkyzy, A (2021). Migration attractiveness as a factor in the development of Kazakhstan cities. *Вестник КазНУ. Серия психологии и социологии, 78*(3), 148–156.
Shatkin, G. (2007). Global cities of the South: Emerging perspectives on growth and inequality. *Cities, 24*(1), 1–15.
Shi, X., Williams, C., Sutherland, D., & Rong, K. (2022). Patent-and trademark-seeking outward foreign direct investment by Chinese firms: The role of business group affiliation. *Industrial and Corporate Change, 31*(3), 838–862.

Simon, C. J., & Nardinelli, C. (2002). Human capital and the rise of American cities, 1900–1990. *Regional Science and Urban Economics, 32*(1), 59–96.
Song, T., Sun, M., Liang, Y., Ngampramuan, S., Wuzhati, Y., & Zhou, K. (2021). Variegated transnational partnerships: Multi-scalar actor networks in China's overseas industrial parks. *Journal of Geographical Sciences, 31*, 664–680.
Stephenson, M., Eden, L., Kende, M., Kimura, F., Sauvant, K. P., Srinivasan, N., & Zhan, J. (2022). How to be smart: Leveraging digital FDI to address risk through growing capacity and competitiveness. In *International business in times of crisis: Tribute volume to Geoffrey Jones* (Vol. 16, pp. 193–251). Emerald Publishing Limited.
Su, Y., & Liu, Z. (2016). The impact of foreign direct investment and human capital on economic growth: Evidence from Chinese cities. *China Economic Review, 37*, 97–109.
Tallman, S., & Chacar, A. S. (2011). Knowledge accumulation and dissemination in MNEs: A practice-based framework. *Journal of Management Studies, 48*(2), 278–304.
Tang, L., Zhang, Y., Gao, J., & Wang, F. (2020). Technological upgrading in Chinese cities: The role of FDI and industrial structure. *Emerging Markets Finance and Trade, 56*(7), 1547–1563.
Tao, Y. F. (2005). A Catch-up Strategy? China's policy toward foreign direct investment. *Japan and China in the World Political Economy*, 130–150.
Te Velde, D.W., Ahmed, M.M., Alemu, G., Bategeka, L., Calí, M., Castel-Branco, C., Chansa, F., Dasgupta, S., Foresti, M., Hangi, M., Ingombe, L., Iqbal, A., Jalilian, H., Jemio, L.C., Kabuya Kalala, F., Keane, J., Kennan, J., Khan, T.I., Lunogelo, H.B., and others, 2008. The global financial crisis and developing countries. ODI Background Note. London: Overseas Development Institute, 62(24), pp.156–168.
Todd, R. H. (1977). A city index: Measurement of a city's attractiveness, *Review of Applied Urban Research, 5*(7), 1–16.
Tsang, E. W. (2002). Acquiring knowledge by foreign partners from international joint ventures in a transition economy: Learning-by-doing and learning myopia. *Strategic Management Journal, 23*(9), 835–854.
Tsenkova, S. (2006). Beyond transitions: Understanding urban change in post-socialist cities. In *The urban mosaic of post-socialist Europe: Space, institutions and policy* (pp. 21–50). Physica-Verlag HD.
Turkina, E., & Sultana, N. (2023). FDI and cities: Network dynamics in cleantech innovation. *Competitiveness Review: An International Business Journal, 33*(3), 557–578.
Van Tulder, R., Rodrigues, S. B., Mirza, H., & Sexsmith, K. (2021). The UN's sustainable development goals: Can multinational enterprises lead the decade of action? *Journal of International Business Policy, 4*(1), 1.
Visnjic, I., Neely, A., Cennamo, C., & Visnjic, N. (2016). Governing the city: Unleashing value from the business ecosystem. *California Management Review, 59*(1), 109–140.
Vongpraseuth, T., & Choi, C. G. (2015). Globalization, foreign direct investment, and urban growth management: Policies and conflicts in Vientiane, Laos. *Land Use Policy, 42*, 790–799.
Wang, D. T., Gu, F. F., David, K. T., & Yim, C. K. B. (2013). When does FDI matter? The roles of local institutions and ethnic origins of FDI. *International Business Review, 22*(2), 450–465.
Williams, C. (2024). Peacebuilding by MNE subsidiaries: The role of intangible capital and local initiative. *Business Horizons, 67*(6), 711–725.
Williams, C., & Du, J. (2014). The impact of trust and local learning on the innovative performance of MNE subsidiaries in China. *Asia Pacific Journal of Management, 31*, 973–996.

Williams, C., Hailemariam, A.T., & Allard, G. (2022) 'Exploring entrepreneurial innovation in Ethiopia', *Research Policy, 51*(10): 104599.
Williams, C., & Steriu, R. (2022). MNE market entry and social investment in battle-weary countries: Evidence from Heineken. *Journal of World Business, 57*(4), 101342.
Williams, C., Van Eerde, W., & Thé, D. (2012) 'Infusion's Greenfield subsidiary in Poland', *Ivey Publishing* (product ID: 9B12M076).
Williams, C., & Vrabie, A. (2018). Host country R&D determinants of MNE entry strategy: A study of ownership in the automobile industry. *Research Policy, 47*(2), 474–486.
Williams, C., & You, J. J. (2021). *Organizing for resilience: Leading and managing risk in a disruptive world*. Routledge.
Wu, L., Sutherland, D., Peng, X., & Anderson, J. (2023). Are Chinese MNEs more strongly attracted to global cities and knowledge intensive city clusters than developed market MNEs when undertaking greenfield strategic asset seeking related FDI? *Competitiveness Review: An International Business Journal, 33*(3), 534–556.
Xie, Q., & Sun, Q. (2020). Assessing the impact of FDI on PM2. 5 concentrations: A nonlinear panel data analysis for emerging economies. *Environmental Impact Assessment Review, 80*, 106314.
Ženka, J., Novotný, J., Slach, O., & Ivan, I. (2017). Spatial distribution of knowledge-intensive business services in a small post-communist economy. *Journal of the Knowledge Economy, 8*, 385–406.
Zhang, H., & De Beule, F. (2024). The impact of contextual distance on the investment locations of Chinese multinationals in countries along the Belt and Road initiative. *Asia Pacific Business Review, 30*(2), 220–250.
Zhang, H., & Van Den Bulcke, D. (2014). China's direct investment in the European Union: A new regulatory challenge? *Asia Europe Journal, 12*, 159–177.
Zheng, S., Kahn, M. E., & Liu, H. (2010). Towards a system of open cities in China: Home prices, FDI flows and air quality in 35 major cities. *Regional Science and Urban Economics, 40*(1), 1–10.

INDEX

Note: Page references in *Italics* refer to the figure, **Bold** refer to tables and with "n" refer to endnotes.

FSC
www.fsc.org
MIX
Papier | Fördert
gute Waldnutzung
FSC® C083411

Kolibri 360 GmbH
Ferdinand-Jühlke-Straße 7
99095 Erfurt, Deutschland
produktsicherheit@kolibri360.de